SECRET DIARY of a LIVERPOOL SCOUT

Sport Media
A Trinity Mirror Business

SIMON HUGHES

For my mother Pat . . .
Hal and Taylor,
a grandpa they never
got to know

— William Twentyman

Sport Media
A Trinity Mirror Business

Acknowledgements

(From William Twentyman)
Simon Hughes: Speaking from the heart, this book may never have been written.
My dad Geoff was told by many: "You should write a book."
He would just laugh, he was far too humble to do such a thing. So my deepest gratitude to
you Simon, as my mum Pat would have been very proud.
Norman Clarke: A loyal and true friend to my father.
John Rae Twentyman: Thank you for your support throughout this book.
Alan Kennedy and Peter Hooton: For your encouragement from the start.
Carra: Thanks for putting up with me! (Are you definitely sure I wouldn't suit that toupee?)
Ken Rogers, Steve Hanrahan and Paul Dove at Trinity Mirror.
My wife Jeanette.
My mum and dad. I was so privileged to be your son, 'Willy WET'.

Players' glossary researched by Michael Haydock.
Production by Michael Haydock.
Cover and endpapers design: Lee Ashun.

Published in Great Britain in 2009 by: Trinity Mirror Sport Media, PO Box 48, Old Hall
Street, Liverpool L69 3EB.

Produced by Trinity Mirror Sport Media:
Business Development Director: Mark Dickinson. Executive Editor: Ken Rogers. Editor: Steve Hanrahan.
Production Editor: Paul Dove. Art Editor: Rick Cooke. Sub Editors: Roy Gilfoyle, Adam Oldfield, Michael Haydock.
Sales and Marketing Manager: Elizabeth Morgan. Sales and marketing assistant: Karen Cadman.
Designers: Barry Parker, Colin Sumpter, Lee Ashun, Glen Hind, Alison Gilliland, Jamie Dunmore, James Kenyon.
Writers: Chris McLoughlin, David Randles, John Hynes, Gavin Kirk.

ISBN: 9781906802004

Photographs: Courtesy of the Twentyman family,
Trinity Mirror (Mirrorpix/Liverpool Daily Post & Echo), PA Pics

Printed by CPI Mackay

Contents

Foreword: Alan Hansen

I SAT trembling in the deep cavernous stands of Wembley Stadium as 92,500 people bellowed above me. The overwhelming majority dressed in Red. It was 20 minutes before the 1978 European Cup final and I was a nervous wreck.

I thought about all the great footballers to have already played in this special match. I pictured Ferenc Puskas, Alfredo Di Stefano and Francisco Gento in the white shirts of Real Madrid thrashing all opponents that lay in their path.

I thought about Wembley and all the historical games that had taken place on its lush green turf. It was my first game beneath the Twin Towers and the magnitude of the occasion was getting to me. I was 22 years old.

Ian Callaghan was substitute, a man who'd broken all playing records at Liverpool and a legend in my eyes. He came up to me in the dressing room and he could see I was weak in the knees. Cally had played in all of Liverpool's most important fixtures since the late '50s and had seen youngsters like me consumed and overwhelmed ahead of important matches like this one.

He told me that I wouldn't have a problem marking any striker in the world and to treat the 90 minutes as a normal game. "You'll breeze through it," he said. "You deserve to be here." Cally's kind words helped but my hands were still quivering – I was, after all, Tommy Smith's direct replacement as Liverpool's number 4 – and he'd scored the opening goal during the 3-1 win against Borussia Moenchengladbach in the previous final.

By comparison, only a year and five days before, I'd signed for Liverpool from Partick Thistle. Most of our home matches at Firhill attracted no more than 4,000 supporters. Against the Old Firm, we'd usually get up to six times that amount. But we were always underdogs and there was nothing like the same expectation on us to win.

I appreciate that Partick was a steady platform on which to build my career, but the responsibility that goes with playing for Liverpool was enormous, and dealing with that in a pressure situation was resting uneasily with my mind.

I'd scored two goals as a midfielder in front of 25,000 at Firhill in the months before I agreed to move to Anfield, and as I sat inside Wembley's changing rooms I began to think about how far I'd come since that day. That performance had given me a taste of what it was like playing in front of a partisan crowd, but this was completely different.

At Partick I believed that the manager, Bertie Auld, didn't have confidence in me and felt I was lazy. I was naturally a defender but I'd played a lot in midfield back then and because I had quite a distinctive running style it gave the impression that I was slow and didn't have enough pace to play at the back. Sometimes it would make me look like I wasn't trying.

Every footballer needs the confidence of their manager to play at their best and I was no different so my performances suffered.

Luckily, Liverpool's chief scout, Geoff Twentyman, recognised that I was just languid and that my reading of the play would make me a decent centre-back. He had enough belief in me to recommend a fee of £100,000 having watched me half a dozen times. The people at Partick had seen me in more than 100 games but didn't have the foresight to realise centre-back was my natural position even though I did play there from time to time.

Most new players at Liverpool endured at least six months in the reserves before making their debut but I'd already played 25 times in the first team by the time the European Cup final came around against FC Bruges of Belgium.

Geoff told Bob Paisley that I was more than ready to perform regularly in his side's 1977/78 campaign. Liverpool were league and European champions when I signed, so that alone gave me a huge injection of inspiration and confidence.

It took me a while to settle into life on Merseyside, however. I was a home bird and hated being away from Scotland. Years earlier, I'd been for a trial at Liverpool and missed home so much that even when I received a letter saying that I didn't meet the required standard, it came as some relief.

It took me well until the second full season before I finally did settle. Even after the final against Bruges, I spent the summer pining for Glasgow and spent the whole time travelling back and forth.

Everyone at Liverpool did their best to help me focus and relax in my new surroundings. Throughout this difficult period, Geoff Twentyman helped me greatly and made sure my form didn't suffer too much by boosting my self-belief.

"Hansen is the best one I've brought to the club," I'd often hear him telling others around Melwood.

Geoff always took a massive interest in the players he'd spotted, and if he hadn't recommended me to the club, I really don't know where my career would have gone.

I believed that I was good enough to play top-level football in England, but whether a club would have taken a chance on me and whether I would have achieved the same levels of success as I did at Liverpool is very doubtful. Geoff was sound in his judgement with me and proved time and again, as you will see in this book, that there was no better judge of talent in the English game.

In the changing room that day, I thought about all of these issues and realised I was where I was supposed to be. I was good enough to be a European Cup winner.

Once the team and I reached the tunnel, I was calm. In those days the referee kept the players waiting there for 10 minutes before walking out. All I could hear was a crescendo of Scouse noise. A Red roar.

Victory was never in doubt.

Author's preface

HIGH summer in Liverpool, 2008. The season has just started and I should be filled with the curious juices of anticipation, expectation and nagging doubt. Instead it begins to drizzle.

It's 8.35am. The phone rings. Still half asleep, I pick it up.

"Hullo, Simon." An uncertain pause on my part. "It's Stephen Nicol."

Steve Nicol, one of the most versatile players ever to wear a Liver bird on his breast, refers to himself as Stephen. I have been chasing him for almost three months. Emails, phone calls, answer phone messages. Now we finally talk.

Nicol is coaching in the United States. He's manager of New England Revolution as well as the MLS All-Stars. If the working day has just started in lifeless Liverpool, it must be the twilight zone in balmy Boston where he is based. America's eastern seaboard is five hours behind. I point this out.

"So it is!" responds Nicol with glee in his voice, "...and I'm on a high!"

Now, Nicol always seemed a joker to me – ever since the 'Anfield Rap' where his grooving and over-enthusiastic hand gestures made him look like Ayr's answer to Vanilla Ice.

It transpires that the night before, Nicol's Revolution side became the first US team to lift the SuperLiga – North America's extravagantly named answer to the UEFA Champions League. Only teams from Mexico and the USA are allowed to take part.

Whether Nicol has been out with the lads and is in a state of inebriation is uncertain at this point, but it is clear that match-day adrenaline is still impelling through his veins. "I couldn't get to sleep and I thought it would be a good time to ring you!"

Midway through the interview, there is a faint sound that can only be described as fine constant water. Then a toilet flush. He's definitely been on the sherbets.

Weeks later, I pick up the phone on a Friday morning. "It's John Toshack." I'd only contacted the press office at the Welsh FA the day before. The quickest response yet.

"You sound like a good Scouser, Simon...how old are you?" Responding,

I'm panicking. I didn't expect the call. Trying to locate a notepad and cobble together some questions, Toshack saves me by talking: "I had to ring straight away…I loved Geoff. It's about time he gets recognition for all his work at Liverpool…"

Writing a book about a deceased former scout of the most successful club in English football is no easy task. Gaining contact details for more than 50 retired footballers is a major operation in itself. I know few of them, so why should they speak to me? I didn't even meet Twentyman before his death in 2004. Where do you start?

The players Twentyman spotted and recommended to Liverpool are kind, though, and can't do enough to help. Most that he recommended to Liverpool endorse Phil Neal's comments when he said: "I owe my life to Geoff."

Soon, pen is sliding voluptuously over smooth paper.

When I speak to players that he watched, however, but who didn't, for one reason or another, ever sign for Liverpool, a familiar conversation ensues as soon as the initial contact is made: "Geoff Twentyman? Ah yeah, he's the former Bristol City player isn't he?" The interviewee is not far wrong. Geoff Twentyman Jnr played with distinction for Bristol Rovers in the late '80s and early '90s. He's a Pirate rather than a Robin.

After a quick explanation about the real identity of Geoff Twentyman Snr, they usually all do the same thing. Fall silent. Few know of his existence, mainly because he went about his job in an understated and professional way.

When Twentyman died, the *Liverpool Echo* opened its obituary with the line: 'If hindsight is the cheapest commodity in football, then foresight is the most valuable.' On that principle, therefore, Twentyman's contribution to the history of Liverpool Football Club is priceless. The career of almost every player that pulled on the Red shirt during the most successful three decades of the club's history began when pen touched paper in Twentyman's notebook. The list of names he recommended to first Bill Shankly and then Bob Paisley, Joe Fagan and Kenny Dalglish during his 19 years as Anfield's head talent hunter reads like an almanac of Liverpool legends.

Kevin Keegan, Alan Hansen, John Toshack, Phil Neal, Ray Clemence, Terry McDermott, Larry Lloyd and Alec Lindsay were just a few of the players he introduced to Liverpool in the late '60s and '70s. In the '80s, he continued with Ian Rush and Steve Nicol, and if he'd had his way, other greats like Trevor Francis, Stan Bowles and Davie Cooper might have followed.

Twentyman used contacts from all over Britain to unearth players for Liverpool. Watching five matches a week, he would travel from north to south, west to east and back again in his distinctive orange Ford Cortina – a club car which had previously been registered with Bill Shankly.

His scouting book is packed with some of the most famous names in modern football. Yet when he started pencilling them into Anfield history more than 40 years ago, most of them weren't even known beyond the confines of their own club's dressing room.

On Keegan, then a winger at Scunthorpe, he wrote: 'A good player, shows a lot of promise.' By the end of that season he'd become a Liverpool player for a fee of £35,000. On Hansen, he noted: 'Does a good job but gives the impression that if faced with quick forwards would struggle.' Liverpool later signed him for £100,000.

Twentyman's scouting diary resided permanently in a room used by groundstaff next door to the manager's office at Anfield until he left the club in 1986. "It was not the kind of room you would want to spend any amount of time in," Twentyman's second son William told me, referring to the characterless breezeblock walls that enclosed it. The original diary, though, which has been reproduced in this book, is an artefact of football history. In appearance, it is unremarkable. Racing green in colour with a thick red bind, it looks more like an aged family photo album rather than a record that decodes Liverpool's transfer activity for the best part of 30 years. It even boasts that musty pong that goes with an item that spends any duration of time in the same place. There's a personal touch, too, with notes of how much money Twentyman was owed by Liverpool for travel expenses as well as a phone number for the DSS in Bootle.

This book, however, is not merely a collection of memories or solely a tribute to one man who worked behind the scenes at Liverpool Football Club. It is a set of stories from people involved in football who one way or another have been influenced by Twentyman, Liverpool, Shankly or the clubs they stayed at after Liverpool dropped their interest.

The book isn't claiming that Twentyman had a more important role than other employees of the club either. It is highlighting that he did his job better than any other scout around. Liverpool's success was spawned from the collective responsibility Shankly instilled in his staff. Each person's job was just as important as the next. It was the 'bootroom spirit' he created by placing the right people in the appropriate positions.

Shankly didn't just modernise Liverpool, he personified everything it came to represent. He imposed the modest but confident manner in which players, coaches, directors, supporters and indeed scouts conducted themselves for the 16 years he was at the club and for the two decades after he left and departed this world.

Twentyman conducted his profession by Shankly's unwritten code, and this bore the richest of hidden treasures when he decided to put his name to a player in the transfer market.

Stephen Nicol being just one of them.

SIMON HUGHES

GEOFF TWENTYMAN WAS A PLAYER
BEFORE HE BECAME A SCOUT. HE SIGNED
FOR LIVERPOOL ON 17 DECEMBER 1953.
THIS WAS THE LEAGUE TABLE IN THE
ENGLISH FIRST DIVISION

	P	W	D	L	F	A	PTS
1 West Bromwich Albion	22	15	3	4	60	30	33
2 Wolves	22	14	5	3	55	31	33
3 Huddersfield Town	22	12	5	5	40	23	29
4 Burnley	22	14	0	8	50	39	28
5 Bolton Wanderers	21	8	8	5	37	31	24
6 Charlton Athletic	22	11	1	10	46	42	23
7 Arsenal	22	9	5	8	43	41	23
8 Cardiff City	22	9	5	8	27	37	23
9 Manchester United	22	6	10	6	35	32	22
10 Blackpool	21	9	4	8	38	38	22
11 Preston North End	22	9	3	10	49	33	21
12 Tottenham Hotspur	22	10	1	11	36	39	21
13 Sheffield Wednesday	23	9	3	11	40	51	21
14 Aston Villa	21	9	2	10	35	37	20
15 Newcastle United	22	6	7	9	35	40	19
16 Chelsea	22	7	5	10	37	47	19
17 Sheffield United	21	7	4	10	36	42	18
18 Portsmouth	22	6	6	10	46	54	18
19 Manchester City	22	6	5	11	28	43	17
20 Middlesbrough	22	6	4	12	32	47	16
21 Sunderland	21	6	3	12	42	56	15
22 LIVERPOOL	**22**	**5**	**5**	**12**	**42**	**56**	**15**

1. Carlisle

Cumberland wrestling,
tragedy at Brunton Park and Shankly

MAY 1977. Liverpool are in Rome for their first European Cup final. Opponents Borussia Moenchengladbach have been champions of Germany for the last three years and are white-hot favourites to lift the trophy.

The teams enter the resplendent and roofless Olympic Stadium. The seven hills of Rome shimmering in the distance. If the Liverpool players are nervous, they aren't showing it. Backed by 30,000 Scousers, Merseyside has plonked itself on the banks of the Tiber. During the pre-match handshakes Kevin Keegan and Ray Clemence are pictured peeking along the line. Berti Vogts, captain of club and country, is blond, German and smiling. He is one of four from the 'Gladbach side that featured in his nation's World Cup-winning squad three years earlier. Unimpressed Keegan and Clemence re-focus and stare back into the flashing photography.

Liverpool are confident. Six of their own starting XI share something in common. Each player has been signed for the club on the recommendation of chief scout Geoff Twentyman: Phil Neal, Joey Jones, Steve Heighway, Terry McDermott, Clemence and Keegan.

Ninety minutes later the word 'LIVERPOOL' stretches proudly across the scoreboard. Bob Paisley's side are the winners. Two of the goals have been scored by Twentyman signings: McDermott and Neal. The Germans have been outplayed, and the role of their fans was reduced to that of an intruder, such was the noise from the travelling Kop. Keegan, a former Scunthorpe player, was at his impudent best. Voted man of the match, he gave Vogts a torrid night. The German's smile now a grimace. "What a night that was," recalled Terry Mac. "I knew the club was on the verge of greatness in Europe. Everyone had the same feeling."

McDermott was right. Seven years later, Liverpool were lifting ol' big ears for a fourth time, again in the Olympic Stadium. Nine Twentyman signings featured in that 16-man squad. The penalty shoot-out victory against Roma on their own front lawn meant Liverpool collected their 26th senior trophy since Twentyman took charge of the club's scouting system in 1967. By the time he left the club in 1986, they'd won another three. Twenty-nine titles in 19 seasons.

Liverpool's unparalleled success in the '60s, '70s and '80s is rightly attributed to the men on the front line: Bill Shankly then Bob Paisley, Joe Fagan and Kenny Dalglish. They were the drivers of the Red tank that flattened almost everything that lay in its path, plundering the whole of Europe without mercy and devouring countless trophies on the domestic front as well. Beneath the drivers, though, were the technicians, and without their help the tank may have been steered on a different path.

Liverpool's success in the three decades after the appointment of Shankly was based on a style of play that the whole club embraced. From the first team to the youth teams, every Liverpool side played with the same philosophy.

Shankly said: "We learned in Europe that you can't score a goal every time you get the ball, so we play in groups that can leave room for others to sneak in. It's cat and mouse waiting for an opening. It's been built up over the years. It's improvisation, using players that can adjust. To play 60 or 70 games a season, you can't run flat out. It's designed to lull and confuse the opposition and to be economical. Everyone at

Liverpool does their share; they're all in the pattern. At kick-off, the main aim is to give everyone a touch as quickly as possible. If everyone's done something simple and done it right, you're off on the right foot. They can all do the basics, control and pass, control and pass, so there's no delay, which gives us more space and time. At Liverpool you have options, two or three players willing to take the ball, somebody to help you run. You're forcing the opposition to chase and change their pattern. You don't run into no man's land. Terrible waste of energy. When you've passed the ball, you've only started, you have to back up. In three passes."

Shankly, always keen to learn from others' successes and failures, may have adopted this approach after a harsh lesson in the Amsterdam mist when Liverpool were thumped 5-1 by Ajax in the 1966/67 European Cup. In his book, *Brilliant Orange*, David Winner says of the Dutch: 'Total football was, amongst other things, a conceptual revolution based on the idea that the size of any football field could be altered by a team playing on it. In possession, Ajax – and later the Dutch national team – aimed to make the pitch as large as possible, spreading play to the wings and seeing every run and movement as a way to increase and exploit available space.' Quite simply, Shankly had his own equivalent of this: the less ostentatious description of 'pass and move'. He believed in common human values and that everything in life, especially football, was over-complicated.

'The Dutch pressed deep into the other side's half hunting for the ball, defended a line 10 yards inside their own half and used the offside trap aggressively to squeeze space further,' Winner continues. If this sounds familiar, it's because Liverpool adopted the same approach. Even in the '80s, Ian Rush worked harder than any other forward by scurrying across the front line and pressurising defenders intent on hoofball. An expert at squeezing the space, Rush was at Chester City before he was scouted by Geoff Twentyman and brought to Liverpool for a world record fee for a teenager.

"Arie Haan was a midfielder before the '74 World Cup, but I was a midfielder too before Bill converted me to a centre-back," adds Phil Thompson. "The key to the way Liverpool played was swift passing from the back. Alan Hansen and Mark Lawrenson played exactly the same way, with Hansen linking defence and midfield."

The build-up of play was key to Liverpool's success, but for that to happen, the club needed the right players. Shankly instilled the values and those that worked with him adopted the simple belief. In the scouting department, the policy towards style was the same. Only players who first of all could pass the ball properly were watched more than once. Then, they had to have the intelligence to move into space. Alan Hansen was considered an undervalued midfielder with Partick Thistle before Twentyman scouted him and recommended to Paisley that he would be perfectly suited to Liverpool's system if he led from the back.

Football dynasties are founded by managerial partnerships. Matt Busby used Jimmy Murphy as a soundbox, Don Revie had Syd Owen, while Brian Clough leant on Peter Taylor, especially for advice on potential transfer targets. Whereas these teams were double acts, Shankly's bootroom was the congress to his unique socialist presidency. And this is what made Liverpool different from the rest. Beneath the manager, there was a network of people – each made to feel as important as the other – in whatever their function. This is what made Liverpool's period of domination sustainable. Shanks held trust in others and after he was long gone, this ideal was maintained. Twentyman, in particular, was the Midas of the transfer market for Shankly, Paisley, Fagan and Dalglish.

It is true that Shankly masterminded Liverpool's success. But to gain a greater understanding of how the club reached immortality, you have to look back to 1949, when Shanks formed perhaps his most meaningful relationship in football. Well before the Anfield revolution. In Carlisle.

*****

CARLISLE is a historical city that evolved into a military stronghold owing to its position on the Anglo-Scottish border. Its castle, which was built in 1092 by William Rufus and once served as a prison for Mary Queen of Scots, is still relatively intact. Caar...lisle (with an emphasis on the first syllable) has played an important part in British history – and, curiously, an integral part in the history of Liverpool Football Club.

In 1949, when Bill Shankly plunged into football management for the first time with Carlisle United, one of his first acts was to appoint Geoff Twentyman as his captain. Twentyman, who'd previously played as a wing-half (a left-midfielder to children of the 21st-century), having made fewer than 100 league appearances in the old Division Three (North), was soon converted to centre-half as Shankly sought to build a spine through his team.

A farmer's boy, Twentyman was big boned and broad shouldered and had enough physical strength to deal with barrel-chested lower-league centre-forwards. He was, after all, a Cumberland wrestling champion in successive years at the age of 14 and 15, and therefore boasted the testicular fortitude to deal with any kind of argy-bargy, although Twentyman himself later said that another player by the name of Paddy Waters was the toughest in the Carlisle team. Waters once played a full 90 minutes in boots two sizes too small for him after leaving his own pair at home.

What set Twentyman apart from the rest of the rag-tag bunch that perennially ensured Carlisle were strugglers in England's lower leagues, though, were his mental attributes – most notably his loyalty. Shankly demanded loyalty, and years later as manager of Liverpool he would inspire the same quality in anyone he worked with, whether it be players, backroom staff or indeed supporters, with whom he frequently interacted.

When Shankly became Liverpool manager in 1959, all of his backroom team expected to be asked to leave. Considering this staff comprised two future Liverpool managers in Bob Paisley and Joe Fagan, as well as Reuben Bennett, a fellow Scot and integral part of the

Liverpool story over the next three decades, it wouldn't have been the shrewdest of decisions to dispense with their services. Wisely, Shankly had a belief that people deserved a chance. As long as they worked hard and more importantly remained faithful to him, he told the trio there would always be a job for them at Anfield. Shankly, a socialist and a believer in human nature, demanded fidelity from every single player and staff member under his charge.

In equal measure, he returned the faith. Sometimes he was too loyal, sticking by the squad that had served him so well in the mid-'60s when Liverpool endured a trophyless six-season spell between 1967 and 1973. But this was how an exceptional trust was forged at Liverpool. It was this belief that made him appoint Twentyman as his first-ever captain at Carlisle, and why, in 1967, he would call on him again, this time as chief scout of Liverpool Football Club.

*****

IVOR BROADIS, manager of Carlisle between 1946 and 1949, first spotted Geoff Twentyman playing football in the Carlisle and District League for a team called Swifts FC at the age of 16. "How could I forget someone with a name like Twentyman?" he says. "Even then when there were all kinds of unusual surnames, Twentyman was probably one of the most distinctive."

Broadis, who to this day remains the youngest-ever player-manager in professional football (he was 23 when he took charge at Brunton Park shortly after the war) adds that Twentyman was a player whose imposing stature made him more noticeable than others. Never mind his name. "I heard about Geoff through a friend of mine and went to have a look at him. I already knew that he was a champion wrestler because I lived up in Cumbria for many years so I know quite a lot about it. It's not wrestling as you would imagine it. You start stooped and hold the opponent by the waist and try and throw him. They call it a World Championship, but I think it's only held in Cumbria. Being a big farming lad as well, Geoff was a tough wrestler. You don't forget someone when they say they are a wrestler, do you?"

An east Londoner by birth, Broadis arrived in Carlisle after being posted to a nearby military barracks shortly after the war. Prior to being sent north, he worked as a navigator on Lancaster and Wellington bombers but didn't see any action as the war ended before he could be deployed in the Nazi skies above Germany.

Despite his tender years, Broadis' pedigree in football was already impressive. Before the war, he'd been a junior at Tottenham Hotspur and played for them regularly in the wartime league. Then, after leaving Carlisle, he became an England international and netted eight goals in 14 matches while also appearing in the 1954 World Cup in Switzerland – scoring twice in a 4-4 draw against Belgium. One of his best strikes in an England shirt came against Hungary. Unfortunately, the Magnificent Magyars, then inspired by Ferenc Puskas and Sandor Kocsis, scored seven. "I wish you hadn't mentioned that," he jokes. After retiring from a playing career that included spells at Sunderland, Manchester City and Newcastle (where he played with the great Jackie Milburn), Broadis became a football writer in the north-east. Even from a short conversation, it is clear that he has more tales to tell than an Anfield pub regular holding service on a matchday.

"Geoff had a natural ability with two feet," Broadis continues. "I know he was very proud of that because there were few players who could do it in those days." Years later, when scouting for Liverpool, Twentyman would eulogise over players who were blessed with similar attributes. "The only thing Geoff didn't have to his game was acceleration over the first 15 yards. He was a bit of a loper and better as a long-distance runner. But I was quite pleased and regarded it as one of my first achievements in management to improve his speed."

Twentyman's lack of pace was a concern for his parents who believed it would be more appropriate for him to take up a traditional trade in the farming industry. Although Twentyman agreed at the age of 16 that he must have a contingency plan if his football career failed to develop in the way he wished, he desperately wanted a chance to play for the club he grew up supporting.

In an interview he gave to Billy Butler on Radio City in the early '80s, Twentyman said that he began following his local club by chance after stumbling across Brunton Park when working for his father on New Year's Day some time in the 1930s. Carlisle were playing York City, and Twentyman and son had been transporting sheep from one side of the city to the other. Job done, they made their way back to the farm. Then young Twentyman heard the roar of the Carlisle crowd as the teams took to the pitch ahead of the match so he decided to go and have a look at what was going on.

Once inside, though, there was nothing but silence and the faint sound of a hymn. Weeks earlier, a Carlisle player had died after his appendix burst on the pitch. It was the first game back at Brunton Park since the tragedy, so the fans and players observed a minute's silence before singing 'Abide With Me'. The sentiment struck a chord with Twentyman, whose own brother died in a shooting accident years earlier. From then on he was obsessed with football and the interaction it fuelled between people, playing the game at every opportunity on ferret-infested farmyards with anyone who would take part in a kick-around.

To satisfy the wishes of his parents and his own aspirations, Broadis came up with a plan. "There was always a feeling, even amongst his mother and father, that he might not make the grade, even though I had a lot of confidence in him. We arranged that he would take an apprenticeship with a garage that were the main Ford dealers in Carlisle working as a panel beater. It was an insurance against not making the grade. The bonus was that the boss of the Ford dealers was the chairman of Carlisle Football Club and the secretary was also on the board of directors."

Within months, Twentyman made his debut in the final game of the 1946/47 season at Chester City. Carlisle lost 4-0. Aged only 17, he performed admirably in a struggling team that was to finish the campaign in 16th place. The following year, he played another eight league games and 29 the season after that. Then, by the turn of 1949, Broadis was running out of patience with a board that refused to back his ambitious plans with cash.

"Carlisle United in those days didn't have two pennies to rub together," Broadis laughs. "It was incredible. We used to have to train in the dark because the club wouldn't pay for lighting. I wanted to sign players to improve the team, because we were going nowhere. The press regarded me as the best player in the team and speculated how much I was worth. So I went to the board and asked them how much they thought I was worth. They told me that they valued me highly, so I asked if I could have half of the money I was worth to spend on new players, just to give the team a chance. If it didn't work, they could sack me as a manager and sell me as a player, then they would be no worse off. But they wouldn't play ball, so I told them I wanted to leave. Four big clubs came in for me – Sunderland, Man City, Preston and Blackburn – but the only club that showed serious interest in me was Sunderland because the manager came to see me in person. So I went there."

Broadis, not contented with being the youngest player-manager in the history of the game, also became the first manager to sell himself to another club, leaving for Sunderland in an £18,000 deal. Management, he says, just wasn't for him at that stage of his career. "I was too young for it. There were players who were playing for me that were a lot older – and a lot cagier too. It was a great experience, though. I learnt a lot more about the game in my two years at Carlisle than I did in the rest of my career. There was a great affinity between me and Geoff because he had a different attidtude to that of the of the senior pros. He was coming into the game and was always eager to learn, whereas the older players weren't interested in listening to a manager who was 10 years younger than some of them. Even back then, Geoff appreciated skill and effort and I think he took those qualities throughout his career – especially into scouting."

Despite leaving Carlisle, Broadis' Cumbrian odyssey wasn't over just yet. His replacement at Brunton Park, a certain Bill Shankly, was a reasonable man and the pair respected each other. Realising that Broadis was keen to continue living in Carlisle (where he still owned a two-bedroomed semi), Shankly offered him the opportunity to continue training with the club during the week, while playing for Sunderland at weekends. Broadis was delighted with the invitation, which he accepted.

"I left Carlisle in January of 1949 and Bill Shankly took over in March. Bill was a great man – although his uncle wasn't. There were pubs in Carlisle that were run by a state management scheme and Bill's uncle, Billy Blyth, worked as a publican. He was the first chairman I worked under at Carlisle too and we didn't get on. He once vetoed a transfer for a good player called Jackie Connor from Ipswich who only wanted £300 for him. Mr Blyth rang up Ipswich and told them the deal was off. That was when I started to think management wasn't for me. I had made an enemy. But soon after, he stepped down from being chairman and took a seat on the board. Shankly was different though. He was a great, honest man – much like Geoff, although they were polar opposites in terms of character."

Like most people who have spent time in Shankly's messianic presence, Broadis spins off a number of original tales about the great man. "I remember Bill came up to me one day and said: 'Ivor, tell me, are you doing anything this afti…noon?' I told him I had no plans, so he said: 'Come and meet me for a game of fitball then.' So I went back to the training ground in the afternoon and he put two pieces of chimney pot in the car park and he went: 'Come on Ivor, it's a game of one-a-side.' He always insisted on calling people by their forenames. You had to hit the pot to score. He was keen but I was younger. If I didn't let him score, we would have been there until dark. His hunger was unbelievable. I think it ended in an honourable draw.

"Another time, not long after we came to our training arrangement, Bill was still living in a hotel. I said to him: 'You'll have to come and have something to eat at my house with me and my wife.' Later that night, there was a firm knock on the door. 'We've come for our dinner, Ivor.' It was Bill and his wife Nessie. I never meant for him to come that very night! Bill was a man of his word, and when he said something, he meant it. He expected other people to do the same.

"That's why he and Geoff got on so well. They both had very similar values about honesty. When Bill became manager, he immediately moved Geoff to centre-back and made him captain – a position and role he considered very important. He did a similar thing with Ron Yeats as soon as he joined Liverpool 15 years later. 'He's a colossus. Try and walk round him,' he said. Although Geoff wasn't as big as Ron, Bill held him in a similar regard and wanted to build his team around him. Under Bill, he played 30 games in 49/50, then 28 games the season after. He was a big player in Bill's team and it was only when Bill took charge that Geoff really flourished as a player."

Twentyman too once commented that he could feel himself improving under Shankly. "It was much more professional. I was a part-timer and within a week, he'd arranged with my boss that I should take two mornings off a week to train with the first team. That carried on into the summer. Most teams come back and do a lot of roadwork to build up stamina, but he wouldn't have any of it. 'You play on grass so you train on grass,' which was far better. I think it stopped a lot of injuries later on." Shankly had changed a chore that was endured to a pleasure to be enjoyed.

Despite the pair's admiration for one another, Twentyman wasn't exempt from Shankly's sharp tongue. Twentyman's son William said that he was told by a family member that on the night his mother and father announced they were engaged, the whole Carlisle squad met in a pub to toast the happy couple. "Bill heard about the gathering and decided to attend himself. When he walked in, apparently every single player jumped up like soldiers and Bill ordered them out. It must have been a sight to see grown men leave full pints of beer as they made their exit."

At the start of the 1950/51 season, Twentyman, now an integral part of Shankly's plans, was called up to complete national service in Oswestry (where he featured in the same army team as John Charles and Tommy Taylor). One day, in a moment of Shankly-esque theatre, Twentyman was summoned to his Camp Adjutant's office to be asked: "Gunner Twentyman, does the name Shankly mean anything to you?" Then: "He's been on to the War Office. He's told them that Carlisle United can win the Third Division North provided he can get you off to play. We've decided to let you go, but once you're out of the running, it will stop." He was duly made available and appeared in 32 games, only for United to finish nine points adrift of the leaders in third position.

Unfortunately for Twentyman and for Carlisle, the season's achievements weren't enough to match Shankly's aspirations, so the manager left in the summer of 1951, accepting an offer to take charge of similarly unfashionable Grimsby Town.

Shankly's flirtation with Carlisle had been brief and for the club ultimately unmemorable. But for Liverpool, it was significant. "Bill was a tremendous fella. One of the best in my lifetime. It was great playing under him just for his enthusiasm," said Twentyman years later in the same interview with Billy Butler. "The way Geoff used to talk about Shanks was quite incredible," adds John Keith, the *Daily Express'* former Merseyside football writer. "Shanks made Geoff his captain at Carlisle because he had all of the qualities that he looked for in a human being first and as a scout second. He was honest, loyal and wasn't flashy. Geoff used to love telling people how Shanks would run up to the press area and grab hold of the public address system before the game and speak to the crowd. Anyone around Liverpool Football Club who didn't know this story soon found out.

"There was one game Geoff always used to talk about when Carlisle were 2-0 down at half-time. When the team got back into the dressing room, Shankly rounded on Geoff and said (in a distinctive Scottish cackle): 'Geoff, what did you call in the pre-match toss-up?' Geoff replied (in a distinctive Cumbrian accent): 'I called heads.' So Shanks said: 'Jesus Christ son, why didn't you call tails?' He bollocked him and even if he'd called tails, he would have done the same. Geoff dined out on that one, but it was a wonderful story."

The relationship forged between Twentyman and Shankly at Carlisle was lasting and one that would have a major contribution towards the second great revolution of the 20th century. The rise of Liverpool Football Club.

2. Playing Days and Management

Anfield nearly man, a player-manager
and getting the push for Brian Clough

WHEN Bill Shankly left Carlisle for Grimsby in 1951, so did a wave of optimism that had previously swept across the club. Shankly took the Cumbrians from 15th in Division Three (North) to the verge of promotion in little over two years. After he departed, Fred Emery took over and they steadily tumbled down the table.

Under Shankly, the team's league form carried across into the cup competitions. After holding Arsenal at Highbury in January 1951, they were beaten 4-1 at Brunton Park, although according to one Carlisle fan, the game was a lot closer than the result suggests.

"We drew 0-0 down at Highbury. There were no floodlights in those days so the replay was on a Thursday afternoon." says Hunter Davies, who is one of Britain's most prolific journalists, having written the autobiographies of Wayne Rooney and Paul Gascoigne as well as the only official biography of the Beatles. "I went to a high school quite near the ground and luckily my school and a few others were given a half-day holiday so the children could watch the game. I believe the headmaster of my school sent a letter of complaint to the football club saying it was disgusting that children should miss out on their education for a stupid football match. Everyone in Carlisle was loving it. Shankly really whipped the team into shape – although we eventually got whopped."

Twentyman was now forging a name for himself in the lower leagues with consistent performances in the heart of the Carlisle defence and his display against Arsenal brought him to the attention of clubs in the First Division. "Twentyman was a hero to all Carlisle fans," recalls Davies. "I liked him because he was brought up in the same Brampton area of Carlisle as Derek Batey from 'Mr and Mrs'. He was probably only behind Ivor Broadis in terms of how much the supporters revered him. The fact that he had big curly hair made him stand out to me as well."

By 1953, the optimism from the Shankly era had dissipated. Wolverhampton Wanderers placed a £10k bid for Twentyman when their chief scout, a man called Stan Noakes, who sported an eye patch, was impressed by his rugged approach and felt it would complement the emerging talent of future England captain Billy Wright. Had he chosen Molineux over Anfield, it is possible Twentyman would have been a part of the great Wolves side of the late '50s that appeared in the inaugural European Cup.

Instead, he moved to Liverpool for £12k. The deal came in at just the right time for Carlisle, as their main stand had burnt down only months before. "The money was a godsend to the club. The fire may have been deliberate," says Ivor Broadis, half joking. "I was at Newcastle United but I knew from my days at Carlisle that the club's financial state was dire and I am sure some people in charge of the club wanted to get rid of certain records. Geoff's transfer fee virtually paid for the new grandstand, so everyone was happy."

The first person to salute Twentyman was his old manager at Carlisle. A day after signing for Liverpool, he wrote to him:

'Dear Geoff.

'Congratulations on your stepping up to the big stuff, it's taken these people a long time to make a move for you. However, Geoff, it has probably been worth it for you because you have gone to probably the finest club in the game, with the most ardent supporters ever, behind you.

'You have no need to worry, just keep on looking after yourself, that's what counts, you will probably find the first division much easier than *the third, but a fit, strong, confident Geoff Twentyman can play in any class. Go out there Geoff and concentrate the whole time, and the very best of luck.*

   'Sincere wishes, Bill Shankly'

Twentyman later told Billy Butler that he only chose to move to Liverpool because he held an affinity with the people of the city. "Before I signed I knew a lot about the club through the time I spent with Scousers in the forces [during national service]. They were passionate people. It made me want to go to a place like Liverpool."

For Twentyman, he couldn't have arrived at Anfield at a more difficult moment as Liverpool faced relegation for the first time in 50 years. The forlorn disposition in the Red half of the city is best summed up in an article published in the *Daily Sketch* ahead of the busy Easter football schedule in April 1954: 'You expect long faces, funeral gloom. You've just checked with the First Division table. No doubt about Liverpool's position at the very bottom of the table. No possible doubt whatsoever.'

Liverpool, managed by Don Welsh, almost achieved the same dubious feat a year earlier before a final-day victory over Chelsea kept them up, finishing 17th. This time, though, the prospect of the drop was made worse by the fact a Dave Hickson-inspired Everton were on the verge of promotion back to the top flight after three years in the Second Division wilderness.

A tea stain-coloured page from the *Sketch* (which later became the *Daily Mail*) featured a photograph of a dejected-looking Liverpool team ahead of a game in which they were probably beaten such was their insipid record that season (they lost 23 in 42 games). In the background, an ocean of flat-capped heads stood across uncovered, expansive terraces. Although the photo is in black and white, it is imaginable, anyway, that the pitch is blanketed in a Lancashire fug of factory/mill pollution haze. Grey smoke enveloping the entire scene.

Pictured with the team, which wore red shirts, white shorts and hooped stockings, is trainer Albert Shelley. Donning a knee-length white cloak, he looks like a cross between a mad scientist and Albert Arkwright from 'Open All Hours'. An uneasy smile stretches across his weary and wrinkly face.

Standing next to him is a recently signed centre-half. Arms folded like the rest of his team-mates, Geoff Twentyman became a Red shortly before Christmas 1953, along with four other new players. Don Welsh thought Twentyman would plug a hole in Liverpool's defence after conceding 50 goals in only 21 league games. But in his first game at Old Trafford against Manchester United, Liverpool conceded another five, and scored only one. A week earlier, the Reds lost by the same scoreline at Portsmouth. These were desperate times and Twentyman was brought to the club in a final hope to stop Liverpool's slide towards the Second Division.

It didn't work. It took four months and 12 games for Liverpool and Twentyman to score a victory, drawing four. Liverpool used 31 different players and a late winning streak only fuelled frustration as the Reds beat Middlesbrough twice, but lost at home to Cardiff in a game where visiting full-back Alf Sherwood was forced to go in goal after first-choice custodian Ron Howells fractured his thumb in the early stages of the game. Sherwood's man-of-the-match performance also included a penalty save from the usually reliable Billy Liddell. The *Echo* ran with the headline: 'Penetrate Sherwood Forest! Deputy 'Keeper's triumph.' The signing of Twentyman failed and Liverpool were relegated.

*****

ARRANGING an interview around Ronnie Moran's weekly social calendar isn't easy. "You can't come Tuesdays or Fridays," he says over the phone. "Why?" I ask cheekily.

"Well, I go up to Melwood those days."

"How about Wednesday or Thursday?"

"I'm with the wife..."

"Monday then..?"

Ronnie Moran, a man who served Liverpool for 49 uninterrupted years and played a major part in the Anfield revolution that was started by Shankly in 1959, still can't shake the football bug. Like Shankly and, as I later find out, Geoff Twentyman, Moran spends two days a week rambling round the fields of Liverpool's training ground. "It's mainly to keep the old knees moving," he says.

Moran was 20 years old and on the fringes of the first team when Twentyman signed for Liverpool in 1953. "What do you wanna know about Geoff then?" he continues when I meet him at his home in Blundellsands. It's clear that Ronnie still relishes the opportunity to talk about football. After five decades in the game, it's understandable why. At Liverpool, he was a player, youth-team coach, reserve coach, physio and manager (albeit on a temporary basis). He was a founding member of the bootroom and played a part in every Liverpool success between 1952 and 1999.

"Geoff was a decent lad, y'know?" he says. "He was quiet and kept everything close to his chest. He could play a bit...scored a lot of goals, too. He was like me and Shanks in that he wasn't the quickest, but his brain took him into good positions. He was a good player for Liverpool, played a lot at left-half. Of course, it was different back then with the formations. There was a goalkeeper, a right-back, a left-back, a centre-half, then a right and left-half with five different forwards. There were no midfielders as such, at least not what we have like now. I remember Shanks seeing Leicester play with four across midfield and liking it, so he did the same with Liverpool."

Moran was paid £14 a week by the club when he signed his first professional contract and £11 in the summer months – just the same amount as Twentyman, who he also lived opposite in the days when staff were given club houses, along with eight other players all on the same

Huyton street. "It was the only time I moved away from Crosby," he points out. "Apart from a four-month stint up in Birkdale about 10 years ago. Me and the wife didn't like it up there."

Given that it's more than half a century since he made his debut for Liverpool, Moran could be forgiven for overlooking one or two details about his debut season in a Red shirt. Not Ronnie. He remembers well the time when Liverpool were facing relegation, although he is keen to relinquish any responsibility for being a part of the squad that sent the club down.

"Everything about Liverpool was very different to what we know now," he says. "We weren't actually that bad, though. Lots of things went against us – mainly luck. But you can't blame me for it – I was only an amateur that season. I think I only played one game. I got paid £5 in the season and £3 in the summer and I only trained on Tuesday and Thursday nights. So I wasn't really a part of the team that took us down." Joking, he adds: "Maybe you could blame Geoff – he played near enough every game after he signed that season."

Moran is correct. History books suggest that Twentyman started in all 19 games after signing in the December of '53. Once again, Moran's memory has served him well.

*****

ANOTHER man who remembers Geoff Twentyman during his Liverpool career is Johnny Morrissey. Morrissey, who is revered by Evertonians for his direct and aggressive style, made 314 appearances at Goodison Park, scoring 50 goals. Tommy Smith, the Anfield Iron, has gone on record as saying the winger was his toughest opponent. 'He was fearless. The Everton fans called him Mogsy. He looked more like a boxer than a footballer,' he whimpered. Morrissey, though, grew up as a Liverpudlian and played for the Reds during their years in the Second Division before being sold against the wishes of Bill Shankly.

Upon signing for Liverpool as an apprentice in 1955, he swept the Kop and repainted its crush barriers during the day, training at Melwood in the evenings. When he reached the first-team squad two years later, with Liverpool still in a Second Division quagmire, he found the transition difficult, with most teammates older and distant. He says only one made him feel at ease amidst more professional surroundings. That teammate was Geoff Twentyman. It was in Paisley's treatment room where Morrissey first spoke to the defender. "The room acted like an illegal bookie's at one point, so much money was changing hands," laughs Morrissey, now retired and living in Crosby. "When anyone signed as a schoolboy then, it meant they'd become part of the ground-staff as well. That meant we'd spend afternoons doing maintenance on the ground. The smell of tobacco and urine was terrible on the Kop.

"We had to get the kit out for the pros in the morning, although we never trained with them. There was a big separation between the pros and the youngsters because there was a generation gap. I grew up with Billy Liddell as my idol, and when I was a kid I'd imitate him, but when I met him he was quite stand-offish and remote. He was a bit of a let-down to me as a person to be honest because he kept his distance and, like a few of the others, didn't go out of his way to make me and the younger lads feel at ease. He was like that with everybody, though. Billy was a dour Scot, but he was a wonderful player. That was the way it was. The older fellas didn't speak to you in the same way you never questioned your father back then. I think it also had something to do with the fact they didn't want you to take their place in the team.

"There were a couple of Cockneys and they were horrid. They'd only talk to you to embarrass you in front of their mates – especially if like me you had a Liverpool accent. I always thought Liverpool Football Club was for the people of the city – not a bunch of Cockneys – so their attitudes to young local lads annoyed me."

By comparison, Morrissey found Twentyman hospitable. "Geoff was never like that. He was more experienced than most of them, but he always treated everyone with respect. Geoff was a great example to aspiring youngsters like me. I'd go to all the home games and even though me and him played in different positions, I'd watch him because of the way he'd conduct himself on the pitch. He was not the tallest defender you'd ever see, but he had tremendous strength and he'd attack the ball harder than anyone else on the pitch. Whenever the heavy weather came, he'd come into his own and would revel in the adverse conditions. I tried to adopt that approach when I played later and I think it was quite successful."

Morrissey, who later became the original equivalent of Jamie Carragher (except Morrissey's shift was from Red to Blue), is venerated by every Evertonian that saw him play. In the same way that Liverpool later missed out on the left-wing talents of Kevin Sheedy when they allowed him to make the same move, they missed out on the best years of Morrissey's career. In modern football, there is no winger of his kind. Given the nickname 'Alehouse', if any rugged full-back tried to hurt him with an early challenge, Morrissey knew that he'd have the best part of 90 minutes to clatter him back. Twice as hard.

This aggressive approach, Morrissey says, was instilled by Twentyman, who gave him an unwitting snippet of advice on the day he made his debut for Liverpool at Sunderland as a 17-year-old. "Alan A'Court was on the right wing, Billy Liddell in the middle and me on the left. I was delighted and full of the joys of spring when I was told about it. That was until I walked into the dressing room. There was a fella I was coming up against called Billy Elliott – don't get him mixed up with the tap dancing boy, though, this guy was a monster. He was a thug and kicked everything that moved.

"I didn't even know he existed until I walked into the room and there was Bob Paisley having a chat with Geoff about me. Then I heard Geoff say: 'Little Johnny Morrissey…the only kick he'll get tomorrow will be on his legs.' I walked in with my face as white as a ghost. Geoff later explained that he didn't mean it in a nasty way. But he was right.

Elliott was tough. From then on, I said that I was never going to let a defender intimidate me."

Morrissey only played another 35 times for Liverpool over the next five seasons, scoring five goals. After the Reds achieved promotion back to the First Division in 1962, he grew tired of trying to stake a regular place in Bill Shankly's starting XI and demanded a move from Anfield. It proved to be one of the most protracted and controversial transfers in Liverpool's history and one that ultimately had consequences later on for Twentyman's scouting role.

"Shanks offered his resignation because of me," he explains. "He was completely fed up with the situation because the board was having too much influence over the transfers and team selection. Shanks wanted me to stay and play but because I was a bit outspoken, some board members weren't happy with me. It was the final straw and eventually Shanks got his way and took full control of team affairs as well as transfers. He broke the mould. Because Liverpool had just won the league and the board was afraid of losing him they agreed to his demands.

"From then on, any football matter had to be approved by Shanks. In some ways, that led to modern-day football as we know it. It also meant Shanks could later send Geoff Twentyman where he wanted on a Saturday afternoon when he became a scout rather than have the board question his every movement."

While Morrissey's Anfield career didn't go according to plan, Twentyman cemented his place in the side. He made the number six shirt his own during nearly six years as a Liverpool player. Despite arriving as a centre-half, he was soon moved to left-half owing to the form and longevity of Laurie Hughes. This switch enabled him to attack, scoring 19 times in 184 games, supplementing the goalscoring threat of Billy Liddell. In 1956/57 season when Liverpool narrowly missed out on promotion, finishing third, he netted seven times in 42 league games. Later, another of his strikes came from the penalty spot in the humiliating FA Cup defeat to Worcester City which eventually led to the sacking of Phil Taylor and the appointment of Bill Shankly.

However, by 1959, Twentyman was on his way to Northern Ireland with Liverpool remaining in the Second Division. He agreed to become player-manager of Ballymena after struggling with an arthritic hip for years. The release from his contract was one of Shankly's first acts in charge of Liverpool. It was an old pals act. Shankly understood that his old friend from their Carlisle days needed to prolong his career to support his family and the slower pace of the Irish League was the perfect place to do that.

Twentyman managed and captained Ballymena to their first-ever Ulster Cup success in 1961 before missing out on an Irish League title by two points a year later. He then returned to Carlisle in 1963, playing another 10 games. Short spells as a player at Penrith and manager at Morecambe followed before he arrived at Hartlepool (then Hartlepools) in the summer of 1965, where he lasted only three months, being replaced by Brian Clough.

Clough was one of Twentyman's oldest adversaries in football. As players, they lined up against each other in many a bloody Second Division clash as Clough strove to score the goals for Middlesbrough that would make England international selectors and Walter Winterbottom take note, while Twentyman sought to stop him for Liverpool and help the Reds to promotion. As managers, Clough took Twentyman's job as boss at Hartlepool after help from friends in higher places. Then, as scout, Twentyman spotted many of the players that enabled Liverpool to dominate the '70s, thus preventing Clough, then in charge at Derby County and Nottingham Forest, winning even more silverware than he did.

There is a photograph that has been reproduced in this book which reflects their rivalry. Clough, forever remembered as confident and rapier witted, is pictured on muddied knees being helped to his feet by the goalkeeper, a physio and a St John's ambulanceman after a robust challenge from Twentyman. The heads of both players are bandaged in towels, probably to stem the flow of claret, though Clough looks shaken and in pain, as Twentyman, muscle-bound, marches behind him in front of the Kop ready for more action. Neither Twentyman nor Clough achieved their ultimate ambition as footballers. Although Clough did play for England on two occasions, he didn't earn enough caps to reflect his performances on the pitch, which saw him score a total of 251 goals in 274 games. He later said that this failure inspired him as a manager.

Twentyman, meanwhile, never won promotion with Liverpool. His achievements as a player were similarly modest. He was a nearly man. He nearly signed for a Wolves side prior to them becoming great in the late-'50s. He nearly avoided relegation to the Second Division with Liverpool after an all-too late upturn in form over Easter. He nearly won promotion back to the First Division only to miss out four times. He nearly played under Bill Shankly when he took charge at Anfield, instead opting to leave.

According to Norman Clarke, a winger who played with Twentyman at Ballymena and Brian Clough at Sunderland, the only reason why Twentyman was fired by Hartlepool was because of an arrangement between their dictatorial chairman, Ernest Ord (a loan shark by trade) and several high-profile names in north-eastern football. "The only thing I have in common with Brian Clough is that we were both given a free transfer on the same day, 30 June 1965," Clarke says, cuttingly. "Clough had a testimonial match at Sunderland in September '65 and it was well known that he was trying to get a managerial job in football. He'd previously been looking after Sunderland's youth team while staying on a player's contract. George Hardwick was Sunderland manager and a famous England international. He and Clough had both come through the Middlesbrough system and had grown up in the same area of the town. Clough knew he wasn't going to play anymore so he was chuntering for something else to do. George gave him a job to keep him quiet for a while. Clough did well and took the team to the semi-final of the Cup where they lost to Everton with Jimmy Husband playing. But at the end of that season, his contract was up and it wasn't renewed because he'd annoyed too many people. He was an insufferable bloke. The press liked Clough, though, because he talked a lot. He also had fingers in many pies and was friends with a few powerful people, notably Jackie Milburn and Len Shackleton. They managed to concoct the job at Hartlepools for Clough by speaking to Ord. Unfortunately for Geoff, he was in the way."

After eight games in charge where 'Pools won three, drew one and lost four, Twentyman was sacked by Ord and given a month's notice on the house he was living in, which was being paid for by the club. Although Twentyman still had a property in Carlisle, he'd let it out to another family and was having problems ending their tenancy. It was a matter of some concern. "My mother was pregnant with me," explains William Twentyman. "We had nowhere to live. Brian Clough wanted to move into our house in Hartlepool and had my mum and dad turfed out before the end of the month's notice. My mum hated Clough for that. She resented him for the rest of her life and wouldn't hear a good word said about him." Twentyman returned to Carlisle, working as a van driver, something that was very "demeaning," according to Clarke. He couldn't get a job in football. "Geoff was thinking about going back to Liverpool to look for work because there wasn't much going on in Carlisle. He thought about Fords in Halewood. He was planning to travel to Liverpool with the family's last £5 in his pocket, then, on the very same day, Norman Lowe, Liverpool's chief scout, left for America. Soon after, Geoff got contact from Shanks and he offered him the job as Norman's replacement. Geoff was in the right place at the right time. So was Shanks."

3. A Liverpool Scout

Spotting Shanks, shopping in the north
and three great teams

BILL Shankly handed Geoff Twentyman a lifeline when he made him his Chief Scout in 1967 but there is a suggestion that Shanks might have been repaying a favour. When Shankly was appointed manager of Liverpool, the club was in distress. After relegation in 1954, Don Welsh pledged that his team had skidded down a crevasse and would scramble back to the summit of English football within a year. Instead, they slid into a chasm of no return. Welsh was sacked, then Phil Taylor took over before departing too. Despite finishing third and fourth it wasn't enough to win promotion, so the directors, led by chairman TV Williams searched for new inspiration.

Upon Shankly's appointment on 1 December 1959, the *Echo* described him as a 'bullet-headed Scot' and said: 'Whatever the future holds, it certainly won't be dull', in reference to his habit of getting his own way at former clubs. 'What sort of a man is Shankly?' the paper questioned. 'He'll be very much the players' boss…if he has a fault it is that he is likely to be too conscientious. He's football daft, as they say he spares neither himself nor anyone who does not give him 100 per cent effort.' Conversely, they inaccurately point out: 'He is not a man with the gift of the gab, but he's none worse for that.'

The *Echo* pictured a stern-faced headshot of Shankly with the caption: 'The face of a man with a mission. Bill Shankly has a solitary aim – to put Liverpool back in the First Division. If he succeeds, he's the friend for life of all Liverpudlians.' Shankly's self-confidence prompted him to work without a fixed contract. 'How far would he be prepared to go, one wonders, to tempt his old club [Huddersfield] to allow Denis Law to join him?' the *Echo* speculated.

With little money available to him in the transfer market (as well as interference from some board members – something that nearly made him resign again) Shankly didn't sign Law and instead focused on getting the best out of those players that were good enough and already there, as well as weeding out those who didn't conform to his leadership. "When Bill took over, the club was in an even worse position than when we went down in '54," Ronnie Moran says. "The players weren't good enough, but Bill didn't have any money to spend, so he had to work with what he already had. The players were lacking confidence, but he would go round, even after losing some games, and tell everyone individually: 'Christ son, you're doing well.' Deep down, he knew that they weren't doing well and that they weren't good enough in the long term, but he tried to boost the confidence of the lesser players at the club to get us through the hard times in the short term. He did it even though he knew he was going to get rid of them as soon as he had the opportunity to."

In every revolution, blood is spilt. Moran sensed there was going to be a great purge of players but believed he was going to be one of those kept on at Anfield. "No, no. I was a worker and I knew straight away Bill liked that. Although I didn't play all the time under Bill, I knew he liked having me around because of my effort and because I enjoyed being there. There was a time when every week two or three players were leaving, so it wasn't a nice period for some of the lads."

Geoff Twentyman had stayed with the club through their years in the Second Division. Johnny Morrissey said that Twentyman led the team through this period and was a 'Goliath' amongst men, recalling a game when he was hit full-on in the face by the ball – "an old proper leather type with stitching that could take your eye out" – making the crowd collectively gasp as he fell backwards onto the mud-caked turf. "The ball was hit so hard that it would have knocked a lesser being out, but Geoff got straight back up and kept heading the ball throughout the match whenever it came his way."

Twentyman played his last game for Liverpool in October 1959, two months before Shankly was appointed manager of the club. When Shankly was appointed, he told the *Echo*: 'Bill Shankly is one of the finest men in football. I think the world of him. The club couldn't have got a better man.' Despite this glowing praise, Twentyman decided to move to Northern Ireland only days after Shankly was announced as Liverpool boss, becoming player-manager of Ballymena United. Twentyman's legacy, though, was perhaps greater than anyone knew at the time. Ronnie Moran says that Geoff was a "quiet lad, y'know", but the kind of person in a dressing room that when he did speak, everyone would stand to attention.

Over his years at Anfield, he'd struck up a healthy working relationship with TV Williams, the club's chairman. Liverpool was a different club to the one we understand today and players frequently mixed with board members freely. Twentyman sometimes acted as a chauffeur for Williams, who could not drive, and on many occasions he took him to the home of John Moores where the trio would play bridge together. Williams and Twentyman respected each other's views on football and would regularly share post-match conversations in Southport's Prince of Wales Hotel – a favourite eating and watering hole of both families. It was here that Williams learnt about the genius of Bill Shankly, according to Ivor Broadis and Norman Clarke, a trusted friend who later scouted for Twentyman after they met in Northern Ireland. Shankly had applied for the Liverpool job in 1951, but instead the board chose Don Welsh (who didn't apply) as a more experienced alternative at top-level football.

"Geoff told me that he spoke a lot about Bill with TV Williams," explains Clarke. "Geoff was and always had been a football person. It was the only thing he knew and Mr Williams recognised his ability to spot a leader. Geoff had always spoken to me about Bill ever since I first knew him and I am sure he did the same with Mr Williams. Bill and Geoff respected each other because they both valued honesty."

Broadis backs this up: "It was clear, even back in the late '40s that Geoff respected Bill a massive amount. Even after we'd both left Carlisle and I was at Manchester City and he was at Liverpool, he would talk about Bill all the time. He was one of his closest friends in football."

Whether or not the kind words of Twentyman influenced Williams is uncertain, but altogether quite possible. Ronnie Moran says that before Shanks's arrival, he wasn't aware of Twentyman's admiration for the great man, but also adds: "This is how it works in football. People talk and those who are respected are always listened to. I'm not saying TV Williams made his decision based on Geoff's opinion, but maybe he was impressed by what Geoff had said beforehand."

If Twentyman's constant nattering to Williams championed his decision to appoint Shankly in 1959, then his credentials as a scout were established long before he spotted Hansen, Rush and Clemence. Shankly's arrival at Liverpool is the single most important point in Liverpool's history as we understand it today, and if Twentyman did propose Shankly to Williams, it was a more important spot than any player he later recommended to Shanks himself, Paisley, Fagan or Dalglish.

*****

WHILE Geoff Twentyman took his first steps in management, Liverpool under Shankly thrived. Despite early struggles – and his ruthless attitude towards people he felt weren't up to standard – Shankly quickly earned the respect of all the players as well as the fans who had been starved of success throughout the '50s.

Liverpool won promotion from the Second Division in 1962 before lifting the First Division title two years later, as well as the FA Cup in

1965. Shankly's first great team consisted of a spine of Scots. The manager understood that all of his achievements with Liverpool branched from the closely knit and humbling team spirit – as well as the fanatical idea that Liverpool were destined for greatness. Shankly also realised that this belief could be shattered given ill-advised moves in the transfer market.

Shankly's first great team, with its foundation of Lawrence, Yeats and St John, was unified by failure then triumph. The team in the main had been formed while the club was in the Second Division, and those very same players rose to become First Division champions in a relatively short space of time. Shankly knew that this team would one day get old and he would have to replace them – but he also appreciated that these players would have to be traded for equally talented or better replacements. Now that Liverpool were considered an emerging power in the top division, they could attract the country's best players. Potentially, though, these players could arrive with the grandest idea of self-worth. Shankly was aware that if he signed a player with a bigger head than Birkenhead, he could break the carefully carved team spirit in the dressing room.

To maintain this atmosphere inside Melwood and Anfield, Shankly decided to place his trust in someone he knew well. By appointing a scout that shared similar beliefs about human qualities as well as how football should be played, he would ensure that the equilibrium inside the dressing room would remain as fervent as ever and Liverpool would continue on their long path to glory. This is why he appointed Geoff Twentyman as his chief scout, in place of the departing Norman Lowe.

"Shanks wanted people around him that wanted to be winners," says Ronnie Moran. "He also wanted people who loved their job and would work hard. That's why the likes of Bob, Joe, Reuben, me and Geoff were around the club for such a long time."

"Shanks and Geoff had similar views on life and football," Ivor Broadis adds. "Shanks realised that he needed someone he could trust to sign the players that would make Liverpool great again, and Geoff's character suited that role perfectly."

Shankly's philosophy towards the transfer market was to target the young. With financial restraints imposed on the club, youngsters were the only players he could afford. He also wanted to sign able players with time on their side and mould them the Liverpool way, so eventually there was a transparency between the way the first team, the reserves and the youth teams performed. If a first-team member was injured or suspended, he wanted a younger equivalent to replace him with seamless ease.

William Twentyman later said that he could tell exactly what his dad used to look for in a player, because of the things he used to tell him before playing football matches as a child. "He'd go through a couple of things. 'Concentrate all the time, roll your sleeves up, look like you want to play, get your arms up for balance.' I could imagine Shankly telling his players the same thing."

And this was Twentyman's guideline for targeting players. They must not only be able to fit into the Liverpool way, but Shankly's way. Twentyman had to pinpoint players who above anything else could simply pass and move. Practically, this seems an achievable task, but as we later find out, not all clubs had the same philosophy about the game, as long-ball tactics in the First Division were common and just getting the ball on the ground was a task in itself for some teams. Twentyman would have to display all of his scouting nous to sign players such as Alan Kennedy, who eventually fitted into the Liverpool way, but before was only used to the kick-and-rush per-centage football at Newcastle.

Years later, Twentyman talked of Shankly's penchant for "getting them young so he could mould them into what he wanted". Shankly would train his squad hard during the week and allow Joe Fagan, Ronnie Moran and eventually Roy Evans to shape the same players into match winners on Saturday afternoons when reserve league games were held.

Shankly repeatedly admitted that the first result he wanted to know after the first team had finished their match was the reserves'. "Get the boys into the habit of winning; it's a good habit," he said.

Despite his intentions in the transfer market, Shankly also grasped he couldn't sign youngsters at a hefty price and then take time moulding them with reserve-team football. The first player Twentyman recommended to Liverpool was Francis Lee, but Liverpool never had the sort of money to afford to pay Bolton Wanderers' asking price. Besides, not even Shankly could leave a player with such reputable ability in the second team, could he?

So Twentyman's brief was to find the best young players Liverpool could afford with the potential to develop in the future, or to make "Liverpool successful by the cheapest way possible", as Shankly said, who knew that the only monies he had available were through personal guarantors made by TV Williams and friends at the bank. The fact that Twentyman wasn't charged with bringing in world-renowned players to the club might suggest that it made his job easier. Far from it. Twentyman's prolific record for spotting young talent in the lower leagues might also suggest that the job was easy pickings for any top-division scout. If that was the case, where were the Arsenal, Manchester United and Leeds United scouts when Twentyman plucked out Ray Clemence, Kevin Keegan and Phil Neal?

The creation of a successful football club is an unending evolution, and one main point sticks out about the way Shankly, with the help of Twentyman, managed to turn the average into brilliant. Players who were regarded elsewhere as no more than ordinary, lacking enough potential to attract interest from any First Division clubs, blossomed into European champions at Liverpool. Until Twentyman came looking, no one thought enough of Clemence, Neal, Steve Heighway or later Steve Nicol to actually commit money towards their purchase.

Equally, when Twentyman did recommend a considerable amount of money for an unknown youngster, as he did with an 18-year-old Ian

Rush (£300,000 and a world record fee for a teenager), he was putting his reputation on the line. Allegedly, when Rush didn't break into the first team for 12 months, without tearing up any trees in the reserves, one club director asked Twentyman: "Why have we wasted so much money on this dud Rush?"

At the beginning there were other problems for Twentyman as well. In Bill Shankly's official biography, Dave Bowler describes how Shanks had previously used 'reliable' contacts around the country before Twentyman arrived in '67. On one occasion he ironically used someone else from Carlisle to cast an eye over Cumbria. The scout went to see a young player at his home just outside the city and ask whether he wanted to sign for Liverpool, because he'd heard of his great potential. Then the boy's father involved himself in negotiations. "There's a vacancy coming up outside Liverpool with my company. Could Mr Shankly fix it for me to get the job? There's a lot of clubs after the lad." Shankly realised he was being blackmailed and told the boy's father that he could sign for someone else. The thought that Shankly had to involve himself in instances like this made him realise he needed someone trusted like Geoff who could make the initial contact before leaving the rest of the deal to someone on the board – usually Sid Reakes, who was a director and the money-man.

With Shankly focusing on his players and Twentyman in control of the scouting system, the pair also agreed that Liverpool would target players with a northern soul – initially an idea to help players adapt quickly, especially if they were young and living away from home for the first time. Twentyman said: "We concentrated on Lancashire and other players nearby, and we picked up Alec Lindsay and Steve Heighway…Bill wanted locally based lads, and even fellas like Clemence and Keegan weren't too far away. We didn't bring them from hundreds of miles away and that helped them settle." Over time, it also seemed a wise idea to sign players with a northern heritage because it not only made them identify with the club more – in turn wanting to be successful – but also pleased the ever-more demanding crowd who loved to see local lads play for the first team. No southern-born footballers played for Liverpool with any distinction throughout Shankly's reign and then after him until Paul Walsh signed for the club (against the recommendation of Twentyman) in 1984, unless you include Phil Neal, who was born in Irchester.

Considering that Neil Ruddock (born in Wandsworth), Phil Babb (Lambeth) and David James (Watford) were all signed in the '90s, achieving non-success as well as not really feeling like Liverpool players, it's clear that Shankly and Twentyman had foresight and it's easy to understand why they preferred to shop in the north.

Under this premise, Twentyman set about building up a countrywide network that successfully provided Liverpool with a steady stream of talent for more than three decades. A quick look inside his scouting book suggests that he used numerous scouts across the country – people who would watch players first and, if they were good enough after an initial report, Twentyman would follow up the lead. Andy Beattie, for instance, made the first call on Kevin Keegan. 'This player is fancied by A Beattie,' it says, scrawled across the notebook.

Another person, whose role as youth development officer often overlapped with Twentyman's, was the legendary Tom Saunders. 'Our system was basically that we signed players who were three-quarters of the way there and then nursed them through to the first team,' Twentyman told *The Kop* in 1996. 'No one could say that the system didn't work. Most people are looking for ready-made articles today, but it's much better to spot a player while he's still developing.'

With Twentyman in charge of first-team recruitment and Saunders leading the youth development system, Liverpool quickly accrued the best talent, predominantly picked from the north, of footballers aged between 15 and 23. There was some transparency between the roles of both Twentyman and Saunders, however, and neither exclusively focused on finding players of a particular age. While Twentyman spotted David Fairclough (then 14), Saunders eyed Bruce Grobbelaar – the first non-British player to become a regular at Anfield in more than 50 years.

Tom Saunders was Liverpool's youth development officer between 1968 and 1986. He was appointed by Bill Shankly and, like Geoff Twentyman, remained in a job throughout the reigns of Bob Paisley, Joe Fagan and Kenny Dalglish. Saunders also spied on Liverpool's European opponents and made dossiers on lesser-known players and clubs across the continent.

Although his main role was overseeing the development of youth players, he also scouted potential transfer targets. He enjoyed similar powers to Twentyman and deserves credit in his own right for nurturing the talents of local boys Jimmy Case and Sammy Lee, especially. Later, Saunders recommended Phil Thompson to Gerard Houllier for the appointment as assistant manager at the club in 1998, and two years ago a lecture theatre at Liverpool's Youth Academy in Kirkby was named in his honour.

*****

LIVERPOOL had three great teams between the '60s and the end of the '80s. Each one can be defined by its strike force. Hunt and St John, Keegan and Toshack, Dalglish and Rush. Shankly and his successors understood that the replacement of each side should be executed carefully. The steady turnover of players meant Twentyman's search for talent was constant.

Shankly learnt this lesson the hard way. When Liverpool won the league title in 1973, the first time in seven years, the *Echo* argued that the shock FA Cup defeat to Watford in 1970 was the day their latest championship success was conceived. Liverpool believed that the cup was theirs for the taking that season after a moderate league performance where they eventually finished fifth (Everton, inspired by Alan Ball, won it). A sixth-round draw against Watford, a side struggling to avoid relegation from the old Second Division, seemed like a passport to the semi-finals. In the line-up at Vicarage Road that day – a team that as they passed Wembley on the train on the way to the match had sung: "We're on our way to Wembley" – were great Liverpool servants such as Ron Yeats, Tommy Lawrence and Ian St John.

They were instrumental in the side that had won two league titles and an FA Cup, but on that winter's day in 1970, dusk was setting in on their careers. While he never admitted it publicly, Shankly knew changes would need to be made – younger men brought in for the old and a new team born. But with Liverpool rolling steadily on in the league and in the sixth round of the cup, he had no excuse to start making those changes mid-way through the 1969/70 season. But the result at Watford finally gave him an excuse. The Hornets swarmed around them in their mustard yellow shirts and almost-brown shorts made filthy by a pitch that resembled a no-man's-land in Ypres. Shankly felt the sting.

A week later against Derby County at Anfield, Yeats, St John and Lawrence were all missing from the Liverpool starting XI. Ray Clemence, who'd signed three years earlier from Scunthorpe, had served his apprenticeship under Lawrence and came in to become a regular. Shortly afterwards, Larry Lloyd replaced Yeats and within a year Steve Heighway arrived from Skelmersdale to add attacking flair in place of St John. Alec Lindsay, who tried more positions than a devotee of the *Kama Sutra*, finally found a regular place at left-back.

Liverpool's defeat at Vicarage Road prompted Shankly to make changes – in turn, placing extra emphasis on his scouting system. Only Tommy Smith, Ian Callaghan and Chris Lawler remained of the veterans from the Watford debacle through to Liverpool's title-winning side of 1973. In the meantime, Twentyman needed to be able to judge a player on his current ability as well as his potential ability if placed in the environment of Melwood. Toshack and Keegan were added to the squad and quickly established themselves as first-choice picks. Liverpool's movement in the transfer market during this time was revolutionary. Wholesale changes needed to be made. Shankly, inspired by Paisley, was aware that Liverpool suffered relegation in 1954, seven years after being champions of England, because the team had collectively grown old.

Although in recent years, with the advent of rotation and the need to have a minimum of 23 players in each squad, at least three or four players arrive at Anfield each summer, in the late '70s Liverpool never made more than two signings who were considered ready for the first team in the close season. After the dramatic turnover in players between 1970 and 1972, Shankly, then Paisley, believed that they had a squad of players that would take Liverpool on to a platform that would create years of success, meaning only a small change here and there was needed later on in the decade.

This approach was one of the reasons why Liverpool outlasted any challengers that came their way. Derby County, Leeds United and Nottingham Forest were all constant threats throughout the '70s before for different reasons, falling away in the '80s. Years after winning successive European Cups in 1979 and 1980, Brian Clough admitted that he ought to have copied Liverpool's best practice of replacing one or two players a season and leaving the rest alone. He hastily replaced influential stars such as Kenny Burns, Martin O'Neill, Trevor Francis, Archie Gemmill and former Liverpool centre-back Larry Lloyd with over-priced dross like Justin Fashanu.

Liverpool imposed a measured, ever-continuing restoration programme – so augmented that it was barely visible. The transition between Keegan's departure and Dalglish's arrival, for instance, was flawless. Clough and Forest, meanwhile, ripped everything away that had made them so successful and tried to rebuild the squad in one swoop.

Clough's attitude towards team rebuilding was in part down to his own ego. He fell out with Peter Taylor, his assistant and the man that did most of his talent spotting (he brought in Garry Birtles from non-league Long Eaton United for £2,000 and within three years he was a European Cup winner), and took on the duty of eyeing targets up and bringing players in himself. As he constantly told everyone: "Forest would be nothing without me", and he unwisely felt he could dictate anything and everything around the club.

There were no 'Big 'Eads' at Liverpool, though, and each member of the staff trusted one another's ability in their respective field. Shankly and Paisley managed first-team affairs, Twentyman got along with his scouting, Tom Saunders took care of youth development and Sid Reakes moderated the bank balance. "It was communism with a small 'c'," as Shankly once put it.

Shankly understood early on in his managerial career that it was harder to maintain success than achieve it. (Clough only realised it retrospectively). Shanky's protocol for success was basic: "Keep it simple and there's less chances of things going wrong," he would say on and off the pitch. His teams were well organised and compact, yet fluent and stylish, playing effortless football. On the training ground the attitude was the same and he trusted players to practice as they wished in preparation for matches. They were, after all, professionals.

4. An Eye for Talent

The boss's old Cortina, signing players
and the bloke with the trilby

THE BALKANS, December 1998. Phil Thompson has been back at Anfield for less than a month. This time he's assistant manager to Gerard Houllier. In his first week on the job he passes through customs at Amsterdam's Schipol Airport three times in four days. In a country where the darker pleasures in life are free and easy, Thompson's activities may appear suspicious. In reality, the Liverpool squad, which allegedly lacks discipline, is in need of a major overhaul and Thompson has been charged with the duty of scouring the continent for new players.

On this occasion, he's watching Croatia Zagreb play Olympiacos. It's freezing. The kind of East European winter that scuppered Nazi dreams of Lebensraum. Maksimir, the home of Zagreb, is suffering from glaciation. The pitch, the stands, the seats and the half-time Vipava soup have all turned into ice. Zagreb are playing in the Champions League group stages for the first time. Victories over Porto at home and Ajax away have placed them in a position to qualify for the next round. All they must do is defeat the Greeks – who will surely not relish a trip north to a rime-gripped city, which only years earlier was at the epicentre of a war zone. Deep beneath the vast concrete terraces, Thompson waits for the game to begin. He leaves it until the final moment to move outside – such are the harsh weather conditions.

"It was Baltic," Thompson recalls, confusing his geography. "I went over there with Sammy Lee to watch Igor Biscan. He was very young but he had a good game on one of the most difficult pitches I've ever seen. The Greek players were all wearing tights and gloves because the temperature was sub-zero. There was snow in the stands and ice on the seats so you couldn't sit down. The pitch was bone hard, too. I remember Sammy went to go for a piss. His shoes had leather soles and he fell down 10 flights of stairs. When he came back, he looked like a little snowman. The game ended 1-1 and Zagreb ended up finishing third in the group and didn't qualify."

In the immediate months after his return to Liverpool, Thompson spent as much time in the air as he did at Melwood as he jetted across Europe in an attempt to suss out potential signings. "It was a very tiring time," he says. Thompson, who as a player won every major competition in the 1970s and early '80s, was tempted back to Liverpool as assistant manager six years after leaving when Graeme Souness was appointed manager. "He sacked me. There's no two ways about it. We never got on when we were players and, for whatever reason, he bore a grudge."

Thompson's acrimonious departure made him even hungrier for success when he returned under Houllier. "There were a lot of changes going on at the club. Staff were moving about, players were coming and going, so I ended up doing a lot of scouting with Sammy as a short-term measure."

The tiring nature as well as the hidden pressures of the role put Thompson off scouting for some time – "I went to watch Cristiano Ronaldo when he was playing in Portugal," he said, "but United moved for him very quickly. That was a hard one to take." Such examples of the competitiveness in the transfer system today indicate that it is harder than ever to snare elite European players. But Thompson is keen to point out that even back in the '70s, when Geoff Twentyman was the chief scout of Liverpool, it wasn't any easier. The talent of seeing potential is a "natural skill."

"Geoff did most of the groundwork himself. There were no computers, so he was on the phone and at the post office all the time. He didn't delegate too much either because he knew the system well and did it all on his own. But like I later found out, the travelling must have been the hardest part. I remember going to games in Sheffield as a reserve-team player and having to go over Snake Pass. It took hours and hours to get there because there weren't as many motorways, so we'd even have a stop off in Manchester to have some lunch pre-match, then have a dinner on the way back, too. Geoff made this kind of journey a couple of times a week just to check out a player that might be a false lead. He did a lot of miles."

*****

IN THE time before avant-garde fashion emporiums, retro boutiques, state-of-the-art retail malls and Liverpool One, the residents of Merseyside would find everything they needed in the shops and street markets on Bold Street and in the surrounding area.

Every family made the weekly trip for fruit, veg and new clothing. Even Bill Shankly and his wife Nessie. As a firm believer in being amongst the throngs, Shanks would drive his gaudy Ford Cortina or Corsair from his home on Bellefield Drive in West Derby, wearing a withered brown flat cap and cloak.

Trawling through the inevitable Hanover Street traffic en route to his parking space, he would take time to salute any pedestrians or motorists that noticed him. Shankly may have been a great football manager, but if he had one failing, it was that he wasn't a great driver. Stirling Moss he was not. Onlookers have recalled how on these trips he would acknowledge anyone who recognised him, in turn taking his giant hands off the wheel and veering onto the kerb.

Shanks's misadventures behind the wheel inadvertently created problems for Twentyman later. To complete his job, Twentyman needed a car roadworthy enough to drive thousands of miles a year across the length and breadth of Britain. Although he was later placed on the official list when Liverpool issued cars at the beginning of every season, in his early days he had to accept the manager's hand-me-downs. Unlike Phil Thompson, he never flew anywhere and was more likely to go to Alloa than Amsterdam.

Every two years, Shankly would get a new motor – usually a different model and colour of Cortina or Corsair – and the old one would be passed on to Twentyman. Shankly loved garish, wicked colours, so most would be bright orange or canary yellow complete with fluffy dice and 1600 engine. Twentyman would run them into the ground before they paid a final visit to a scrap yard in the Liverpool docks.

'The second car he passed on was much the worse for wear,' Twentyman once told the *Weekly News*. 'One door had obviously been bashed in and re-sprayed a different hue. Unfortunately, the damaged door never fitted properly. There was always a draught. When I gave a director a lift in the car one day, he couldn't understand how I managed to travel any distance in such an icebox.'

Many of Twentyman's journeys would follow a similar route. The M6 to the Scottish borders or Snake Pass over to South Yorkshire. Sometimes he would drive via Scotch Corner on the way to the north-east. Such was his pride in his job, he rarely told anyone where he was going, at least outside the football club. Geoff Twentyman Jnr (his first son) said that he was constantly badgered in school by classmates asking who Liverpool were going to sign next. "There was an unwritten rule in the house that you couldn't ask who he was looking at. If he wanted you to know, he would tell. Once you'd established that they were the rules of engagement, although it wasn't like signing an official secrets act with the family, you accepted it."

Young Geoff explained that he only became privy to golden snippets of Liverpool blether long after signings were made and long after players became regulars in the first team. He recalls the time when his dad told him about the deal to bring Alan Hansen to Anfield.

"Sometimes he'd come back and tell me about an unnamed player. 'Unbelievable, what a player, nobody could get the ball off him. He does things players shouldn't be able to do.' Then he'd come back the next week and it would be: 'Oh, he's a liability, got the ball taken off him on the edge of his own 18-yard box trying to dribble.' Alan Hansen was definitely one of these players. At the end, he was decisive about him, but at first, he wasn't so sure.

"The one thing I remember him telling me particularly about Hansen was that it got to the end of the financial year and Liverpool had a certain amount of money to spend to avoid a tax liability. In the end, they had a bit of a punt on him really and spent £100,000. Hansen was a fine footballer and would have made it elsewhere, but the deciding factor of him coming to Liverpool was because they had a bit of spare cash that had to be spent – otherwise, it would have ended up with the taxman."

Twentyman rarely displayed any level of excitement about a player, at least not to his family. Down at Melwood, though, without naming names, he would wax lyrical to various members of staff when he saw someone who could "go both ways". "It meant to Geoff that he was a complete player," says Kevin Keegan. "It was the kind of player who if you showed him left, he would still go left, then if you showed him right, he'd do the same. Why he picked me then is anyone's guess because I was one-footed."

Every person at Melwood knew about Twentyman's role and understood that it was part of his job description to search for talent that was good enough to eventually replace particular players. "We'd all shout to him: 'Who have you found that's better than us today, Geoff?'" says Alan Kennedy, who goes on to explain that he and his teammates would take the mickey out of Twentyman because of his repetition of the idiom "he goes both ways". "He said it so many times about different players that it became his catchphrase. The fact that there was an innuendo in it made it even funnier because Geoff was so honest and innocent – a typical Liverpool FC character."

Countless players and coaching staff add that Twentyman had a slight but noticeable tremor in his voice, highlighted by a broad Cumbrian burr. " 'Carlisssle…goes both waaaays,' " replays Phil Thompson. "One of the lads thought he sounded like a sheep."

Twentyman played in the famous five-a-side games that took place at Melwood against the apprentice players up until the early '70s (by that time the pain in a longstanding hip problem became too apparent). Along with Shankly, Paisley, Ronnie Moran and Reuben Bennett, Twentyman would be an "integral" part of the staff team, according to David Fairclough. "Geoff would usually play in midfield and was the steadiest of them all," he says. "Shanks would operate in the right-half position as a link between the defence and midfield, not moving out of the centre circle. That was his area and nobody else went in it. Joe Fagan would be the centre-half – he didn't move much and Reuben would be the goalscorer. His head was like a magnet and he would sweep home any cross that came his way. Ronnie Moran had the strength and the stamina so he would do most of the running, playing everywhere. Aside from that they all had their little zones and each one knew their position inside out. There were no real referees for the games. Shanks and Joe would do that. If any of them lost the ball in a dangerous position, there would be a whistle blowing for some obscure decision."

Even after retiring from Melwood's legendary matches, Twentyman would often occupy his free afternoons by walking round the fields of the training ground, gathering his thoughts – much like Ronnie Moran does to this day. On one occasion, Fairclough recalls how Twentyman stopped him – "He had a soft spot for me did Geoff" – before telling him about a player he'd been watching at Chester City. " 'Rush is the boy's name. He's got a lot of potential…but don't worry, he's not a better player than you.' "

Away from Melwood, Twentyman would spend three days at a time travelling day and night over weekends to watch players mainly in the north of England and Scotland. It is ironic that while Liverpool were playing some of the greatest football in their history, he would be away from Anfield watching some struggling teams for players with a glimmer of talent at a dung heap in the old Fourth Division.

Geoff Jnr says the one and only time his father took him on a scouting mission was at the age of 10. "Shrewsbury were playing Bournemouth or someone like that. If anyone thought it was a glamorous job, that experience put it into perspective. But that was the level of football he watched. There must have been a tremendous level of satisfaction when one of his players came through. He rarely saw Liverpool play on Saturday afternoons, but it didn't bother him. He was happy just watching any level of football."

One of the perks of Twentyman's job, however, was that he did manage to attend most of the showpiece cup finals that Liverpool were involved in at the end of each season. By that time of year, his campaign, like that of the players, was more or less complete. Son William remembered panic gripping hold as he searched for his father in TV pictures during Heysel only to see him sitting calmly with other club dignitaries away from the horrors of the pen in section Z.

Eight years earlier, after the 1977 European Cup final, Twentyman brought the trophy to their home in Maghull. "I remember returning from school at about 4.30pm and it was really hot," recalls William. "The sun always hit the back of our house, so my mum drew the curtains to keep it a bit cooler. At least that's what I thought. I saw a green velvet jacket on the couch and I wondered what my dad had been buying. I looked a bit closer and then in this darkened room I could see the gold Umbro emblem stitched into the cape. I opened it up and there's the European Cup shining at me. I was only 10 and it was all a bit surreal. I would liken it to seeing Elvis Presley in my living room. It was unusual on the eye because it was such a massive trophy and only a few weeks earlier I'd seen Emlyn Hughes lift it in Rome. The trophy was nearly bigger than me. Dad did the same thing when we won the UEFA Cup the year before. He left it in his Cortina overnight."

As the sons of a renowned scout like Twentyman, there was a pressure to perform on the football field for William and Geoff Jnr. William admits that he was never really good enough to make it in the game professionally and ended up playing for the reserve team of local non-league side, Marine. Even during games at that level, his father's knowledge of the game would come in handy.

"He knew something about every single player on the pitch," William laughs. "He would know their strengths and weaknesses, and everything would be up there in his mind. All the players at that level would have nicknames. For instance, if there was a lad who they called 'Fitzy', my dad would still know who he was. 'Oh yeah, that's Fitzgibbons – he's a really handy right-winger,' he would say to me. 'But make sure you get him on his left foot – he can't use it.'"

Geoff Jnr, meanwhile, forged a long career with Bristol Rovers in the West Country, where he now works as a radio presenter for the BBC. In his teens he was good enough to play for Liverpool's youth teams, but was later released. He then joined Chorley where he was spotted by Preston North End scouts. He made his debut at Deepdale as an auxiliary centre-forward against Jim Smith's Oxford although he'd previously made his name, like his father, at centre-half.

"I asked dad on the off-chance whether he fancied coming to watch me play, but I thought he'd be out watching someone else for Liverpool. Unbeknown to me, he paid and sat in the stands at Deepdale. I did ok and won a few headers. He was sitting among the Preston fans saying: 'Who's this number nine? He's doing ok isn't he?' So he was enhancing my reputation. 'You've got a good 'un there,' he told them."

Twentyman would give his sons all kinds of unconventional advice when they were preparing to play games as teenagers, too. "Bathe your feet with methylated spirits to toughen your soles..." William and Geoff Jnr recall. "Shave the hairs off the top of your toes...train on grass...keep off the road...warm your legs up...leave the ball alone and get the blood flowing...roll your sleeves up and get your arms out for balance…grit your teeth and concentrate all of the time. You'll easily beat this lot…" You can imagine Shankly telling his squad the same thing deep beneath the Main Stand before a training session or on a match day, each one simple in reasoning yet rarely thought out practically.

Liverpool's success was born out of simplicity. As Barry Davies said: "Neal against Knuyp…[before tucking away the penalty]…and with such simplicity surely now the European Cup is won." Twentyman's approach to scouting was just as uncomplicated. 'If I see the slightest hint of ability I will compile a report on a player. Go back to check him out again. Make certain he doesn't slip through the net,' he told the media. 'One secret is that I invariably watch a player away from home. See how he reacts to foreign surroundings. Ian Rush was the exception to this rule. But he was only 18 when he burst so brilliantly onto the league scene. Because of that I was prepared to give him the benefit of the doubt.'

Observers of Liverpool history have often said that their success in the golden era was down to humble attitudes and trouble-free methods. "It was modesty to an extreme," Steve Nicol says. It is unsurprising, then, that Twentyman's criteria for spotting players followed common sense and honesty. 'If you go anywhere expecting to find the perfect player, you're going to be disappointed every time,' he said. 'I've a simple set of rules when I watch players. First, they must be clean strikers of the ball. I've never looked twice at any prospect who couldn't perform the basic function of kicking the ball correctly.'

Second on Twentyman's list: 'Can they pass properly?' After that comes the ability to be involved in the game, to want to be on the winning side. 'Pace and attitude are also essential,' he said, referring to the fact he would ask members in the crowd what players' reputations were like off the pitch. 'I look for craft in a player, someone who is crowded in but can still poke a little ball out of the ruck to set things moving. Those little things tell you if a player has got brains. I've one other rule. I never look at the programme before the match to see who's playing. You see a name that is familiar and suddenly you find yourself watching that player. If he's supposed to be good then somehow he becomes good. It's psychological.'

Few of the players Liverpool signed during Twentyman's time at Anfield were lacking in any of those departments. His record of backing winners meant that his selections were often signed without any pre-warning. 'The manager and coaches would do their best to have a look themselves, but sometimes they would bring them in on my word alone,' he said. 'A lot of players came in just on my recommendation, although as in every business a lot of it depended on finances.'

In interviews with *The Kop* magazine (November 1996) and a number of national newspapers who recognised Twentyman's aptitude for eyeing talent at the beginning of the 1980s, he explained how he was prepared to travel anywhere to find one player – even if it means dozens of wasted journeys. Twentyman's job was not only concerned with searching for good players, but keeping the bad ones away from Anfield as well. He quickly found out which people to trust on players and which ones would lead him down a blind alley. Many tips turned out to be players who just weren't good enough for Liverpool.

'I received a hot tip from a fellow in Dundee about a youngster he rated "the best kid ever seen in Scotland". I drove north to see this boy play. When he ran out his socks were around his ankles. He looked slovenly. Something I don't like. After only 10 minutes I left. The trip was a complete waste of time. The kid didn't deserve the rave reviews. He was never going to make the grade. There are many bad scouts sending in reports to clubs. Claiming expenses for their efforts. Many clubs would do better sending the expenses to charity! Their scout's judgement isn't up to scratch. I admit I'm not infallible. But I hope to be right 80 per cent of the time.'

Twentyman didn't even have to travel that far to find some players. Together with Tom Saunders, he found Jimmy Case playing for non-league South Liverpool and followed his progress in Sunday League football with Dockers side Blue Union while serving an apprenticeship as an electrician (which he continued when he was playing for Liverpool reserves). Twentyman and Saunders were impressed by Case's tenacity and single-mindedness, adding that his natural enthusiasm impressed them more than other players who followed misguided instructions from wannabe managers.

'I first saw Jimmy Case on a parks pitch. He went on to win a handful of medals with us. But the amateur coaching that goes on throughout the country is killing natural ability. I want to see kids passing a ball. Showing skills. Just enjoying themselves. Tactics can come later. The saddest sight is watching a team of talented kids being told how to play by a tin-pot coach. I can't bear watching youngsters play an offside trap. Usually they don't understand it anyway. So why teach them those things?'

Even when watching parks football, Twentyman attempted to continue the pretence of merely being an interested onlooker. Unlike today, when scouts arrive at kids' Sunday league matches wearing official club attire and their initials festooned across their shoulder blades, Twentyman's approach was diffident and he lapped the pitch slowly, watching from behind the parents and over-enthusiastic try-hard coaches. Soon enough, though, kids, especially in Sefton where he lived, came to recognise him for one distinctive piece of clothing. Peter Daly, a former apprentice at Liverpool, now living in Bootle, told me that despite Twentyman's role as a nationwide scout every kid in the area eventually knew about him because of one piece of distinctive clothing – a recollection that is backed up by Jimmy Case.

Daly says, "We'd be playing a match on Buckley Hill and there would be this guy standing on the side watching our matches for weeks and weeks. We didn't have a clue who he was and we all hoped he was a scout from one of the big clubs. Then one day, he turned up wearing this hat. We all knew it was Geoff Twentyman from that point because every kid in the local leagues recognised him as 'Twentyman…the bloke with the trilby'."

5. What Might Have Been

A Spanish superstar, the new McGarvey
and the ones that got away

SUNDAY league fields like Buckley Hill may have been the final destination for a few of the careers that Twentyman tried to launch, but other players finished their careers in more salubrious locations. Madrid, for instance.

Michael Robinson, who lives in the Spanish capital, might not be one of Liverpool's greats, and his status in English football circles is modest. But in Spain, he's a megastar presenter and an Iberian cross between Gary Lineker and Jan Molby owing to his regular TV appearances and his proclivity for mastering a foreign tongue while immersing himself in local culture. This mightn't have been possible had it not been for Twentyman – not that Robinson was sure whether the scout had a role in his move to Anfield when I met up with him ahead of Liverpool's Champions League game with Atletico Madrid in October 2008.

His home, concealed within a golfing estate 25 minutes from the centre of Madrid on a northern road to the distant barrack town of Burgos in the Basque country, is something from a Mills and Boon novel. The restored farmhouse stands abaft tall, ivy-encrusted stone walls. Fresh berries dangle on the end of every leaf. Each villa in the area is different from the next. Robinson's, however, is by far the most picturesque, lying in the milieu of a sweeping mountain range. Only the buzzing noise of a hedge-strimmer fractures the tranquillity, although the scent of freshly chopped pine is most refreshing.

After being welcomed by his son Liam, Robinson Snr wobbles down the varnished stairs inside his home looking pie-eyed. "I was out last night. Until 5am," he smiles, with one of his peepers almost popping out. "A neighbour had a party and he plays the piano. So I had a go and it became a bit of a Beatles tribute night. Anyway, I've had five hours sleep and I'm dying for something to eat. Let's go get some tortilla."

Robinson drives to the clubhouse at the golf course just up the hill from his house where the conversation takes in a whole range of sociological, cultural and sporting issues. "Basketball," he says, "is zoological." Robinson is certainly not your average ex-professional footballer. Later, we sit on his veranda. By now the midday heat is at its peak. His garden stretches into the Castilian countryside and is green and lush despite the lack of rainfall.

Robinson, now working for Canal Plus, is the face of football on Spanish TV after making his fame with 'El Dia Despues', which for 15 years was the country's most-watched sports programme. And, as it turns out, in his playing days he was scouted by Geoff Twentyman more than five years before he actually signed for Liverpool. "Twentyman, you say…I'm not sure whether he had anything to do with my transfer…"

Resting back in his wicker garden furniture with quilted cushion, Robinson reflects on precisely how important a role Twentyman played in his career without him knowing about it. In his book, the scout noted Robinson's potential in 1978, but it wasn't until 1983 when he actually signed. After leaving Liverpool, he spent two seasons at QPR before agreeing a move to Spain to play for Osasuna, even though he and his wife didn't know where the club was based. "The missus thought that Osasuna must be a real backwater because we couldn't find it on any maps at all. We even looked on one of those novelty table cloths but, of course, it wasn't there." (Osasuna hail from the city of Pamplona.)

Despite an uncertain start to life in Spain, he quickly settled and scored regularly for Osasuna in La Liga. He enjoyed the experience so much that after retiring he stayed and has been living in Spain ever since. "Whether or not Geoff remembered me from my Preston days and recommended me to Joe Fagan, I really don't know," he says. "What I do know is that my short spell at Liverpool gave me a reputation across Europe and when I arrived in Spain I was the only player in the top league with a European Cup winners' medal – the English teams had dominated the competition for so long. Without my time at Liverpool, I probably wouldn't have earned a move to Spain, and without the move to Spain, I probably wouldn't be sitting here now talking to you with the sun on my back. Maybe I have a lot to thank Geoff Twentyman for."

Robinson is uncertain whether Twentyman played any part in his £200,000 transfer from Brighton in the summer of 1983, adding that he wasn't at Liverpool long enough to find out. "I knew I had limitations to my game. But few players can say they've won a league title and a European Cup in their one and only season at a club, can they?"

Robinson was 20 years old and playing for Preston North End when Twentyman initially went to watch him at the beginning of the 1978/79 season. 'Looks a good player if playing in a good side. Has to learn a little more on positional play around goal,' the scout noted. Instead of moving to Anfield, Robinson, unaware of Liverpool's interest, signed for Manchester City having scored 15 league goals in 48 games at Deepdale. Robinson grew up as a Liverpool fan and says that although he would have relished signing for the club at the time, it was probably best he ended up at Maine Road. "I averaged something like one goal in every three games while I was at City. The move might not have really worked out because I didn't get on with Malcolm Allison, the manager, but I was glad I went there because it allowed me to develop my game before I moved on to Brighton."

Months before Twentyman first looked at Robinson, Liverpool signed Frank McGarvey from St Mirren for £300,000. Although it is unclear on whose recommendation Bob Paisley signed him, there is no mention of anyone by the name of McGarvey in Twentyman's notebook. It was a huge fee for an unproven striker and he flopped badly, moving back to

Scotland a year later with Celtic (at a loss of £25,000) having never made a first-team appearance at Anfield. It is quite possible Liverpool realised McGarvey wasn't good enough soon after signing him and that Twentyman looked at Robinson as his potential replacement.

However, it looks like he signed Ian Rush instead. Rush moved to Liverpool from Chester City in 1980. Once again the fee was £300,000. Like McGarvey, Rush struggled to settle at Anfield and people behind the scenes at the club questioned Twentyman's acumen for spotting talent. "Why have we spent so much money on a striker that doesn't score goals?" one board member asked Twentyman after Rush failed to find the net during his first season at the club. "Just you wait," responded Twentyman.

"It's an interesting thought," says Robinson on this issue. "Even Rushie struggled in his first season. Although I didn't struggle, I wasn't a prolific scorer. If Geoff saw me as a potential answer to the problems caused by McGarvey all those years before, maybe I was a little better than I thought I was. Who knows?"

Robinson isn't the only player who might wonder what would have happened had a move to Liverpool materialised. A quick glance through Twentyman's notebook reveals that he targeted names such as Stan Bowles and David Mills (both players were unavailable for interview during the writing of this book), while he also looked at Davie Cooper and Keith Weller who are now sadly deceased. Cooper later became a great with Glasgow Rangers, but for a period in the mid-'70s it seems that Twentyman was watching him every other weekend while he was at Clydebank. Often regarded as one of the most gifted players in Scottish history, Cooper was blessed with balletic grace and an elegant left foot. Graeme Souness, his former manager at Rangers, rated Cooper a more naturally gifted player than Kenny Dalglish, and was convinced he could have achieved worldwide fame if he had moved south of the border or to Italian football. Quite why Liverpool never made a bid for the winger is unclear because he was two-footed and could 'go both ways'. Each one of Twentyman's entries on the player is a positive one:

04.01.75: 'A lot of skill, will watch again' (GT)
11.08.75: 'Very good player gifted with skill. A real crowd pleaser' (GT)
17.08.75: 'A promising player who can take on defenders and is comfortable with both feet' (GT)
1975/76: 'Plays on the flanks. Can pick up a ball any part of the field and beat defenders. A very useful player' (GT)
1975/76: 'A good player in possession. Can beat defenders easily and cross a good ball' (GT)

Cooper wouldn't have even commanded a hefty transfer fee, and given that he was Scottish, Glaswegian and tough to go with it, the only sensible reason why Liverpool didn't sign him is because they already had better players at their disposal. Steve Heighway was well on his way to becoming an Anfield legend, while Ian Callaghan still had one or two years left in him and Ray Kennedy had been signed for a considerable transfer fee in the summer of 1974 – another player recommended by Twentyman and Shankly's last signing before leaving Liverpool. Meanwhile, Jimmy Case was soon to make his debut and Sammy Lee was emerging through the youth development system installed by Tom Saunders.

Keith Weller was a player Twentyman looked at in the late '60s when Shankly toyed with a number of strikers and deep-lying link-men. Weller was a player I remember watching in BBC's 'Match of the '70s'. He was gifted abundantly with finesse and ease of movement, frequently deployed on the right wing but more effective in a central position. Unswerving and resolute, he had the dexterity and speed to leave markers dithering in his shadow. His energy seemed infinite and he boasted a wicked shot which generated some memorably stunning goals.

'I saw him at Millwall and thought he looked excellent. I put in glowing reports,' Twentyman said of him. 'But it was decided that we didn't need a player of his type at the time. I was asked by another scout how much I rated Weller. I told him to start bidding at £80,000. Soon afterwards he went to Chelsea for £100,000.'

As with most of the obviously talented players that Liverpool didn't decide to sign, Weller was a victim of the era – a period where money didn't tell as much because squads were much smaller than today. He surely would have been a success at Anfield. Weller was blessed with all of the innate ability needed to become a top footballer with either Tottenham Hotspur, where he previously played, or Chelsea. However, Weller agreed a transfer to the less highbrow, altogether more humble environment of Filbert Street where he matured during the 1970s into one of the most venerated players in Leicester City's history. He deserved more than the four caps he was offered by the England caretaker-manager Joe Mercer, and surely would have won more if he had he gone to Liverpool.

Two other players that Twentyman scouted but never signed were Martin O'Neill and Malcolm Macdonald (Twentyman refers to them as O'Neil and McDonald). O'Neill was watched in the winter of 1970 while playing as an inside forward for Distillery in Northern Ireland. Despite two positive reports by a scout with the initials 'JD', when Twentyman, or 'GT', went to have a look at him, he left the note: 'Not enough pace, does not strike the ball.'

Aston Villa's current manager undoubtedly proved Twentyman wrong by becoming a part of Nottingham Forest squads that won two European Cups and a First Division title later in the decade. He eventually played in midfield.

Macdonald, meanwhile, was a goalscorer at Luton Town when Andy Beattie scouted him on behalf of Twentyman. At first, Beattie noted: 'Useful around the box, could hold his own in 1st Div', before visiting Kenilworth Road again a month later and adding: 'Scored 3 goals, useful in box.' Less than six months after that, Macdonald signed for Newcastle in a deal worth £180,000. He continued scoring goals there (95 in 187 league games, three of which came on his debut against Liverpool) before later moving to Arsenal where he was equally prolific, averaging exactly one goal in every two. 'Supermac' then retired at 29 after a serious knee injury having never won a major honour.

There were other players that Twentyman scouted, of course, who might not have been successful at Anfield. In April 1973, the scout travelled to Glasgow to watch Alan Rough play for Partick Thistle. 'Done nothing wrong. Good prospect,' he noted. Some fans would say that it was either lucky or wise that he didn't pursue the interest any further after a series of high-profile mistakes while keeping goal for Scotland, although he was at the time their most capped player in that position (Jim Leighton has since taken that mantle).

Paul Rideout was another one he looked at but didn't sign. This, however, was more down to Rideout's own personal decision after he agreed to join Aston Villa ahead of Liverpool in 1983, citing that he felt he wouldn't get the chance he deserved at Anfield. Rideout had scored consistently in his teens for Swindon Town and was pictured outside Anfield after what the *Echo* described as 'productive negotiations'. Instead, the following day, he signed for Tony Barton's Villa before failing and moving to Italy, China and the USA (as well as Everton).

Right at the back of Twentyman's notebook, a list of names that includes Gary Owen, later of Manchester City, also mentions a schoolboy player by the name of 'Reid, Huyton'. That youngster is of course Peter Reid – someone who supported Liverpool before much later moving to Everton from Bolton. Reid is the one player that Liverpudlians would have loved in their side in the mid-'80s, without replacing any of their own. Unfortunately, no comments are made alongside his name. "I knew Geoff well," Reid, now manager of Thailand, says. "After hearing some of the names he looked at but didn't sign, I don't think I'd have had the legs to even get into that side. There's no way Kopites would have swapped me for Steve McMahon, anyway."

6. The Players 1967-1970

Francis Lee, Ray Clemence, John Gidman,
Alec Lindsay, Gordon McQueen, David Fairclough,
Alan Birchenall, Larry Lloyd, Kevin Beattie,
Steve Heighway

GEOFF TWENTYMAN'S scouting diary is not definitive. But it is unique. There could be more records that reveal which players Liverpool were targeting between 1967 and 1986. They, though, have since disappeared. This is the only diary to remain in his family's possession.

The diary shows that over a period of more than 15 years, Twentyman and his band of scouts spied on nearly 200 different footballers in matchday action. The chief scout had many of those players watched at least three or four times, taking in hundreds, possibly thousands, of games. The name, club, age, height, weight and a brief report on the player's performance is included in the majority of entries made by Twentyman and the dozen different scouts working underneath him. Many of the scouts are only identifiable by their initials.

A small 'X' marked in red pen at the end of a comment meant that a player was good enough to be signed by Liverpool. Toshack 'does the job we want – AB', noted Andy Beattie, one of Bill Shankly's oldest friends and a key member of Liverpool's scouting department. Other subjects were deemed not up to the standards of the club – players such as Martin O'Neill, then of Distillery in Northern Ireland, whose scouting trail ended in January 1971 with Twentyman's remark: 'Not enough pace.' There were others that caught the eye and were watched over a number of games. But they were not always signed. Players such as Davie Cooper, as we have seen, fall into this bracket.

The first entry in Twentyman's diary is at the beginning of the 1970/71 season. That means that there are more than three previous years of unaccounted scouting activity. Whether or not Twentyman used a diary in those years is uncertain. What is certain is that during that period, Liverpool made some of the most influential signings in their history, all of which were shaped by Twentyman's opinion.

The reason we know Alec Lindsay, David Fairclough, Larry Lloyd and Ray Clemence were all signed by Bill Shankly on Twentyman's recommendation is because they have spoken about it in the press before. Steve Heighway was also watched by Liverpool's chief scout after Tom Saunders made the initial discovery. The stories of other players that Liverpool had watched but chose not to sign, such as Francis Lee, were revealed in exposés Twentyman gave to various national newspapers in the late-'70s and early-'80s.

Twentyman conducted his scouting during the '60s while Shankly's Liverpool side aged slowly. The Reds won the league title in 1964 and 1966 as well as the FA Cup in the year in between. But it took another seven years to lift the championship, which had as many different winners during that time. Players such as Ron Yeats and Ian St John were nearly 30 years old when Twentyman arrived in 1967, and Shankly was slowly coming round to the idea that he would eventually have to replace those that had served him so well in the past. It meant a lot of work for the club's chief scout.

FRANCIS LEE

Lee won league championship medals with Manchester City and Derby County during his career, which began at Bolton. He scored more than 200 goals and won 27 England caps.

Birthplace: *Westhoughton, Lancashire*
Position: *Forward*
Clubs: *Bolton Wanderers, Manchester City, Derby County*

THE FIRST player Geoff Twentyman recommended to Bill Shankly was Francis Lee. 'I rated Lee as fine a player as I'd seen,' Twentyman once told the national press. 'I reckoned he was being wasted at Bolton as an orthodox winger. I felt if we could let him run free, as he did later with Manchester City, he'd be brilliant. But at that time, Liverpool were not looking for big-money players and it was obvious that Lee was going to cost a fortune.'

Another player Twentyman spotted at Burnden Park was Roy Greaves. Shankly, though, ended up spending his money elsewhere. 'We were looking for a midfield player of his type and the other candidate was Alec Lindsay of Bury,' Twentyman continued. 'We watched Greaves on a foggy night. I was willing him to do well but he had an average game. So the decision was to sign Lindsay. It was ironic that he turned out to be a great buy, not in midfield but as a full-back. I reckon Greaves would have been ideal. But that was the magic of Shanks – he could pick the wrong horse and turn it into a winner.'

If Alec Lindsay was the wrong horse, Francis Lee was undoubtedly already a thoroughbred by the time Liverpool started looking at him, at least in reputation. Lee was a rotund little player of angry disposition. Like a Yorkshire terrier chasing a ball on a beach, he was tenacious, so much so that opponents were often aggravated by his approach. He holds the English record for the greatest number of penalties scored in a season, with 15 of his 35 in 1971/72 being converted from the spot. This feat earned him the nickname of 'Lee One Pen' and such was his propensity for earning them himself, he was often damned for going to ground so easily. The tag infuriated Lee and one such accusation from Leeds United's Norman Hunter led to an on-pitch punch-up, which the *Observer* later named as sport's most spectacular ever dismissal.

Whether or not Lee, a striker of infamous repute, would have suited Liverpool's way at the time is debateable, but few can argue with his goalscoring record of more than 200 career strikes with Bolton,

Manchester City and Derby County (he also won First Division Championships with the latter two clubs). He was a leader on and off the pitch, and in 1994 he became chairman of Manchester City. Liverpool in the '60s was full of tough players. Tommy Smith need only glance at an opposing striker to bow him into submission, while Kevin Keegan also won several controversial penalties during his six-years at Anfield.

Ironically, Liverpool mightn't have needed to pluck Keegan from Scunthorpe in the first place had they earlier signed Lee. Lee was originally targeted to partner John Toshack after numerous strikers before him had failed to convince Shankly that they were the answer to Liverpool's goalscoring problems. Geoff Twentyman said that he scouted Lee in 1967, months before he signed for Manchester City. He was 23 and had been in Bolton's first team since he was 15, thus accruing enough experience to be considered as a Liverpool target.

Instead, Lee moved to City for a club record £60,000 while Liverpool signed Tony Hateley, spending £96,000 – another record fee. Despite scoring 28 in all competitions in 1967/68, Hateley's direct style didn't suit Shankly's pass and move philosophy, and within a year he'd moved on to Coventry City. His replacement was Alun Evans from Wolverhampton Wanderers who became Briton's most expensive teenager in September 1968 after impressing Shankly in a match where he outwitted Ron Yeats, prompting the manager to spend £110,000. But he didn't fulfil his potential either and soon moved back to the Midlands with Aston Villa.

Had Liverpool signed Lee in '67, then maybe they wouldn't have suffered six trophyless seasons until they lifted the title again in 1973. Lee, however, doesn't see it like that. "People look back now and say that between '67 and '73, Liverpool didn't win anything. But they were always there or thereabouts," he says. "I don't for a single minute remember going to Anfield and expecting to win. I still considered them to be a top club – one of the top three in the country – and they were always verging on winning things. The games against Liverpool were always the toughest. People go on about not getting penalties at Old

Trafford when visiting teams play Manchester United now. At Liverpool, you never even got a free-kick. At least it seemed that way.

"I remember in one game we got a throw-in and I thought the referee was bent – I couldn't believe it! The crowd was so hostile. I know referees never parked in the streets near Anfield. They always arrived by train and got a taxi to Lime Street. They used to fear for their lives! It always made for probably the most difficult game of the season. It's only now when people look back and see that they didn't win anything for a relatively short period that they say: 'Ah, they mustn't have been as good.' Let me tell you that any Liverpool side of Bill Shankly's was a good side. Sure, they had a few problems in the striking department, but it wasn't like they didn't score goals. I remember many teams going to Anfield and being on the end of a hammering."

Lee may have only been 23, but he'd played at Anfield more times than most top professionals do in a lifetime. "I remember going there when I was 15 and Liverpool were on the verge of promotion from the Second Division," he continues. "Boy were they tough opponents. They certainly created an impression on me and it made me wonder what it would be like playing there regularly.

"That was 1959/60 and they had a strong team even then. Throughout the '60s, they became a wonderful team and enjoyed tremendous success. Even before then, I'd enjoyed a couple of Central League matches at Anfield as well. They were always on a Wednesday afternoon. I remember playing against Billy Liddell. It was a massive thing for me then because Billy was a living legend. I just remember the game being tough because I was trying to get around Ronnie Moran. He was so stocky and fast. He was a big lad. I was worried all day that they were going to kick lumps out of me because I was the youngest player on the pitch, but at the end of the game, Ronnie and Gerry Byrne came over to me and ruffled my hair. Ronnie said I would be a good player and one day make the first team. He was right because not long after we were playing against each other again – this time in a first-team game."

Lee scored 92 league goals in 139 games for Bolton – a record that surely would attract interest from most top clubs. By the time he was due to leave, though, only Manchester City made a bid for him, while Liverpool, Manchester United and Stoke City all made only tentative enquiries. "There was lots of speculation in the papers – although it's nothing like the kind of speculation you get today. The season we got relegated, I could see that there were lots of scouts sitting in the directors' box at Burnden Park, but I wasn't always sure whether they were looking at me. All the players knew they were there.

"There was some speculation that Liverpool were interested in me around the time we played them in a cup match. We beat them in a replay and I heard that I'd impressed someone at Liverpool and that they were preparing an approach for me. Within a matter of weeks, though, Manchester City came in and I agreed to go.

"Bolton were relegated to the Second Division just before. I'd been the leading goalscorer for the club for about five seasons and I really wanted to see how far I could go in the game. If Liverpool had come for me, I would have gone there straight away. There's no doubt about that. I was keen to leave and because Manchester City made the first approach, although Stoke made enquiries as well, I went there. It was as simple as that. It was quite an easy decision to make. Manchester United were linked with me too but I think City had a couple of bad results and took a gamble on me because they wanted to change things round quickly. Maybe if Liverpool had been on a bad run or something like that they would have moved quicker like City. I had no preference where I went."

Quite why Liverpool decided not to move for Lee is unclear. Lee thinks it was just timing and adds that Shankly told him it was one of his biggest regrets in management. "Whenever I saw Shanks from then on he always made a point of coming over to me (cue Shanks impresson) and said: 'Eh, sin. That was the worst night's work I ever did. I should 'a signed ye the night ye scored at the Kop end!' I used to hide from him because he'd always say the same thing. He was quite scary to someone who didn't really know him. He was a lovely guy, but the aura about him made him intimidating because I didn't want to say something that would upset him."

Now semi-retired after his flirtation with chairmanship at City, Lee is insistent that he wouldn't change any aspect of his career. "I was lucky that at the beginning of the '70s I played with a lot of great players at City, so I don't feel like I missed out at all. We were a strong side, but Liverpool pushed on and left everyone else behind them. I can't complain at all what happened at City because within four months, I got picked for England. You can never tell what would have happened had I gone to Liverpool. I was 23 and had scored regularly for five seasons, but I had never even been called up for the under-21s or anything like that. Also, I felt I was a first-team regular and I wanted to play every week. Maybe if I'd gone to Liverpool I would have had to wait in the reserves and maybe things wouldn't have worked out. You can never tell with football. Just look now. Who would have thought that Manchester City would become the wealthiest football club in the world? Not me! It's strange how things work out."

RAY CLEMENCE

Clemence spent a long time in the reserves after Shankly bought him from Scunthorpe in 1967 – he had to wait until 1970 for his full league debut. Once he took Tommy Lawrence's place, Clemence only missed six league matches in the next 11 years. In 665 appearances he kept 335 clean sheets, winning five league titles, the FA Cup, three European Cups, two UEFA Cups and one League Cup in the process. He subsequently moved to Spurs, where he won the FA Cup again.

Signed: *from Scunthorpe for £18,000 in June 1967*
Age when signed: *18*
Total LFC appearances/goals: *665/0*
Seasons spent at Liverpool: *13*

Birthplace: *Skegness*
Other clubs: *Scunthorpe United, Tottenham Hotspur*

WHENEVER Liverpool moved in the transfer market in the 1960s or '70s, the intention was always to manipulate the player until he was no longer of use. Ron Yeats, Ian St John, Phil Neal and Tommy Smith were prime examples of footballers that came to the club as unknowns before leaving or retiring a decade later, having amassed hundreds of appearances with their best years behind them. It took its toll on many, particularly Smithy, who now struggles on his feet, such were his toils for the Red shirt.

The idea of rotation was taboo and players, especially at Liverpool, would have to bide their time before a position in the starting XI became available. Terry McDermott waited almost two years before he was given a chance in the centre of Bob Paisley's midfield. Once a player had signed for Liverpool and proved himself worthy of a first-team shirt, it was his for keeps providing he met the standard every weekend. Take a quick glance at teamsheets over the years and the same names appear. Ian Callaghan and Smith between them played in more than 1,500 games.

Only three players in the 30 years between Shankly's appointment in 1959 and the last league triumph in 1990 left the club with at least a few good years still ahead of them. The first was Kevin Keegan who departed for Hamburg in 1977 at the age of 26 having just played a major role in Liverpool's first-ever European Cup triumph. The last was Ian Rush, signing for Juventus, also at 26, before returning to Liverpool barely a year later. On both occasions, the Reds made mammoth profits – Rush was signed for £300,000 and sold for £3m and Keegan was signed for £35,000 and sold for £500,000 (both at least 10 times their original amount) – although it is worth remembering that Keegan chose to leave and Liverpool generally weren't interested in selling players who still had some of their best years ahead of them.

The only other player that departed Anfield and achieved any note of success elsewhere during that era was Ray Clemence, who left the club for Tottenham Hotspur at the age of 33 – a goalkeeper's peak in those days when many played until they were 40. He still made 665 appearances as the Reds' number one, playing 337 games in a row between 1972 and 1978. Once again, Liverpool engineered a huge profit of around 20 times the original fee they paid 14 years earlier, selling Clemence for £300,000 after signing him in a deal that was quoted between £15,000 and £18,000. The goalkeeper that succeeded him, Bruce Grobbelaar, played for 13 seasons too, making 628 appearances.

"The team never changed when I played," concedes Clemence who now works as England's goalkeeping coach and talks to me days before the national team's 4-1 World Cup qualifying victory in Croatia. "But each player, including me, knew they had a shelf-life. By the time Bruce came along, it was time for me to move on."

Clemence was one of Twentyman's first signings as Liverpool chief scout, arriving at the club as an 18-year-old from Scunthorpe in 1967. Twentyman had been impressed by Clemence's maturity in the lower leagues, as well as his unique ability to kick with his right foot and dive to his left side.

"I had the perfect balance for a 'keeper," Clemence says. "There was no secret behind it, I was just very, very lucky. It was the way my body was made to work. Diving one way or the other felt just the same for me. I didn't feel any noticeable difficulty diving either way and it was never something I consciously thought about – or even believed would make me a top goalkeeper later on. When I went to Liverpool to speak to Shanks I was in awe of him, but he just told me that they saw a lot of potential and believed I could become the first-choice 'keeper in years to come and that was why they were signing me."

Clemence may have only been a rookie by goalkeeping standards, but it still didn't stop Liverpool from going out of their way to entice him to Anfield. "Personally, I couldn't believe that Liverpool were making so much of an effort to impress me. They showed me round everywhere and introduced me to everyone. It made me feel like I was part of the club already – before I'd even signed. It summed up the way the club was. They took me onto the pitch, into the dressing rooms and up to the training ground, all of which were better than anywhere else. They gave me no reason to go anywhere else because Shanks saw everything about Liverpool as being the best.

"Liverpool had won the league and the cup in the years before, but Shanks told me Liverpool were only going to go up from there. He said that Liverpool would become the champions of Europe and I was going to be a part of it. It was his vision.We did, of course, win the European Cup. It's sad in some ways that Shanks wasn't the manager at the time. His enthusiasm and passion for the club and the city shone through from the moment I shook hands with him. It was almost as if he was in awe of the city and couldn't quite believe that he was the man to get Liverpool back on its feet.

"Bill Shankly appreciated the fact that he was Liverpool manager and wasn't going to let anything get in the way of his aspirations. His attitude didn't change at all from that very first day I met him until the day he shocked us all by retiring."

Clemence admits that he didn't have any specific leanings when it came to supporting a football team as a child. "Skegness, where I was born, was a backwater when it came to football," he says before revealing that his father took him to watch Leicester City and Nottingham Forest. He also doesn't recall a great deal of his debut season in a Scunthorpe shirt. "All I can remember was that I had a lot to do," he jokes. "Scunthorpe were struggling a bit, so I suppose that helped me. Maybe if we were doing well, I wouldn't have played or had less to deal with in games, so Geoff could scrutinise me a little bit more. I remember making a few errors that season too, so it may have been good for Geoff to see how I reacted to those mistakes. That's one of the marks of a good goalkeeper, or a good outfield player even, to react positively when things aren't going so well. That's why Pepe Reina is proving to be a good goalkeeper for Liverpool now. Whenever he makes a mistake, he doesn't let it affect his game at all. You learn so much more about yourself in the hard times than you do in the good times. Maybe Geoff thought if I was reacting well to bad results or even a couple of mistakes, then maybe I would have the strength of mind to do well at Liverpool as well."

Clemence attracted the interest of Sheffield United and Southampton when Liverpool lodged their bid, although he was just happy to be playing regularly. "I felt privileged to do so at a young age. Then towards the end of the season, I read in the papers that there were other clubs supposedly interested in me, but I didn't really believe any of it because it was my first year in the game and I didn't think any big clubs would come all the way to Scunthorpe just to watch me play. I got on with my own game and never paid any attention to what was going on in the press."

Upon signing for Liverpool, Clemence became the first player to be educated through the system, the Liverpool way. He could see, even then, that the learning curve was intentional and equally beneficial to his own game. "I only played occasionally in the first team in my first two-and-a-half years," he explains. "I quickly realised how high the standards were because I thought I might have more of a chance initially. In some ways, I was the first player of this kind that learnt the Liverpool way in the reserves. People like Terry McDermott had to do it after me. It was all about watching what was going on around the club, taking in the atmosphere and learning from those in front of you. Shanks knew not to throw people in at the deep end, but in the meantime, I was learning how to swim, so the system worked well."

What helped Clemence the most, though, was experiencing success with Liverpool's all-conquering reserve team. "I settled into this way very quickly. It helped that I was part of a very successful young reserve side that won more or less everything in its path. Everyone made me feel very welcome, all the way from the top to the bottom, and I keep in touch with a lot of the people until this day because that's the way you should be treated as a person."

These basic human skills nurtured at Melwood helped Clemence later in his football career when he took charge of Barnet in the mid-'90s. "At that level, you have to be out scouting even more of the time. I had quite a lot of success at Barnet, signing players for next to nothing before eventually earning the club £2m. Dougie Freedman, Maik Taylor [who in the summer of 2008 was linked with Liverpool] and Linvoy Primus all came through with us, so at that level, you were scouting for young players who you felt could excel and probably sell at a profit.

"It wasn't Liverpool's mentality to sell players at their peak, but it was at Barnet, so the scouting was slightly different. You have to buy players who can more than cope with the demands of the division you are in, but with a little coaching could go one or even two levels higher. At Liverpool, a player had to be ready for Liverpool and nobody else. All of the players I brought in, though, were first and foremost good, hardworking people and that's why they achieved some success later – just as Liverpool did."

JOHN GIDMAN

Gidman won the League Cup with Villa in 1977 before joining Everton in 1979. He became Ron Atkinson's first signing at Manchester United in a swap deal that took Mickey Thomas to Goodison Park, and he played his part in their 1983 and 1985 FA Cup triumphs. After leaving United, he suffered relegation with Manchester City and Darlington, playing for Stoke in between. He made one England appearance.

Birthplace: *Liverpool*
Position: *Right-back*
Clubs: *Aston Villa, Everton, Manchester United, Manchester City, Stoke City, Darlington*

"THEY might as well have written 'this player is F***ING SH*TE' in big letters when they let me go. It knocked the life out of me and I felt like I'd let my parents down."

If John Gidman's account of the moment Liverpool tried to release him as a 16-year-old seems inelegant, it probably is. But it's also a candid reaction to what it is like suffering rejection at such a young age.

Before forging a lengthy and sometimes tumultuous career with Aston Villa, Everton and Manchester United, Gidman, who was a boyhood Red, got off to a false start at Liverpool.

Gidman had signed apprentice forms in 1969 when Liverpool appointed Tony Waiters, a former Blackpool goalkeeper with five England international caps, as a coach in the club's burgeoning youth development programme (the same Tony Waiters that later managed Bruce Grobbelaar at Vancouver Whitecaps).

"Everything changed for me when Waiters came in," Gidman says from a bar near his home on the Costa del Sol. "He did not like me at all. Within six months of him arriving at the club, he wanted me out. I don't know why. He never told me. I had long hair and looked more like a rock star than a footballer – maybe that pissed him off. I still have the letter he wrote to my dad saying that I didn't have the standard of skill or levels of ability to become a top-flight professional to the standard of Liverpool and that they wanted to release me ahead of the expiration of my contract."

Earlier that year, Geoff Twentyman spotted Gidman playing for Liverpool Schoolboys, but the chief scout could do little to help him out of this predicament. "I liked Geoff and he was a lovely fella," Gidman concedes in a Scouse accent mellowed by decades of living far away from the shores of the River Mersey. "He liked me as a player, too, and believed I would be a good player for the club. I know Geoff knew about Waiters trying to force me out, but he was a scout and couldn't influence the managerial decisions of those in charge. Geoff wasn't around the training ground when I was there with the youth lads and didn't train us, so it was solely down to this guy Waiters. If your face doesn't fit in life, you don't get anywhere, no matter who you are."

Gidman was brought up in Garston. His father, who worked for the Post Office as a draughtsman, had a season ticket in the Kop and took Gidman to matches in the boys' pen. Before Waiters' arrival, Gidman had signed a two-year contract and still had another 14 months to run. So he refused to accept the termination and the stubborn resistance resulted in him playing for the club's C team.

"My late father told me that because I had so much time left on my contract and because there wasn't much work going in Liverpool, I should stick the contract out and refuse to leave. So they had to keep paying me, and Tony Waiters decided to put me into the C team with kids off the park. That's how bad he was to me. The C team was full of players fresh off a school field and I was being forced to play with them."

By 1970, Waiters had ended his short association with Liverpool by taking up a player-coach role with Burnley. Later, he managed Plymouth Argyle (for five years) before emigrating to North America, taking charge of Vancouver Whitecaps as well as the Canadian national team at the 1986 World Cup. Waiters' departure from Liverpool came as a "massive relief" for Gidman, although his reputation at the club still caused problems – eventually forcing him to be released.

"Ronnie Moran wasn't pleased about what was going on with me and Waiters. Ronnie and me had always got on really well. As soon as Waiters left, my life changed. Ronnie took control of the situation and put me back into the B side before putting me in the A side. One day at Melwood he asked me to do a favour for him and play right-back because they had a player shortage. He knew I was a bit small, but said he had confidence in me, and from then on I played right-back. I went on from there to play in Joe Fagan's reserve side. I was getting good reports from then on and I was told that the staff were telling Shankly to keep me on as pro. It didn't happen though, and because they'd proposed the contract to be terminated, there was some kind of ruling that meant they couldn't go back on it. So I was left without a club."

Gidman says that another obstacle in his way at Liverpool was the presence of Chris Fagan as Liverpool's first-choice reserve-team right-back – Chris being the son of Joe Fagan. "It's funny, because Phil Thompson came on a trial while I was there and he didn't have any more fat on him than a chip, but Waiters loved the bones of him and he just went on and on. It didn't help that Joe Fagan's son, Chris, was playing in the reserves at the time in my position too. I think it just wasn't meant to be for me at Liverpool. It tore me apart at the time because I knew my dad had his heart set on me playing for the club we both grew up supporting."

After walking out through the gates of Melwood for a final time, Gidman considered quitting football altogether and burying his head in rock music – his other passion. Instead he decided to go on a holiday to Devon with a friend. Then six days into the break he received a call from his father, saying that he must come home before travelling to Birmingham. Aston Villa wanted to take him on trial with a view to a permanent deal.

Geoff Twentyman later claimed in a radio interview that he'd recommended Gidman to a Villa scout called Neville Briggs who'd contacted him at the end of the 1970/71 season. "This bloke [Briggs] called me saying he knew me from his playing days when he was at Rotherham and I was at Carlisle,' Twentyman said. "He was asking me what apprentices we were letting go of and whether any of them were any good. I liked John Gidman, so I told him and he went down for a trial there and they liked him too. This guy [Briggs] then said he'll be in their first team within 12 months and fair enough he was. I never even got a thank you off him, mind."

Gidman says that he is unsure if this conversation ever took place, for the reason that he became quite close to Briggs during his time at Villa, without him ever mentioning that he'd spoken to Twentyman. "That's f***ing rubbish. I had never heard that story," Gidman says, almost as if he refuses to believe that an employee from the club that ditched him actually played a part in his rejuvenation.

What is certain, with Liverpool looking for a long-term replacement for Chris Lawler who was coming towards the end of his career, they could have saved themselves some money had they decided to keep Gidman. Instead, Twentyman ended up scouting Phil Neal before spending £66,000, which as it transpired didn't turn out to be a bad bit of business anyway.

Gidman, meanwhile, impressed in his trial at Villa Park so much so that Chelsea made enquiries about him after an energetic display in a pre-season youth-team friendly match. "Frank Upton, who was in charge of the youth team at Villa then, came up to me and said: 'Look, if the Villa don't want you, I've had a guy at Chelsea who really liked the look of you in the friendly so you could go there.' Frank Upton used to play for Chelsea, so his connections were good. Instead, Villa signed me on the same day as Brian Little."

Gidman settled down quickly at Villa Park, "without any coaches having any preconceived opinions about my ability". Soon, he was in the same England youth team as Trevor Francis and Phil Thompson. "After eight or nine months at Villa, I was knocking on the first-team door," he says proudly. "I played against Stan Bowles on my debut and not long after that Ron Saunders got the manager's job and we won promotion. I think in our first campaign back in the First Division, we played Liverpool at Villa Park and won 5-1. We were five goals up after 40 minutes. Liverpool won the league that year. (It was the Reds' heaviest league defeat since losing 4-0 to Chelsea 11 seasons earlier). I was 19, and only two-and-a-half years earlier I was at Liverpool as an apprentice.

"I was playing against Keegan and Emlyn – all the lads I used to clean boots for, and we were thrashing them. It felt good personally because I thought I'd proven a few people wrong, although I was still a Liverpool supporter and always wanted them to win. After the game, Shanks came up to me in the tunnel. He was there that day after retiring a year earlier and put his arm round me. All he could say was: 'Son, son, son…' He was speechless. Maybe he thought he was wrong in letting me go."

Although Gidman felt that he'd proven one or two people wrong at Liverpool, he emphatically proved that point later when he moved to Everton for a club record £800,000 fee – even though it was a move he wasn't all that keen on. "If I am honest in my heart, I didn't want to go to Everton. My dad insisted that I made the move. He wanted to prove that Liverpool had made a mistake by letting me go. The fee certainly proved that. I spoke with Gordon Lee and I had my reservations straight away and my form proved I was right because I couldn't play the football that I wanted because Everton were very defensive-minded and afraid of losing games. They weren't the best defence in the world as well with Billy Wright and Mick Lyons, who used to head-butt the wall really hard to get wound up before matches. But my game was going forward and I told Gordon this. I was better bombing on and creating things. If you don't create, you don't score.

"There were some funny stories at Everton, though. Freddie Starr was a Blue and came inside the dressing room a few times. Because I was a talker, he took the piss out of me by acting queer and getting his cock out. Even I blushed that time. After one game I was being filmed and he mooned at me behind the camera. I was in stitches – Freddie was wild and he cracked me up. In the end, Howard Kendall came in and didn't fancy me. All managers have their own fancy things. I went to the Far East on a pre-season tour with Everton and on the way back we stopped off in Los Angeles. That was where I got a phone call off Ron Atkinson. 'Giddy, I've got the Man Utd job. Do you want to join me?' F***ing hell, I was on the next plane home and signed in a flash. Sixteen months of sh*t at Everton – then moving to Man Utd, who were one of the biggest clubs in the world.

"By then, the feeling that I wanted to prove Liverpool wrong, or Tony Waiters wrong, had gone. That ended when I pulled on that England shirt when Don Revie picked me. When I lined up and sang the national anthem, the only thing I could think of was Bill Shankly and how he'd not done enough to keep hold of me. I thought: 'Right, if you're watching now, it's finished with.' I had the greatest respect for Shanks, having said that, and I would always want to talk to him if we bumped into each other."

Gidman's honesty on the issue of Liverpool's pusillanimous attitude is admirable as much as it is resentful. It is obvious that he respects Shankly by the way he talks about him – just like any other Kopite from that generation. But it seems he also begrudges Shankly for not doing enough to tie him to the club when his reputation had been tarnished. Shankly, it seems, more than any other character at Liverpool (even Waiters) was the person Gidman wanted to prove wrong. After all, his opinion counted more than any other.

"I've got no regrets," Gidman says reflectively. "Even though I played for loads of other teams, I still feel like a Scouser. Whenever I watch Liverpool on TV, I always see the Kop and think: 'F**k me, I used to stand there.' I love the club, and my 17 months as an apprentice opened my eyes and it put me in the frame of mind to think that if I get the chance of doing something, never let it go. That helped me throughout my career. But probably my heart is now at Villa. They're the ones that gave me the break. It took them a month to decide they wanted me, whereas Liverpool had me for more than two years and nothing happened."

Gidman enjoyed more than five years at Manchester United, and became a crowd favourite, despite hailing from Liverpool. "Stevie Coppell knew all about this and he told me on the day I signed that they'd give me a hard time at the start, but if I got my head down and attacked and excited, they'd begin to appreciate me. It was true and I think I had a decent understanding with the fans."

During his time at the wrong end of the M62 Gidman moved back to Liverpool and commuted every day. "This posed a few problems because everyone hates United in Liverpool. Back then there was more animosity from Evertonians towards United as well because Everton and United weren't far apart in terms of success. Now, I think a lot of Blues don't mind United because they're stopping Liverpool winning things. Back then it was different. I've had to have police escorts home from Goodison and Anfield because of the animosity in the rivalry. I could understand, though. If I was a fan, I'd give me stick!"

Living in Liverpool also meant Gidman could enjoy a drink away from the local media glare in Manchester. "This was the great thing about living back home. I was good mates with Warky (John Wark) and went out with Graeme Souness quite a bit too. Liverpool and United were both club's filled with drinkers and I think it's no surprise that we had better team spirits than other teams and were successful off the back of it. All the lads at United agreed that you should never trust a footballer who doesn't drink. Maybe that's why Peter Beardsley never cut it at Old Trafford. He was teetotal and never touched a drop. Some of our behaviour when we were on the beers wasn't the best and the media now would go crazy over it. But I don't think a single player who played would change that era."

One of the few regrets Gidman does have in his career, however, is that he didn't win more caps for England, his only one coming in a 5-0 World Cup qualifying victory over Luxembourg. "I didn't really help myself," he concedes.

"I played for England under-23s in a match against the Soviet Union in Moscow. On the flight home, Alan Ball got us on Jack Daniel's and by the time we arrived at Luton Airport I was falling all over the place. If you were outspoken or did rebellious things with England, all of the heads didn't like it and you didn't fit in. Look at Brian Clough. I wasn't the kind of fella to toe the line just for the sake of it and if I saw the chance for a laugh, I just went for it."

Gidman believes that if he'd become a regular at Liverpool, maybe he'd have been an international regular as well. "I know Ron Saunders didn't like his players playing for their country. That included Andy Gray, myself and Brian Little. He was renowned for that at Man City too. He didn't like older players or players who were in the press more than him getting the limelight. Don't get me wrong, his record was very good, but I don't think he pushed me and Andy especially on the international scene. Back then, the First Division managers were closer to the managers of England, Scotland and Wales. Maybe if I'd been at Liverpool, it would have been different, because that wasn't a problem between Phil Neal and Bob Paisley to my knowledge."

Gidman now spends most of his time playing golf in Spain with Andy Gray, another Twentyman target. "We ended up living in a house together after Andy signed for Villa. Ron Saunders rang me up and told me he had signed a young lad from Dundee United. I was single and living alone, so he said to me: 'He's moving in with you.'"

ALEC LINDSAY

Lindsay was bought after impressive wing-half displays for Bury but grew frustrated in the Liverpool reserves and nearly left the club before he was given the chance to make the left-back role his own.

Signed: *from Bury for £67,000 in March 1969*
Age when signed: *21*
Total LFC appearances/goals: *248/18*
Seasons spent at Liverpool: *7*
Birthplace: *Bury*
Other clubs: *Stoke, Oakland Stompers, Toronto Blizzard*

"CIME on sinny, let's see some of them goals we saw you scoring when we watched ye," was the cackle across the field at Melwood on a crisp autumn morning in 1969. "But I'm a midfielder, boss," cowered the non-plussed newcomer who'd signed for Liverpool the previous afternoon.

According to several onlookers, Bill Shankly thought that he'd brought in Bury striker Bobby Kerr in his search for extra competition for Roger Hunt and Ian St John. By accident, he'd signed wing-half Alec Lindsay.

It's a tale well known to Liverpool supporters. It's also one that Lindsay dismisses flatly. "Bluddy hell," he says, pronouncing in a deep Lancastrian accent. "It's a load of rubbish that. Shanks knew exactly who I was. It's a joke if you think about it. I don't think Shanks would make a mistake about signing someone. You know what he's like, he said a lot of things as a joke and because he was such a god, everyone took it as the gospel truth, like."

Considering Shankly earlier threatened to resign from Liverpool after club officials tried to interfere with his transfer policy, it is unlikely that he would allow such a boob to take place – even if it did turn out to be cute business later. Lindsay, though, admits he was an unlikely footballer and a social misfit in his early years, so much so that it affected his confidence during his first season at Anfield. Having played for his hometown club since he was 17 years old, amassing close to 200 appearances, he grew up not supporting any particular team and worked as a part time pig farmer.

"I don't think I spoke for 12 months at Melwood," he jokes. "I loved playing football, but I wasn't used to professionalism. I was overawed by Bill and the whole thing. Sometimes even when I think about it now, especially the way the game has gone today, I still find it hard to believe that Liverpool signed me from Bury. It was bolt of lightning because one minute I was watching them in Europe on the TV then the next minute I was sharing a dressing room with all these great players. On the first day, I sat next to Roger Hunt and I was thinking: 'What the bluddy hell am I doing here?'"

Twentyman had no such doubts that Lindsay was good enough. Speaking about the player in 1982 he said: "He was one of the finest passers of a ball I've seen in recent years and proved to be another bargain buy for Liverpool.

"We paid out a modest £60,000 fee to Bury for Alec. He had one of the sweetest left feet in the game. At Anfield, Alec was switched from wing-half to full-back where he played for England. He had the type of touch to his passing that I rate almost priceless."

However, Bob Paisley once said that it was 'a case of once bitten, twice shy' in relation to Liverpool's move for Lindsay. Paisley cited that the club were weary about doing business with Bury who'd auctioned centre-half Colin Waldron to Tommy Docherty's Chelsea after previously agreeing a fee with the Reds. (There was a suggestion in the Manchester media that Liverpool also wanted to sign City legend Colin Bell who played for Bury at the same time, although this is unsubstantiated and not included in Twentyman's scouting book.) 'Admittedly Chelsea's gain didn't turn out to be our loss, but after Waldron we played transfer dealings very close to the chest,' Paisley added. 'Our policy is that we do our talking at a press conference to introduce any new signings. That's why we kept as quiet as possible when we were negotiating with Bury to sign a player with as sweet a left foot as you could hope to see in Alec.'

Lindsay says that he was unaware of any interest from other clubs, "mainly because I've never read newspapers", but concedes that he found the move to Liverpool uneasy at first. "I didn't know whether I was in a dream or a nightmare," he states, adding that he struggled to deal with the pace of training and first-team matches.

By his own admission, Lindsay lacked dynamism to play further up the field, although he did score 22 goals as a striker in his first season in Liverpool's reserve team. "I didn't enjoy it there. In the end it got to the stage where I'd played everywhere on the pitch other than in goal. We had a few problems at left-back and luckily I managed to make it my position. I was in the last chance saloon."

Peter Wall and Gordon Milne both unsuccessfully passed on the opportunity to take up the left-back position made vacant by Gerry Byrne's retirement. Lindsay had all the attributes to finally nail-down a regular starting place with his enthusiastic attitude and will-to-win, something Twentyman would have spotted in a Bury shirt. He was also ferocious in the challenge. "I'd always played like that since I were a kid, y'know." What set Lindsay apart from the rest, however, was the ability he had with the ball at his feet. Like every other player with an educated left peg, he was garnered for it. 'Naturally left-footed players aren't easy to come by,' noted Paisley, who also commended Lindsay for his ability to break forward. In some ways he was a left-sided Phil Neal, only finding his position by default before making it his own.

Lindsay carried his goalscoring form from the reserves into the first team, linking up effectively with Steve Heighway who he describes as the "most underrated player I've played with", owing to the winger's ability "to hit that byline more times than any other bugger going", netting 18 times in 248 games from full-back. It would have been 19 had Lindsay's volley in the FA Cup final of 1974 not been ruled out when the score was 0-0. "I was gutted about that one," he says, "but it was all forgotten about when we got on the train home.

"We had a good drink and by the time I got on the bus to go on the parade, I was drunk as a skunk. We were somewhere on Queens Drive and I was dying for a pee so I jumped off the bus at an area where it was a bit quieter and knocked on a front door. I asked the lady who answered whether I could use her loo. I could have been Jack the Ripper or anybody but she was very hospitable. By the time I'd done my business, I went outside and there was a crowd gathering. Luckily, a policeman had noticed what I was doing and took me on his motorbike back up to the bus, which was now about half-a-mile up the road. So I clung on to this policeman and sang 'Liverpool, Liverpool', as we sped up the street."

Like every other person at the club, Lindsay has no explanation for Shankly's retirement from Liverpool a month and a half after the Newcastle match, but suspects he was weary after so long in the game.

"The one thing about Bill that stands out for me is that he was such a funny guy," he says almost laughing as he tries to explain why. "He'd have us in stitches and he'd look at us and wonder what we were laughing at. He'd say things that were so profound and he didn't realise it. He was so honest it was untrue."

Lindsay reveals how Shankly would prepare for matches on Friday afternoons by calling the team into the dressing room at Anfield. It would be dominated by a green-clothed Subbuteo table and the manager would lay out two teams, one in red and the other usually in white. "He must have painted them himself because there were no shorts, shirts or socks. The whole figure was painted in red." Shankly would then explain how he wanted his team to play the following day. "The meeting only lasted a few minutes because he'd end up just flicking all the opposition off the board. Some of them would snap in half as they hit the wall and he'd say they weren't good enough to play on the same pitch as us. By the end, these little players were all over the room and Liverpool won about 11-0."

Lindsay left Liverpool for Stoke City in 1977 after a series of off-the-field problems, which he is reluctant to discuss with me. "I wouldn't speak to Bob Paisley about it, so there's no point bothering you with it," he says. Legend has it that he was treading a thin line at Liverpool as far back as the reign of Shankly. According to one newsman, he skipped training one day and was caught for driving with undue care. Allegedly he had baldy tires on his car. Shanks, apparently, was enraged when he heard about it and told Lindsay that "a professional footballer should never have baldy tyres".

Since retiring, he has returned to Anfield only once. "I started a pub in Leigh and this guy came in haranguing me to death for a ticket. He was a Liverpool fan so I went with him. I didn't enjoy it because there's too many comments from people who don't know what they're taking about and I can't just sit there and let it go. I will always side with the players, y'see. Maybe I'm naïve, but I think any player who pulls on that Red shirt doesn't give the ball away on purpose. It gets me wound up. Players don't go out and intentionally try and make mistakes, do they?"

Lindsay, who's 60 now and lives in Dumfries, sounds older than his years. Maybe it's down to his deep accent, which is thicker than the gravy in a Lancashire hotpot. Throughout this interview he uses phrases such as "any road" and "by 'eck". Given that he hails from the same part of the world as Gary Neville, to the untrained ear, you would believe he was a Man Utd sympathiser. Then again, maybe he sounds older because of the daily pain he suffers after a recent operation to mend a slipped disc, which means his legs feel like jelly and some days he can't walk as much as he'd like to. "I used to have a some Labradors and take them for a walk. I also enjoyed shooting, but I can't any more.

"I watch a lot of football in the comfort of my own home, but when I sometimes go the pub, I see a lot of United supporters. You'd think it would be Rangers or Celtic up 'ere, but it's full of United. I hate the bluddy bastards and spend most of my time putting them straight. It feels like me against the whole bluddy world."

GORDON MCQUEEN

Scouts circled McQueen while he was at St Mirren, and Leeds had a £30,000 bid accepted in 1973. McQueen partnered Norman Hunter as Leeds won the league championship in 1973/74 and enjoyed a run to the European Cup final the following season (which they lost 2-0 to Bayern Munich). In 1978 he signed for Manchester United and won the FA Cup in 1983. During his career, he won 30 Scotland caps. He is now working as Middlesbrough's chief scout.

Birthplace: *Ayrshire*
Position: *Central defender*
Clubs: *St Mirren, Leeds United, Manchester United*

LEEDS United – every rival fan in the 1970s detested them. Don Revie's side included a collection of players that instantly evoked scorn. They were successful, too, and that made it worse. It's like Drogba, Diouf, Neville (either one), Lampard and Cristiano Ronaldo all playing in the same team today and winning the Premier League. Instead, Leeds had Bremner, Giles and Hunter. To a lesser extent, there was Reaney, Clarke and McQueen.

Gordon McQueen was an obvious figure of disdain for Kopites. He played for Manchester United after leaving Elland Road, infamously stating that "99% of players want to play for Manchester United and the rest are liars". Years earlier, he was very close to becoming a Liverpool player. Along with Francis Lee and Kevin Beattie, Twentyman said that McQueen turned out to be someone that he missed and regretted not persuading to become a Red. 'In McQueen's case, I don't think I could have done any more,' Twentyman said in a newspaper interview. 'I was told there was a very raw kid called McQueen in Scotland, and as I'd known McQueen's father I invited him for a trial. Rangers had also heard about him and they had first bite. But after two weeks they decided not to bother. So down he came to Liverpool. He arrived without boots, explaining that when he got to Rangers he'd thrown his old ones away. But when he left Rangers they asked for the boots back. McQueen played for our A-team at Rochdale, and though he was still very raw, I saw enough to offer a month's trial, which I thought was the best we could do at the time. He went home to think about it and decided he would prefer St Mirren. I wasn't really that convinced about him to feel as upset as I did about Kevin Beattie. To be fair, it was a long time before McQueen came good.'

McQueen's reasoning for not signing for Liverpool was simple. Like Alan Hansen after him, he missed home desperately. "I was a country boy," he says. "I was playing for a men's team called Largs Thistle in Ayrshire. Bill Shankly was from the same area and he took a shining to me. He taught me a few things later in training. I went down to

Liverpool on trial for nearly four weeks and stayed in the Lord Nelson Hotel. Alun Evans had just signed from Wolverhampton and he was staying there too. Bill picked me up most days because he wanted to take care of one of his own. He'd take me to Anfield, where we'd get changed, then get on a bus and go to Melwood.

"I enjoyed it at Liverpool but found it really tough. It was full-time training and something I wasn't really prepared for. They wanted to sign me but I was a little bit homesick. Ron Yeats was still there, but they'd just signed Larry Lloyd and I thought it was better that I went home. I was only 17/18. I went back to Scotland to think it over and once I was there, I didn't want to leave again. England seemed like going into space for me, and even though there was a big Scottish contingent at the club with Ian St John and Bill Shankly especially, who were both fantastic with me, I couldn't bring myself to leave home. The St Mirren manager was a friend of my dad's, and I ended up signing for them instead."

In his early teenage years McQueen had the physique of a stick insect on a body fat prevention programme but by the time he went to Melwood at 17, he'd developed dramatically in height. These growing pains made it more difficult for him to impress, although he believes that Twentyman, in particular, was taken aback by his pace.

"I grew a lot between 14 and 16 and by the time I was 17 I was still unbelievably weak, which was a big problem for me – especially when I went to Rangers and Liverpool with the intensive training. I think Liverpool were shocked at how quick I was. People don't associate me with having pace, but I was really quick back then. I was incredibly raw, though, and other clubs weren't prepared to take a chance on me. Geoff was the first one that did."

Liverpool and Twentyman were on the lookout for a long-term successor to Ron Yeats by the end of the '60s so it is possible that McQueen could have filled that huge void. Instead, he became Jack Charlton's replacement at Leeds – an equally daunting task – and

Top: Geoff Twentyman, aged 19, with future wife Pat, 18, discussing the finer art of how to clean football boots

Left: A young Twentyman standing next to his Under-15 Westmorland & Cumberland wrestling trophy

Below: Swift Rovers, 1946-47, where Ivor Broadis first scouted Twentyman, who is pictured back row, second from right

SWIFT ROVERS. 1946-47.
League Champions + Charity Shield Winners

Learning from the master: A fitness test at a snowy Brunton Park conducted under the watchful eye of Bill Shankly in 1951. Below: Listening intently (centre) during one of Shankly's training ground talks at Carlisle

Carlisle United line up on one of the greatest night's in the club's history – the third round of the FA Cup against Arsenal in 1951. Twentyman is back row, second from right. Paddy Waters – 'the toughest man in the Carlisle side' is pictured back row, far right

Right: The letter sent by Bill Shankly – then manager of Grimsby – when Twentyman clinched his move to Anfield. Above: In Liverpool kit

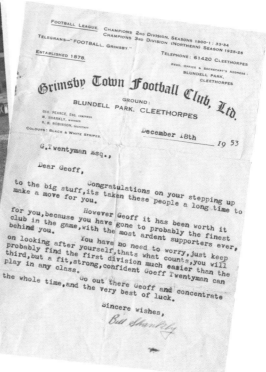

FOOTBALL LEAGUE, CHAMPIONS 2ND DIVISION, SEASONS 1900-1 : 33-34
CHAMPIONS 3RD DIVISION (NORTHERN) SEASON 1925-26
TELEGRAMS—" FOOTBALL, GRIMSBY "
ESTABLISHED 1878.
TELEPHONE: 61420 CLEETHORPES
REGD. OFFICE & SECRETARY'S ADDRESS :
BLUNDELL PARK,
CLEETHORPES

Grimsby Town Football Club, Ltd.

GROUND:
BLUNDELL PARK, CLEETHORPES

GEO. PEARCE, ESQ. CHAIRMAN
W. SHANKLY, MANAGER
R. E. ROBINSON, SECRETARY
COLOURS: BLACK & WHITE STRIPES.

December 18th _____ 19 53

G.Twentyman Esq.,

Dear Geoff,

Congratulations on your stepping up to the big stuff, its taken these people a long time to make a move for you.

However Geoff it has been worth it for you, because you have gone to probably the finest club in the game, with the most ardent supporters ever, behind you.

You have no need to worry, just keep on looking after yourself, thats what counts, you will probably find the first division much easier than the third, but a fit, strong, confident Geoff Twentyman can play in any class.

Go out there Geoff and concentrate the whole time, and the very best of luck.

Sincere wishes,

Bill Shankly

*Liverpool v Barnsley 1955: Twentyman looks on as
Ronnie Moran beats Bobby Brown to the ball*

*Training (far left) at Melwood with Bob Paisley
and teammates including (heading the ball) Billy Liddell*

Above:
Relaxing
(third from
right) with
fellow Reds
players

Right:
Ready for
action:
In the
Liverpool
team line-up

Left:
Winning the
Ulster Cup
at Ballymena
United in
1961

*Twentyman on his return to Carlisle in 1963.
The grandstand behind him was built with
money generated by his £12,000 sale to
Liverpool 10 years earlier – the previous
stand had burnt down (inset left)*

Two worlds colliding: Brian Clough and Twentyman are treated after a clash of heads during a match at Anfield. Their paths would cross many times in the future as Liverpool and Clough's Derby and Nottingham Forest sides battled for supremacy. Right: The 'bloke with the trilby'

Team behind the team: Pictured (centre, back) with Bob Paisley and the backroom staff

National treasures: A newspaper cutting showing how much the Army team, featuring Geoff Twentyman (back row, second from right), would be worth. Shankly arranged for Twentyman to be discharged to help with Carlisle United's 1950/51 title challenge

Below: Signing autographs for fans in Liverpool. It was the strong bond Twentyman developed with the people of Liverpool that brought him back to the city. Below right: An Anfield scout

The Army's team against Aston Villa. Back row, left to right: Pte. W. Webb, RAOC (Leicester City), Pte. N. E. Gunter, RAOC (Portsmouth), Pte. A. V. Marchi, RAOC (Spurs), Pte. W. Fraser, REME (Airdrieonians), Gnr. G. Twentyman (Carlisle United), Pte. D. J. Hines, RAOC (Leicester City). Front row: Gnr. L. Simpson (Huddersfield), Gnr. G. E. Nutt (Coventry), Pte. A. Kaye, RAMC (Barnsley), L/Cpl. A. E. Fenton, 4/20 King's Hussars (Blackpool) (captain), and Pte. J. Parry, 2nd Sherwood Foresters (Derby County)

THE ARMY'S £100,000 TEAM

Bringing the Cup home: On the train back from Wembley after winning the FA Cup in 1974. Ronnie Moran is far left, Tom Saunders seated centre and Joe Fagan seated far right

partnered Norman Hunter at the back. "I didn't really think about it to be honest. I was just proud to be playing at Leeds. Me and Norman formed a good barrier. If I'd have signed for Liverpool, maybe I'd have said the same thing about Tommy Smith, who was equally tenacious!"

Don Revie was said to be obsessed by tactics, particularly those of the opposition. Brian Clough famously lamented his rival for keeping files on opposing players and allegedly had them torched after taking charge at Elland Road when Revie became England manager. McQueen believes Revie's fixation with the opposition wasn't as dramatic as it has been portrayed in the years since, but adds that all Leeds players were made aware of certain strengths and weaknesses. Especially against Liverpool.

"Usually Don would tell me to make sure I got John Toshack into wide areas and compete well in the air," McQueen explains. "Norman had to deal with Kevin Keegan, thankfully, because still to this day when people ask me who was my most difficult opponent, I will say Kevin. He was the most difficult to pin down because he was so energetic, lively and sharp. A lot of people go on about Don being consumed with tactics, but as far as I was concerned, he just told me to mark Toshack.

"You were made well aware of the strengths and weaknesses of every single player you were up against. Whether they were physical – whether you could give them a whack – whether that whack would keep them quiet, or even whether it would make them play better. Don knew all these things and he would pass on all types of different information about different opponents."

McQueen was involved in countless battles with Liverpool over the years, and despite Revie's approach, the Reds usually prevailed. "All the way through my career, I ended up being the rival of Liverpool. At both Leeds and Man Utd. All the way through, Liverpool always had the edge, although we pipped them to the title in '74 with Leeds. I can't remember too many games when I came out on top against Liverpool. We knocked them out of the cup with United, but in the biggies, especially at Leeds, Liverpool were too strong. Definitely at Man United, we were always a poor second.

"Despite all the battles, though, and even years later when Leeds and Liverpool were clashing in the league, Bill Shankly would always make a point of coming over to me and ask me how I was keeping. That's a measure of the man. He knew I was doing well at Leeds and he was genuinely pleased for me, despite the fact we were rivals."

McQueen must be one of the only players in the history of football to have been coached by the three great managers of the '70s: Bill Shankly, Don Revie and Brian Clough. These managers changed the way club bosses were viewed and, like a state of matrimony, an audience with either one was not to be entered lightly.

"To have been associated with people like that is something I will take with me forever," says McQueen. "They were the legendary managers of the time. It was something else for a young kid like me. They were all very different, and although Brian Clough's reign at Leeds was a disaster, it was clear that he was a winner in his own right.

"Even when I was back at Liverpool, at Melwood, I was in awe of the names and the faces that surrounded me. Peter Thompson, Ian Callaghan, Ian St John and Tommy Smith – people like that – I just feel honoured to have shared a dressing room with them, although it didn't last. When I eventually went to Leeds, it was the same there with Peter Lorimer, Eddie Gray, Billy Bremner and Jack Charlton. It was a lot to take in for a younger player. It was a privilege."

Now working as Middlesbrough's chief scout, McQueen informs me that he's due at the airport for a flight to Greece to look at a transfer target, but before he goes, he explains his "99 per cent of players would want to sign for United" quote. "Manchester United in the '70s went year after year without winning a single thing," he says, laughing. "But they still stayed massive because of the following they attracted. People talk about Newcastle being a big club now and their fans think everyone wants to sign for them, but that's rubbish. There was a time when their crowds were low – even Glasgow Rangers, pre-Souness, their crowds were poor.

"United's crowds had always stayed big and the majority of players would have found it difficult to turn them down – although I have since been told by an awful lot of players that they did turn United down.

"Some of them were later associated with Liverpool Football Club…"

DAVID FAIRCLOUGH

Fairclough's arrival in the Liverpool first team was crucial to the club's league title challenge in 1976 – his seven goals helped them overcome QPR's challenge. However, he is best remembered for his tie-winning goal at Anfield against St Etienne in the quarter-final of the European Cup the following season. Despite his excellent goals-to-games ratio, Fairclough struggled to make the starting line-up on a regular basis, instead coming off the bench during Liverpool's glory years.

Signed: *Came through youth ranks*
Age when signed: *17*
Total LFC appearances/goals: *154/55*
Seasons spent at Liverpool: *8*
Birthplace: *Liverpool*
Other clubs: *Toronto Blizzard (Canada), Lucerne (Switzerland), Norwich, Oldham, Beveren (Belgium), Rochdale, Tranmere, Wigan, Knowsley (amateur)*

'SIGN THAT RED HEAD,' was the headline on page 33 of the *Sunday People*, 10 September 1978. The opposite page ran a story about Brigitte Bardot, 'the sex nymph of our times', who'd announced that she was 24 years old when she decided she wanted a baby.

The redhead in question was not, ironically, the subject of Bardot's desires. It was David Fairclough, Liverpool striker and super-sub (a nickname he later came to resent).

Geoff Twentyman spoke to the *People* about how he'd spotted Fairclough. The story ran as follows: 'If Geoff Twentyman had £1 for every father, schoolmaster or fan who thought they'd found a star, he'd be a millionaire. But there's one Liverpool supporter who made up with one simple tip, for all the pestering Twentyman endures. "There's this little red-haired lad called Fairclough who's magic. You've got to see him." That was on a Thursday. On the following Sunday Twentyman saw Fairclough, who was then 14 play for a local junior side and by Tuesday he'd signed a schoolboy form and was on his way to stardom. "I don't often get advice as good as that, and I don't often act as impulsively as on that occasion," said Twentyman. "But I decided to watch the lad and having seen him I didn't hang about. I had a long chat with his dad, explained that for both David and the club it would be a gamble, but it could do neither of us any harm. Young Fairclough was keen and signed the form. A week later he scored nine in a schoolboy match. I'm sure that if I'd not acted when I did, every scout in the country would have been on his doorstep."'

Fairclough says now that he never even thought about a career in professional football until Twentyman knocked on his front door one day. "I was from Everton originally. I remember playing in a local tournament in Stanley Park where the car park is now. As I walked off the pitch in the direction of Goodison Park, someone came up to me and asked me my name. He introduced himself as a scout of Liverpool Football Club. I didn't think anything of it and didn't even tell my parents about it because it seemed like he was just having a chat with me to see who I was, rather than making an approach.

"Within a year I'd moved to Cantril Farm. By that time a friend of my dad was doing some scouting for Geoff Twentyman as one of his networkers, a guy called Wally Burgess. I believe that he threw my name into the mix after he saw me play well in a Bootle and Litherland Sunday League match. One morning on a Saturday there was knock on the door. Geoff had come to my house to speak to me, but I wasn't around unfortunately. Luckily for me, my dad told them I was playing the next day in a Sunday League match and Geoff was dead keen to come and have a look at me. Geoff brought another guy with him to watch me play for a team called Littlemoss. The deal was sorted soon after."

The striker was one of the youngest players to have signed associated schoolboy forms at a time where players didn't usually arrive at Melwood until they were 15 years old. Fairclough believes the attribute that set him apart from other players was his rapid pace – something Twentyman said would enable him to race in the legendary (in Cumbria, at least) Powderhall Sprint.

"I was very direct and quick and my timing at arriving in the box was quite good too. More than anything, though, I was lucky. Maybe if Geoff watched me on another day, he'd have seen something that would have put him off and someone else would have come under his radar. I may have done enough a bit later to attract Liverpool because even up to the age of 16 I was scoring goals for Liverpool schoolboys. Anyone who played and was doing well for the schoolboys team was always of interest to different clubs. The Powderhall Sprint was an event that people from Cumbria entered because it was just over the border into Scotland. Geoff told me it had a lot of history and that I was so quick I could compete in it even as a teenager. That was one of the first things he said to me…he'd always try and bring Carlisle into conversations."

Born into a rabid Reds-supporting family, Fairclough's father used to ask Twentyman for favours getting tickets for high-profile matches such as the Leeds United title decider in 1973, which Liverpool won at Anfield. "My dad had a season ticket but I only went when I could. Dad was a modest, shy fella, but he plucked up enough courage to ask Geoff for help when he needed to."

Less than four years after watching history unfold in front of his own eyes, Fairclough was making history himself as he scored a late winner to see off St Etienne and put Liverpool through to the semi-finals of the

European Cup. The progression from youth team to first team, Fairclough says, was seamless and something he didn't spend time thinking about.

"Everything just fell into place for me quite comfortably. It was a natural progression because at first I never stressed about being spotted as a teenager, then luckily it happened. I'd always been selected regularly for Liverpool boys and select teams, but being a professional footballer wasn't something I consciously thought about. I never felt like I should be chasing a future in football and believed that I would end up doing an average job and leading an average life. Even when I got to Liverpool, everything flowed easily. I never worried about making the next step. I worked hard and just tried to take every opportunity I had to impress without getting intense about it."

Despite scoring 55 goals in 154 games for Liverpool, Fairclough never truly established himself as a first-choice striker. "The 'supersub' tag didn't help me because I felt it meant the manager would be more inclined to leave me on the bench and have an impact later in the game. Because of my pace, I was a good asset to have when teams were tiring late in games, especially on the heavier pitches. In some strange way and from a selfish point of view maybe I'd have started a lot more games if I didn't score that goal against St Etienne and other late goals as a sub in league matches early on in my career. It pigeonholed me."

The nickname did, however, build up his reputation, especially on the continent where he moved after leaving Liverpool in 1983. "A call came from Canada one summer and I agreed to go over there and play while I was still at Liverpool. Then when I decided to leave for good there were plenty of offers abroad because of my exploits in the European Cup. I decided on a move to Switzerland with FC Luzern. I ended up living next door to Ottmar Hitzfeld [the current Switzerland manager and two-time European Cup winner with Borussia Dortmund and Bayern Munich]. He'd just started his managerial career with FC Zug back then.

"Ottmar was a really nice bloke. We got to know each other really well over the two years, but of course I had no idea what was in store for him during his managerial career. Ottmar was not soft. He was a very hard and organised coach, a typical German really. I loved it over in Switzerland, but in some ways it was a little bit too peaceful. Luzern had beautiful forests, lakes, architecture, but just didn't have the buzz of Liverpool." After deciding to return home to play for Norwich City then Oldham, Fairclough decided to move abroad again. "I was on the verge of signing for a team from Larnaca in Cyprus, but while I was over there finalising the deal, we were on the beach one day and a big Scouse family were sitting there. They owned the famous Blue Star chippies around Liverpool and they were all going: 'Come on Dave, you're well too good for Cypriot football.' So I decided there and then to go to Beveren in Belgium."

His time in the satellite town just outside Antwerp initially proved successful, with Beveren reaching the third round of the UEFA Cup after knocking out Athletic Bilbao. The squad included the brother of the fabled Jean-Marie Pfaff (the former Bayern Munich keeper soon became a good friend of Fairclough's), as well as Eugene Ekeke who scored against England in the 1990 World Cup.

Fairclough's performances didn't go unnoticed and Ajax lodged a bid for the striker who was now nearing his 30th birthday. Beveren's president rejected the offer and the Dutch masters signed Frank Stapleton instead. Within a year, Beveren's fortunes slumped, their manager replaced and Fairclough was left looking for another club. A move to French Club Quimper fell through, and despite interest from Bastia and Gueugnon, he eventually returned to live in Liverpool.

"A lot of people don't really know what happened to me after I left Liverpool," Fairclough laughs. "In terms of playing time and learning a different cultural experience, they were some of the best days of my life. Living in Canada, Switzerland and Belgium was very different from growing up in Cantril Farm, anyway."

ALAN BIRCHENALL

Birchenall was an attacking midfielder who started his career at Sheffield United in 1963, where he won his first two of four England Under-23 caps. He was one of the first £100,000 players when he joined Chelsea in 1967, and after three years there he moved to Crystal Palace. His career also took him to Leicester, Notts County and the US before he retired in 1983.

Birthplace: *East Ham*
Position: *Attacking midfielder*
Clubs: *Sheffield United, Chelsea, Crystal Palace, Leicester City, Notts County, San Jose Earthquakes, Memphis Rogues, Blackburn Rovers, Luton Town, Hereford United*

WHEN Liverpool lifted the First Division title in the Easter of 1973 the swash of the Kop was at its most tidal, fans swaying back and forth in celebration. Bill Shankly, wearing a deep red shirt, walked slowly around the perimeter of the pitch in a "great communion between players and supporters", as commentator Gerald Sinstadt piously described it. Shankly raised his hand in acknowledgement to the crowd and picked up scarves laid in front of him. "That…" he barked to a policeman who kicked one from his path, "…is someone's life." They might as well have been palms.

Liverpool had won the league for the first time in seven long years. The Sabbath had ended. Kopites clambered and surged forward like a great ocean wave just to get closer to the man that had given the city back its swagger. "Being involved no matter where the ball is is the essence of the game," Shankly said later, pointing towards why Liverpool were champions again. The opposition that afternoon, Leicester City, had scraped a 0-0 draw but it was enough to spur a title party. While captain Emlyn Hughes hoisted the trophy around Anfield and his team-mates sloshed champagne on the pitch, one Leicester player remained at the tunnel entrance to the Main Stand and witnessed the scene. He could have been celebrating with the Liverpool team had Geoff Twentyman decided to recommend him to Shankly a few years earlier.

Alan Birchenall was a silky ball-playing midfielder, not too different in appearance to the blonde-locked Alun Evans. He'd played for Sheffield United, Chelsea (where he was watched by Twentyman), and Crystal Palace before joining Leicester in 1971.

"When I look back over my career, it is something I savour," Birchenall says enthusiastically in a quasi Cockney-Midland accent. "We gave Liverpool a good game and wanted to win, but they held out. There were 55-60,000 people inside Anfield and another 20,000 outside wanting to get in. Liverpool, for once, played nervously in front of their people. After the game, we made a guard of honour and let the players run out onto the pitch. Then Shankly walked out. He was a messiah. I can visualise it now. I was just yards away and Bill was walking towards the Kop. People were throwing scarves at him and he picked every single one up. Watching the Kop and Bill interact that way was awesome."

Twentyman targeted Birchenall towards the end of the '60s, around the time when Roger Hunt and Ian St John were coming towards the end of their Anfield careers. Norman Clarke, who was one of Twentyman's many scouts in his web of contacts, says that he went to watch Birchenall on behalf of Liverpool in a game against Sunderland at Roker Park not long after he'd signed for Chelsea. Although Birchenall eventually evolved into a midfielder, he was considered a striker in his formative years and Twentyman believed he had the movement and touch to be a success at Anfield, unlike Tony Hateley, who despite scoring consistently in his one and only season with the club, didn't fit into Shankly's pass and move approach to the game.

"Tony was a nice fella and a good player in the right team. However, his arrival changed our style of play," Tommy Smith later said. "From being a passing team, we suddenly started launching the long ball up to the big man. It is not something you plan. It's just that a centre-forward who is good in the air becomes a magnet for the long, high ball."

By comparison, Birchenall, who played virtually the whole of his career in the First Division, frequently scoring more than 10 a season, would have stylistically been the kind of player Shankly would have liked. "I was never really a prolific striker but I always fed off the prolific ones and played off the main guy – like the way the so-called 'second striker' does today," Birchenall says. "Had I moved to Liverpool, I would never have scored the number of goals that Rushy or Aldridge did a bit later on. I know Liverpool endured a bit of a barren spell in the late '60s and didn't win the title until '73. Maybe it's a good thing they didn't sign me because the barren spell might have gone on a bit longer! They were probably wise not to sign me. They got Keegan in 1970 and he turned out ok didn't he?"

Birchenall's apprehension about the prospect of a move to Liverpool is probably a result of his reputation off the field – a reputation that Shankly or indeed Bob Paisley wouldn't have tolerated. During the '70s he was regarded as aloof and a bit of a funster. David Beckham may strut around his kitchen playing up his metrosexual status today, but he certainly wasn't the first English footballer to be afforded such a title. Birchenall shocked the football establishment when a picture was taken of him kissing Tony Currie after the pair collided in a challenge. But to Birchenall, it was just a case of mates having a laugh – like the rest of his career. "I don't want to sound like an old fart, but I wouldn't swap playing in that era [the '70s] for anything. The game's fantastic today but no one's allowed to have a laugh anymore. I used to trip up referees, throw snowballs at the crowd; I even played in the p***ing rain at Highbury holding an umbrella – it took the ref ages to spot it!"

Unlike many of the players featured in this book, Birchenall says that he'd heard of Liverpool's interest through a friend that worked for one of the Sunday papers. "He knew Twentyman and had seen him at Stamford Bridge one day. Everyone knows that football has changed dramatically in terms of the media involvement, but even back then we knew when other clubs were sniffing around. There was still a lot of rumour, but it wasn't publicised like it is now. When I heard about Liverpool, I tried to take it as a pinch of salt, even though I was very happy because until something happened I was helpless. A journalist told me that Liverpool made an approach but Chelsea didn't tell me about it, so if Liverpool did, the club must have rejected it. Whether it was true anyway, I don't know. Back then the clubs had all the power and players stuck around at those clubs for a lot longer than they do today, so I didn't really think about it at all."

Birchenall was brought up in East Ham and predictably followed West Ham until he moved to Nottingham as a child where he watched Notts County at Meadow Lane and his hero Tommy Lawton. Since retiring after a spell playing in the NASL in the late '70s, he has been adopted by Leicester City and their fans as one of their own and has worked in variety of roles at club for last 28 years. Now an official ambassador, he describes himself as a "general Leicester City busybody."

Despite not being a consistent goalscorer throughout his career, he insists that his strike rate against Liverpool was particularly "remarkable", although he also recalls featuring on the losing side in an FA Cup semi-final in 1974 when Shankly, in one of his last games in charge, master-minded a 3-1 replay victory at Villa Park after Leicester and Birchenall frustrated the Reds to a 0-0 draw at Old Trafford. "I never thought Shankly would leave at that point," he says. "Liverpool looked like they were on the crest of a wave." Liverpool, of course, later defeated Newcastle in the final – Shankly's last competitive game in charge, discounting the Charity Shield the following season.

"It would have been brilliant to play for Liverpool," Birchenall adds. "Look at all those great players. Cally, Steve Heighway, Tommy Smith...Lawler, you can go on and on. Everyone who has ever played at Anfield says the same thing, I know, but playing there was something I will never forget. I played there for several different clubs, but I know that everyone used to raise their game by 20-25 per cent when we went there."

Birchenall, whose affable nature comes across even over the phone, then concludes the interview by referring to himself in the third person. "When people have a pop at me and say I was bloody rubbish, now I can say: 'Hold on son, Liverpool nearly signed me, so shut up.' I'll be going into the pub tonight and I'll say: 'Hunt and St John were nearly good enough to play with the Birch!'"

LARRY LLOYD

Bought by Shankly in 1969, Lloyd was an uncompromising defender and a natural leader. However, injury meant that he forfeited his place in the side to Phil Thompson, and he never recovered it. Lloyd later won the league title and the European Cup at Forest.

Signed: *from Bristol Rovers for £50,000 in April 1969*
Age when signed: *20*
Total LFC appearances/goals: *218/5*
Seasons spent at Liverpool: *5*
Birthplace: *Bristol*
Other clubs: *Bristol Rovers, Coventry City, Nottingham Forest, Wigan Athletic*

IF YOU have ever witnessed a post-match press conference after your team has slumped to another miserable defeat, you will know that certain journalists think they know more about football than managers. Clever questions are often (rightly or wrongly) met with cool responses. Even wittier remarks are fired back. According to the *Times*, Larry Lloyd is one of the 50 worst footballers to have ever played in English football's top division. This is certainly a case where a journalist has got it wrong. This is the same Larry Lloyd that was signed by two of the most iconic managers of all time in Bill Shankly and Brian Clough, and the same Larry Lloyd that was the cornerstone of the two great teams of the '70s: Liverpool, then Nottingham Forest.

Lloyd won two First Division championship medals, two European Cup medals, two League Cup medals and a UEFA Cup medal, making more than 400 league appearances in the top division. Yet he is rated 43rd in the Times' list, just better than fellow centre-back David May (who owns a European Cup Winners' medal after appearing on Man Utd's bench in 1999 and made 93 appearances in nine years at Old Trafford), but apparently worse than Claus Lundekvam [Southampton] and Roque Junior [Leeds], who are both merely noted for suffering relegation with their respective clubs. Now this is not just speaking through Red-tinted glasses. After all, the Times quite rightly placed two other former Liverpool players, Istvan Kozma and Torben Piechnik on the list. They deserve to be there.

Lloyd, though, was an Anfield stalwart, not missing a single minute of the 54 matches in Liverpool's double-winning 1972/73 season. He was, however, a player of devilish strength and minimal grace, thus making him suffer a degree of mockery throughout his career. Geoff Twentyman once told a newspaper that he was so impressed by Lloyd after watching him play for Bristol Rovers, that their manager Fred Ford said: "You've got more confidence in him than I have." Twentyman then added: "I reckon Lloyd did a great job for Liverpool and even when he left they sold him at a very handsome profit."

Liverpool signed Lloyd in 1969 as a long-term replacement for Ron Yeats. "It was a monster task replacing Ron because he was a monster player," Lloyd says from his probably monster sized home in Marbella, Spain. "I didn't realise, being in Bristol, how much he was revered by Liverpool fans. But after a week or two up there I discovered just how important big Ron was. He was club captain and a damn good player as well. It was a monster job in front of me and I found that out very early on in my time at the club."

Bill Shankly labelled Yeats a "colossus" and told waiting journalists to "come in and walk round him," after signing the Scot from Dundee United in 1963. Lloyd certainly felt a sense of intrepidation at succeeding such a recognisable figure. "Liverpool were looking for a replacement for big Ron. As I was a big lad and a left-footer, I came into the equation. Shanks wanted a young and tough no-nonsense centre-half, and Geoff Twentyman saw that in me. I knew about Ron and his build and I knew how much Shanks liked him. I also knew that one day it would be me who they were replacing. I knew Geoff and Shanks had a lot of confidence in me and that settled me down straight away."

Twentyman took a special interest in centre-halves. He was one himself and Larry Lloyd was the first he guided towards Anfield. Lloyd, speaking with a husky Bristolian accent that has never left him despite leaving the south-west nearly 40 years ago, explains that by the time he signed for Liverpool, he'd already played for the England amateur side at 17 as well as making more than half a century of appearances for Bristol Rovers.

"We had two big lads at the back: me and Stuart Taylor. Stuart was a gentleman's centre-half, if that's possible – he wouldn't hurt a fly. I would have kicked my granny for a fiver. In fact, that's exactly what Shanks said to me when I went up there to sign for Liverpool. I knew what Shanks wanted, and I said: 'No, I'd kick her for half of that!' I think Shanks liked the fact that I was a left-footer as well."

Recalling the game that made Twentyman decide that he was the player to replace Yeats, Lloyd, now 60, says that like many of his signings it was only after the scout had seen him at his worst that he decided to make a move. "I remember the game well. I have spoken with Geoff about it. He went all the way up to Hartlepool to watch me. There was a man and his dog watching the game because no Rovers fans travelled up there because of the distance.

"The main thing I remember though was having an absolute f***ing nightmare. I had probably the worst game I ever had in my professional career. When I asked Geoff why he still signed me after that performance, he told me that he knew my intentions were good, but it wasn't coming off for me. He also said he believed I couldn't play any worse. That speaks volumes for Geoff Twentyman because he wasn't put off by one bad game. He'd obviously watched me months and months before and he'd already done his homework. I think we lost the game 2-1. The worst thing about it for me was the trip home afterwards. I knew Liverpool were watching me and I was thinking if they'd seen me play on that night, they would never be interested in signing me. It was such a long way home, I think I got in with the milkman."

Lloyd believes that Liverpool had been keeping an eye on him since his first-team debut and reveals how his move north was nearly scuppered by the demands of the then Rovers manager, Fred Ford. "I know they'd watched me for a long time before I signed. They wanted to buy me after about 20 games but Fred, who was mates with Shanks from well back (they played together at Carlisle), asked Shanks whether he could keep me until the end of the season because we were struggling desperately in the league. Fred didn't want to let me go until we were safe. By April '69, we'd secured safety, so Bill made the phone call again and Fred agreed to let me go. It became apparent that the deal between Liverpool was never in doubt. Fred and Shanks were as thick as thieves together and they had an agreement in place for a long time. I later found that Matt Busby wanted me for Man United. I'd have never gone there anyway. Liverpool were a bigger club and I liked the things I'd heard about Shanks's treatment of his players, so it was a no-brainer."

Eventually, Lloyd arrived at Anfield in a deal worth £50,000 after travelling to Merseyside alone to seal the deal. "I got to Lime Street and this taxi driver was going on and on, cracking joke after joke. He was swearing his head off, but it was clear he was a mad Liverpool supporter. Scousers always were and always have been very open people and he started telling me he was a part-time taxi driver and a part-time comedian. I wasn't sure whether that was a joke in itself. He was giving it all the 'German this, and German that!' He recognised my face from the paper and wouldn't charge me. So I asked his name to look out for him on the comedy scene. He went: 'It's Stan.' So I went: 'Stan who?' It was Stan Boardman.

"When I met Shanks, he didn't say a thing to me until I'd signed the contract. He just came up to me and said: 'Son, you'll want to be signing this…' and left it on the desk. 'In 20 minutes' time, there is another train at Lime Street back to Bristol. If you don't sign it son, you'll be on it.' So I signed it straight away. I was a bit disappointed what they were offering, but I didn't want to disappoint my new friend Mr Shankly."

KEVIN BEATTIE

The heart and lungs of Bobby Robson's Ipswich team in the '70s, Beattie made over 200 appearances and was integral to the club's FA Cup triumph in 1978 and their UEFA Cup win in 1981 (although he missed the final with a broken arm). Beattie won nine England caps and was nicknamed 'The Diamond' by Robson because his scouts had discovered a real 'gem'.

Birthplace: *Carlisle*
Position: *Central defender*
Clubs: *Ipswich, Colchester, Middlesbrough*

THE story about Kevin Beattie and his brief flirtation with Liverpool Football Club is a tale of myth and legend. Beattie, who was later described by Bobby Robson as a player who matched Ronaldo (not the winker) in terms of natural ability and speed, was due for a second trial at Melwood after impressing Liverpool scouts, notably Geoff Twentyman.

Twentyman had known about Beattie for a long time, having lived on the same Carlisle street as Beattie's parents, and he was stunned by the young Cumbrian's physique. He was a brute of a boy and had built up his strength after years of working in the meat industry with his father. 'I remember we had 22 lads on trial and chose two to come back the following week. One was Kevin Beattie,' Twentyman told the *Sunday People* in September 1978. 'I was really keen on him and on his second visit we played him in a B team game. He came through that no bother and I was convinced he would make it. He returned to Carlisle and was due back in two weeks when I was convinced we'd signed him. When the day arrived I turned up at Lime Street Station at 1pm to meet him. But Beattie was not on the train. I called Carlisle, was told he'd missed the train and would be there later. I waited all evening, but he never made it.'

Norman Clarke, one of Twentyman's scouts, says that his friend told him he'd methodically searched every passenger that passed through the station that night. 'Next thing I knew he'd signed for Ipswich,' Twentyman added. 'You spend the rest of your life wondering where you went wrong. Should I have signed him when he first arrived? Should I have gone to Carlisle and dragged him back?'

Beattie originally went to Liverpool following a recommendation from somebody Twentyman knew who had scouted for Liverpool for several years. But by the early '70s the person was also scouting for Bobby Robson's Ipswich Town. "Whether or not he did a deal with Ipswich, nobody's sure," says Clarke. "But it's a bit of a coincidence, isn't it?"

Beattie, though, has his own story. "Geoff must have checked on a different bloody platform other than the one I was on," he chuckles. "The truth is that I did go to Liverpool. My dad put me on the train from Carlisle and I couldn't wait to get there. I had a successful week, so there was absolutely no way I'd turn them down. I was disappointed when nobody met me, although I would have said at the time that football wasn't my main love. When I left school, I did an apprenticeship and didn't set out to become a footballer, it just happened really because it was something I enjoyed doing and had a bit of ability. Maybe there was a problem his end – maybe hc arrived there late and made up a story just to keep Shanks happy, I don't know!"

Beattie, who has in the past refused to speak about the issue of his failed move to Liverpool with several magazines and newspapers, continues, adding that it's about time he set the story straight. "I really liked Geoff, so I will never understand why he didn't turn up. My family knew him well too, so neither could they. My dad, Tommy, was a bit of a scallywag and the Beattie family was quite well known around Carlisle. Everyone enjoyed a few beers and a game of darts. Everyone in Carlisle knows one another and even when I go home now I can't walk around without being stopped. I grew up on a really rough estate in Botcherby and Geoff knew my dad from there because it's a notorious area of the city.

"When I was 15, I was as strong as a horse and Geoff liked that. I was made up when he told me that he wanted me to go to Liverpool. I spent a week down there and I loved it. All we did was five-a-side and we played against Shanks every day. I really did love it. It was absolutely brilliant. Meeting Mr Shankly was something special. I thought I'd done quite well. The following week, I got a letter off Geoff saying that he wanted me to come and play in a game. That was no problem at all. So I got the train on a Friday from Carlisle to Lime Street, got off and there was no one there to meet me. I remember to this day that one of the porters on the train was a big Everton fan and he was going: 'Ah bloody Liverpool, you know what they're like.' I waited, waited and waited, but I didn't have any numbers to contact anyone, so I got back on the train and went back home to Carlisle. The following couple of days, I got a letter saying something like: 'Sorry son, you didn't turn up. That's it.' A week later, I signed for Ipswich. They'd watched me as well and moved quickly. So I didn't even have time to dwell on what happened with Liverpool."

Several years later, Beattie recalls playing in Shankly's testimonial at Anfield in 1975. "Shanks came up to me, you know the way he speaks, and said: 'Aye son…I've only made a few mistakes in my life…but you were one of the biggest…but don't tell anyone that!' He was great with me, though. He handed over a brown envelope and wanted to pay me for turning up. I said: 'Mr Shankly, I don't want it…I don't want it.' He said: 'Eh, I've made a few bob lad – put in your pocket.' The guy was something special and I can see why he achieved so much success – the players loved him. Anfield was my favourite away ground, even though I never won a single game there in my career. Liverpool were always Ipswich's bogey club. But talking to Mr Shankly – I'd always call him that – was a pleasure. He'd always reminisce. 'Ah lad, you slipped through our net.' It meant a lot to me, it really did."

Beattie says that he has also spoken to Twentyman on many occasions about the mysterious occurrences that led to his botched deal with Liverpool. "I always told him the same thing. At the end he just said it was water under the bridge – there was no grudges, although he was disappointed the way things turned out. He was always adamant he was on that bloody platform!

"Liverpool were an absolutely massive club. When I came to Ipswich, I didn't have a clue who they were, or even where it was in the country. Everybody had heard of Liverpool, though. It wouldn't make sense to turn a club like Liverpool down would it? It's just circumstance that I didn't go there."

After moving to Portman Road, Beattie reverted from his then more natural centre-forward position to left-back and finally centre-back. All this after he started playing as a goalkeeper in his teens. "I still hold the record for goalscoring in the Ipswich youth team after all these years," he adds proudly. "I ended up playing at the back on the off-chance really. Our left-back, Colin Harper, was injured in 1971 and we played Man Utd at the start of the season away. Bobby [Robson] just told me that I was playing left-back in the game and that was it. I did quite well and before long I was a left-sided centre-half and I never looked back."

Reflecting on games he played against Liverpool, Beattie insists that Kevin Keegan was without doubt his toughest opponent. "It's funny because I believe Kevin wasn't really an out-and-out forward when he signed for Liverpool, but we both ended up playing in different positions to when we were scouted. I played against Kevin many times and played with him for England. He was always so quick over the first 10 yards – but so was I. I used to love playing against Kevin. We'd come off black and blue but we'd still have a smile on our faces and have a drink afterwards."

If Beattie had signed for Liverpool back at the end of the '60s, he could have replaced Ian St John or Ron Yeats, which sounds strange given their different builds and abilities. But that was what singled Beattie out from the rest. His versatility. Still living in Suffolk to this day, Beattie says that he sometimes wonders about what would have happened if he'd moved to Merseyside during his career.

"I am big, big mates with Phil Thommo through my England days and he always used to tell me what it was like at Liverpool. I don't have any regrets about playing for Ipswich because I had great times there, but I often think what it would have been like at Liverpool. I went to Ipswich in '69 around the time Bobby Robson turned up so I experienced Ipswich's most successful ever period. They were the glory years and we had a great team with a fantastic manager. I won the UEFA Cup and the FA Cup at Ipswich. But if I went to Liverpool and made the first team, I would have won a lot, lot more. It doesn't half make you think. When I went down to Liverpool, I stayed in digs on Prescot Road and whenever I go past them now, I always think about how different things could have been. Liverpool are my second favourite club, and whenever the vidiprinter starts on a Saturday, I always look out for their results."

Before the end of the conversation, Beattie mentions the nickname he was given by Bobby Robson, 'diamond', in reference to the fact that he was chiselled out of an obscure, humble Cumbrian upbringing. "God, I got so much stick for that. God knows what Shanks would have called me! He must have wanted to call me a gobsh*te after what happened…"

STEVE HEIGHWAY

An economics graduate who became one of the greatest wingers Anfield has ever seen, Heighway was spotted playing for Skelmersdale United in 1970. Heighway helped Liverpool win four league titles, an FA Cup, a League Cup, three European Cups and two UEFA Cups. He left Anfield for the US in 1981.

Signed: *from Skelmersdale United for free in May 1970*
Age when signed: *22*
Total LFC appearances/goals: *475/76*
Seasons spent at Liverpool: *11*
Birthplace: *Dublin*
Other clubs: *Skelmersdale United (amateur), Minnesota Kicks (USA)*

IT HAS been 18 months since Steve Heighway ended an association with Liverpool that lasted into a fifth decade. Infighting caused by issues concerning the club's youth policy with first-team hierarchy at Melwood allegedly made Heighway decide to clear his office at the Academy in Kirkby. He announced his retirement, somewhat untypically, in a dramatic manner, live in front of Sky TV cameras on the pitch at Old Trafford after his Liverpool youngsters had defeated Manchester United in the FA Youth Cup final. Heighway is an archetypal Liverpool character of his time. Modest and grounded. Nothing, it seems, has ever gone to his head.

"I'm finding things now to keep myself busy that compare with my career in football – it's difficult," he says from his home near Southport. "I play a lot of golf and I have a lot of grandchildren so I have focused a lot of my energies there. I've been spending lots of time in America too as well as keeping an eye on the Academy. I still go down and watch the young lads and do the odd job here and there."

Heighway arrived at Liverpool in the summer of 1969 after being looked at by a number of club scouts including Geoff Twentyman. The former winger was told that Tony Waiters and Ronnie Moran had the biggest part to play in his scouting, although it is likely that Twentyman went to watch him owing to Skelmersdale's close proximity to Liverpool.

"Ronnie [Moran] said that they had me watched on many occasions," Heighway explains. "Apparently they'd seen me in games against South Liverpool – they were a really tough non-league outfit – and I did enough to impress and persuade them to sign me. I'd never heard of Geoff Twentyman's role before. But he probably had something to do with it because scouting was always done in a quiet way behind the scenes. As a player, I wasn't even aware that someone was watching me until Skem told me they'd had direct contact from Liverpool."

Heighway was only turning out for Skem in the first place because Roy Reece (not to be confused with Roy Race), Skem's boss, was also managing the English Universities side for which Heighway played. "I was at Warwick University studying in politics and economics while living in digs in Coventry. My long-term ambition was to become a teacher. But Roy liked me and asked me to go to Skem so I agreed because all I wanted to do was play football for fun. Things started to change from there. I never ever thought about football in a professional way. Not for one minute. My path was clear for me. I never set out to be a pro player and I'd already arranged to take part in a teaching diploma at Birmingham University in 1970. I'd always played football without thinking too much about it.

"Warwick University was only founded something like three years before I started there, so it didn't have any background in sports or a history in footballers. We had quite a strong team, but none of the other players were even playing semi-pro. Just because I was playing at a level higher than any of the other players didn't mean I was considerably better than anyone else. It just meant I prepared to travel for a game of football rather than going for a boozy session on a Friday night."

The distance Heighway had to travel just for a match with Skem in the Cheshire League would suggest that he took football a bit more seriously than his teammates at university, especially when you consider the lengths he went to just to arrive at the game on time.

"Some weekends I would travel to Manchester and grab a lift from my parents, but when that wasn't possible, I'd hitch-hike. I wasn't driving and I was only 20, I was engaged and because the train ticket was £4, I thought it would be better if I saved the money towards something worthwhile and risk it. I remember I had an evening game at Skem once and because it was late, the furthest I could get on the way home was the Bull Ring market in Birmingham. I didn't get there until midnight and from there I managed to get another lift off someone, then had to walk the remaining five miles home. I didn't get back until 3am."

Heighway, who was born in Ireland and spent time in Sheffield before his parents moved to Bramhall near Stockport, continues: "I was 22 when I was approached by Liverpool. I was getting along with my studies and at the same time playing as much football as I could. I played for British Universities, English Universities, Warwick University and Skelmersdale all at the same time. Skem always played with wingers and that obviously favoured me. I used to get knocked around a lot by tough full-backs, but it never bothered me. I was too quick for a lot of them so the only way they could stop me was by kicking. The Cheshire League was very tough and players weren't afraid to give you a good kicking if they felt it was necessary to stop you. The fact that I scored a lot of goals from the wing as well didn't help because it made me a bit of a marked man. In each of the two seasons I was there, I scored around 20 each year, so I always felt that the opposition would know about me – but never thought my record would attract interest from clubs higher up that wanted to sign me."

Heighway played in the same Skem team as Mickey Burns, later of Blackpool and Newcastle, as well as Peter Hardcastle who also moved to Blackpool. "There were quite a few other players as well who were good enough. I was just very lucky."

After the first move came from Liverpool, Bill Shankly decided to travel to the Midlands in an attempt to convince Heighway that Anfield was the right destination for him. But negotiations weren't as straight-forward as most fans would imagine. "I was told that Bill Shankly wanted to come and see me. So I told my parents and they said I would have to make a serious, life-changing decision about what I wanted to do, because I was really enjoying my studies and was looking forward to a career after I finished in university.

"I was also told that Coventry were watching and had planned to come and knock on my door pretty much the day after Liverpool had done the same thing. Shanks came down to see me and tried to persuade me that Liverpool was the best place for me by offering me a one-year contract. I sent him away and told him that I'd think about it. He found that a bit strange because I think he was used to people falling at his feet.

"It pleased me that Shanks was prepared to travel in order to sign me, but I'm not the impressionable type so I wasn't really, really amazed by the whole experience. I was just thinking that I had everything mapped out and because it came out of the blue, I was thinking: 'Blimey, is this the right thing to do?' Maybe some people would say that they couldn't get hold of the pen quick enough but it wasn't the same in those days and I'd gone through so much studying and done well that I thought if I gave it up, I might regret it in the long run.

"I spoke to my girlfriend and the family and they agreed that as long as I completed my degree, I'd have nothing at all to lose. If it didn't work out in the year at Liverpool, I'd go back to university and take another year to become a teacher. Two or three days later, I travelled to Liverpool and signed the contract there. But I was straight back to university to finish my studies and focus after that."

When asked what he believes prompted Liverpool to sign him, Heighway's answer, as always, is pragmatic. "I've always felt that Liverpool saw a strength in my pace and dribbling and thought they could use that as an advantage, rather than focus on improving a weakness. That's why we were successful because the management always made sure we got the very most out of each player's strength. Because I never thought that I would make myself a career in football, I never focused consciously on improving the weaknesses in my game. I could never head the ball that well and that stuck with me throughout my time at Liverpool. I think the other doubt Liverpool may have had would be whether I could take to a professional life, training day in and day out because I'd never done that before. Because I was a quiet lad with a degree and wasn't used to being in a football environment, football clubs higher up might have thought I wouldn't be good enough to deal with the cut and thrust of a football environment. But Liverpool could see past that."

Heighway admits that he had reservations about switching to full-time football, however. "I didn't find training particularly easy. But I was never a natural trainer. I could run and run all day but I'd never done any proper training in my life. I'd just played loads and loads of football and learnt my skills there. I never even trained with Skelmersdale because I lived so far away.

"But the one thing I always noticed about myself was that I never sustained any injuries. Not in training or in matches. The longest I ever spent out of the team was something like three weeks. I never had any muscle tears or ligament twinges at all, so it would suggest that I trained well. Anyone who plays for more than a decade without a serious injury must be doing something right in his preparation. It was hard going the first year because I needed to understand what it was all about being a professional and representing a club like Liverpool. It was my first year of marriage, too…"

Heighway completed his degree, and within six weeks of pre-season he'd made his full competitive debut. "I wouldn't say that I didn't expect to play so soon because I genuinely didn't know what to expect. I knew I had a one-year contract and had nothing to lose. I came in and did the pre-season training and worked as hard as I could. I'd got married around the time that I signed so I wanted to make it a success for the stability of my relationship first and foremost. But I'd done enough in pre-season to earn a place in the squad when we travelled away for the first game of the season against Burnley. I was the 13th man, but I was pleased that I'd impressed enough to share a dressing room with all these great footballers so soon."

Heighway played his first league game in a 1-0 win over Chelsea after Bobby Graham broke his leg. "I took to the game like a fish to water and proved I was good enough to deal with the pressure." Before long, Heighway had claimed Liverpool's number nine shirt as his own – despite it traditionally being the number of a striker. "The only reason why I became Liverpool's number nine was because it was Bobby Graham's shirt before me and because he was injured it was the only number to take. When I made my debut, everyone else had their established shirts so I just took Bobby's number. Before I was at Skem, I played mainly on the right wing and wore seven, then when I moved to the left, I wore 11.

"The system at Liverpool was different, though, and it made you build respect for your team-mates. Even later when bigger name players came in, including quite a few traditional number nines, they never demanded the shirt and just took what was given to them. It shows you that there were no egos at Liverpool then. As long as you got a shirt, it didn't matter what number was on the back."

Heighway went on to make 33 league appearances in his first season and quickly earned the nickname 'Big Bamber' after the scholarly Bamber Gascoigne. "The media called Brian Hall 'Little Bamber' as well because we'd both been to university. It was definitely something the papers invented, because none of the lads in the squad ever referred to us by those names. They were far worse than that."

Aside from nicknames, Heighway also established himself as a favourite of Bill Shankly's and the club's first choice left-winger. "Bill never said anything to me particularly, but it was always clear that he rated me. He didn't spend a lot of time talking individually with players but I always felt he thought highly of me. I think he had a soft spot for me because my route in had been different to everyone else's. He made it clear that I was his number one choice and that inspired confidence in me – as long as I was fit, I was always going to play. Don't get me wrong, though, he never did anyone any special favours."

Before going to university, Heighway played for Manchester City's youth sides. Despite enjoying his time at Maine Road, he was never offered a professional contract. He says that he probably would have rejected it anyway, such was his desire to follow education.

"I was there from the age of 17 for about two years. The club treated me brilliantly and I haven't got enough nice things to say about them. Malcolm Allison was the manager at the time. I'd play for my school on a Saturday morning and City's A-team in the afternoon. But I thought that university was the way to go for my long- term prospects even though they'd given me a chance at an early age to play in their reserve team. When I told them I was planning to go to university, they never came back to me and offered a contract as a professional player. Whenever I went back there as a player with Liverpool, the people at City would always make a point of saying hello. When we parted company, it was amicable so the club always acted positively towards me."

Heighway enjoyed 10 years of unbroken success at Anfield, leaving in 1981 for a short spell in NASL with Minnesota Kicks before living in Florida for eight years. Upon his return to England, he took charge Liverpool's youth system, remaining there until May 2007.

"My playing career ended in 1982 and I could never say that my enjoyment in life has dipped in any way since then. Other than eight years in the States, I've been at Liverpool since 1970. It's a long time and the only employment I've ever had – which is surprising when you think how keen I was on university and different career paths. I take an overall pride having been there for so long rather than one particular moment in my career. First of all, being good enough to play for Liverpool and then of course being responsible for helping build a fantastic facility for young players. Working with those lads has been a great experience and I take just as much enjoyment from that as I do from my playing career."

Heighway isn't keen to talk about his reasons for leaving Liverpool so he finishes by explaining what he believes is important in the making of a competent scout. "You can mix with a lot of devious people in football generally – especially in scouting – because people are so keen to make money from the next big thing. I have experienced this during my time at the Academy – you get offered players all the time. So it's very much about the quality of person that was going to be representing the club. I always felt that they were representing me as well so it was important to conduct themselves in the right way with honesty and integrity." Just the same qualities Heighway used throughout his Liverpool career.

7. The Players 1971-1980

Trevor Francis, John Toshack, John Connolly,
Kevin Keegan, Terry McDermott, Martin Buchan,
Jim Leishman, Gerry Francis, Joey Jones, Andy Gray, Phil Neal,
John Gregory, Alan Hansen, Kevin Sheedy, Steve Ogrizovic,
Gary Gillespie, Alan Kennedy

THE '70s was Twentyman's busiest decade as a talent spotter. His scouting diary has a comprehensive review of each year's work and is packed with players on every page. Liverpool's loss in the FA Cup to Watford in 1970 prompted Shankly to make radical changes to the Liverpool team and it comes as no surprise that Twentyman's job was at its most demanding in the months after this game.

He travelled everywhere from Cardiff to Cowdenbeath in a long and exhausting search for the players that would make Liverpool great again. Although Everton, Arsenal and Derby were the first three Football League champions during the decade, Liverpool wrestled the title away from Leeds United in 1973 before winning it on another four occasions by the time the '70s became the '80s.

TREVOR FRANCIS

Brian Clough splashed out to buy Francis from Birmingham City in 1979. At Forest, Francis won the European Cup in 1979, but his career was hampered by injuries. High points included winning the Coppa Italia at Sampdoria in 1985 and the Scottish League Cup at Rangers in 1987. Francis won 52 England caps.

Birthplace: *Plymouth*

Position: *Striker*
Clubs: *Birmingham City, Detroit Express (USA), Nottingham Forest, Manchester City, Sampdoria, Atalanta, Rangers, QPR, Sheffield Wednesday*

Scouting diary notes:
02.01.71: 'Very promising player. Worth noting' (EB)
16.10.71: 'Lurks up front. Could become good?' (GT)

BRIAN Clough was always one for trumping rivals. But his decision in February 1979 to burst the British transfer record surprised even the most excitable football fan. Had Sky Sports been around then, it would have surely sent their reporters into a deeper level of hyperventilation than we now ritually witness on transfer deadline day.

Just one month after West Brom boss Ron Atkinson made David Mills Britain's first half-a-million-pound footballer, Clough spent £1m to take Trevor Francis to Nottingham Forest. Given that Geoff Twentyman scouted both of the aforementioned players in the early '70s, it is possible that Liverpool could have either prevented such excessive prices being paid at the end of the decade, or indeed broken the transfer record themselves. On Francis, Twentyman noted: 'Lurks up front. Could become good?'

Whether the chief scout, however, would have recommended such exorbitant fees or, indeed, whether Liverpool's board would have commissioned funds on just two players, is very doubtful. Francis in particular had been touted as a star of the Football League ever since he made his Birmingham City debut at the age of 16.

'He moved effortlessly past defenders, as if he were gliding,' noted Duncan Hamilton in his book *Provided You Don't Kiss Me: 20 Years with Brian Clough*. 'Half-close your eyes and you might think that his studs never touched the turf. If Clough could walk on water, Francis could run on air, with a hint of vapour trail from his boots.' Francis was a player who probably more than any other mentioned in this book was good enough to play for Liverpool without ever signing. Today, though, close to Christmas, he has other matters at hand, rather than wondering what might have been more than 30 years ago. "My wife thinks I'm faking it..." he says, cautiously. "I'm meant to be writing all the cards and because I'm on the phone, the wife thinks I'm trying to avoid it. Which, of course, I am!"

By scoring four goals in one game against Bolton Wanderers soon after making his debut as a teenager, something else that Francis couldn't avoid was attention from other clubs. "Any scout that didn't know about me as a 16-year-old wasn't doing his job properly. I'm not being arrogant or conceited when I say that, but those goals put me on the radar of a lot of clubs. Sometimes I thought people believed I was going to do it every time I set foot on a pitch after that. But I didn't let the pressure get to me."

Despite growing up in Devon, Francis moved to Birmingham at 15 after being spotted playing in the English Schools' Trophy. "We were playing up in the Midlands," he explains. "I played quite well, scored three goals, and luckily there was a scout at the match from Birmingham City. He invited me to come to the club and I didn't have too many options with professional clubs where I came from. Realistically, there was only really Bristol City and Plymouth and they never paid any definite interest in me. I decided that Birmingham was a good option."

So in the summer of 1969, Francis moved north, although he didn't expect to play in Birmingham's first team so quickly. "My first season was mostly in the youth team. Towards the end of that season I had one or two games in the reserves. Then at the start of the second season when I was still 16, I was selected as a substitute for an away game at Cardiff. John Toshack was starting for them. I thought I'd just be there to make up the numbers but at half-time one of our players, Johnny Vincent, picked up an injury and I was on. I had no time to think about it so I just got on with it.

"The following week, I was given my full debut against Oxford United and I was up against the Atkinson bothers, Ron and Graham. They didn't call Ron 'The Tank' for nothing. He gave me a bit of a kicking but I managed to get a goal and I was in the team from then on." Francis then appeared on the teamsheet for a game at St Andrews against Bolton Wanderers. In a 4-0 win, he scored all four goals. "I only played for the first 70 minutes, then I got a whack on my thigh so I had to come off. If I'd stayed on, I felt that I would have scored a couple more."

By the end of his first full season as a professional, Francis had scored 15 goals in as many games. "I have no doubt that playing in the Second Division gave me the chance I needed," he insists. "If we'd have been struggling at the foot of the First Division, like we were a few years later, they probably wouldn't have risked someone as young as me. The second season we reached the FA Cup semi-final and that raised my profile even further and we won promotion as well. So for a 17-year-old to be part of that, especially at a time when there were few youngsters playing at that level, it was something special."

Francis adds that he became such an integral part of the Birmingham team because of his pace and speed of thought. "Above anything I didn't have any fear," he says. Although he is unaware of any direct interest from Liverpool, Francis admits he would have had a difficult decision to make had Birmingham accepted an offer.

"I really don't know what I would have done. I would never have demanded to leave Birmingham because I was young and doing what I'd always wanted to do. I don't see the point, even now, when young kids make a couple of appearances then leave to a bigger club just to stay in the reserves without ever progressing. There was a lot of speculation but I never read into it. The clubs were in control of the players and I was completely at their whim. We were locked into contracts. If Birmingham decided to let me go then I would have gone but only because it was the wish of the club. When I got into my early to mid-20s, there were times when I wanted to move on with my career and asked the club whether it would be possible to see if there was interest elsewhere. When I was 14 and playing for England Schools, I trained quite often with Plymouth Argyle when Billy Bingham was manager. He liked me, but the club never got round to offering me anything, so I ended up at Birmingham. By the time Billy took over at Everton, he was linked with me every other week. As far as I know, he never bid for me, but the board would never have told me anyway. Around the same time, Brian Clough wanted me to join him at Derby County. But I knew that without the club agreeing, it was completely impossible for me to leave."

It was only when Jim Smith was appointed Birmingham manager in 1978 that Francis finally earned a move away from St Andrews. "Jim pulled me to one side pretty much on the day he arrived and said something like: 'Look, I'm new to the football club. I want to do well and I need my best players to be on side with me. You're the best player, but I know you want to move to a big club. If you knuckle down for the next three to four months, I'll give you the chance to go once we get past Christmas.' Jim was true to his word and I respect him deeply for that. He helped me move on and that's why I ended up going to Forest in February '79."

Despite interest from Coventry, a deal with Forest – a club that were reigning league champions and on the verge of European Cup glory – was too tempting. "There were a number of other clubs interested. Whether Liverpool were one of them, I'm not so sure, because Birmingham insisted that I was going for nothing less than £1 million. Liverpool might have baulked at such demands. A lot of people reckon it was Brian Clough who put that price on my head by spending so much, when in reality it was purely down to Birmingham's insistency.

"It was a huge fee and the fact that Birmingham wanted that amount eliminated a lot of clubs' chances of getting me. I think that Coventry could only afford the fee because they had an agreement with Detroit Express, a club in the NASL, that they would share me. I'd already been over to America in the previous summer for a short spell and it wasn't the kind of move I wanted, even though I enjoyed it over there.

"Coventry offered more to me personally, but I was desperate to start winning things and because Forest were league champions, it didn't take very long to decide to move there. Brian Clough didn't really need to do anything to convince me because Forest's results sold the club to me. They were the only club that I felt could seriously challenge Liverpool over the next few years, and because Liverpool didn't make a bid, it made my decision quite easy. Had Bob Paisley come in for me, it may have been different, it might have made things more interesting from a decision-making point of view."

In reality, though, it is unlikely that Liverpool would have ever spent so much money to bring one player to the club. Paisley paid out a record £440,000 to sign Kenny Dalglish in the summer of 1977 and that wasn't broken until three years later when Craig Johnston arrived for £650,000 from Middlesbrough. The following summer, that fee was smashed by the £900,000 spent to lure Mark Lawrenson from Brighton, but it wasn't until July 1987 when Liverpool finally broke the million-pound barrier for Peter Beardsley from Newcastle in an extravagant £1.9 million deal (a fee made possible by Ian Rush's departure to Juventus for £3.2 million). Ironically, Beardsley arrived at Anfield after being recommended as a teenager to Twentyman in 1979 by former player and current Academy director Hughie McAuley, who was then playing with the Geordie at Carlisle.

"Geoff dismissed Beardo because he felt he was too similar to Kenny Dalglish," McAuley says. "I argued the toss, but Geoff wasn't interested."

Francis continues: "I would have seriously considered Liverpool if they'd have come in. My only reservation would have been the depth and quality of their squad. I was at a stage where I was pushing on with England and wanted to play every week. By the time I left Birmingham, Kenny and David Johnson were the forwards, so I would have had a real fight on my hands to get into the team because they formed an effective partnership. They hardly needed me with Kenny Dalglish there."

When Francis agreed to move to Forest, Liverpool were enjoying arguably their greatest-ever campaign in the league, winning the title by eight points and winning 19 of their 21 home matches, conceding only four goals. Birmingham, by comparison, were relegated on 22 points (finishing above rock-bottom Chelsea), having only gained four points away from home all season.

Within a matter of months, Francis travelled from a relegation battle with Birmingham to the European Cup final against Malmo with Forest – a game in which he netted the winner. He then scored regularly in his first full season at the City Ground, but was shifted from a role as central striker to a more unorthodox position on the right wing by Clough, and his form suffered as a result. After missing the second of Forest's two European Cup triumphs in 1980 against Kevin Keegan's Hamburg because of an Achilles injury (rather than travel with the team to the final in Madrid, he was banished by Clough to the south of France for a holiday, so his absence from the starting XI wouldn't affect Forest's preparations), Francis agreed to move to Manchester City, this time for £1.2 million. Again, this deal wasn't without its controversy, with City manager John Bond threatening to resign if chairman Peter Swailes didn't broker a deal even though the club claimed they couldn't afford the fee.

"I rejected Man United for City," Francis says. "Ron Atkinson was the manager at United and the deal wasn't as straightforward as it should have been because Ron was putting obstacles in the way. When you're dealing with Brian Clough, messing around isn't an option, so I ended up at Maine Road." Francis was later part of the City team that beat Liverpool 3-1 at Anfield on Boxing Day 1981; a result that meant the Reds plummeted to 12th in the table. It was a landmark game for Liverpool because afterwards Phil Thompson was stripped of the captaincy and replaced by Graeme Souness. 'I felt Phil had been going through a rough patch playing-wise and I thought the extra responsibility of leading the team was having an effect,' Paisley later said.

It was also a match where City dignitaries sneered at Liverpool's title hopes in the bootroom. "All these know-it-alls came in after the game, saying: 'Ah, you'll never win the league now – not in a million years,'" Ronnie Moran told me. "I didn't respond, other than saying: 'Just wait and see – there's still half a season to go yet. We'll see who's top at the end of May.' So I returned to the dressing room and told the players what the City bods were saying. Such arrogance annoyed them and I thought it would spur us on."

Moran's opinion was proven correct and by the season's end Liverpool were four points above Ipswich at the top of the league and nine ahead of Manchester United in third, having won 20 of their remaining 25 matches. "I have to admit that I didn't think Liverpool would make up the points after we beat them at Christmas," Francis says. "But that proves what a great side they were – such a deficit would never be recovered now."

After leaving City, Francis spent five years in Italy with Sampdoria and Atalanta before ending his career with spells at Rangers, QPR and Sheffield Wednesday. "If I'd gone to Liverpool in the early '70s, I probably would have ended up with a lot more medals than I did. Maybe Forest wouldn't have won the European Cup. Nobody knows. Maybe it would have all been very different for a certain Brian Clough as well."

JOHN TOSHACK

Shankly bought Toshack from Cardiff City and he formed a formidable partnership with Kevin Keegan at Liverpool, often providing the knock-downs for his partner to score. Niggling injuries meant he was in and out of the team, but he still played a vital role in the club's triumphs during the '70s. He became player-manager of Swansea in 1978.

Signed: from Cardiff City for £110,000 in November 1970
Age when signed: 21
Total LFC appearances/goals: 247/96
Seasons spent at Liverpool: 7
Birthplace: Cardiff, Wales
Other clubs: Swansea City

Scouting diary notes:
31/10/1970: 'Best display to date. 3 goals, good enough Div 1' (AB)
6/11/1970: 'Very good in the air. Does a job we want' (GT)

JOHN Toshack was 16 when he made his debut for Cardiff City. By the time he was 21, he'd scored more than a century of goals for the club as well as appearing in European competition. His achievements at Ninian Park made scouts take notice and Geoff Twentyman persuaded Bill Shankly to travel to south Wales to have a look at him. Earlier, Shankly had tried to sign Frank Worthington from Huddersfield Town, but the player failed a medical after both clubs had agreed a fee.

"I didn't know a great deal about what happened to Frank," current Welsh manager Toshack says as he prepares to take his side to Russia in September '08. "I know the official line was that he'd failed the medical because of high blood pressure. But there was a suggestion that he'd been to Magaluf shortly before the deal was due to be completed. If he'd signed for Liverpool, they probably wouldn't have come looking at me."

According to Twentyman's scouting book, Liverpool watched Toshack only twice. Those games were in the October and November of 1970. Even if the club made a quick decision to sign him, his achievements in a Cardiff shirt over the previous four seasons had surely not escaped Twentyman's attention. Toshack had all the attributes to become a classic Liverpool signing, especially after playing in the Cup Winners' Cup at such a young age. By the time he was 18, his performances attracted a bid from Bobby Robson's Fulham, but Toshack was reluctant to leave the Welsh valleys and decided to stay at home.

"The offer was for £80,000," he says. "I made my debut when I was a schoolboy. I had a lot of hardened Second Division professionals around me and that helped a lot. Then the bid came in from Fulham. Bobby had Allan Clarke up front and he wanted me to be his partner. But I didn't want to leave Cardiff. I was desperate to stay, in fact. Luckily for me, Cardiff won the Welsh Cup every year and back then it meant automatic entry to the Cup Winners' Cup, so I was getting European experience year after year, 18, 19, 20.

"When Fulham came in, we were due to play Torpedo Moscow in the quarter-finals and I didn't feel I was ready to move to London. I was so excited about being a regular and being a local lad at Cardiff, so I turned it down even after the club accepted the bid. I think some of the board were disappointed because they thought they were in for a windfall. £80,000 was a lot of money. Some people thought I was crazy but I liked being at home. It was close-knit in the village where I lived and I thought it was too much of a big step at such a young age. In the end, we beat the Russians and we went to the semi-final against Hamburg, drawing 1-1 in Germany and losing at home. It was a terrific experience for me just playing in Europe.

"These days, 18-year-olds go for ridiculous money to big clubs and sit on the bench for three years. The standard of reserve-team football isn't strong enough, so it's stemming the flow of talent. It's definitely not the ideal thing to do. I know the world has changed for different reasons, but I always tell young players I coach to get experience before you sign for a big club. It's beneficial for both parties. Besides, Fulham were in the First Division back then, but they were struggling. Soon after they bid for me, Bobby left the club after a disagreement with the board. With hindsight, it was probably one of the wisest decisions in my life."

Eighteen months later, though, Toshack was finally ready to move on. "I was told that a Liverpool scout was having a look at me. The word to me was that Shanks was coming too and the press eventually got hold of it because they saw him at the ground. Liverpool had an injury crisis with Bobby Graham and Alun Evans both spending time on the sidelines. Tony Hateley had just left and Liverpool tried quite a few things up front with none of the combinations really working. The Saint was also coming towards the end of his career.

"I think Liverpool, Geoff and Shanks all realised that my European experience would stand me in good stead when I moved to Anfield. I had more European experience than some of the senior pros lurking around the First Division so maybe that's why Liverpool ended up paying over £100,000 for me. I was a big number 10. I was young. I could play as a target man. I had experience and I had years on my side. I think Geoff saw a game at Wrexham for Wales against Scotland where I scored. The main thing, though, was that I had scored more than 100-odd goals for Cardiff before the age of 21. At that particular time, too, I was injury free – that's why Liverpool signed me."

Initially, Toshack found the weight of expectation too heavy on his young shoulders as Liverpool's lack of success on the pitch over the previous five years got to him. Shankly's first great team had broken up and their replacements, including Toshack, were expected to be successful immediately. "When I went up to Liverpool, the first thing Shanks said to me was: 'You're coming out of Sunday school and going into church.' He was right because a lot of young players came in at the same time to replace the great team of the early to mid-'60s. Shanks decided that was it and me, Emlyn, Kevin, Ray Clemence, Alec Lindsay and Larry Lloyd all came in as new signings. It was tough early on, I must admit, and I found the step up very difficult. The massive difference was that I was playing in front of 54,000 people every week instead of 25,000. The expectation of the Kop week in week out made the step up difficult, but that's what happens when you play for a big club."

Toshack's Liverpool debut came on 14 November 1970 against Coventry City. A week later he scored his first goal in a memorable derby comeback against Everton. But it wasn't until Kevin Keegan arrived from

Scunthorpe in the summer of 1971 that the player and the team really started to look the part on the pitch. Toshack says it was a natural progression. "Nobody told us what to do at Liverpool and that was the key. Nobody told us how to play. We just signed players and it was part of a jigsaw. The management knew how we'd perform and how well we'd do. There wasn't a single time when someone came up to us, Bill or anyone, and told either me or Kevin to do things a certain way. Bill, the coaching staff and the scouting departments all knew which players would fit Liverpool's way and that's why we were successful. The management had enough confidence in his signings just to let them play the way things came naturally. We were slung in together and everyone got on with it.

"I remember when Steve McManaman was at Real Madrid a few years ago and he said that the manager Vicente del Bosque just let the players decide what to do in training. They were the best players in the world and they were professionals so they knew exactly what to do for their own benefit and for the benefit of the team. We were exactly the same at the beginning of the 1970s. That stemmed right throughout the club. Shanks had terrific confidence in Geoff's work and Geoff knew what football was all about and how to spot and sign a player. These days, you get clubs and scouts shouting from the rooftops – they even go into player lounges – I have seen that. Geoff only came into the players' lounge at home matches. It was like he had carpet slippers on because he felt so at home at Anfield that you didn't even realise he was there."

Despite not being a regular at Anfield on match days (he was usually watching potential targets elsewhere), Toshack recalls Twentyman in the bootroom. "He was always round Melwood too. 'Went to Gillingham yesterday [with a definite sound of GILL rather than JILLingham]. Lovely player…goes both ways,' he always used to say. I remember one time when Geoff had a bad hip, so he had an operation to get it mended. After a while, it got better and he started walking around Melwood. A few months passed and he started jogging with Tom Saunders, Reuben and Bob as well as Ronnie. He was fine by then.

After time, Reuben developed a problem with his hip and he went in for the same op. He came out and I asked him how it was. 'Aw, it's f***ing creasing me. Terrible, terrible pain I'm in.' He was struggling for months and it wasn't getting any better at all. One morning, Bob came in and asked Reuben about his hip again. It was no good, and Bob went: 'No wonder, son…they've put Geoff's old one in there!' Geoff loved that and he was running round everywhere, while Reuben struggled. (Laughing) That was typical Bob. He was a funny man and all the fellas there were the same. They were like that all the time."

Toshack says that although football is very different in the 21st century to the game he knew when he started playing, he believes that the fundamentals to success are just the same. "People talk a lot about unsung heroes. It's a pity that the Geoff Twentymans of the world just aren't about now. His way, I am told, is not the way to do it. It's all 'modern this, modern that', but I tell you what, I was very lucky to have eight years up there with all of them. Their methods have stood the test of time.

"It's 30 years since I left Liverpool and I have been a manager in six different countries, managed Real Madrid, and I still work exactly the same way which I was taught by Shanks, Bob, Reuben, Joe, Geoff and everyone else up there. Shanks used to say that what's important now should still be important 50 years from now, and I still believe in that. If you're talking about honesty, trust and hard work, I think that gets you a long way in life and those good habits were instilled into all of us at Liverpool. Treat people the way you would want to be treated. They were the best days of my life."

JOHN CONNOLLY

Connolly played in the St Johnstone team that reached the Scottish League Cup final in 1969. Harry Catterick took him to Everton in 1972, and it was while he was at Goodison that Connolly earned his one and only full Scotland cap.

Birthplace: *Barrhead, Scotland*
Position: *Outside left*
Clubs: *St Johnstone, Everton, Birmingham City, Newcastle United, Hibernian, Gateshead, Blyth Spartans*

Scouting diary notes:
3/10/70: 'Very impressive big improvement on last season' (WF)
7/9/71: 'Back to his best form' (WMc)
10/1/72: 'Disappointing'

JOHN Connolly was the first in a line of strikers to have been scouted by Liverpool only to sign for Everton. Barely two months before moving to Goodison Park from St Johnstone, Geoff Twentyman travelled north to watch him, only to leave the word "disappointing" in his notebook. Like many Twentyman signings, Connolly was Scottish, playing at an unfashionable club, and had gathered experience by performing in European competition. St Johnstone were once regulars in the UEFA Cup and even knocked out Hamburg, who of course, later signed Kevin Keegan.

Given his lack of success after signing for Everton, most Liverpudlians would argue that the club was wise not to sign him. Connolly scored only 16 times in 108 league appearances as a Blue, but saw his goalscoring opportunities decrease by playing most games as a left winger. Yet if you look at Connolly's record in Scotland, it would have suggested he would have been a hit at Anfield. Forty-one goals in 96 games is almost a strike rate of one in two and is impressive for a forward who had just entered his early 20s. Especially at a club that rarely challenged for domestic titles.

"One in two isn't bad for any striker, considering I was a young boy too," Connolly insists. "St Johnstone were only a provincial side, but we were very good. We qualified for the old Fairs Cup, which is now the UEFA Cup. We went across to Hamburg, who were one of the best sides in the Bundesliga. We lost 2-1 over there, but won 3-0 at home. That shows you the calibre of our side. We were the type of team that if we lost three goals, we were still capable of scoring three or four. We played a lot of exciting football under Willie Ormond (who later managed Scotland), and in 1969 we reached the final of the Scottish League Cup, losing 1-0 to the Celtic team that won the European Cup a few years earlier. A couple of the players from that St Johnstone team went on to other clubs, like Jim Pearson who came down with me to Everton. The main goalscorer was a guy called Henry Hall, but he stayed up in Scotland for one reason or another despite lots of interest from clubs down south."

Connolly didn't have an inkling that Liverpool were scouting him, but explains that he was invited by Tottenham Hotspur to watch them play Nottingham Forest as a guest ahead of a potential move. Undoubtedly, he says, his experiences playing in Europe raised his profile. "Everything just passed me by. I was only 19-20 years old when I played in Europe. I learnt a lot just from the Hamburg game. Uwe Seeler was starting for them and Willie Shultz was the German centre-half and played in the 1970 World Cup as well as the final in '66. I was St Johnstone's centre-forward, so it was a tough game, but I fared ok when you consider the opposition we were up against. We knocked out Vasas Budapest as well on that run and I scored our only penalty in the home leg. Unfortunately we got knocked out by Sarajevo in the next round, but to play against this calibre of opposition made me a better player."

Eventually, Harry Cooke, Everton's chief scout and equivalent of Geoff Twentyman, told Harry Catterick to sign Connolly. "I met John Toshack the night I agreed terms with Everton. He was 6ft 4 and I was a wee boy. We were both in the Lord Nelson Hotel, so we had a chat. It was a funny one. When I signed for Everton, there was a ruling that you could only play in games that didn't affect promotion or relegation, so in that first season, I only played one game against Leicester City.

"Everton played a 4-3-3 with Jimmy Husband on the right, big Joe [Royle] in the middle and Johnny Morrissey on the left. I was a centre-forward and Joe was the main man, so the season afterwards I was converted to a winger. Maybe if Liverpool signed me, I would have stayed as a forward and scored more goals. I was at Everton for five years and I don't think we ever beat Liverpool in my time. Mr Fairclough used to come on in every game and score the winner. They were great occasions, though."

Connolly suffered two double breaks in one year at Goodison Park as Everton struggled in the league. Liverpool, meanwhile, dominated the domestic game and became a major player in European competition. But Connolly has no regrets. "You can't look back can you?" he says. "These things happen. I was lucky to play for Everton and Newcastle who were two massive clubs – I'm not going to turn around to you and say I wish I'd have played for Liverpool because I had an unforgettable time at Everton and I loved my time in Merseyside. I think the Liverpool folk have a similar mentality to the Scots. It seems to be more of a northern thing because it's not the same relationship with the southerners and I loved that."

The only regret that Connolly did have was that he didn't add to the single cap he gained with Scotland after moving south of the border. He says that this is down to the fact that he chose to sign for an English club over a Scottish one. "When I moved, it all happened very quickly. Willie Ormond said the clubs had agreed a fee with Everton, but Rangers came in with a bid too. Rangers offered something like £40,000 and Everton offered nearly double that. I didn't have a choice to make because St Johnstone were never going to accept a bid of £40,000 when they could get more from an English club. It seems silly talking about that money when you see what is spent today.

"I always wanted to try England. But had Rangers matched Everton's bid, who knows what would have happened. I think history has told us that if you play for Rangers or Celtic, you have a far better chance of playing for Scotland than you have down in England. There was a wee thing going on about English-based players getting knocked back a bit in terms of playing for the national side. Maybe it was the media asking: 'What is wrong with our home-based players?' A lot of players suffered from this – maybe Alan Hansen did too. I only made one cap against Switzerland and was on the bench against Brazil in '73. When you think about Alan playing only 26 games for Scotland, it's ridiculous. I'm not sure everyone would feel that way about me, though."

KEVIN KEEGAN

A right-midfielder at Scunthorpe, Keegan was pushed forward by Shankly to partner John Toshack, and the experiment brought rich rewards. In 1973 he helped Liverpool win their first league title in seven years, as well as the UEFA Cup, and a year later he scored two in the FA Cup final against Newcastle United to secure victory. Keegan picked up three league titles, two UEFA Cup winners' medals, one European Cup and one FA Cup before he moved to Hamburg.

Signed: from Scunthorpe United for £33,000 in May 1971
Age when signed: 20
Total LFC appearances/goals: 323/100
Seasons spent at Liverpool: 6
Birthplace: Armthorpe
Other clubs: Scunthorpe United, Hamburg SV, Southampton, Newcastle United

Scouting diary notes:
'No 8. Mid: A good player shows a lot of promise' (AB)
'This player is fancied by A. Beattie' (GT)

WITH MORE listed buildings than any other city outside London, contrary to national perception, Liverpool isn't short of historical structures that are easy on the eye.

The Queensway Tunnel, however, isn't one of them. Built in 1934, the underwater burrow connects the rear end of Scotland Road with the Wirral peninsula. Although it is an impressive feat of engineering, it could never be described as one of the city's major tourist attractions. A black hole, it is fuelled with smog and belches out that kind of uneasy heat reserved for unearthly places, particularly in the summer months.

But there was a time when the tunnel was a major end-of-year day trip for thousands of school children. Back then, it was something that no other city in the north of England could boast. Something that Kevin Keegan went to see with his school from his home town of Doncaster. Keegan remembers the day well, especially as it was the only time that he had been to the city, prior to signing for Liverpool in 1970.

"Bearing in mind it was an exciting and exotic place with the music revolution just starting, there might have been some more dramatic places to go and see in Liverpool." Keegan says only weeks before he left Newcastle as their manager for a second time. "I believe a lot of schools did a similar thing. We didn't have tunnels like that in South Yorkshire. It was memorable solely for the reason that I was bored. It was an impressive tunnel, yes, but a long way to travel from Doncaster just to see a tunnel."

The next time Keegan set foot on this side of the Mersey was for a second FA Cup replay against Tranmere Rovers while playing for Scunthorpe. The sides were inseparable in the first two games and after drawing at Prenton Park they had to toss for the location of a neutral venue in the replay. Had Scunny won the toss the game would have been played at Hillsbrough. Luckily the coin fell on the side of the Tranmere captain and Goodison Park was chosen instead. So Geoff Twentyman took Bill Shankly along to watch.

"Everton played a major part in me coming to Liverpool." Keegan jokes. "If the game was played elsewhere, then maybe Shanks wouldn't have been so quick to sign me. That was the match that probably swung it. That's when Bill came to see me for his own eyes, so I have been led to believe. He didn't like leaving home and he let Geoff do all the travelling to watch people. But he saw it as very convenient to go to Goodison, so he agreed to go along with Geoff. Luckily, I had a blinder."

Keegan, who'd been playing in Scunthorpe's first team for three years, says that he only became aware of Liverpool's interest after they lodged a bid for him. It came just in time because only a few months earlier, Arsenal had asked him to go on trial at Highbury. "It would have been great for a young lad like me to train with Arsenal, but the FA wouldn't let me go because I was already contracted to Scunthorpe. Scunthorpe were willing to let me go, but it was at the time when the FA had more power than the clubs and the players, so they didn't let it happen. If Arsenal offered me a deal, I would have gone there.

"Despite the interest from Arsenal, I wasn't pulling any trees up at Scunthorpe, but I was doing ok. Anybody who was under the age of 20 and playing in the lower leagues had a bit of talent because youth policies weren't really implemented. In those days there were probably only five players in the whole of the Fourth Division that were still in their teens. Most of the players that were playing at that level were old experienced pros that had dropped down the divisions and had experienced top-level football. Scunthorpe had Bill Punton and people like that. So just holding a place in the Fourth Division felt like an achievement. I never thought I would attract the interest of a club like Liverpool."

Keegan felt nervous as he waited to be called into the temporary manager's office at Anfield ahead of finalising the deal. He was told that Liverpool had made an approach in the morning and he travelled across the Pennines that very afternoon. "Liverpool paid £33,000 for me. The Main Stand was being refurbished so all of the management team were based in temporary offices down at Anfield. They later became the development centre near the Shankly Gates.

"I remember sitting down on a dustbin outside and waiting for the call to go in. Shanks called me and the first thing he asked me was if I ever thought of becoming a boxer because I was quite stocky. Boxing was Shanks' first love. He kept on grabbing my shoulders and sizing me up. At one stage he even started sparring with me. God knows what would have happened if I'd properly hit him.

"The strange thing about the deal was that my manager at Scunthorpe, Ron Ashman, came with me to Anfield and even watched me complete the medical. That would definitely not happen now. He was keen to get it all done so he'd have some money to spend. As soon as everything was signed Ron looked made up and wished me well."

During the first meeting between Shankly and Keegan, there were no talks between manager and player about how he would fit into the Liverpool team. Such was Keegan's eagerness to sign, he didn't even bother speaking to Ray Clemence, a former teammate at Scunthorpe. "I wasn't in any position to negotiate. I grew up in Doncaster and played for Scunthorpe. This was Liverpool. I just signed."

Keegan's eventual role within the team highlights how crucial the scouting process was to the whole transfer because before he signed for Liverpool Keegan predominantly featured as a right-winger for Scunthorpe. In Twentyman's scouting book, Andy Beattie notes this and says that he might be more suited to a striking role. 'No 8...might be better as a forward,' it says. Less than six months later, Keegan was pulling on the number seven shirt at Anfield against Nottingham Forest and played alongside John Toshack in a new-look Liverpool attack. By the end of the match, the Reds had won 3-1 with Keegan grabbing a debut goal after only 12 minutes. History would prove that Beattie, one of Twentyman's most trusted scouts, was correct in his judgement and Keegan would never play on the wing again.

"I played everywhere when I was at Scunthorpe and filled in wherever the manager wanted me to play. I was on the right-wing until the manager (Ron Ashman) realised I could play a bit and wanted me to get a little bit more on the ball, so he put me inside depending on whoever we were up against. Andy Beattie spotted me playing in midfield, and I'd never in a million years considered myself a striker. That really shows you how good these scouts were. People like Andy and Geoff could see something in a player like me that nobody else could see.

"Maybe I would have made it somewhere later on if I'd stayed at Scunthorpe, but I doubt anyone would have seen enough in me to pull me into a different position. It was only really afterwards that I realised how Liverpool spotted me. I used to speak to Geoff all the time at Melwood. He was a funny guy. One of his favourite ones was to say that if a player was injured he described him as having 'a cold in his knee.'"

Keegan is arguably Twentyman's greatest-ever signing. A lot of the credit must go to Andy Beattie for spotting his potential as a striker. While Scunthorpe manager Ron Ashman was so reluctant to place Keegan in the firing line in the Fourth Division, Beattie's strong mindedness encouraged Shankly to take a gamble and make him Liverpool Football Club's first choice frontman.

Later in this book, Keegan tells me about the difficulties in scouting today, something that ironically led to his resignation only a matter of weeks after this interview. "Back then, most of it was done with the aid of a car and a map – it was a lot harder," he said. "Now, it's hard for different reasons. A lot of clubs are all trying to sign the same player and you have to speak to the technical director to see what's what and who's who in the transfer market.

"I prefer the old way when you had to place your trust in someone to travel the distance and unearth a gem. Now people rely on video cassettes and DVD players to look at players. Ninety-nine per cent of the players are rubbish and the other one will usually have an agent only in it for himself. Transfer deals were a lot simpler when I was a youngster.

"I wish for my sake things could go back to the way they were..."

TERRY MCDERMOTT

After stints at Bury and Newcastle, Bob Paisley bought 22-year-old McDermott in 1974, and despite a slow start over the first two years, he then flourished alongside Graeme Souness in the Liverpool midfield. His trophy haul included the UEFA Cup, four league titles, three European Cups and two League Cups. McDermott returned to Newcastle in 1982.

Signed: *from Newcastle United for £175,000 in November 1974*
Age when signed: *22*
Total LFC appearances/goals: *329/81*
Seasons spent at Liverpool: *8*
Birthplace: *Kirkby*
Other clubs: *Bury, Newcastle (two spells)*

Scouting diary notes:
24/10/1970: 'A good prospect. Worth watching' (VG)
19/9/1972: 'An improved player. Will watch again' (GT)
4/11/1972: 'Played well. Will definitely follow up' (GT)
23/12/72: 'Played well might have scored two goals' (GT)
12/11/72: 'Bad conditions. Showed a lot of skill' (KK)

RATTLING south along the A1 in his recently purchased sky blue Ford Capri, Terry McDermott couldn't believe what was unfolding. Eight years earlier he'd joined Bury after Liverpool failed to spot him playing for a Kirkby boys' team that was stuffed with raw talent.

Fifteen-year-olds were plucked by talent scouts from Everton, Bolton Wanderers, Wolves and Liverpool. Only two players in that Kirkby squad remained unsigned. McDermott was one of them. For a fluffy-haired teenager, and a boyhood Red who used to watch games from the boys' pen before climbing over the fence to be in the Kop, the rejection hurt. But that pain was at an end. Today he was signing for Liverpool.

"I went to Bury because no one else wanted me," McDermott reflects when he speaks from Newcastle United's Darsley Park training base (he soon left the Magpies at the same time as Kevin Keegan). "The Kirkby Boys team was full of great lads. John McLaughlin, who later played for Liverpool, had already been signed up. There were only two players left from that team who didn't have a professional club. I was one of them. Dennis Mortimer was the other. It's ironic because the last two players in that team to be tied up to a club ended up having arguably the most successful careers. Unfortunately for John, he suffered with injuries, and for one reason or another didn't really have a massive impact – although at first he was rightly regarded as a potential star of the future. I ended up winning three European Cups with Liverpool and Dennis went on and did the same with Aston Villa, albeit only once!"

McDermott concedes that he probably wasn't good enough to sign for Liverpool at the age of 15. Given that Geoff Twentyman mainly scouted players between the ages of 18 and 23 (McDermott was 22 when he eventually signed for Liverpool), he agrees with Twentyman's idea that the maturity of a footballer can only be judged after the player enters adulthood.

"Maybe it's a blessing in disguise that I didn't go to Liverpool or one of the bigger clubs straight away," McDermott wonders. "Geoff always said to me that he would judge players when they have matured a bit. I agree with that and, in a way, my example and Dennis prove that there are late developers. Maybe if I'd gone to Liverpool earlier, I would have fallen by the wayside because I wouldn't have played as many games and I wouldn't have developed in the right way.

"I see it even now at Newcastle when people make judgements on kids at 15 or 16. But I defy anyone who says at 16 a player is or isn't going to make it, unless they are an extra-special player like a Gascoigne. A lot of them take more time to develop until they are 18 or 19. It's unfair to judge a player when they are so young. I was at Bury from the age of 16 to 21. So even when I signed for Liverpool when I was 22 or 23, it shows you it takes time. By the time I arrived at Melwood, I'd learnt my trade and that helped."

Back when he was 15, though, McDermott felt differently. Desperate to sign for anyone after remaining unattached to a club for so long and after leaving school with no qualifications, he was delighted when Bury's chief scout came calling – literally, at his front door. "I wasn't big on education, so I left school with nothing. Before I went to Bury as an apprentice, I had about four or five jobs in the space of six weeks. I was crap at them all. I stacked wood, worked in a paint factory and anything else I could get my hands on. I remember working in Kirkby as a cabinet-maker, but I was one of the first people to be sacked from there because I kept on walking out the gates and talking to my mates. One time I did it, I walked back in and they told me to leave. I needed some direction. Then Bury came in.

"I remember going to watch a game at Anfield and when I got home later that night, I was told by my mam that a guy called Colin McDonald had knocked on our front door and was looking to speak with me. He was the chief scout at Bury and he'd seen me play and wanted me to sign that night. In fact, he wanted Dennis [Mortimer] to sign as well, so he went to his house and spoke to his parents. He left forms at both of our houses, hoping we'd both agree to go. Nobody else wanted me, so I grabbed a pen straight away. At that age, I just wanted to play football, so I didn't even think about it. I never felt disappointed that Liverpool or even Everton didn't come in for me, because I just wanted to play for someone and be a part of something. Dennis ended up signing for Coventry instead."

McDermott was at Gigg Lane for three years before making his Bury debut. Soon, he was attracting the attention of scouts from clubs across the country, including Twentyman and Liverpool. In his scouting book, it is clear that Twentyman liked McDermott. He started watching him in his very first professional season (1970/71) and continued to monitor his progress over the next three years, taking in five games. Twentyman, in fact, liked McDermott so much that he told Bill Shankly to sign him, but Shanks was content with his midfield and felt he would be better spending his money elsewhere. Even if he did want to sign him, it would have been too late as Newcastle made the earliest move for a then 21-year-old McDermott in early 1973.

"I'd heard that Liverpool were interested, but it was only after I left Bury that it became clear that they wanted to sign me. I took it all with a pinch of salt because it's what dreams are made of. I never really believed that Liverpool wanted me at first, but having spoken to people at the club like Geoff, he told me that he watched me quite a lot and really liked me all along. At the time, Liverpool were strong in midfield and that wasn't an area of the team that needed strengthening."

It took just longer than a year acclimatising to top-flight football as well as a dynamic display for Newcastle during a 0-0 draw at St James's Park in February 1974 against Liverpool, for Shankly to admit that he made an error by not signing McDermott. 'Aye, he was a cracking player. We made a mistake on that one,' Shankly later admitted in an interview with his autobiographer, John Roberts. Unfortunately for McDermott, Shanks retired soon after. Ironically, his last competitive game in charge was against Newcastle at Wembley in the 1974 FA Cup final. Liverpool won easily 3-0.

Five months later, though, with Bob Paisley now in charge, McDermott received a telephone call that he thought was a wind-up. "I was the victim of an illegal approach!" McDermott jokes. "This kind of thing happened all the time. I'd been playing for Newcastle down in London, October time. I was lying on my bed in the hotel and the phone went. It was Phil Thompson. He went [in Phil Thompson's unmistakable accent]: 'Errr, Terry? It's Phil Thompson 'ere.' I was like: 'Yeah, yeah, y'alright?' Then he goes: 'Terry, do you fancy playing for Liverpool? They really want you!' I couldn't believe it. It took a few days to sort out, I think they were haggling over the fee. But I think Newcastle didn't know that I already knew about it.

"If I'm honest, I didn't want to leave Newcastle because I was really happy there. It was the same when I was at Bury. I loved living in Newcastle and I still do. I would never have left for any other club but

Liverpool. I could not turn down my hometown team. I remember Alan Kennedy, who was only a kid at Newcastle, came to me and said that Joe Harvey, the manager, wanted to speak to me. So I went to the ground at one or two in the afternoon and Joe said that the club had agreed a fee with Liverpool for me. Would I want to go? I said yes and Joe gave me an envelope and told me to drive to Liverpool."

Within minutes, McDermott says he was spinning out of St James's Park as he began the long journey south. "I must have done it in record time," he adds. Halfway down the motorway, McDermott, whose mind was in a whirl after realising he was about to fulfil a childhood dream, became curious of the brown envelope sitting on the passenger seat next to him.

"I slowly opened it with one hand and kept the other on the wheel. I was driving down the A1 and the traffic was heavy. When I finally managed to open it, I read that the transfer fee was £166,000. Twenty months previously I'd left Bury for £22,000, so in the space of 18 months, my price had risen by almost eight times. It was a hell of a lot of money and I nearly veered off the road. I wouldn't have minded a bigger cut of that money myself too because I'd done my bit for Newcastle. When I got back into Liverpool, I went straight to Kirkby to my mam and dad's house and they came with me to Anfield where I had a 10-minute talk with Bob Paisley, John Smith and Peter Robinson. Then the contract was signed, no messing around and it was all done and dusted."

Despite the euphoria that goes with signing for team you supported as a boy, McDermott would once again have to prove himself to Liverpool, spending two years in the reserves before finally becoming a regular in Paisley's midfield. It was during this time that McDermott starting questioning whether he'd made the right decision to return home, but thanks to the help of people like Geoff Twentyman, he decided to stay.

"It was getting me down big time," McDermott reflects. "Luckily, I had the likes of Roy Evans, who was the reserve-team manager, and especially Geoff to get me through it. Geoff was there at Melwood most afternoons and he was a funny guy. He'd offer little words of encouragement that would keep my morale going. I can still hear him say: 'Keep it going Terry; you know what you're good at. Don't change.' Roy Evans was the same. Geoff was a fantastic guy and a big influence on a lot of players.

"Geoff understood football. When you talked to him, he always understood how the players felt, mainly because he'd played at the top level as well. It's not hard to understand why Liverpool were so successful. Yes, there were a lot of great players around the club, but they were only there because of the judgement and characters of the coaching staff. Reuben Bennett, Tom Saunders, Bob Paisley and Roy Evans were all fantastic characters, and there was continuity and they understood what it took to be successful."

MARTIN BUCHAN

Buchan signed for Manchester United from Aberdeen in February 1972, and swiftly became captain. United suffered relegation in 1973/74 but bounced back immediately, and Buchan helped them to FA Cup victory against Liverpool in 1977. He won 34 caps for Scotland and is the only player to have captained both Scottish and English FA Cup-winning sides.

Birthplace: Aberdeen
Position: *Central defender*
Clubs: *Aberdeen, Manchester United, Oldham Athletic*

Scouting diary notes:
10/1/72: 'Looks very good in back four' (GT)

ENMITY between Liverpool and Manchester United was not always as vitriolic as it appears now. The cities have always shared antagonism dating back to the building of the Manchester Ship Canal, which swiped trade from Liverpool and made Manchester an emulous power through the cotton industry. But until the late '60s the Reds and their devilish equivalent on the football pitch from 30 miles away embraced a comparatively respectful rivalry. Matt Busby was a former Liverpool player and had a close friendship with Bill Shankly – both of them came from Lanarkshire mining stock – and Shanks famously enjoyed regular telephone conversations with United's tough-tackling midfielder Paddy Crerand. Like some other Manchester United players, Crerand even went to Anfield to watch Liverpool when United didn't have a game on a Saturday afternoon, and stood on the Kop.

Despite the unlikely love-in, it should come as some surprise that another former United player, in fact United captain, has a 'soft spot' for Liverpool. And it's not Paul Ince. The player in question is Martin Buchan, a defender whom Geoff Twentyman recommended to Bill Shankly before he instead chose to move to Old Trafford. Later in 1977, Buchan inspired United to an FA Cup final victory, in turn denying Liverpool an unprecedented treble.

"It's true, I always saw Liverpool as a special club and I still enjoy going to Anfield on European nights just as a football fan to this day," Buchan reveals. "Bill Shankly was one of the best human beings you could meet. After retiring, he used to come through to Old Trafford to see John Toshack whenever he brought his Swansea team to play us. Tommy Docherty (the United manager) and Shanks both played for Preston, so they'd be together after the game with their heads together in the corner of the players' lounge. Shanks always seemed to like talking about history and his enthusiasm for football was infectious. I had a great admiration for him ever since he described fellow Aberdonian Ron Yeats as a 'colossus'. I enjoy listening to people who have leadership skills and Shanks was the best at that."

If Buchan holds Liverpool and Shankly with such reverence, why then didn't he join the club when the Reds made an approach to sign him at the turn of 1972? "Leeds United also came in for me," he explains. "Manchester United were the first team to make a concrete offer, though. They wanted me to replace David Sadler who was suffering with knee problems. In those days you needed to open the knee up to have a go at it. There were no MRI scans or anything like that. It was their idea that I would come in as his medium to long-term replacement.

"Liverpool and Leeds had great players already in my position. I was never going to displace Norman Hunter, Gordon McQueen, Tommy Smith or Larry Lloyd, and because I was nearing my 23rd birthday, I didn't want to risk not getting into the first team. I was club captain at Aberdeen and I'd played European and international football, so I wanted a regular place in the starting XI wherever I went. Many people have said over the years that I should have chosen to go to Liverpool because I'd have won lots of medals. I always say to them that there's a chance that those medals could have been Central League medals because that was the competition and that was the risk."

Buchan was spotted by Twentyman while playing for Scotland under-23s in a match at the Baseball Ground against England, "I am sure I was up against Kevin Keegan that night," he questions. Reuben Bennett, the Liverpool coach, who was also Aberdeen born, knew Buchan's father and the player suspects that is how Twentyman first became aware of him. "I did ok in the match at Derby and I was told afterwards that a couple of English clubs were watching me. It would have been easier for them to watch me there. Nowadays you get dozens and dozens of scouts at under-21 games but back then hardly anyone watched the under-23s. The main thing I can take from the game is that there was mud up to my ankles."

Although infrequently used as a midfielder, Buchan evolved into a natural leader and canny interpreter of probing through-balls during his time at Pittodrie. "There was a tradition to play four at the back. One of the middle two would be a big stopper and the other one was more of a reader of the game. I was the latter. I considered myself to be a central defender rather than a centre-half because I was only 5ft 11in. I read the game well and for that reason I think I appeared quicker than I actually was. I wasn't a slouch, though. I was a good talker and I could organise a back four."

Like near enough every other Twentyman target, Buchan was fed a rich diet of domestic, European and international football in his late teens, playing against Juventus and Fabio Capello in the Cup Winners' Cup as well as making his full international debut lining up alongside Kenny Dalglish against Belgium in 1971. "I met Capello not long after he became England manager," Buchan says. "I don't think his recollection of me lived long in his memory..."

Like Alan Hansen later, Buchan, despite being a captain of two different clubs and having undoubted class, never became an undisputed fixture in the Scotland side. "I always felt that because I played for Aberdeen and Manchester United and never played for either of the Old Firm, I was keeping a Rangers or Celtic player out of the team, especially when we played in Glasgow, so I didn't enjoy playing there as much. They didn't look too kindly on the Anglos, or the players that had gone down south to further their careers. Perhaps the fans didn't get behind certain players in the team as they should have done."

Buchan's development and importance to Aberdeen, though, was marked quickly by boss Eddie Turnbull, who awarded him with the captaincy on his 21st birthday. "I had the most wonderful education by Eddie. He was the best coach I ever worked with. He was particularly good with young players. When he came to Aberdeen, it was like a retirement home for old players that were well past their best from the Glasgow clubs. He came to the club in February 1965. By the summer he'd released 17 players. He revolutionised the place by bringing in appropriate experience and giving youth its chance.

"Eddie left Aberdeen in the summer of '71 to go back to manage Hibs. He'd been a Hibs player all through his career and they were his first love. I saw it as a sign to move on myself. I was a Manchester United player by March '72. When the opportunity came to leave Aberdeen, I could have played anywhere in the world in any kind of defensive formation from what I had been taught by Eddie. Lots of people know the game but he could explain it, put it across and teach people. That's a special skill."

Irish manager Frank O'Farrell paid a club record £125,000 to take Buchan to Old Trafford. The fee was also a highest for any Scottish player moving to England. "I was delighted when a few days later United signed Ian Storey-Moore for £150,000 from Forest," Buchan jokes. "Then Man City signed Rodney Marsh for something like £200,000 so my record was in the papers for all of a week. I had no control over the fee so I didn't really think about it. I was told later on that United had budgeted £150,000 to sign me so they did a good bit of business by getting me for 25 grand less."

Buchan then captained United in only his second game against Everton at Old Trafford after Bobby Charlton picked up an injury the week before against Tottenham. O'Farrell was sacked the following winter after a stormy relationship with George Best and a stuttering start to a campaign where United eventually finished eighth. Tommy Docherty took over and gradually steered United towards relegation, finishing 18th, then 21st thanks to the back heel of Denis Law, then of Manchester City.

"I found it tough under Doc," Buchan concedes. "He'd play me at left-back and I didn't enjoy it. While I was competent defensively and was quite good going forward with my left foot, Ryan Giggs I was not. Eventually things got sorted out and I was back in the centre. In fairness to Tommy Doc, when he took over there was a lot of dead wood in the squad. There was a curious mixture of superstars when I initially joined like Law, Best and Charlton and players who wouldn't have got a game for Aberdeen reserves. For me that was a cold and hard fact.

"In some ways, relegation gave Tommy Doc the breathing space to get rid of a lot of bad players and rebuild the squad. To the extent that in the first season back in the First Division in 1975/76, we almost won it (United finished four points behind Liverpool who won the league on the final day by beating Wolves 3-1 at Molineux). The problem that season was that some of my colleagues got carried away with our FA Cup run where we eventually lost to Southampton and it took our mind away from the league. We took a lot of teams by surprise..."

Buchan is quick to add that in the second season back in the top flight, United stopped Liverpool winning the treble by winning the FA Cup thanks to a fortunate deflection off Jimmy Greenhoff's paunch. "That Liverpool team was one of the greatest. A mark of greatness is how you respond to defeat and they did by winning the European Cup four days later. That makes our achievement even better as well. We had some key players and could rise to big occasions. Unlike Liverpool, we lacked consistency. If we played Coventry at Highfield Road on a wet Wednesday night, we'd struggle. Maybe it was the character of the players."

Tommy Docherty, trumpeting around Wembley with the cup lid on his baldy crown as the United fans – as ever magnanimous in victory – yelped "Liverpool, Liverpool," believed his position as club manager was indomitable after the victory. He'd reformed United from the rotting carcass they became in the post-Busby years and was rewarded with a new four-year contract worth the then unheard-of sum of £25,000 a year after promotion in 1974.

The FA Cup final build-up on the BBC that day portrayed a man shining in self-belief. At the team's hotel he was filmed performing a pre-rehearsed comedy routine with Gordon Hill, extracting the urine out of Lou Macari about his un-footballer-like teetotal approach to his career, and sitting down at breakfast chatting genially with Laurie Brown, his team physio. What nobody at the club realised was that Docherty was carrying on an extramarital affair with Brown's wife, Mary. A fortnight after the cup final he announced (at a press conference, sporting a black eye) that he was setting up home with Mrs Brown. A month later, United fired him. Buchan still wonders what might have been had the Scot remained in charge. "It was a mess really. If he'd have stayed, I believe the team would have emerged, especially after lifting a first major trophy for a long, long time."

Buchan was an integral part of United's team and held on to the captaincy for more than five years. He was once described by David Fairclough as his toughest opponent – "He was a thinking man's foot-baller, and had so much style and class" – and he is still remembered by United supporters as one of those players they could not bear to see missing from the line-up, in much the same way as Bryan Robson's absence was dreaded later years.

A man of forthright principles, Buchan also upset some people with an unbending attitude and professionalism. He expected those around him to meet his own high standards and could be fearsome when they didn't. Norman Whiteside describes Buchan as 'frosty' in his autobiography, adding that he remembered a time when he was caught leaning on another player's car in a designated space at the Cliff (United's old training ground). "What do you think you're playing at? Step away!" Buchan allegedly barked. 'He was a classic "know your place, stay behind the rope" kind of guy,' Whiteside wrote. During this interview, Buchan is nothing but polite and helpful, and before putting down the phone, he invites me to call him again if there's anything else I want to talk to him about. Why should any United player agree to partake in a book that in part charters the halcyon days of Liverpool Football Club?

Then when I mention the possibility that Twentyman could have been looking to sign either him or Jim Leishman – they were both of similar build, position and upbringing, and they were scouted at the same time – he responds coldly: "I was a lot better than Jim Leishman."

In total, Buchan made 458 appearances for United, scoring four goals. He also appeared in two World Cups for Scotland in 1974 and 1978. He won two major medals, collecting the Second Division championship in 1974 and the FA Cup two years later. Had he moved to Liverpool in

1971 and left in 1983, as he did with United, there's a chance he could have won seven First Division titles, one FA Cup (it could have been two if Buchan had not played so imperiously at Wembley in '77), three League Cups, two UEFA Cups and three European Cups. That's 16 medals in total. But as he emphasises once again: "It could have been reserve medals instead." (Liverpool won the Central League nine times in that period.)

Given that Buchan was respected as a player of self-belief, it is surprising that he feels this way. If he'd chosen Anfield over Old Trafford, there is every chance he could have superseded Alan Hansen as a majestic Liverpool centre-half, albeit with a game based slightly more on upward mobility, as he was a firm rather than ferocious tackler, while also blocking the potential development of Phil Thompson who only made his league debut, ironically against Buchan's United in a 3-0 win at Anfield, in 1972 (Lawler, Toshack and Hughes scored the goals). Take away initial thoughts of him in a United shirt and Kopites would have taken kindly to him. He was a cultured defender who played with a sense of responsibility to himself, his club and its fans. "I could have left United after we went down," he said, "but I wanted to prove I was good enough to captain a team back to the top of English football." He may have been aloof off the pitch, but Liverpool supporters would have respected his professionalism on it.

Buchan, though, is pragmatic on this issue. After a long pause, he adds: "You know what...I lived the dream. I always wondered playing in Scotland what it would be like if I moved away. I lasted 11-and-a-half years at one of the biggest clubs in the country, so I can't complain. I took the road that I felt was right for me at the time." Bearing in mind that Norman Whiteside said that Buchan 'took his responsibilities very seriously and could be quite dour and protective about his players' status', maybe it's no surprise that he now works for the Professional Footballers' Association. After leaving United for Oldham, he managed Burnley before working for Puma. In the '90s, his unspoken veneration for Liverpool grew stronger by signing Robbie Fowler, Jamie Redknapp and David James to boot deals.

"Liverpool were in decline and although they played some good football in spells, there were too many players in the '90s who weren't fit to wear the shirt." (There goes that outspoken nature again). "I'll honestly say that watching Liverpool suffer broke my heart because it's not nice to see an institution with all its great history suffer at the hands of lesser clubs. It's good that they are back towards the top again. I am pleased two great clubs like United and Liverpool are two of the best in England and Europe. It doesn't stop me having a soft spot for you boys too."

JIM LEISHMAN

Leishman's professional career was cut short by injury. He spent most of that time at Dunfermline, where he has also been manager and is now director of football.

Birthplace: *Lochgelly, Scotland*
Position: *Defender*
Clubs: *Dunfermline, Cowdenbeath*

Scouting diary notes:
'Useful player could be better as a centre back' (GT)

ONE player that truly regrets a move to Liverpool not happening is Jim Leishman. The Dunfermline defender was only 20 years old when he was forced to retire from the professional game after breaking his leg in a Scottish League Cup match against Hearts. He later managed the club on two separate occasions, and had a spell in charge at Livingston, now struggling in the Scottish Second Division. If he'd moved to Anfield, his career may have been very different.

In the months before sustaining his injury, Twentyman made several trips up to Fife to watch Leishman and was suitably impressed, noting that although he was playing as a right-back, he would be more comfortable playing at centre-back. Leishman, a softly spoken Scot, who was given an MBE in 2007 for his services to Dunfermline (he also has a street named after him in the town), reveals that Twentyman was right about his best position.

"Not long after he watched me, I was moved into the middle and Dunfermline won promotion," he says. "The only thing Geoff seems to have got wrong was my age. When he watched me, I was 19, not 21 as he says in the scouting book. I'd retired by the age of 20, so I was definitely younger than he thought!"

Now director of football at Dunfermline, Leishman adds that he didn't know Liverpool were looking at him and talks with a genuine surprise in his tone after being told that they were. Yet he also explains that he'd been down to Liverpool in the mid-'60s for a week-long trial and maybe the club had followed his progress from then.

"I thought I was a decent professional but I never dreamed a club like Liverpool would pay any interest in me. I think I was strong for my size and maybe that's what they liked about me. I was quite quick too, but most of all, I was a good passer of the ball. I was different from Hansen, though. If we'd played together I would have been in front of him and tried to win the headers and he would have mopped up behind me."

Maybe Leishman is surprised because at one stage it looked like he was bound for Elland Road after Don Revie offered Dunfermline £50,000 to take him to Leeds. "I had my heart set on the move. It was at the same time Gordon McQueen signed for the club. I was going down as an understudy to Paul Reaney. Leeds were a great team. Tottenham Hotspur and Celtic were also looking at me. But then I got injured and that was it."

Although Leishman didn't know Twentyman personally, he'd heard of him by mixing in football circles and believes it is possible that the scout remembered his name after a trial at Melwood as a teenager. Leishman trained with Liverpool for a week, along with another friend from the same Sunday league team, and did enough to prompt an offer of a youth contract. Instead he agreed to sign for Dunfermline, his local club. "Dunfermline had just won the Scottish Cup and were in the semi-final of the Cup Winners' Cup, so I decided to stay at home and play for them," he says. "Quite a few years passed after that and I thought Liverpool had forgotten about me. Obviously not."

Leishman says that not long after ending his career he bumped into Phil Thompson and Terry McDermott on holiday in Benidorm. "They were great lads. They used to go every year at the end of the season for a blow-out." Then, after deciding to enter management at the age of 29, Leishman used Thompson as a valuable contact in the loan market south of the border.

"I went down to watch Liverpool's reserve team two or three times to see if we could pinch a few players in the short-term. Phil was always happy to advise me on certain things. One of the players I tried to sign was John Durnin. When we won promotion again back to the SPL, I thought he would have been a good player. But I couldn't afford him. What we could have offered Liverpool, he wanted for a signing-on fee.

"The Liverpool reserve team on that day we went to see Durnin was phenomenal. Paul Walsh was up front with Durnin. Craig Johnston was on the right. Molby and Dalglish played in midfield and Stevie Staunton was on the left. They played 4-4-2, with Alex Watson and Mark Lawrenson at the back and Bruce Grobbelaar in goal. I would have fancied some of those players. They won five-nothing and I said afterwards that the Liverpool team that day could have won the Scottish Premier League. It really could have, no problem."

Leishman took charge of Dunfermline when they were bottom of the old Scottish Second Division, leading them to successive promotions in the mid-'80s and back into the top flight (he also later took lowly

Livingston into Europe). To Liverpool fans, though, he is perhaps best known as the man who brought Istvan Kozma to Britain. He signed the Hungarian, regarded as one of Liverpool's all-time flops, from Bordeaux in 1989 for £550,000, a club record fee at Dunfermline that still stands. Kozma, who played only 10 times in two years at Anfield, was earlier recommended to Leishman through one of his closest scouts who'd followed the midfielder's progress since his time at Ujpest in his homeland.

"They're a special breed, aren't they, the scouts? When I was manager, I looked for a scout who had a positive attitude towards football and wanted to win games. That meant the scout would look for the right player because you need winners. Every time you look for a player, you need the perfect player. Personally, the one player I developed and saw move on was Jackie McNamara. I liked what I saw in him and he moved on to Celtic for £625,000.

"The other player I liked was Istvan Kozma. It's funny you know, because he was a big player for Dunfermline. Then Graeme Souness took him to Liverpool and he didn't do it at all. When I brought him to the club from Bordeaux, he already had 37 caps for Hungary and he put another thousand people on the season tickets. David Fernandez was another player I brought to Livingston and he was a fantastic find and he made a lot of money for the club. The reason why these players were found was because I trusted the scout I was working with."

Today, over 35 years after Liverpool scouted him, Leishman ponders what might have been. He enjoyed his managerial career ("I doubt I'm going to go back into it now," he says), and although he certainly isn't bitter about the abrupt end to his playing time – "I was just dealt a duff card" – he wonders whether he would ever have left East End Park and enjoyed a career in England, had his playing days transpired differently.

"I have been very lucky because I've won seven promotions as a manager and that has brought me a lot of joy," he concludes. "But I still think about how far I would have gone had my career lasted longer. By the time I was forced to retire, I'd already played more than 90 first-team games, which was an awful lot of games for a young lad. Playing against Willie Henderson from Rangers and other great Scottish players at the time made me feel like I was progressing in the right way. I had three years as an apprentice in the first team behind me and I was gaining lots of experience along the way, although there was lots of room for improvement too. Sadly for me, I never got the opportunity to fulfil my potential."

GERRY FRANCIS

Francis was the captain of QPR when they pushed Liverpool all the way for the league title in 1976. During his time at the club he won 12 England caps.

Birthplace: *London*
Position: *Midfielder*
Clubs: *QPR, Crystal Palace, Coventry City, Exeter City, Cardiff City, Swansea City, Portsmouth, Bristol Rovers*

Scouting diary notes:
17/2/73: 'Strong and has ability. Appears in need of training' (GT)
24/2/73: 'Was QPR best player. Worked hard with ability' (GT)
3/3/73: 'Looks capable of playing in Div 1. Best player on field' (GT)

"YOU'RE gonna have to be quick mate, I'm busy today…" insists Gerry Francis over a crackly phone line. "In fact, can you call again tomorrow?" Francis, someone who has served football for five decades, was out of the game for five years when he was asked to coach Stoke City by manager Tony Pulis. Then, suddenly, Joe Kinnear wanted him as well after he took charge of the train wreck that is Newcastle United. Inundated with offers and media opportunities, his life became busy again. "I'd have spoken to you for hours and hours if you'd called the other week. It's a slightly different situation now."

The following afternoon, he's on to his way home to his house in the south when he speaks (hands-free of course) on the M1. Twentyman looked at Francis on several occasions, months before Liverpool secured their eighth league title in 1973. Francis was 22 years old and unaware that any other clubs were looking in his direction until Bill Shankly approached him after a game at Anfield.

"That's what Shanks was like," Francis says. "He was always very respectful towards the other club in that he wouldn't directly ask you to sign – otherwise that would be tapping up. Instead, he'd just say: 'Eh, sinny. You're good enough to play for Liverpool Football Club.' It was very flattering. But that's as far as it went as far as I know. As a Londoner, I was very happy playing for QPR. I'd been there all my life and didn't really think or know about any other clubs. Although I was very flattered that a club like Liverpool were interested in me, I decided not to think about it until a proper offer was made."

Twentyman was looking at Terry McDermott around the same period (they were both the same age, too), suggesting that central midfield was an area Shankly was keen on strengthening. By the time McDermott did sign for Liverpool in the summer of 1974, QPR were making strides themselves in the First Division and by 1976 were rivalling Liverpool for the title, so Francis didn't have any further thoughts of leaving Loftus Road.

"I played against three different Liverpool sides under Shanks and Bob Paisley, from the Roger Hunt and Ian St John days when I started in 1968, through to the Keegan/Toshack days, then the Dalglish and Rush team. During those two decades, I was used to Liverpool being top of the tree. The thing that set them apart was that they could play good football, but they were also all tough physically and mentally. Tommy Smith and Graeme Souness were the two toughest – but everyone knows that don't they? You could really tackle back then, so when I was playing in the middle, I was on the receiving end of a few tasty ones. You had to know how to look after yourself against most teams, but when you went up to Anfield, I played with one eye at the back of my head. Tommy and Graeme were two players you had to look out for.

"There was always forward-planning at Liverpool, and even now clubs are trying to replicate that. I remember playing against Peter Thompson – he was a truly great and underrated player – who was replaced by Stevie Heighway. As soon as they built one team, they were always thinking about building another one. Maybe that's why Shanks had an eye on me – as one for the future. In '76, though, I felt we matched Liverpool all the way through the season and even bettered them. They just had that bit of experience that helped them. We had a really excellent team. I am obviously a bit biased but we felt we'd done enough to win the league. We had 10 internationals in that team and for those couple of years we gave Liverpool a very tough run for medals. Unfortunately, we could only ever finish second at best."

Francis will never forget the final game of the 1975/76 season. QPR had completed their season and were top of the league. Because Liverpool were playing in Europe, their season finished one week late with a game at Wolverhampton Wanderers. If they gained all three points, the title would be theirs, but anything less and Shepherds Bush was poised for unbridled celebration.

"We'd won the league as far as I was concerned," sighs Francis, clearly still hurting from the memory. "We all genuinely believed that we were going to win the league. Because Liverpool were in Europe, they were allowed to play their final game a week or so later – now that would never happen now, would it? We sat in a television studio and watched the match against Wolves. It was a bit unique, but when I think about it now, it breaks my heart. Wolves were leading for about an hour and I thought we were champions. Then Kevin equalised. The rest is history, as they say. Liverpool won the European Cup the year after. It could have been QPR!"

Instead, the Londoners played in the UEFA Cup, reaching the quarter-final where they played AEK Athens. Francis scored two penalties in the first leg but missed the return match after pulling his hamstring while scoring a goal against Arsenal. QPR lost 3-0 and were knocked out on pens. "We'd have played Juventus in the semi-final. It just shows you how much luck you need to win things and how narrow the margins are."

Francis's performances in a hooped shirt re-ignited interest from other First Division clubs, although he is unsure whether Liverpool registered an enquiry. "I knew there was definite interest from Man U, Man City and Tottenham, but our chairman Jim Gregory wasn't having any of it, Jim was a local businessman and he'd built up the club over the years. He had a couple of favourites there like Stan Bowles and myself and he never ever wanted me or Stan to leave the club. If Shanks was alive now, he'd tell you whether there was a bid, but Jim would never have told me. He was always adamant that we would not be leaving.

"Even when my contract was finished, I couldn't leave because QPR still held my registration and could command a fee. There was no freedom of contract with the player and the club was in total control. Arsenal were fined for making an illegal approach for me and Phil Parkes in 1972/73. Jim took them all the way to the top of the FA and got them fined. So it doesn't surprise me that other clubs were interested in QPR players. I loved my time at QPR. They're my club. But it's good that players now have the right to move on, despite what people might think."

Francis later became a player, and then manager at Bristol Rovers during the time Geoff Twentyman Jnr was there. He in turn met Geoff Twentyman Snr – the man that scouted him for Liverpool years earlier. "Maybe if Liverpool would have signed me, Terry Mc wouldn't have arrived at Anfield," he concludes. "I think that most of you Scousers would have preferred a local lad like Terry over a southern boy like me, wouldn't you?"

JOEY JONES

Jones only spent three seasons at Anfield, but he will be remembered for his excellent displays at left-back as Liverpool conquered Europe and won the league in the 1976/77 season. Jones rejoined Wrexham in 1978.

Signed from: *Wrexham for £110,000 in July 1975*
Age when signed: *20*
Total LFC appearances/goals: *100/3*
Seasons spent at Liverpool: *3*
Birthplace: *Llandudno, Wales*
Other clubs: *Wrexham (three spells), Chelsea, Huddersfield*

Scouting diary notes:
1/9/73: 'Played well. To be followed up' (WJ)
8/9/73: 'Good display. Will bear in mind. Good material' (GT)
8/2/75: 'Looks ungainly but is effective. Plenty of heart for the game'

PRIOR to Jean Tigana there was Michel Platini. Before Platini there was Joey Jones. Each player, with his socks resting barely above his ankles, was iconic in his own right. Whether or not Liverpool's Llandudno-born left-back was an inspiration to later Gallic expressionism is doubtful, but few can argue that Jones's rumbustious style and laissez-faire attitude to his appearance made him just as distinctive as the French pair in the blue of their national team nearly a decade after the Welshman's time at Anfield.

Whereas Tigana and Platini had the balance, poise and vision to add to their unkempt allure, Jones, however, with his shirt out and hair all over the place, looked like Worzel Gummidge on a football pitch. As Twentyman notes in his description of the player, Jones was 'ungainly'. This isn't doing the European Cup and First Division title-winner a disservice. It's something he agrees with by his own admission. "I was once told by John Flynn, the father of Brian Flynn (Wrexham's legendary manager) that when he first saw me play for the Welsh Under-21s at a game in Newport that I looked like I had been dragged in off the road," he jokes. "Everyone else looked neat and tidy, but I just looked like a scruffy get."

Football in the 1970s may have been full of Lotharios, playboys and champagne guzzlers, but Jones was the first to go rock and roll with his socks. "That was just my style," he says. "Not that I was stylish or anything. I wasn't consciously a non-conformist or anything like that. I looked how I naturally was and I played like I naturally was. I was ungainly, but I didn't care because I played football to enjoy it."

One of the reasons why Jones appeared and played as he felt was because he never thought he would leave Wrexham and progress up the league pyramid. "I didn't think I'd be good enough to play any higher than the Third Division, never mind winning the European Cup. People used to tell me that I was a lot better than I thought I was, but I laughed it off because I didn't believe it."

Jones insists that there were plenty of other players at the Racecourse Ground in the mid-'70s that he felt would earn moves to top clubs ahead of him. Ironically, only he and his best mate Mickey Thomas, who later played together with him at Chelsea, were the only two to really make a mark on the game at the highest level.

"I was ungainly on the pitch. Mickey was ungainly off it. He also had hair that had never been combed, so we were an unlikely pair. Mickey was talented and with hindsight was always destined to play at a higher level if he had some luck, but I would say there were a few players better than me in that particular Wrexham team and in the youth team as well. Graham Whittle was one, Alan Whittle's brother [the former Everton player]. Dave Smallman signed for Everton and he was probably rated the highest of everyone. Everton never saw the best out of him and he was really unlucky [Smallman broke his leg on two occasions keeping him out of the game for more than three years at a time when Everton played drab unimaginative football]. There was Billy Ashcroft, too, who was a Scouser and played in the top flight for Middlesbrough."

Before Jones, Liverpool had signed Wrexham full-backs Peter Wall and Stuart Mason, two players who'd graduated through their esteemed youth system built up by manager John Neal. Months prior to the offer from Liverpool, Sheffield United made a bid for Jones and offered right-back Len Badger, a player who'd previously been close to a place in the England squad, in an exchange deal.

"Wrexham weren't keen on the swap and wanted straight money for me so the deal fell through. I didn't want to go there anyway because I was happy living at home. I actually said to Wrexham that the only team I wanted to move to was Liverpool. Their response was: 'Well that's never going to happen, is it?'"

Far from taking umbrage with Wrexham's denigrating response, Jones, somewhat typically, put his heart and soul into the club's faltering Third Division 1974/75 campaign where they finished 13th, despite Bill Shankly's proclamation that they were the best passing side in the lower leagues. Badger, meanwhile, moved to Chesterfield, and Sheffield United looked at other targets.

Jones was sea fishing off the coast back home in Llandudno with a group of friends when he found out about Liverpool's interest in him. "We were making our way back to shore after catching a couple of fish when I saw my dad standing on the beach waving his arms. I thought something was wrong at home but when he told me Wrexham had phoned to say Liverpool wanted to sign me I almost fell back into the sea."

Back on dry land, Jones travelled to Chester by train (he didn't drive) and quickly agreed a deal with Bob Paisley and John Smith. Months earlier, he'd signed a contract worth £65 a week at Wrexham. "The first thing they asked me was whether I wanted to sign. I thought it was a strange question to ask. They offered me £100 a week, but if they'd offered me half of what I was on at Wrexham, I still would have signed."

The following day, Paisley told the papers that Jones had the same enthusiasm for the game as Emlyn Hughes and that's why he made a move for him. "I know I was never as good as Emlyn mind," says Jones. "But I had the same passion for the game whether I was in Liverpool reserves or Liverpool's first team. I would say that my strength was winning the ball and giving it to someone else who could pass it."

Still only 19, Jones had posters and Liverpool memorabilia decorating his room at home of all his favourite players, including Kevin Keegan whom he idolised. Suddenly he was sharing a changing room with these superstars. The following week he made his debut against Utrecht of Holland in a pre-season friendly, then scored his first Liverpool goal against Borussia Dortmund in a 2-0 win in Germany. Unlike many players that signed for Liverpool from the lower leagues, Jones bypassed reserve-team football and was immediately thrust into Bob Paisley's first team for the league campaign. This, he says, may have been to the detriment of his career in the long run.

"I did things back to front and I think that's why I only lasted two years at Liverpool," he explains. "Maybe if I'd learnt my trade in the reserves my game would have become more rounded. Instead, all of a sudden, a Third Division player was a First Division player playing for the best team in Europe.

"Maybe my game didn't have the opportunity to develop. With hindsight it would have been better for me to do what the others did and go in the reserves first and settle down. Kevin Keegan had more time than me to settle down and even he would have found it hard to adapt in the time that I had."

Jones has no definitive explanation why Paisley was so keen to throw him into first-team action – especially because he was considered to have flaws in his game, even by the coaching staff at Wrexham. "Bob was a better judge than anyone, so who could argue against him?" he questions forcefully. "Bob felt I deserved to go in because of my attitude. That's the only thing I can think of."

Liverpool, though, had been scouring the lower leagues for a long-term successor to Alec Lindsay. According to his notebook, Twentyman travelled to East Fife, Huddersfield, Partick Thistle and Dundee to watch half a dozen different left-backs in the months before signing Jones. The position had become one of some concern for Paisley and Phil Neal was initially used as an auxiliary option on the left-hand side. Even though he failed to win a trophy in his first season, Paisley spent only £100,000 in the summer of '75, and all of that money went on Jones – with Phil Boersma leaving in a deal worth £72,000 to Middlesbrough. This indicates that Paisley either had little cash to spend after a debut campaign that finished trophyless (after winning the FA Cup in '74, Liverpool spent more than £500,000 on Ray Kennedy, Phil Neal and Terry McDermott), or that he had so much confidence in Jones that he genuinely believed he could make the left-back position his own.

The only thing certain about his move, Jones says, was that he was forced to sharpen up his appearance as soon as he appeared at Melwood for his first day of training. "Ronnie Moran was particularly insistent on tie-ups. I managed to get away with wearing my shirt out, though."

Jones's first full season at Anfield saw him make a dozen league appearances, but in his second year he played in all but three matches, ending the campaign famously in Liverpool's first-ever European Cup-winning team. Despite his full-blooded approach to the game – an approach that endeared him to the Kop – Jones was sold back to Wrexham in 1978 for £210,000, almost double what Liverpool originally paid for him. After spells with Chelsea, Huddersfield and Wrexham again, he retired in 1992 as Wales' most-capped player ever, having played 72 times for his country – although he has since been overtaken by six other players, including Ian Rush.

Today, as first-team coach back at the Wrexham, he is proud that his move to Liverpool sparked a special relationship between the two clubs. During the past decade the Reds have taken a team to the Racecourse Ground as part of their pre-season preparations near enough every July, a match which generates much needed revenue for the hard-up club who last season struggled in the Conference with former Red, Dean Saunders, as manager. And over the years several other players have moved directly between North Wales and L4, Mike Hooper and Lee Jones being just two, while Alan Kennedy and Jimmy Case have also played for both clubs. In September 2008, Steve Cooper, the head of youth development at Wrexham, joined Liverpool's academy staff at their base in Kirkby.

"It's the way it should be," insists Jones. "Although Wrexham aren't a feeder club to Liverpool, they still maintain strong links and I think it's beneficial for both parties. There are a lot of young lads coming through at Wrexham at the moment and although it's harder for them to reach the top these days, there's still hope for them because scouts are down at the Racecourse all the time. If they want to be Premier League footballers, the one thing they must make sure they do is knuckle down and live their lives the right way. And yes, that probably means pulling their socks up too..."

ANDY GRAY

At Dundee, Gray played in and lost the 1974 Scottish Cup final, before moving to Villa in 1975. In 1976/77 he picked up the golden boot after scoring 25 goals. A year later, he scored 29, and won the PFA Young Player of the Year and Players' Player of the Year awards. Gray moved to Wolves, where he scored the winner in the 1980 League Cup final, then Everton, where he won the FA Cup in 1984 as well as league and European Cup Winners' Cup medals the following year. He returned to Villa in 1985 and made several subsequent moves before retiring in 1990 and turning his hand to punditry.

Birthplace: *Glasgow*
Position: *Striker*
Clubs: *Dundee United, Aston Villa, Wolverhampton Wanderers,*

*Everton, Notts County, West Bromwich Albion, Rangers,
Cheltenham Town*

Scouting diary notes:
3/11/73: 'A good prospect who will probably move south' (WF)
**1975/76: 'Fights for every ball looks useful in the air. Could do
better regards making space'**

ANDY GRAY isn't liked by Liverpool supporters. Yes, he's a big
appreciator of Steven Gerrard's talents – "Yeee beautyyyyyyy" – and yes
he always gives the Reds backhanded compliments for gallant defensive
performances on faraway European fields. But most of the time there's an
Evertonian burbling beneath his words. He's knowledgeable, regardless,
and a damn sight better than some people who get behind the mic. Yet,
for most Liverpudlians, it's Gray that gets lodged up Kopite noses. He's
been with Sky since the beginning of the Premier League in 1992 so the
suffering has been long.

It could have been different, though. Gray might have been a
Liverpool player. Back in the winter of 1973, Geoff Twentyman had a
good look at him and predicted that he would move to England, should
his progression continue. He was 18 years old and leading Dundee
United's front line in the rough and tumble of Scotland's Premier
League. "I know that some Liverpool fans don't like me," he says, only
too happy to talk. "It's natural that they wouldn't. I don't think it's a
personal thing, it's just down to my links with Everton."

Gray scored 46 league goals in 62 games in his first two seasons at
Tannadice, leading to speculation that he would leave for Rangers or
Celtic. But it was the English scouts that made their interest known first.
"I read a bit in the papers about it, not long after I signed for Dundee
United [pronounced 'Dindee']. I must have only played in the first team
for about six weeks. Therefore he [Twentyman] must have seen me very
early on. I started scoring goals quite quickly and that probably made him
come and watch me. Certainly in the first two years, people mentioned

Liverpool, but I thought nothing of it. Nothing was concrete and I was too busy trying to make a name for myself as a footballer and make sure I kept on playing for the Dundee Utd side. I dinnae bother worrying about whether any single club in England was coming in for me."

Gray, more than most, is happy to dismiss any links with Liverpool, maybe understandably. He was, after all, the Everton signing that transformed Howard Kendall's fortunes in the mid-'80s. The week before he moved from Wolves to Goodison Park, Liverpool thrashed Everton 3-0 in the derby and that defeat prompted Kendall to spend in the transfer market. Tellingly, he backed out of a deal for Brazilian striker Joao Batista Nunes and swooped for Gray instead. In the same week, he appointed Colin Harvey as assistant manager, and later that season Everton won the FA Cup, challenging Liverpool for league titles over the next few years.

"Ye have to remember that Everton were interested me in 1973 as well ye know," Gray adds. "Liverpool and Everton were the first two clubs to make their interest known. I think Nottingham Forest also had a look at me. When I actually signed for Everton those years later, the scout Harry Cooke, who was Geoff Twentyman's mate, showed me what he wrote about me." Gray then rustles round his house looking for the document. "It says: 'Andy Gray, Dundee Utd, 13 August 1975: CF aged 19, has made progress and is becoming more mature. He was up against a good centre-half and their duel was a feature with honours about even' – Gray laughs – 'I think he would be an asset to the club and I wouldn't hesitate recommending him.'"

When Twentyman went to watch Gray, he also took note of Hamish McAlpine, Dundee's most Scottish-named of Scottish goalkeepers, as well as David Narey, who famously scored against Brazil in the 1982 World Cup before the Scots typically capitulated and lost 4-1. "Hamish was a really good goalkeeper, but like most keepers he was eccentric. He had great agility, his distribution was excellent – he had good feet for a goalkeeper and could ping the ball 70 yards right onto its target time and time again. I'm not surprised Liverpool were looking at him because he was a top goalkeeper in Scotland. He ended up staying at Dundee Utd for the whole of his career mainly because he had such a good life up there. He came from the area and he married a local girl so I don't think he ever really had ambition to move on. David was a good lad too and he is a Dundee United legend. He was still playing in the mid-'90s and ended up playing something like 1,000 games for them."

Although Gray, like McAlpine and Narey, was content in Tayside, the club couldn't resist the overtures of several English clubs and decided to cash in on their prized asset. "Early on in pre-season training in the second year, Jim McLean the Dundee Utd manager pulled me in pre-season training and said: 'Look son, I am going to have to sell you this year. You are going to have to go, because if I don't let you go, I am only going to hold you back.' That was flattering because it was a big compliment for me. When that season started I knew I was definitely going because there was talk about freedom of contract for the first-ever time. Jim was worried about players walking out and the club getting absolutely no money and I think he got a little bit pressurised by that. I never thought I'd go as quickly as I did, though.

"In the end, Manchester United, Liverpool, Villa and Leeds came in for me. They were all massive clubs and I wasn't sure which one to go to. I trusted Jim McLean's opinion so I asked him which club might suit me. Jim told me Villa would be a good move, so off I went. I didn't even know where Aston Villa was. I had no idea it was in Birmingham. I will never know if things would have turned out differently if I'd moved to Liverpool or England earlier on. All I do know is that I got my chance earlier by staying in Scotland. Jim McLean had a reputation as a manager that gave youngsters an opportunity and I was one of many that he gave that opportunity to. Two or three of us took the shirt and kept hold of it."

Everton moved for Bob Latchford instead of Gray, while Liverpool, who still had Keegan and Toshack up-front, later signed David Johnson.

Eventually, Dalglish and Rush became the chosen pair. One attribute, though, according to Gray, held each striker in common. "Football has changed so much in recent years, but the thing that is exactly the same as 35 years ago is the desire of football clubs to find strikers that will put the ball in the back of the net. I was scoring goals early on and that is undoubtedly what Geoff must have liked in me. Finding a striker who is young and has the ability to be composed is probably the hardest thing a scout has to look for. Goalscorers have always been worth their weight in gold."

When asked whether he feels a Dalglish and Gray partnership would have been successful at Liverpool, he jokes: "I think Liverpool supporters would prefer Dalglish and Rush." Instead, Gray became the partner of Graeme Sharp after he moved to Goodison Park in a deal worth £250,000. "It takes all sorts of things to make a side successful. We had probably one of the unlikely mix of players to reach success. The player that set us apart was Kevin Sheedy and we nicked him from Liverpool. When he started doing well for Everton, I am sure Liverpool would have loved to have him in their side [Sheedy, too, was a Twentyman signing for Liverpool]. Kevin was an amazing player for us, so maybe if he'd stayed at Liverpool, we wouldn't have achieved what we did."

Predictably, Gray has no regrets about the way his career turned out. An Everton legend isn't going to admit he wished that he signed for Liverpool is he? "I could have been like Alan Hansen with lots of championship medals and four European Cups. But it wasn't to be. If I'd signed for Liverpool straight away from Dundee Utd, I would have been competing for a place with Keegan and Toshack who were a brilliant partnership, so I may have never broken through.

"There was talk of me moving to Liverpool when I left Villa in '79. Keegan and Toshack had left then and Liverpool had Johnson and Dalglish instead. But Liverpool were frightened off by the price tag of £1.5m. It would have been a good move to go to Anfield, but I can't complain. I had a fantastic career, played lots of big games, won lots of medals, represented my country and met lots of great people along the way over 17 years. So I didn't have a bad innings."

PHIL NEAL

Phil Neal is one of the most decorated English footballers ever. The full-back was an integral part of the Liverpool teams that won eight league titles and four European Cups. He scored in two of those European Cup finals, slotting home the winning penalty against Borussia Monchengladbach in 1977 and scoring the opener in the 1-1 draw with Roma in 1984 (which Liverpool won on penalties). Neal had played almost 200 games for Northampton Town when he became Bob Paisley's first signing.

Signed: *from Northampton Town for £66,000 in October 1974*
Age when signed: *23*
Total LFC appearances/goals: *650/59*
Seasons spent at Liverpool: *11*
Birthplace: *Irchester*
Other club: *Bolton Wanderers*

Scouting diary notes:
18/9/74: 'Done well. Worth a quick follow-up' (GT)
21/9/74: 'Satisfactory game'
1/10/74: 'Done well all round. Good prospect' (GT)
5/10/74: 'Played as central defender. Done well' (GT)

WHEN Rotherham United announced they were to play their home games at the Don Valley Athletics Stadium in Sheffield during the 2008/09 season, travelling fans and lower-league professional footballers collectively exhaled. That's because Millmoor, their former home, is a relic of soccer stadia that even the most romantic fanatic would struggle to fall in love with. (The writer can vouch for that having 'experienced'

Millmoor several times during four agonising years studying in South Yorkshire.)

Whether it's the urine-scented cobbled alley path leading to the away end, the steely view of CF Booth Scrapyard behind the same goal, or the corrugated sheltered terraces, Millmoor was a ground that holds few fond memories. If it wasn't for the pies.

One former Liverpool player, though, has a fondness for the place. That's because Millmoor was the ground where he clinched his move to Anfield. "I remember my last game for Northampton when Geoff came down to watch me with the money man, Mr Sid Reekes," Phil Neal says. "I didn't know Liverpool were interested in me and that they were coming to watch me on that day. Liverpool were preparing a bid for me and I think Geoff just wanted to show the club what they were getting. But within 15 minutes of the game starting, I'd gone from right-back to in goal because our keeper was carried off injured. We were already 2-1 up and we still managed to win the game. I didn't concede any goals, too.

"So they came to see me, a player they were going to invest £60,000 on and they only saw me play for 15 minutes. It was quite funny really looking back. I think Geoff made the point that it reflected well on my character that I had the balls to go in goal, especially away from home. 'Can he handle it away from home in hostile arenas?' I remember Geoff saying to me. Some might say that Millmoor may not be the most hostile of places, there was less than 5,000 that day. All of them Yorkshiremen. But the fact that I went in goal and actually played well sealed the deal from Geoff's point of view."

Neal had been a jack-of-all-trades at Northampton. Sadly, he admits, he was master of none, even when Liverpool came to sign him. "I was a utility player for Northampton when Geoff spotted me. A couple of years before my move to Liverpool, I scored eight goals in nine games, and a lot of clubs came watching me. I thought that I might get a big move elsewhere, but it never materialised. Geoff watched me back then and must have decided not to sign me, but he kept coming to watch me over the next few years. During those years, I played at full-back, centre-back, midfield and up-front, so I think Geoff must have seen something in me to play regularly as a right-back."

Twentyman, though, spotted fundamental attributes in Neal that made him a natural target. 'I saw him take a free-kick at Blackburn. I was impressed by how cleanly he struck the ball,' he later told the press. 'He had the ability to hit accurate passes long and short distances which is a true art. Like a golfer, a footballer must be able to chip passes, drive the ball, bend the ball. Be in complete control. Many players have certain of those talents. Few have them all. Just as it's only a top golfer who can combine all the talents.'

Despite his stellar goalkeeping performance, Neal still wasn't aware of Liverpool's approach until the following Monday when he arrived for training. "I played the game on the Saturday, then on the Monday I went into the dressing rooms straight away to get ready for training. The assistant manager at Northampton came up to me and said that the boss wanted to speak to me. So I had to walk out of the dressing room and 20 yards up the street to the manager's office. When I got there, the first thing he said was: 'How do you fancy going to Liverpool?' Open-mouthed, I said I was ready to go straight away. I didn't even want to get changed even though I was wearing scruffy jeans. But I went back home, sharpened up and the Northampton secretary whizzed me up to Liverpool and back in the day. I agreed the deal as soon as I arrived at Melwood. I got £10 a week more than I was on at Northampton and I was made up to finally get the move that I had wanted for some years prior to that.

"Apparently Newcastle and Tottenham looked at me too, but Liverpool was what I wanted. It didn't take me much to put pen to paper. On the day I signed, my wife was in hospital having our son, and I couldn't even consult her. It was completely out of the blue, so I had no option but to sign. I was 23 years of age and I wondered what I was going to do for the rest of my life. I was playing Third Divisi and going nowhere really and I thought that time had already passed me by. Luckily, Geoff believed in me and everything I have achieved since then is really down to him. In any walk of life you need people to open doors and Geoff opened the most important one for me."

Neal says that he passed a straightforward medical before negotiating a salary with Peter Robinson: "It was a sign of the times. I received five per cent of the transfer fee, as arranged by the PFA in those days. The prospect of playing for Liverpool was quite daunting, but I wasn't daunted by the fee.

"I came into the team and replaced Alec Lindsay initially, although some people saw me as the long-term successor to Chris Lawler. It was only 15 months after I joined that Chris retired, so they started looking for a right-back. Because of my versatility, and Geoff had told Bill that I could play at right-back, I was moved from the left to the opposite flank. I was always more right than left, but I was two-footed, so playing for the first year and a half on the left wasn't a problem at all. Later, I found that Geoff loved players who could strike the ball cleanly. The fact I could use both feet was an added bonus, because I am told he loved two-footed players as well. I think he realised that when I integrated into the simplicity of Liverpool's play, it would bring me on leaps and bounds and he was right because I felt a big improvement straight away."

Despite Twentyman's apparent instant influence over Shankly's decision-making regarding Neal, it was only months into his time at Liverpool that Neal actually found out about the scout's influence in his transfer. "I got to know him really well after that. He used to come into the dressing room on a Monday morning and have a chat with Reuben Bennett and Shanks's old brigade, then go round the players, sometimes individually, telling all the lads about stories from Carlisle – or Caaar…lisle as he said it. He'd always be going on about Carlisle. He'd have lunch with us in the canteen, so I'd spend a lot of time with him, especially in the early days. He told me about how he used to go and wear his brown flat cap and sit in the stands at grounds up and down the country watching me. Apparently the Northampton fans really liked me because he asked them what I was like as a person off the pitch and they gave me good references."

One of the reasons why Neal settled so quickly into the Liverpool system was down to the humble nature of the dressing room and management. He'd been playing lower-league football with Northampton, but was made to feel right at home as soon as he moved to Melwood. "When I made my derby debut against Everton, I picked up my boots from Anfield in the morning and walked across Stanley Park early afternoon in my training gear and got changed when I got there. There was no fuss and that's why people like me felt so at home at the club.

"Geoff never really told me why he liked me as a player. Nobody really did that at Liverpool because once you were there, it was assumed you were good enough, so the coaching staff let you get on with your own game. They put faith in players and even though I was in a squad full of internationals and I was from lowly Northampton, everyone thought that if Geoff Twentyman scouted me, I was automatically good enough to mix it with these guys. That alone gave me an unbelievable amount of confidence. There were other players like me, who'd come from lower-league teams that had made a success of themselves at Liverpool, so they set the examples we needed to make players like me believe that we could get into this team and become a prominent member. He always checked on me and the players he spotted. I remember him asking me how it went when I played my first reserve game. Reuben Bennett was the same too. Geoff was always interested in those people he brought to the club."

Recalling several stories about Twentyman and Shankly throughout this interview, Neal says that he, just as much as anyone else in the Liverpool family, deserved European Cup medals like some of the players he signed. "He had a lot of Shanks's habits as well. He loved telling stories and his delivery of the punchline was always spot on. He was very understated, but he had the confidence and the boldness to make statements of intent – like the way he said Alan Hansen would become a world-class player, when people in Scotland had their doubts about him. He'd always be quick to praise his fledglings. He'd say things like: 'I've heard you're doing well,' and just stuff like that would give players lots and lots of confidence."

Neal, more than any other player that signed for Liverpool mentioned in this book, is grateful of Twentyman's role in his career. "Scouting was Geoff's forte. If he was here today, he might say that there were a few that failed, but that is fine because everyone makes a few mistakes in their lives. But Geoff travelled thousands of miles and talked to a lot of people and knew a lot of players in a game. If he got a sniff of a player, he would drive anywhere over a Wednesday, Thursday and Friday just to check him out.

"Geoff needs to be recognised as a formidable force behind a lot of Liverpool managers, particularly Bob Paisley and Bill Shankly before that. He brought in a conveyor belt of talented players that gelled together and I don't think Geoff got the recognition he should have. The list of players is uncanny. I doubt whether there is another scout in the history of football to have brought through players like he did. The players he scouted were dragged from little clubs, big clubs, any kind of team. His record was phenomenal."

JOHN GREGORY

Gregory was a versatile midfielder who played for seven different clubs and won six caps for England. He later managed Aston Villa.

Birthplace: *Scunthorpe*
Position: *Midfielder*
Clubs: *Northampton Town, Aston Villa, Brighton & Hove Albion, QPR, Derby County, Plymouth Argyle, Bolton Wanderers*

Scouting diary notes:
18/9/74: 'Well worth looking at' (GT)

THERE is a shortage of great Liverpool players who have later become great managers. Graeme Souness may have enjoyed total domination of Scotland with Rangers and coached in five different countries, but the only former Red to have achieved enduring success is Kenny Dalglish.

Succeeding illustrious Liverpool managers such as Shankly, Paisley and Fagan may or may not have made his job easier. The foundations for greatness were already there, it can be argued, yet there also followed expectations of epic proportions – quite a prospect for a footballer that had not managed a team before and vowed to play his part on the pitch for as long as he could.

Dalglish performed as critical a role as any other player when Liverpool became First Division champions in 1986, before retreating to the dugout for further successes in '88 and '90. He also won the FA Cup on two occasions ('86 and '89). Souness, meanwhile, lost the hearts of many Liverpool fans by selling established stars such as Beardsley, McMahon, Venison, Staunton and Houghton, and replacing them with dross such as Walters, Stewart and Tanner. The moment he agreed to be interviewed by *The Sun*, Souness the manager would never be regarded in the same light as Souness the player.

John Toshack has taken charge of Real Madrid on three occasions, and that is no mean feat, but he could never be marked as someone who has established himself as a manager in England's top flight. Maybe he just hasn't had the opportunity. Phil Neal, Ian Rush, Kevin Keegan, Ray Clemence, Steve Nicol and even Bruce Grobbelaar have all had a go at management without ever winning football's grandest prizes, although Nicol is currently highly regarded in modest North American coaching circles.

Quite why this has happened is bewildering. John Gregory, former boss of Aston Villa and one of Geoff Twentyman's targets for Liverpool, believes it is a result of football becoming over-complicated. "In terms of management, maybe it has gone against some of the former Liverpool players," he says. "I ended up playing with Phil Thompson for England as well as Sammy Lee and I'd ask them what their key was to success. They were winning everything in sight and nobody could figure out what they were doing to make them so successful. It wasn't that they were so successful; it was also because they were so difficult to play against. You could never get the ball off them. It was impossible.

"I always asked Phil: 'What do you do during the week? Give me the secret.' There was no secret, though. Everything was just so down to earth. I remember going to Anfield as a player with the Villa and 10 minutes before kick-off, all the Liverpool players were drinking cups of tea in the tunnel. Ray Houghton told me that on his debut at Luton he said to Kenny Dalglish that nobody had told him what to do from corners and set-pieces. So Kenny told him to ask Ronnie [Moran] what to do if they get a corner. Ronnie just told him to f**k off! There was no secret to it, there was no masterplan and everything was made simple for the players.

"That meant they could play their own game and focus on their own strengths. Everyone knows that all they did was five-a-sides, getting it, giving it and moving. I think a lot of managers who have played that system at Liverpool have tried to re-create it at their own clubs later on in management and it hasn't worked. Even Kevin [Keegan] in his last spell at Newcastle tried to go back to the old days and keep it simple in approach to everything, but it's difficult to implement that now."

Why, I ask Gregory? "I remember the story about Shankly and Paisley walking out of an FA coaching course muttering the words: 'This is complete and utter bollocks.' They were probably right at the time. I think a lot of managers go for the scientific approach with pro-zone and things like that. My view is that there needs to be a balance. When I was a player and early on in my management career I was under the misapprehension that every player thought like me. I went to training and ran my bollcks off. I used to love training and I thought everyone else thought like that. I also thought when everyone else went home after a game, they would sit and talk about the game and then watch 'Match of the Day.' I'd talk to my teammates at Villa and ask them about what they thought about other teams and players. Some of them would look at me and wonder what I was talking about. It made me realise that everyone was different.

"Some players need people like sports scientists and psychologists – it's a crutch to them. Some players need to talk about problems they have during the matches and off the pitch. Some of the time, I think it's a load of bollocks. Just roll your sleeves up and run around for 90 minutes and you'll be fine – that should be the way. A big part of me thinks that. But I also realise people come from different backgrounds and cultures and a lot of the players want that support.

"At the end of the day, football is a very simple game. You can control it and pass it and if you can't you will never make it. Footballers will be footballers no matter what. You only need someone to spot you – like Geoff Twentyman – then everything else will follow. You're not telling me Steven Gerrard would never have left the streets of Liverpool to become the world-class player he is...You can't tell me Jamie Carragher isn't the same. He was born to be a footballer. They are the players that do it simple and they are the ones who are the easiest to manage."

Gregory has a point. Kevin Keegan, like he said, was reported to have brought the Liverpool way to Newcastle during his latest ill-fated spell at St James' Park. In his first game at Arsenal, one newspaper rumoured that players went onto the pitch not being instructed who to mark from corners and free-kicks. John Toshack says in this book that he also uses the same basic philosophy learnt on the field of Melwood more than 30 years ago when he takes charge of the Welsh national team as they attempt to qualify for the World Cup in 2010.

"Some of the academy stuff does my head in as well," adds Gregory. "I remember when Spurs came to Villa for a youth team game and they stayed at Newhall. Whenever the FA Cup semi-final is played at Villa

Park, that's where the teams stay – it's £500 a room or something like that. But Spurs' Under-16s stay there for a morning game. I don't want to sound like some kind of traditionalist, because I am not, there just needs to be some kind of balance. For instance, I remember when I was at Northampton with Phil Neal and we used to drive the f***ing mini-bus and get up at 6.30 in the morning to go to f***ing Mansfield to play at some bulls**t park. It made me and Phil the people we became and grounded us. Phil was a good driver by the way."

Gregory was at Northampton at the same time as Neal. Although Gregory was considered mainly as a central midfielder later in his career, back then, like Neal, he filled in all over the pitch. It is thought by Gregory that Twentyman had to pick between him or Neal when Liverpool were deciding which player to sign as their next full-back.

According to Twentyman's notebook, he was also having a look at someone by the name A Starling. "Ah, Alan Starling. He was our goalkeeper," Gregory reveals. "We used to call him Sparrow [pronounced 'Sparra' in a pseudo Midland/Cockney accent – giving the impression like on TV that he's a Londoner. Although he's lived there for the last 25 years, he was actually born in Scunthorpe].

"I can't remember what I did last week, but I remember everything when I was at Northampton. I was only about 19-20 and everything was very exciting so I remember every game. In the game against Rotherham (when Liverpool decided to sign Neal), we had one substitute, but it obviously wasn't a goalkeeper, so Nealy just said he'd do it when Alan went off. He'd played everywhere for Northampton and tended to get moved around. He was so versatile. He'd be right-back, left-back, centre-half, centre-midfield, up-front. He had that ability and knowledge to positionally adjust to an area of the pitch. If he played as a right back, he knew what a right back had to do and it was the same if he played anywhere else. He was very astute. So when he went in goal, it was natural almost because even there he knew how a goalkeeper was supposed to look."

Neal's show of courage made Twentyman realise that he had the character to be a success at Liverpool. Maybe if Gregory had gone in goal instead, it would have been him and not Neal making more than 600 appearances in a Red shirt and picking up countless winners' medals. "Who knows?" Gregory ponders. "It may have not worked out for me at Liverpool like it did for Phil. I was a bit younger then and maybe the move would have come too soon for me."

Gregory made his Cobblers debut as a 17 year old and over the next five seasons would play right-back, centre-back and central-midfield. "My problem was that I didn't have any pace. That was what let me down. I could read the game and I could pass – that stayed with me all my life. In that sense, I was very similar to Phil. Phil wasn't the quickest, but he was a great two-touch player."

After Neal moved to Anfield, Gregory and his teammates at Northampton used his example as one to follow and it personally made him more determined than ever to sign for a big club. "When Phil went, I actually thought: 'Sh*t, Liverpool have actually sent someone all the way to Northampton to watch him – they must have seen me too.' I was completely unaware that a club would do that. I was so naïve about that side of the game – I didn't know what went on. I just thought the manager went home at 12 o'clock and that was it. I didn't have a clue that scouting went on really. Then it clicked that they must have seen me play too.

"When Phil went to Liverpool it gave everyone at the club, including me, a massive buzz. I got a kick up the backside and started to believe that if Phil got spotted, then there was a chance I could too. It inspired me and I got my head down a bit more and concentrated a bit more and worked a lot harder on the training ground. Phil couldn't have gone to Liverpool at a better time and I was watching him play in FA Cup and European finals, dreaming of emulating him. It made me so desperate to progress and I became almost obsessed by it. I could see how the Liverpool fans took to Phil as well, and I wanted that, although I grew up supporting Tottenham.

"Through Phil, we all became Liverpool fans. Leicester were in Division One back then and me and all the lads went there to see Liverpool play. It was handy because Northampton used to play a lot on Friday nights, so we could go and watch Phil on the Saturday. I remember going to the FA Cup final in '77 when Liverpool lost to Man U. We were about four rows from the front and we managed to get Phil's attention during the warm up and he came over to us. Through all this, we always read up on Phil and we found out about this guy Geoff Twentyman. So for me he became associated with a lot of signings at the club."

Soon, though, Gregory's enthusiasm to emulate his former teammate turned to exasperation and he started to think seriously about his future in the game. "I was still there two years later and at the start of the 1976/77 season I was 22 and I said to myself that if I didn't get a move then, then that'll be it. It was going to be my last chance and I knew that at 23-24, a lot of players got stuck in their ways and found it too hard to move on.

"I was so desperate by the end at Northampton. When I went to bed at night, I always used to hammer the weights beforehand to build my upper body, then tie them to my feet with bandages and sit on the end of the bed and build up my thighs. I was so desperate to get away from Northampton and make a name for myself in the top division, that I figured out if I built up my strength, I would get a chance. Luckily, Villa came in for me because I knew it was my last chance of getting away. I thought that if I didn't get away, I was going to have a testimonial at Northampton in five years time because I'd been in the first team for so long and had already played 187 games."

Like Neal, Gregory contemplated quitting professional football altogether immediately before Villa's interest became apparent. "Phil was actually going to play for Kettering Town under Ron Atkinson. They were the best team in non-league football and Phil had been promised a job in a boot factory. It was the main employment in Northampton. It would have meant he'd double his money. Then the

Liverpool deal pitched up and that changed his life. I could have done the same and it did cross my mind, but I am glad I didn't."

Gregory's move across the Midlands takes us back to successful management techniques. In his first few years at Villa Park under Birkenhead-born Ron Saunders ("Wasn't he a Scouser?" Gregory asks), he learnt the few things that he would take with him on his own career in the dugout.

"If Ron ever said you played well, you must have been f***ing brilliant," Gregory explains. "If ever he gave you a compliment or pulled you to one side and said: 'You did well today son,' it was the ultimate accolade. He was a tough man to please. He could never pronounce foreign names – I remember when Ossie Ardiles signed for Tottenham – he had real problems with his name. 'Ardeeleees,' he'd call him.

"Whenever he got the oppo's team sheet, Ron would walk into the dressing room, look at everyone and screw the paper up and throw it in the bin: 'They're f***ing s**t,' he'd say. There was a little bit of arrogance in him that made him successful. One thing that I learnt from him was that he always had that dividing line between himself and the players. He'd have a laugh and a joke at times but always knew when to step back. The main thing I took from him, though, was never to get too excited about anything. You can never get carried away in management because one day you're the bee's knees and the next day you're a zero. If you look at Liverpool, they were the same – they'd never celebrate anything until it was certain that it was won."

With the conversation drawing to a conclusion, Gregory, who has been an insightful interviewee, admits that he still has aspirations of making a career in management after spells in charge of Aston Villa, Derby County and QPR. "I am out of it and it's hard. A decade ago, I was top of the Premier League with the Villa, if only for a short period of time. Now I can't get a job. I do a couple of media things with Transworld International at the moment as well as running a business that provides mobile phones for professional footballers. One of our clients is Javier

Mascherano – he's a lovely fella. But everything goes so quickly doesn't it? Peter Reid is a good manager, as is big Sam [Allardyce] – people wanted him to be the England manager. Then he goes to Newcastle and it doesn't work out and his reputation slumps.

"After what's happened with Keegan, you can see bloody why can't you? Fans are funny aren't they? Sometimes they don't help. Your lot at Liverpool are the best, though. They're fantastic because they back the manager and the team. Liverpool fans don't make knee-jerk reactions and they give people a chance to prove themselves. Kopites really do get behind the team throughout the whole game – not just for 10 minutes like at some places. They're real fans."

ALAN HANSEN

After an unsuccessful trial six years earlier, Liverpool were finally ready to buy Hansen after he helped Partick Thistle to the Scottish First Division championship in 1976 and a solid mid-table finish in the Scottish Premier Division a year later. The fleet-footed centre-back was an instant success. He won eight league titles, three European Cups, three League Cups and two FA Cups at Anfield.

Signed: *from Partick Thistle for £100,000 in May 1977*
Age when signed: *21*
Total LFC appearances/goals: *620/14*
Seasons spent at Liverpool: *13*
Birthplace: *Sauchie, Scotland*
Other clubs: *Partick Thistle*

Scouting diary notes:
1975/75: 'Does a good job but gives the impression if faced with quick forwards would struggle' (AMc)
1975/76: 'Very good game a good reader and always in command' (GT)
1975/76: 'Looks the best CH in Scotland. Worth buying now' (GT)

DURING the '90s, whenever a Liverpool manager left the club Alan Hansen was usually mooted as a potential replacement. He never fancied the idea. "I'd tried scouting under Kenny when I was coming towards the end of my playing days," Hansen says. "I wasn't starting as many games as I had in the past and I knew I was finished. So Kenny asked me to get out there and have a look at a few players to keep me busy. I was absolutely useless. It made me think twice about staying in football after I retired."

Hansen wishes that he had the foresight of the man that spotted him while playing for unfashionable Partick Thistle in Scotland. If he did, maybe he would have reconsidered his stance, which has resulted in a career of football punditry. "There is a knack for looking at players and knowing their ability and potential for the future. It's hard. I went watching players in the lower divisions and up in Scotland, but I just came away every time not really knowing whether the player had enough ability. I never really had the decisiveness to pin my money on a player. I didn't want the stress either.

"Geoff was decisive. He had the knack. Geoff always told me that you must be able to pass the ball from A to B and I had that ability naturally. But that didn't mean that scouts spotted me and thought they should sign me. I never played for any of the Scotland teams from Under-16 to Under-19 upwards. None of the scouts reckoned I was any good. I remember playing in a trial game at Under-18 level and I felt that I gave one of the best passing displays that I ever had at any time. But I never got through the trial. I was told later that I never got in because they felt I didn't run around much, which is absolutely stupid. All the way through my days at Partick, people felt that. Everyone seemed to think that I was a good player on the ball, but I was a bit slow. That reputation stuck in Scotland.

"Then when I went to Liverpool, my game was set up for the way they played and Geoff realised that. Every now and again, I look at the old videotapes of my early days and I think: 'Christ, I never played like that!' I looked like I could barely move, but Geoff saw through that and realised in the right environment, I could become a real player. It was all down to the way I ran really, because as soon as I signed for Liverpool and bearing in mind I was part-time at Partick, they couldn't believe how fit I was. I was always in the top five when it came to fitness training, so it just shows that Geoff could see beyond my languid style.

"Everyone thought I was too casual. Andy Roxburgh thought it when he became manager of Scotland, even Bob Paisley thought it when he first saw me play. They both said: 'He doesn't play like that does he?' "Luckily Geoff could see beyond my 'weaknesses'. Geoff said to me that never at any stage did he think he was taking a chance on me. He never gave me any advice, he just told me not to worry about anything because he felt I was one of the great passers and if you are a great passer, the place to be is at Liverpool."

Twentyman did have faith in Hansen's natural ability but it's not true to say that he didn't have doubts. Speaking in an interview he gave to the *Sunday People* in 1978, Twentyman revealed: "I had a headache over him. We were watching a few Scottish centre-halves but Hansen was the one I fancied most. I watched him regularly and could never find any fault. He was great in the air, gave a good pass. Above all, he was so relaxed. But, as well as being his good quality, this coolness always worried me. Was he too relaxed? Could he cope with a one-to-one situation where speed off the mark and smart reflexes were vital? That was the one aspect I waited to see but I waited in vain because in Scottish football he was never placed in that situation.

"When Partick played at Bolton in an Anglo-Scottish cup tie I was convinced I'd find the answer. Again I was disappointed because Hansen played as a sweeper and again missed the sort of challenge I was looking for. Finally we had to decide and I plumped for Hansen. It was not until he arrived and I saw him in training that I could breathe easily. I saw immediately that his relaxed manner did not stop him being alive to a player who tried to take him on and go round him."

Ironically, Twentyman inadvertently rejected Hansen years earlier when he went to Liverpool for an unsuccessful trial. "I remember it well. As if it was yesterday," says Hansen. "First of all, I didn't want to be there. I was only a boy at 15 and at that age, it seemed like a long way from home. To be fair, Liverpool looked after me really well, but I had a little corn on the little toe of my right foot and I was in agony for the four days. On the last day, we had a friendly against a local non-league side. I was playing in the middle of the park and I just remember getting kicked everywhere. I never saw the ball. The first challenge came in and someone whacked me and after then, I couldn't get my game together.

"When I got home, I received a letter saying that 'you have not reached the required standard', and it was signed by Geoff. He hadn't seen me play during my trial, and he'd just signed a load of letters because he was the head scout. There were dozens and dozens of other trialists there. When I got home I wasn't too bothered that I didn't get through the trial. I was just happy to be home."

Even years later when Liverpool's interest again became apparent, Hansen was reluctant to leave Scotland. "I knew that Liverpool were watching me and I thought about it. Some kids when they go away from home at that age, they end up staying away forever. I couldn't hack that idea. Even when I did sign for Liverpool at 22, I didn't want to leave home. I didn't want to go to Liverpool and I would have preferred to stay in Scotland. I was a home bird. I'm not saying that I didn't like Liverpool, because they were a massive club and with Bill Shankly as the manager when I went there on trial, there was no bigger club. It was a big thing for any 15-year-old lad, but I wanted to be a golfer. My dad said I should go to Liverpool because it would be a good experience for me. When I walked away from Anfield after the trial, I never envisaged that I would be back there in seven years time and spend the rest of my career there. Never in a million years."

Despite the offer from Liverpool, none of the major clubs in Scotland ever made their interest known to Hansen. "Everyone thought I was lazy. Not long after I started playing in the first team for Partick, people were telling me that scouts were watching me in the stands. But as a player, you cannot afford to worry about that. When I found out Liverpool were watching, the Partick manager, Bertie Auld, always came up to me and said: 'The big boys are upstairs today.' He always called Liverpool the 'big boys'. He thought that I was lazy and that I needed a kick up the backside, so sometimes I think he told me that the 'big boys' were there, even though they probably weren't.

"I'd suffered, and I mean suffered a growth spurt and I grew from about 5ft 7in to 6ft 2in in a very short space of time. It meant that I didn't have any energy and I couldn't run and this probably put scouts off me too.

"My body was just trying to get used to being so tall and it affected my performances, so that was probably why nobody tried to sign me. People were talking about me in England and there's a story that Jimmy Armfield [then manager of Bolton] came up to Glasgow to watch me armed with a chequebook, but my performance was so bad that he allegedly threw it on the ground in disgust. That plagued me throughout my career because I was quite languid in style so when I wasn't playing well, it looked like I wasn't trying."

Even though no Scottish clubs made an official bid for Hansen, there were plenty of offers from clubs south of the border. "When I finally did move to Liverpool, everything was conducted in secret. Bolton finally came in for me five or six weeks before the end of the 1974/75 season. By then, I just wanted to get away from Partick because I was fed up there. There was also a deal done with Newcastle, but they changed managers the day I was supposed to be travelling there.

"At various different times, Rangers and Celtic tapped me up and I definitely would have gone to either one of them. Signing for one of the Old Firm excited me because it meant that I would have stayed at home. Then Bolton made the first offer because they knew Liverpool were in for me.

"But in the end, it turned out that Liverpool had already agreed a fee with Partick well before Bolton came in and well before I'd even known about it. I was the last to find out about everything."

KEVIN SHEEDY

Sheedy played for Hereford for two seasons before signing for Liverpool. The left-winger made his league debut in 1981 but then only made two further appearances in the league the following season from the bench. He played in two League Cup games for the club, scoring in both of them, but after failing to force his way into the side, he moved across Stanley Park to join Everton in 1982. Sheedy became a legend at Goodison, helping them to the league title in 1985 and 1987.

Signed: from Hereford United for £100,000 in July 1978
Age when signed: 19
Total LFC appearances/goals: 5/2
Seasons spent at Liverpool: 4
Birthplace: Builth Wells, Wales
Other clubs: Everton, Newcastle United, Blackpool

WHEN Kevin Sheedy scored for Everton against Liverpool in April 1987 he charged towards the Kop and made a two-fingered salute. The Blues were edging towards the First Division title, their second in three years, with Sheedy, a former Red, one of their most influential performers.

The Kop was surprised just as it was incensed. For someone who was renowned as being mild-mannered and polite, the act was out of character. The newspapers, both sets of supporters, Kenny Dalglish and even Howard Kendall all questioned why he did it. At first, Sheedy pleaded that he was merely recreating a hand gesture made famous by Ted Rogers in his show '3-2-1', which was all the rage in the mid-'80s. Years later, he admitted to Everton fanzine 'Blue Kipper' that it had simply been a rush of blood to the head, adding that 'it was a joyous moment', 'a great free-kick' and 'just how I felt at the time'.

Subconsciously, Sheedy's outburst could have been a release of frustration. It was his first goal for Everton against Liverpool since moving to Goodison Park five years earlier. In his derby debut he was a part of the Everton side that was thumped 5-0 thanks to four goals from Ian Rush. During his time at Anfield, he'd come close to claiming a first-team place after Ray Kennedy picked up an injury, but he got a knock himself while on international duty and his chance went. From then on, he believes that some members of the Liverpool coaching staff treated him as something of a 'sicknote'. It was a tag he never shook off and eventually prompted a move across Stanley Park.

Sheedy joined Liverpool for £80,000 in 1978 after making his debut for Hereford as a 16-year-old, before making a further 50 appearances. "In the first year after I signed for Liverpool, I felt I did enough to merit a chance in the first team," Sheedy says. "Unfortunately, I injured my back, and in those days the club didn't have proper physios. Not like they do now. Ronnie Moran and Roy Evans did all the work and unfortunately their treatment didn't work on me. It got to the stage where my back was suffering for about six months and in the end I think they questioned the extent of my injury. I had a feeling they thought I was a crock, when all I really needed was proper treatment. Unfortunately, they got this idea into their heads and it made it very difficult for me to reach the first team.

"I understood that I'd signed a four-year contract, but my appearances would be curtailed by the injury, so it got to the stage where I had to move on, otherwise I would never develop as a player. It was very disappointing because I thought I was good enough, but circumstances didn't allow me to prove myself."

Sheedy, now coaching at Everton's youth academy, insists that he understood he had to be patient before earning a regular first-team place at Anfield especially after witnessing first hand Liverpool's European

Cup triumph against Brugge at Wembley in 1978. "I left the ground that night thinking how brilliant Liverpool were," he says. "I was still a Hereford player and I watched the game more as a neutral because I'd always watched the big England international games and European games due to the fact that there were no clubs near me to watch that were at such a level. One of my friends got the tickets, so we went down and I ended up supporting Liverpool, purely because they were British. I watched Kenny score and I celebrated the goal and the victory. Then two or three weeks after the game, I had a phone call one morning asking me to make my way up to Liverpool because Hereford had accepted a bid for me."

Sheedy won the Third Division championship during his time at Hereford and he quickly established himself a reputation as a winger with the ability to drop a shoulder and open a can of beans with his left foot. When he put down the phone after being told of Liverpool's offer, Sheedy, unlike many others who couldn't wait to sign, was overcome with anxiety.

"I was obviously excited, but I had mixed emotions really because I knew Liverpool had a record of signing players from the lower leagues before making those players wait their time and learn in the Reserves. I felt I was ready for first-team football. So I went up there with an open mind and wasn't really sure whether I should sign, but as soon as I got to Anfield and Melwood, met Bob Paisley – the man who'd just delivered the European Cup – and looked round the set-up, I knew that I should sign for Liverpool. It was too good an opportunity to turn down. There were no negotiations. They made me an offer and I signed it."

Local papers in Herefordshire previously linked Sheedy with moves to Wolverhampton Wanderers and Bristol City, but he read little into it because he was happy living at home in Builth Wells with his parents and playing regularly for his local club. "This made it harder for me to move because I looked at Liverpool's midfield and saw Case, Kennedy, Souness and McDermott. They were the best midfield in Europe and it was going to be very hard for a young boy like me fresh out of Hereford to try and break into that team."

The scout that spotted him, though, soon allayed Sheedy's fears. "I was a bit younger than some of the players that Geoff Twentyman signed, but he told me at the start that he expected me to be a first-team regular within a year," Sheedy says. "I saw that as a big compliment because Liverpool were European champions and there were a lot of excellent players to dislodge, but Geoff had enough faith in me to say that."

Whether or not Twentyman gave Sheedy false hope, thus heightening his frustration later, is debateable, but it is clear that the scout envisaged him replacing Ray Kennedy before Ronnie Whelan arrived from Home Farm in Ireland. "My success with Everton meant Geoff was right in his judgement," Sheedy points out. Whelan's ascension into Liverpool's first team prevented Sheedy's own progression.

It is ironic then that Sheedy, who played for Ireland with Whelan for more than a decade (with Sheedy on the left of midfield and Whelan in the centre), was the one who helped him settle in immediately after moving to Liverpool. Sheedy initially lived with Alan Hansen at Elsie Road, seven streets down towards Breck Road from the old Kemlyn Road, but invited Whelan to live with him after Hansen moved out when he found a place of his own.

"I was good mates with Ronnie and I knew he was feeling a bit homesick, so I asked the landlady, a Mrs Edwards, if he could move in. It was home from home for me and I never felt homesick at all, but she really helped Ronnie.

"I remember when we both first played for Liverpool's first team for the first time. I was selected against Birmingham one week and was sub against Brighton the following week, then me and Ronnie went off to play for Ireland Under-21s at Anfield, funnily enough, and I picked up an ankle injury. I was ruled out for about a month and in that time Ray Kennedy got an injury and Ronnie took his place. He took his chance with both hands and deservedly made himself a major player. Maybe if I'd have been fit during that time, I would have got my chance instead and history would have been different. Ronnie made the breakthrough and my opportunities were then finished because I had two people in front of me in my position."

Sheedy's success at international level was another reason why he was keen to taste first-team football. Despite being born in Wales, he qualified for Ireland through his father (his mother was Welsh) and could have played for either nation. But Sheedy says the Welsh FA "dilly dallied" for too long and didn't include him in any of their youth squads, even after informing them that he had an offer to play for Ireland.

"I had a call off someone from the FAI to ask whether I would be interested in representing them. So I rang the Welsh FA to find out whether they would be selecting me for an upcoming game and they told me that they wouldn't reveal who was in the squad before they officially announced it. That made my decision for me. So I told the FAI that I would take up their offer.

A few days later, Wales told me that they wanted me to be a part of their squad. It was a good decision as it turned out because we achieved some incredible things with Ireland and I ended up scoring at a World Cup, which for me was the pinnacle of my career. Kevin Ratcliffe gave me a bit of stick about it, though."

By the summer of 1982, Sheedy was, as he puts it, "fed up" at Anfield and decided to move on having started only five games in total. Despite interest from Derby County and Blackpool (Liverpool encouraged him to move to both clubs ahead of Everton), Sheedy was adamant that he wanted to stay on Merseyside.

"It all happened when I received a phone call from a press man who told me that Everton were interested in signing me and asked whether I'd be interested in going. I'd spent four years at Liverpool and during that time a few lower league clubs had come in for me as well as a few top teams, but Liverpool didn't want me to go to any of those clubs. In those days, the clubs had the power, and the player, in this case me, had no power to dictate where I went.

"While I was living in digs, I used to love watching football, so I used to go to Goodison for midweek games. I saw the team that Howard [Kendall] was assembling there with Graeme Sharp, Adrian Heath and Kevin Ratcliffe, and realised he was putting together a good young side. So when Howard came in for me, I knew where I was going and who I was going to be up against when trying to make the first team. I knew Evertonians were thinking that if I wasn't good enough for Liverpool, why would I be good enough for Everton, so I knew I had to get off to a good start and, luckily for me, I did."

Sheedy, like Johnny Morrissey before him, was undoubtedly one player Liverpool missed out on in terms of ability, although Ronnie Whelan, the preferred choice ahead of him at Anfield, was just as good as him if not better, albeit different in style. Liverpool supporters wouldn't have changed Whelan for anyone and Evertonians wouldn't have changed Sheedy. They were two players at the top of their profession playing for the top two teams in the country (although when Sheedy initially signed for Everton, it is worth bearing in mind that anyone with a half decent football brain would have been guaranteed first-team football. Mick Ferguson was their first-choice striker for a time in those pre-glory apocalyptic days).

At Goodison Park, Sheedy flourished, winning two league titles and a Cup Winners' Cup medal as Everton challenged Liverpool's reign as the superpower of English football.

He would have won the FA Cup too, but an injury prevented him from playing in the final against Watford in 1984. Sheedy says that despite not becoming a regular at Anfield, he learnt at Melwood that the best players always exercise good habits, and he carried this mentality throughout the rest of his career.

"Another thing I learnt was never to nutmeg Graeme Souness in training," he jokes. "I did it once and he just laughed. But then a few years later I did the same thing against him in a derby match and he elbowed me in the face."

STEVE OGRIZOVIC

Ogrizovic arrived at Anfield as cover for Ray Clemence after only 16 games in Chesterfield's first team, but Clemence's immovability limited his opportunities. He left for Shrewsbury in 1982, and then went to Coventry where he made his name, winning the FA Cup in 1987 and breaking appearance records.

Signed: *from Chesterfield for £70,000 in October 1977*
Age when signed: *20*
Total LFC appearances: *5*
Seasons spent at Liverpool: *5*
Birthplace: *Mansfield*
Other clubs: *Shrewsbury Town, Coventry City*

STEVE OGRIZOVIC was like any other footballer of his era. He might not have played as many games for Liverpool as other Geoff Twentyman signings, but he owned a Ford Capri. The car for a guy in his early 20s with a bit of cash in his back pocket. Albeit for a short period of time. Oggy's motor was one of a raffish gold and red colour. The Batmobile type. One day, not long after he joined Liverpool, he parked the car underneath some scaffolding at Anfield before heading off to training at Melwood with the team.

When he returned, the car was bare of colour. Paint stripper had fallen from the rigging half way up the Main Stand. Whether it had been dropped deliberately is uncertain, but a week later a decorator came forward and admitted his misgiving. "At least he was honest – in the end," reflects Ogrizovic, now a first-team coach at Coventry. "The club paid for the damage and a couple of weeks later I got my car back. It was as good as gold – forgive the pun."

Ogrizovic says that he has heard a number of stories about his 'decorated' car over the years, including one where it was stolen from in front of his own eyes (as well as several security staff) while he spoke to Bob Paisley in Melwood's car park. "There's a lot of different tales. All I can say is that the person who dropped the stripper apologised and it showed me the people of Liverpool were very honest."

The giant goalkeeper, who was born in Mansfield but was of Serb/Croat decent, had been spotted by Twentyman playing for Chesterfield in the lower leagues. "Geoff told me that he watched me six or seven times in a short space of time," he says. "He also went on record saying that I was his 'biggest' ever signing. In that, he meant that I was the tallest. I was 6ft 4. I was also one of Liverpool's first-ever loan signings. Liverpool didn't need to sign people on loan, but they were a bit unsure about an injury I had, so to play it safe they took me for a month before signing me permanently. That kind of loan was unheard of back then, especially with Liverpool."

Ogrizovic only made five appearances in total during his five years on Merseyside, but he had a formidable task in displacing Ray Clemence as the club's number one. "Geoff's track record with goalkeepers was excellent. He'd signed Ray Clemence before me and I knew he was the best goalkeeper in the country, so I went to Liverpool with the attitude that I would just try my best to push him and be the best back-up goalkeeper in the country. I learnt so much just watching him." After leaving Anfield in 1982, he spent two seasons at Shrewsbury before signing for Coventry City where he played for 16 years, making more than 500 appearances. "When people think of me, they think of my time with Coventry because I was there for such a long time," Ogrizovic sighs. "That's understandable because I played at every ground in the country in a Coventry shirt season after season.

"Obviously, I am a big Coventry fan now because I have strong links with the club. But if someone ever asks me who I played for, I will always tell them about Liverpool. I can't ignore that period of my life because Liverpool instilled so much in me. I loved going back and playing in front of the Kop when I was with Coventry because I always received a great reception. Having said that, it was probably because they knew they were going to stuff us!"

GARY GILLESPIE

Joe Fagan's first signing, Gillespie captained Falkirk at 17 before moving to Coventry where he played for six seasons. At Liverpool he battled with Mark Lawrenson and Alan Hansen for a centre-back spot. He won three league titles and the European Cup in 1984 before moving to Celtic.

Signed: *from Falkirk for £325,000 in July 1983*
Age when signed: *23*
Total LFC appearances/goals: *214/16*
Seasons spent at Liverpool: *8*
Birthplace: *Stirling, Scotland*
Other clubs: *Falkirk, Coventry (two spells), Celtic*

GARY Gillespie had all the characteristics of a trademark Geoff Twentyman signing. Firstly, he was Scottish. Twentyman loved Scots. Secondly, he played first-team football at Falkirk as a teenager, becoming their first-team captain at the age of 17. Twentyman liked to sign players after they had benefited from a couple of years of experience, and Gillespie had it in abundance. Lastly, Gillespie's reputation had dipped slightly after a difficult spell in a struggling Coventry side. Twentyman rarely targeted big names.

"When you look at the people that Geoff signed, a lot of them, including me, had something in common in that we weren't superstars in our own right when we came to Liverpool," says Gillespie. "Geoff didn't go and spend £30m on Shevchenko or £27m or whatever it was on Fernando Torres. The players that came in were from teams like Northampton, Chester or Partick Thistle. They were all unknowns, and through Geoff and Liverpool, they became world stars. That's the difference between being able to spot talent and going and buying that talent at the right price."

Before Gillespie signed for Liverpool, he'd come to the end of his contract at Coventry City after making more than 200 appearances in five years. "I wasn't looking for a move although I was talking to other clubs," Gillespie explains. "While Coventry drew up a new contract, I spoke to a few different managers. West Brom, Stoke and Arsenal had all shown an interest. I'd been down to speak to Terry Neill and Don Howe at Arsenal when I got a call from Bobby Gould saying that Liverpool wanted to talk to me.

"He asked me whether I was interested and I told him that it was a silly question. I was impressed by Arsenal and what they had to say, but I hadn't made up my mind because I wanted to give Coventry the benefit of the doubt and allow them to make me an offer. I hadn't talked contracts with Arsenal, although I was 95 per cent certain I would go there in the end. Had Liverpool not come in, I would have gone there, but instead I drove up to Liverpool the next day and Geoff was at Melwood waiting for me with Joe Fagan as well as Peter Robinson and Tom Saunders. They took me for a meal where what is now the St George's Hotel and that was me hooked, signed and delivered. Job done."

According to his scouting book, Twentyman first scouted Gillespie when he was 17 years old. He must have monitored his progress at both Falkirk and Coventry before signing him for Liverpool six years later. Gillespie sounds surprised when told that Liverpool were watching him in his teens, although he knew that West Bromwich Albion had been to have a look at him.

"Probably the reason why Liverpool never tabled a bid for me was down to the fact that I had no experience at that age," he says. "Centre-backs reach maturity a bit later than other players, at the ages of 28-29 and Geoff knew that new players would spend two maybe three years maximum in the Reserves before playing for the first team.

"If I'd have signed at 17, I would have had a five or six-year wait minimum before I reached the first team, so he probably felt it was better that I gained experience elsewhere first. After getting to know Geoff and how he worked, he didn't just look at the player's football ability. He wanted to know what the player was like off the pitch too. That's a further testament to his ability, because judging a person's character from afar is probably one of the most difficult things to do as a scout. He knew a player that could play particularly for Liverpool, which makes him different from everyone else."

Gillespie made only 22 league appearances for Falkirk, in which time he had become the club's youngest-ever captain. But he says that "it was no big deal" when Billy Little, the manager, offered him the armband. "We were a poor side and I was the only one guaranteed a regular first-team spot!" he jokes. "Being a defender also helped because most captains of clubs were defenders. I captained Coventry a couple of times, but I never captained Liverpool, so maybe I wasn't a born leader. It's just something for the record books."

Despite interest from a host of other clubs (not including Liverpool), Gillespie elected to join Coventry in 1978 in a £75,000 deal. Reflecting, Gillespie believes it was the right move for him. "The biggest thing at Coventry was that the competition to get into the team wasn't as fierce so if you were good enough, you were old enough, so it allowed me to play a lot more games than if I'd have moved to Liverpool. During the years I played there, there were an awful lot of youngsters that came through – Danny Thomas; Stevie Hunt, who came back from America – they were littered with loads of young players who were given opportunities, although it was always a massive struggle to stay up.

"When I moved to Liverpool, it was a massive step up, just in terms of expectation. I could see that the moment I stepped into Melwood. Not just on a weekly basis, but on a daily basis, too, because if you didn't perform in training, it would affect your chances of playing in the first team at the weekend. If you didn't perform well straight away, you didn't play. It was as simple as that."

The pressure was something Gillespie struggled to deal with initially and he failed to break into Bob Paisley's starting XI. Instead, like many signings before him that were accustomed to first-team football, he was resigned to the Reserves. "It was a great education, but it was difficult to take because I was so used to first-team football with Coventry City. I'd like to think that I learnt quickly, though.

"Geoff had an eye for clever players and intelligent players, not just on the football field, but off it too, and I'd like to think I was one of those. I think Geoff realised which players would be able to cope with learning the 'Liverpool Way'. The one thing about me was that I was unfortunate to have Mark Lawrenson and Alan Hansen ahead of me. The team was doing really, really well and it was difficult to change that winning formula.

"When I was given an opportunity and I did play games, the system at Liverpool meant that the transition was seamless. Although Alan and Mark were ahead of me, when I came in I would like to think that there was no downside because the bandwagon just kept on ticking along. When I got my chance to stake a regular place under Kenny [Dalglish], I think it proved that the Liverpool system worked because I enjoyed a good career with the club."

Back at the beginning, however, Gillespie's frustration at his situation forced him into thinking about leaving. "They were all boyhood idols of mine, Souness and Dalglish, so walking in the dressing room on the first day was quite nerve-wracking. But when I signed for Liverpool, I never thought I would be playing in the Reserves. I knew it might be hard work becoming a regular but I seriously don't think any player signs for Liverpool and believes they will be playing for two seasons in the Reserves.

"The situation got to me and I considered leaving at one point. I vividly remember going in to speak to Joe Fagan ahead of the 1984

European Cup final. Joe, being the man he was, listened to me and understood that I was frustrated at not being a part of the first team, but I could understand his point of view as well because Mark and Alan were playing very well. So it was a mutual agreement that if the right offer came in for the club and for me that I would probably move on. It was only a 10 to 15-minute conversation and I didn't put a transfer request in, but I did it mainly to vent my frustration. Joe never really took it further forward. Then things happened, with Joe retiring, Kenny coming in and Mark getting an injury. All the same, I had to be ready to take that opportunity and playing in the Reserves helped me with that."

The Scot overcame his problems and ended up replacing Mark Lawrenson, who by the mid-'80s was struggling with knee injuries. "Us Scots are quite strong when it comes to a fight, so I ended up toughing it out," he says. "That's probably why Geoff Twentyman liked us so much. At that time, it was a good market to exploit because there were a lot of good players up there. Probably other clubs neglected it. The Scottish mentality generally is a winning mentality. Look at Kenny, Bill Shankly, Matt Busby and Alex Ferguson across the way. All winners. Geoff obviously knew what to look for. His biggest attribute was that he could spot a player that could improve himself while at Liverpool as well as improving the team. With Scottish players, he knew what he was getting in terms of character. I can't understand why scouts don't operate more up there these days because I believe there's still the talent around. It's just not fashionable to scout in Scotland today."

Like many Scots from the time, Gillespie remains on Merseyside to this day, living just down the road from both Alan Hansen and Kenny Dalglish in Birkdale. "It will be interesting to see the modern-day guys that come from all over the world, whether they will base themselves in the north-west when they finish," he questions. "I would bet against it."

ALAN KENNEDY

After five years at Newcastle, Alan Kennedy was signed by Bob Paisley to solve Liverpool's problem at left-back. He played 37 league games in each of his first two seasons at the club, and helped the team to the league title (five times), the League Cup (four times) and the European Cup (twice). Kennedy is best remembered for his winning goal in the 1981 European Cup final against Real Madrid.

Signed: from Newcastle for £330,000 in August 1978
Age when signed: *23*
Total LFC appearances/goals: *359/20*
Seasons spent at Liverpool: *7*
Birthplace: *Sunderland*
Other clubs: *Sunderland, Hartlepool*

"WE'VE got Barnesey today. We're bound to win," chuckes Alan Kennedy on a crackly line from a bus somewhere between Dublin and Cork. "Give it a rest," he pleads with Bruce Grobbelaar, who is probably involving himself in some tomfoolery on the back seats.

Liverpool veterans are on the way to play their Manchester United equivalent in Ireland. "We're going to whack them," claims Kennedy at the end of the interview. He was right. Later that day, the Reds rattled home three to United's none. The team included a clutch of players who were originally spotted by Geoff Twentyman before they signed for Liverpool. "It might have been very different if it wasn't for Geoff," says Kennedy. "I might have been playing for Newcastle United Vets, Brucie might have been in the Vancouver White Caps Vets – if they have one – and someone like Gary Gillespie would have been a Falkirk veteran. Of course, we might have all moved on to other big clubs if Geoff didn't scout us, but I doubt any of us would have achieved anywhere near the same amount of success."

Kennedy admits he has a lot to thank Geoff Twentyman for. Before moving to Liverpool in the summer of 1978, he'd fallen out with Bill

McGarry, the then Newcastle manager. McGarry, a disciplinarian who'd played under Bill Shankly at Huddersfield in the '50s, saw Kennedy as a rebel after refusing to shave his beard for the official pre-season team photograph. At 23, Kennedy was desperate to get away, and when Liverpool came calling, it was the 'ideal' escape.

"The people at Newcastle saw me as a disruptive influence. Me and some of the other players managed to get Richard Dinnis the manager's job after being in charge the year before McGarry became the manager. A lot of the youngsters in the team liked Dinnis and thought he was a decent man and we all wanted him to be manager, so we went to the chairman and told him so. The board gave him the job and we we're all really happy. But then we lost something like 10 out of the first 11 games and he got sacked – proving we were wrong.

"Then they gave the job to McGarry and I hated the guy. I didn't care about him and he didn't care about me. In the end I grew this big, bushy, stupid beard just to piss him off, because he didn't like people with opinions. When they took the team photo just before I left for Liverpool, I still had this beard and people sometimes look back at it now and ask who it is. The problem with it was that it had more grey hairs in it than it does now. It looked ridiculous because perms weren't in just yet. McGarry spoke to me like a kid. But I was 23 and I'd already given the club good service. I didn't like the way I was being treated, so I was desperate for someone to come in for me. Anyone."

Luckily for Kennedy, three big clubs had spotted his talent. The papers acknowledged two of the clubs, but didn't realise another one was also preparing a bid.

"I knew that Man City and Leeds were both in for me. I was an up-and-coming player reaching what would be the peak of my career. I'd already played more than 200 games for Newcastle and had represented England Under-21s and Under-23s, so people knew about me and I knew that clubs were looking at me. What I didn't know was that the other club that wanted me was Liverpool.

"The story goes that Bob Paisley told Geoff that he wanted a left-back. I was playing a pre-season friendly with Newcastle against Hull City. The score was 0-0 and I played ok. Apparently Geoff paid for himself to go in the ground and sit in the stands. He knew Leeds were interested, so he didn't want people spotting him there. He sent his report back to Bob Paisley and within days the fee was set at £330,000. It was on Geoff's recommendation that Liverpool paid that amount. I only found out about Liverpool's approach through a journalist in Newcastle who came round to my house and told me about it. That was the first I heard about it and I didn't have a clue Liverpool were looking at me. I didn't know how transfers were conducted, what players were doing and what scouts were doing, so I just played my own game.

"City and Leeds were interested too and if I'm honest, I regarded City as a massive club and even bigger than Man Utd. They had great players like Francis Lee and Mike Summerbee and I remember thinking how much I would have loved to be playing with them. When Newcastle told me about the bid, the chairman went to say 'L' and I was convinced he would say Leeds. But it was Liverpool. Geoff had gone about his business very quietly."

Even though Kennedy had no inkling about Liverpool's approach, he'd always harboured dreams of a move to Anfield. "I'd been on an end-of-season tour with England B across Malaysia at the start of that summer, and as you do when you're a player, you talk amongst each other about what it is like at the different clubs. David Fairclough told me what a great club Liverpool was. He wasn't playing a great deal at the time, so I thought if he was happy when he's not playing, they must be a really good club. In some ways, I always hoped that Bob Paisley would take some pity on me and sign me for Liverpool. He was from the same part of the north-east as my mother and they actually knew each other way back. So deep down I hoped Bob would come in and try and buy me."

This dream was made a reality when Paisley tabled a British record £330,000 bid for the full-back in early August '78. It was a fee that took

Kennedy by surprise, but flattered him in equal measure. "I thought the transfer fee was excessive. I knew Newcastle were desperate for money. They wanted to sell me and Irving Nattrass, who was right-back. When it went to £330,000, I couldn't believe it. I saw the 10 o'clock news and the leading story was 'Liverpool smash the transfer record for a full-back'. I couldn't believe it was me. Negotiations were quite simple when I came to agreeing my contract. Peter Robinson told me what they were offering me and if I didn't accept it, they would go elsewhere. I couldn't grab the pen off him quick enough."

After signing on the dotted line, Twentyman approached Kennedy and explained that he had had his name inked into his scouting book for some time, so when Paisley asked him to find a left-back, he knew exactly where to look. "It was at a city centre hotel. Geoff told me that they'd watched me a little bit the season before, and when Bob had asked him to find a left-back, he looked in his scouting book and I was one of the first players he thought he should come and see. Liverpool had a few left-backs, with Joey Jones and Emlyn Hughes as well as Colin Irwin and Brian Kettle coming through, but he must have regarded it as a bit of a problem position to spend that amount of money on me. Geoff told him my strengths as well as the things I needed to improve on, but Bob knew my family and understood what type of person he was signing. He knew I was raised in the right way. Most of the lads in our area worked down the mines and Bob realised that he was signing a hard-working player in me. The only thing Geoff said directly to me was that I needn't worry about the transfer fee, to play my own game, get up and down the wings and provide crosses for the forwards."

Unfortunately for Kennedy and the club, he struggled to repay the fee straight away. After a less than unimpressive debut at Anfield against QPR, Paisley allegedly remarked: "I think they shot the wrong Kennedy!" But soon enough, thanks to some gentle words from Twentyman and the faith of Paisley, Kennedy soon began to look secure as the club's first-choice left-back.

"Liverpool were taking a little bit of a gamble on me to some extent. The biggest thing for me was that I wasn't used to playing a passing style of football. All McGarry wanted us to do at Newcastle was knock it long into the channels as soon as possible. I have to say, I think Bob was a little bit disappointed in me in the months after I signed for the club. My form wasn't that good. Bob just wanted me to play it short and simple, whereas I was used to playing long-ball. It took me a while to settle into playing the Liverpool way and I am almost certain that Geoff and Bob sat down a couple of times and debated whether they'd signed the right player. But over time, my game got better.

"One of my biggest allies was Tom Saunders. He always said that he would have 10 Alan Kennedys in his team. He always said that if there was a war on, I would be the first to go over the top. But he also said I'd be the first to get shot! Tom said that my attitude got me through my first few months at the club because I would always be the first to volunteer my name. I didn't care who I was playing against because I was playing for Liverpool.

"After time, I think I proved I could be a success because I settled down and began to understand about how important it was to live and play the right way. Geoff helped me with this because I felt I could go to him and speak when I had problems. Geoff would tell me all about Liverpool Football Club and the standards it upheld. Sammy Lee would go to him as well. He sometimes needed an arm round the shoulder and Geoff was good like that. We never regarded Geoff as simply a scout, he was more a part of the backroom staff. It was all part of one family."

Kennedy would prove to be one of Twentyman's most valuable signings for the club. Barney, as he was soon to be known (after his distinctive running style akin to Barney Rubble), scored two winning goals in European Cup finals – a feat that remains unsurpassed to this day.

8. The Players 1981-1986

Ian Rush, Bruce Grobbelaar, Steve Nicol, Simon Garner,
Jim Magilton, Tim Flowers, Tony Cascarino

LIVERPOOL maintained their dominance of the domestic and the European game throughout the '80s, but new challengers came from Aston Villa then Everton. Even though Twentyman remained at Anfield until 1986, his final entry as a Liverpool scout in the diary is in 1982. Two of the last players he looked at were Paul Rideout, then of Swindon, and Simon Garner, the Blackburn Rovers centre forward.

There is a four-year gap between entries in the diary although they follow on seamlessly from one year to another across page. This is maybe because, as we later discover, Twentyman was forced to adopt a more bureaucratic approach and report to his superiors at the club by the beginning of the '80s, providing a broader summary of his findings. Maybe it left his diary resigned to years of gathering dust in his office drawer as he completed lengthier dossiers by other means.

It is possible that he returned to his tried and trusted methods when he moved to Glasgow Rangers under Graeme Souness because by October '86, he'd started making new entries. Twentyman scouted youngsters Kevin Pressman and Nigel Worthington, the former Sheffield Wednesday pair, as well as Everton's Neil Pointon during his spell in Scotland. Only one of his three years at Ibrox is charted in the diary, leaving countless blank pages towards the back. Maybe It indicates that when he bought the diary, he thought he'd be involved in football a lot longer and fill it up with even more names. Twentyman was only 59 when he retired.

IAN RUSH

Liverpool's greatest goalscorer took a while to warm up after signing from Chester, but after he scored against Oulun Palloseura in 1981, the goals started to flow.

Signed: *from Chester for £300,000 in May 1980*
(and again from Juventus for £270,000 in August 1988)
Age when signed: *18 (26)*
Total LFC appearances/goals: *660/346*
Seasons spent at Liverpool: *15*
Birthplace: *St Asaph, Wales*
Other clubs: *Chester City, Juventus, Leeds United, Newcastle United, Sheffield United (loan), Wrexham, Sydney Olympic*

SOUTHERN romantics say that Crystal Palace were the team of the '80s. Not Liverpool. Or even Everton. Despite the fact that between them the captains of Liverpool (and Everton) lifted 10 different major trophies, played the most exciting football and scored more goals than any other teams in England, it was Terry Venables' Palace that were 'the team of the '80s'. Apparently.

They could have been, however, had Ian Rush signed for them barely a year after becoming a Red. Liverpool paid a world record transfer fee for a teenager to snare Rush from under the nostrils of Manchester City scouts, and much was expected from the moustachioed 18-year-old. But he failed to score a first-team goal for more than 12 months at Anfield, and was banished like Terry McDermott before him to the reserves for much of that time.

"There was a point when people were asking why Liverpool had spent all this money on me," says Rush. "That was when Palace put a bid in for me. Things might have been different if I went there. Palace were going places under Terry Venables and maybe I'd have been able to help them. But it's a good job I stayed at Liverpool because before long David Johnson got injured and I got the call to play for the first team."

Geoff Twentyman spotted Rush playing for Chester City and later told the press: 'I watched him six times and finally, at an away game at Rotherham, I decided that despite his youth, we had to strike quickly. A lot of other clubs were holding back waiting for further proof. Liverpool took some criticism at first when people said that £300,000 was too much for a teenager.'

According to his closest friend in football Norman Clarke, a director at Liverpool was one of the people who questioned Twentyman's wisdom, rasping: 'That's a lot of money you've spent on a dud', as he walked past the chief scout in the corridors of power at Anfield. 'He'll prove you wrong,' was the response from Twentyman.

Rush insists that he gave the move to Palace serious consideration, but Bob Paisley was desperate for him to demonstrate his worth and ended up rejecting the approach personally. "Geoff and Bob's words to me at this point made me understand I needed to be patient and made me realise that I would break through sooner or later. Geoff would talk to me at Melwood and tell me to get my head down and graft, and he was right. He probably paid a bit of extra attention to me because of his involvement in my move to Liverpool and he would always tell me just to keep on doing what I was doing. But he was like that with all the young lads."

Rush, however, wasn't aware at all about Twentyman's role within his transfer until long after he signed for Liverpool. "When I moved to Anfield, I didn't even know Geoff existed. Even for a good few weeks or months, I didn't know what role he played in the transfer because he was always away watching players. He must have been very busy because I signed towards the end of the 1981 season, April time I think, so at that time of year he must have been looking at more new players for the following season. I only got to know him when he came down to the training ground, and it was then that I realised he played such a big role in my move to Liverpool, along with Tom Saunders who also came to see me at Chester."

Rush's stock as an up-and-coming player had risen after scoring a goal for Chester in the FA Cup against Newcastle. This strike, he says, raised his profile and soon Liverpool and Manchester City were scrapping for his signature.

"Because Newcastle were top of the old Second Division [now the Championship], it alerted other clubs to my ability. It was a great day that, and it had a massive influence on me going to Liverpool because Geoff realised that he had to move quickly if he was going to sign me. In some ways the goal might have been an annoyance to Geoff because it meant my price would increase while it would also make it more difficult for him to remain unnoticed at games. If I hadn't scored that goal, Liverpool would have signed me for a lot less, that's for sure."

Despite Rush's form for Chester, Liverpool's approach took everyone by surprise, mainly because people in the know presumed that a deal would be arranged with Man City. "It was well known that City were looking at me, and with Alan Oakes [a former City player with more than 600 appearances behind him] my boss at Chester, it seemed inevitable that I would end up going there. People in football talk and it was clear that City wanted me. I remember Trevor Storton, who played for Liverpool and was in his early 30s, said that a move to City would be the best move I could make. But City felt I needed longer to progress and the deal didn't represent value for money in their eyes."

City, according to Rush, weren't the only club sniffing around Sealand Road, Chester's former home. "I was an Evertonian back then and when I found Gordon Lee was coming to watch me, it excited me. But he didn't see anything in me. That was where Geoff was a bit special because he could see something that others didn't and could see that in the right environment alongside Bob Paisley and Tom Saunders, I could develop. Everyone at Liverpool was good at their jobs and above everything they trusted each other. That's why

Liverpool were successful. Bob Paisley only watched me once or twice but Geoff's opinion counted."

Rush then explains that he'd already rejected a move to Liverpool once by the time he finally signed for them. "Liverpool put a bid in for me a few months before. Alan Oakes told me about it and I felt that I needed more time playing first team football, so I turned them down. That's right – I turned Liverpool down!

"I just felt the move wasn't right for me because all I wanted to do was play first-team football regularly. Liverpool were so good then, I never thought I was going to get a game. It was common to sign younger lads and let them learn the Liverpool way in the reserves. I was playing first-team football with Chester City in front of decent-sized crowds and really enjoying it, so I saw no reason to move.

"But towards the end of the season Liverpool came in again. This time I couldn't say no. I realised that they had really big hopes and the fact they were still watching me after me saying no the first time proved that they really liked what they saw. I realised that even if things didn't work out at Liverpool, the experience I would gain would be invaluable for the rest of my career. At Liverpool, even if you didn't make the first team, a lot of players moved on elsewhere further down the leagues and did ok because everyone was after a player who had been lucky enough to have developed their game at Liverpool. So I figured out it was worth a shot."

Rush may have been an Evertonian, but the magnetism of Anfield, Melwood and its history made the move to the Red side all the more easy. "Bob Paisley asked me to go up to the training ground before I agreed anything, just to have a look around. So I went there with my dad and I felt there was something special. I was instantly drawn in about the history of the place and the way people treated me, so I couldn't turn it down. I was sitting next to Alan Hansen and Ray Clemence in the dressing room and at first it was daunting. But after a few months and after realising that everyone else was just as human as me, I found that I was good enough to play for Liverpool and started to believe in myself a lot more."

And then the problems started. "It was a more than a year before I made it into the first team. It was frustrating because I was so used to playing every week, but I'd already prepared myself for it. It's the right way to run a football team from the playing side of things because Liverpool reserves played exactly the same way as Liverpool first team. I don't know who did it first, but it is exactly the same thing that Ajax do now and always have done. It means that a young lad can come into the first team and know exactly what his job is straight away. It means that it's easier to blood young lads and easier to have continuation."

Despite Rush's early problems, he says that the transfer fee never played on his mind – in fact it acted as an inspiration. "Geoff had the confidence to tell them to go and do it. If the fee ever played on my mind, I just thought what Geoff was thinking because ultimately Geoff lived and died on his observations and if I didn't make it, it would look bad on him, probably more than me. He rarely looked bad, though, because of his success rate. I looked at the players he'd previously signed and it gave me a lot of confidence because 99 per cent of them had been success stories."

The signs that Rush's early months at Liverpool wouldn't go to plan were there from his very first day at the club. "When you sign for Liverpool Football Club, you assume that everything is the best. The day I signed, we all got changed at Anfield before getting the bus up to Melwood. But it broke down on the corner of Utting Avenue. It was good because it made me realise that everyone was humble, really. We all went down to Melwood in cars. Terry Mac and Sammy Lee went: 'Jump in the car with us', so that's what I did. They were so down to earth and it made me realise how much of a family club Liverpool was. Everyone there looked after each other and we took that onto the pitch."

BRUCE GROBBELAAR

Grobbelaar debuted for Liverpool in August 1981 and remained ever-present for five years. He kept his place until 1993/94 when David James took over and Bruce went to Southampton. He won League Cup, FA Cup, league championship and European Cup winners' medals with the Reds.

Signed: *from Vancouver Whitecaps for £250,000 in March 1981*
Age when signed: *23*
Total LFC appearances: *628*
Seasons spent at Liverpool: *13*
Birthplace: *Durban, South Africa*
Other clubs: *Crewe (loan), Stoke City (loan), Southampton, Plymouth, Oxford, Sheffield Wednesday, Oldham, Bury, Lincoln*

BRUCE GROBBELAAR was a Rhodesian-born, South African-raised Zimbabwe international that could have represented Canada instead, before getting stranded in Paris' Charles de Gaulle Airport only to settle in Merseyside for 15 years of his life. He also fought for two nations but he was no soldier of fortune.

The former Reds' number one had a long and eventful road to Anfield. It was also the most unusual in the club's history. Before his arrival, the last African-born player to represent Liverpool was Berry Nieuwenhuys, 'Nivvy' for those who couldn't pronounce his unusual-sounding surname. He left shortly after the Second World War, but played in 260 games, scoring an impressive 79 goals from the wing. Before him there was Harman van den Berg, Hugh Gerhardi, Lance Carr and the great Gordon Hodgson. But none of them endured such a colourful journey to becoming a winner of European Cups. Equally, none enjoyed as much luck in being spotted by Liverpool talent scouts. This time, though, it wasn't Geoff Twentyman that found him.

Tom Saunders was Liverpool's youth development officer between 1968 and 1986. He was appointed by Bill Shankly and, like Geoff Twentyman, remained in place throughout the reigns of Bob Paisley, Joe

Fagan and Kenny Dalglish. Saunders also spied on Liverpool's European opponents (the Reds won four European Cups during this time so he obviously did a good job) and make dossiers on lesser known players and clubs across the continent. Although his main role was overseeing the development of youth players, he also scouted potential transfer targets. He enjoyed similar powers to Geoff Twentyman and deserves credit in his own right for nurturing the talents of local boys David Fairclough, Jimmy Case and Sammy Lee, especially. Later, Saunders recommended Phil Thompson to Gerard Houllier for the appointment as assistant manager at the club in 1998. One player he scouted in mind for the first team, rather than the youth team, amongst many others, was Bruce Grobbelaar.

"Tom Saunders, Geoff Twentyman and another scout called Peter Dee came to watch me at different stages," says Grobbelaar. "But it was Tom who spotted me first at Crewe. There were other teams watching me too. The strongest interest came from Manchester City. They really wanted me but took too long."

Grobbelaar arrived at Crewe via the Rhodesian National Guard (where he fought in the Bush War), Jomo Cosmos (based in Johannesburg) and Vancouver Whitecaps. Before his spell in Canada, he'd flown to Britain for a trial with West Bromwich Albion. "The great incredible hulk, Ron Atkinson, was in charge," he jokes. "It all came about because I knew Colin Addison who was his assistant manager. Colin tried to sign me in 1975 for Durban City. I was in the Rhodesian Army at that point and Colin was willing to make the club pay money to buy my contract from the army. I wanted to go, but they wouldn't let me leave and by the time I did get out, Colin had left South Africa.

"I ended up playing for Jomo Cosmos, and within 18 months I had to do National Service in the South African army as well. I was living with a guy in Durban who'd played for Wolves and he knew how keen I was to go abroad, so he contacted Colin, who'd moved to West Brom and he persuaded Colin to pay for me to go over there for a trial. They liked me there and enquired about getting a work permit, but it was rejected. Eventually they had to get an 'alien book', which was basically a pass into the country for an extra two months. But they couldn't sort out a work permit, so it was decided that I would go back to South Africa. Before I left, though, I went to Derby County for a bit, then Colin contacted Tony Waiters, who was manager at Vancouver Whitecaps. The restrictions meant it was easier to get into Canada, so I went there to learn my trade."

Waiters, who John Gidman earlier said played such an instrumental part in him leaving Liverpool, had a more positive influence on Grobbelaar's career. "It was completely different because as everyone knows, the whole of Canada is obsessed by basketball and baseball. It was good for me as a young goalkeeper because it meant I could learn without any outside pressures. The only people who put us under pressure were the people involved in the team, so it meant younger players like me could concentrate on playing football and learning quickly. In my first year over there, I was back-up to Phil Parkes who used to play for Wolverhampton Wanderers and I only played four games in the whole campaign. We won the Soccer Bowl, though, and I got my medal. I played against Washington, San Diego and Minneapolis in the away games, so it meant a lot of travelling."

In his second season, Grobbelaar played in nearly every match. His performances were so good that Waiters included him in his long-term plans – which could have changed the history of Canadian football forever had they come to fruition. "I was really enjoying playing out there. Tony wanted people like myself and Carl Valentine who played for Oldham to stay out there and become naturalised Canadians. I think Tony knew that if he did a good job with Vancouver he would have a good chance of getting the Canadian national job so he wanted the better players to stay for three years – it only took that amount of time before they offered you a passport – and try and qualify for some major tournaments. Tony thought that if youngsters like myself and Carl stayed out there, over the years Canada could get stronger.

"Then Liverpool came in and Tony, a little bit reluctantly, allowed me to speak to Bob Paisley. It was as if he could see into the future because in 1984, he took Canada to the Olympic Games then two years later, they played at the World Cup in Mexico. Tony didn't stand in my way in the end. But had Liverpool not come in for me, I would have been more than happy to stay in Canada. Vancouver is a beautiful, beautiful place and if Tony had told me to take my time over a decision, there is a chance I would have stayed there for another year and get naturalised.

"It was in the interim between going back to Canada after being on loan at Crewe that Zimbabwe asked me to play for them. Tony said: 'Wait, become a Canadian.' The main reason why I chose to play for Zimbabwe was down to the fact that I'd chosen to move to England. It was the place I had grown up and I felt I owed something back, but had I stayed in Vancouver it is likely I would have played for Canada. Now, it's a regret because I missed out three World Cups at the last qualifying round with Zimbabwe."

Grobbelaar was enjoying a spell on loan to Crewe when he attracted Liverpool's attention. The move to Crewe came as a short-term fix to both player and club. Grobbelaar had finished his domestic campaign with Vancouver, while Crewe were in desperate need for a 'keeper on the cheap after struggling in the lower leagues.

"It was a completely different world at Crewe," Grobbelaar reflects. "First of all, the NASL was played in the summer. Coming over to Crewe was a learning curve because I wasn't used to playing in the cold. That stretched all the way back to my days in Rhodesia and South Africa. It was never cold. Even though we played in the winter the only time we experienced different conditions was down in Cape Town, which is a blustery city mainly down to its geographical location. I would never go there in the winter because the temperature drops to nine or 10 degrees with a terrible chill factor. That was the only example of consistently cold weather I'd ever experienced.

"When I made my debut at the terrible Springfield Park against Wigan, the pitch was rock hard because it had been a dry summer. I ended up playing the game in Astroturf boots because the pitch was bone hard. Later we played at Rochdale and it had been pissing down all day. The pitch was muddy and wet and I remember diving to save a shot in the first minute and not having anything else to do in the next half an hour. I was standing there freezing cold and soaked wet through. I was frozen and I started thinking of Vancouver."

Despite Grobbelaar's problems adjusting to the weather, he excelled at Gresty Road and his performances attracted the attention of both Liverpool and Manchester City. "I was told about Liverpool in the March of 1980. Then after a game in Portsmouth the following month, I heard about it again. We drew the game 1-1 and a Northern Irish chap called Nicky Guy scored both goals; one of them was an own goal. It's funny how these back passes from these Irish people go sailing over my head [he is referring, of course, to Ronnie Whelan's own goal at Old Trafford]."

A deal with Grobbelaar's parent club Vancouver Whitecaps was hammered out very quickly (despite the pleas of Waiters) and within weeks, he'd flown to and from western Canada to pick up his belongings. "When I was told I was getting sold for a quarter of a million, I was speechless," he continues. "Is this for real? It was a lot of money for a chap who had only played for a Canadian team for two seasons."

If Grobbelaar thought he'd finally secured a permanent deal in England, though, he was wrong. "The record books say that I signed on the 17th March 1981, but I actually signed the day before," he explains. "Because of problems with my passport and work permit – Zimbabwe weren't in the Commonwealth back then – I had to go out of the country to get back in. Bob Paisley gave me a ticket to go to France, so I flew over there and stayed with one of Peter Robinson's mates for a night. But when I got to Charles de Gaulle, they wouldn't let me in because I needed a visa. I only had a Rhodesian passport. Luckily I saw a woman who told me I could get a shopping visa, which would last me 24 hours before I had to leave again."

It was only when Grobbelaar arrived at Melwood to fully finalise the deal that he realised who had been watching for Liverpool. "I am eternally grateful to Tom," he says. So what did Saunders see in him that others didn't? "I used to catch the ball because I always played wicket-keeper at cricket. I played a lot of baseball too and South African rugby, so I was used to catching different balls in all kinds of positions. This added a spring in my game. I was different to other keepers and the Liverpool scouts really liked that."

Different he certainly was. Saunders had spotted a person that would change the way goalkeepers played. In 24 games for Crewe, he scored a penalty, picked up a booking (apparently for warming up while wearing a face mask of an old man) and impressed sufficiently to catch the eye of Saunders.

Bob Paisley once spoke of seeing Grobbelaar warming up by having one of his teammates blast a ball at him from the edge of the box. "He not only stopped everything, but caught it." Paisley promptly left Gresty Road without even seeing him play, such was his conviction that he was the man to keep goal for his team.

Technically, his ability was never in doubt. "Until Bruce burst on the scene," said former Arsenal goalkeeper Bob Wilson, "it was a rarity for a keeper to go for a high ball beyond 12 yards from his goal or to sweep up behind his defence more than 25-30 yards from his goal-line. His philosophy knows no limits. If a ball is in the air long enough to allow him to catch it 17 yards from goal, then attempt to catch it he will." Bruce Grobbelaar undoubtedly made mistakes during his Liverpool career, but he redefined the boundaries of what was acceptable for goalkeepers to do. Without Anfield's scouts, this may never have happened.

STEVE NICOL

Nicol became one of Liverpool's most versatile players. He managed to fill six different positions in the 1988/89 season. Nicol won four league titles, three FA Cups and one European Cup at Liverpool.

Signed: *from Ayr for £300,000 in October 1981*
Age when signed: *19*
Total LFC appearances/goals: *468/46*
Seasons spent at Liverpool: *14*
Birthplace: *Ayrshire*
Other clubs: *Ayr, Notts County, Sheffield Wednesday, West Bromwich Albion (loan), Doncaster, Boston Bulldogs (USA)*

Scouting diary notes:
22.03.80: 'A good potential player. Strong and looks adaptable. Should make a good defender' (GT)
'Scotland v Sweden under 21. Nicol playing at RB. Was very comfortable and going forward was always a problem for the opposition as in previous reports he appears a player we should sign'

STEVE NICOL sat on a plastic seat. Orange in colour. "The type issued at school." Down a quiet and unremarkable corridor somewhere inside Anfield's Main Stand, he waited for 45 minutes. Time dragged. Like in a dentist's waiting room, Nicol looked around for something to capture his mind, but nothing happened and the longing continued. Eventually, breaking the hush, a wrinkled man and club servant popped his head out of an unmarked door. "Ey Stephen...cup of tea?" he said in an old Scouse croak. "Conversation, finally," thought Nicol.

Ayr United boss Willie McClean had driven Nicol to Liverpool after accepting a bid of £300,000. The young Scot waited outside a room while McClean agreed the finer details of the deal with Liverpool manager Bob Paisley and chairman John Smith. It was done within minutes. After McClean had left the room and driven back to Scotland, telling his now former player to stay in the chair before he departed, Nicol was called into the chairman's office where he promptly signed the contract. "I don't know what took them so long after Willie left the building," says Nicol. "They probably wanted me to soak up the atmosphere of Anfield. It would have been typical of Liverpool. Instead all I did was have a chat with this old geezer."

Nicol says that he'd just been "treading water" at Ayr when Paisley originally made an approach. He could scarcely believe that a club the size of Liverpool had bothered visiting Ayr's Somerset Park just to watch him. "Once again, it was classic Liverpool. Nobody had a clue they were interested, including me. I certainly didn't find out until a long time after I signed for Liverpool how everything worked out. I supported Rangers, but Ayr United were my local team and my dad took me to watch them. When I signed, it made him very proud because I grew up watching players like Ricky Fleming and now I was wearing the white shirt. But I never expected to end up playing most of my career in the red of Liverpool."

Nicol then explains that Geoff Twentyman told him that he'd been informed by a scout that worked for him in the west of Scotland that there were a couple of players coming through the system at Ayr. And he was the one that stood out. "Geoff came and saw me five or six times. I was none the wiser and played my normal game. I think he got one of his scouts to arrange the tickets, so nobody apart from Geoff and the scout concerned would know about Liverpool's interest so it took the club by surprise too when the bid was made. Maybe it was my red hair that made me stand out!"

Twentyman said in an article published in *The Weekly News* in January 1982, shortly after Nicol signed for Liverpool, that he watched him for 18 months before making the decision to recommend a move for him. 'I realised Nichol [sic] had pace, two good feet and sound tactical awareness. But he was playing in a poorish grade of football. Would he do it at a higher level? A performance for the

Scotland Under-21 side convinced me. Alongside players from the English First Division and Scottish Premier League, he held his own. He looked a classy player. I gave Bob the nod. He has a great future...'

The fact that the journalist and Twentyman in his book spells Nicol's name incorrectly is either down to a lack of research, or down to the simple idea that Nicol was an unknown at the time.

Nicol recalls the game for the Under-21 side. It was against Sweden at the home of Hibernian, Easter Road. "I didn't play that well at all," he concedes. "But Geoff saw something in me that others may not have. It was classic Liverpool and classic Geoff. When I left I felt that I definitely wasn't playing at my best. Geoff was brilliant at his job, though. He took good performances and bad performances and treated them the same. Sometimes when you see a player at his worst, you learn more about him. It's very different now, of course. Liverpool have gone public in their pursuit of players like Gareth Barry and it makes no sense to me. Why would you want to let everyone know what you're up to?"

Nicol says that his first position at Ayr was at right-back and although he felt he could play in midfield, he never believed that he would end up becoming one of the most versatile players in the history of Liverpool Football Club. A quick glance across teamsheets throughout the 1980s proves that Nicol felt comfortable anywhere on the pitch. He wore number 2, 4, 5, 8, 10 and 11 for the five years immediately after he signed. Like Twentyman said, he had 'two good feet and sound tactical awareness.'

Nicol says, "I believe that when Liverpool first signed me, they thought I would succeed Phil Neal. Phil was a tough player to dislodge, though, and he never missed a game, so I ended up being moved around here, there and everywhere. Some players say that versatility means you never nail down a position and suffer as a result. But I played in nearly every game once I had established myself, so it didn't do me much harm at all."

Twentyman later suggested that one of the main reasons why he decided to sign Nicol was after he confided in Jock Stein, the former boss of Celtic and Scotland. "I know Jock liked me. But I don't know whether that is true. He picked me for Scotland later on. Jock was one of my heroes. There have only been a couple of people in my life that I have been completely in awe of. So if big Jock spoke to Geoff about me, then that makes me delighted."

After waiting in the corridor for so long before signing the contract, it was only when Nicol stepped out on the Anfield pitch that he realised how far this move had taken him. "I came from Ayr United, a small humble club, to the biggest, most successful club in Europe, which as it turned out was even more humble than Ayr. Given Liverpool's status at the time, I thought it was going to be all razzmatazz, big-time Charlie, that kind of thing. But when I got there, everything was just so down to earth. Run of the mill. Nobody was better than anyone else and everyone was there to do a job. If we did the job, then we would succeed and that's what happened."

Part of Nicol's unassuming introduction to the Liverpool way of thinking was being put into digs with the Pike family, "in a house that was no more than 20 paces from Anfield. If I fell out of bed, I was practically at the Shankly gates.

"Again, it was so humble. The attitude was that you are nothing until you have done something, but even those who had done something acted like they had done nothing. Their attitude was the same: 'Ok, you play for Liverpool. Now let's get on with things.' When I walked into the dressing room the day after I signed, it was clear that this was the way the whole way through the club. I walked in and everyone was down to earth and welcomed me.

"On my left side there was Alan Hansen, to my right it was Ian Rush and Kenny Dalglish. It was so not big time, it was scary. That attitude came from the top of the club and I am sure that Geoff looked for players who had a similar attitude. It was instrumental in why I settled down so quickly. As soon as I walked through the dressing room door, I felt like I was part of the furniture."

SIMON GARNER

*Garner joined Blackburn as an apprentice and turned professional in
1978. He became the club's record goalscorer, with 168 goals in 484
appearances. In his final season at the club, they were promoted to the
Premier League.*

Birthplace: *Boston, Lincolnshire*
Position: *Striker*
Clubs: *Blackburn Rovers, West Bromwich Albion, Wycombe Wanderers,
Torquay United*

Scouting diary notes:
**'Watched on a number of occasions. A useful alround [sic] midfield
come goalscorer. Would do well I think in a better team than
Blackburn' (GT)**
11.10.86: 'Experienced player. Good front player' (GT)

SIMON GARNER was a footballer that smoked 20 a day, drank to the
edge of oblivion, instigated practical jokes, drove his managers to dis-
traction, and spent time in the nick after a messy divorce from his wife.
He is the kind of player that despite his indiscretions is remembered
fondly by all who met him – the hell-raiser that makes you say there
isn't enough of his type in the modern game.

More than that, at least to supporters of Blackburn Rovers, he was an
effigy of everything for which the club stood. While QPR had Stan
Bowles and Wolves had Derek Dougan, Blackburn had Simon Garner.
Liverpool simply didn't have a player of this ilk. Cult heroes, after all,
are usually carved out of periods of non-success as a figure onto which
a supporter can cling for hope. At Everton, see Duncan Ferguson.

Garner is associated with playing for only one club – even though he
also appeared for West Brom and achieved some notoriety with Martin
O'Neill's emerging Wycombe Wanderers team at the beginning
of the 1990s. If you think about him and his Blackburn side, it conjures

images of ill-fitting pale blue and white jerseys, thigh hugging shorts and frantic goalmouth scrambles on boggy pitches. Rovers fans will add that it takes them back to a game when a quick throw-in, assisted by an over-enthusiastic ball girl at Ewood Park, led to an injury-time equaliser from Liverpool in the FA Cup. Jimmy Hill was typically lugubrious on 'Match of the Day' later that evening, blaming the girl who didn't realise her act would create such a whirl of controversy.

Even today, 16 years after he last played for Blackburn, the chant "There's Only One Simon Garner" frequently echoes round Ewood Park. Quite how a man who never played in the Premier League, or even won it as Blackburn did in 1995, could become a kind of virtuous talisman might seem a mystery, especially when you consider Alan Shearer succeeded him as the club's chief goalscorer. To the supporters, though, Garner was always one of their own. Even after he'd sunk a Second Division hat-trick on a Saturday afternoon, he always had time to sink a few pints, have a laugh and enjoy a fag with fans in town centre pubs later that night.

Garner insists that he wasn't alone in his off-the-field escapades, and says that his attitude towards the game was similar to lots of others' during his time: "The difference with me," he points out, "is that I enjoyed all of life's pleasures in full view of the fans on a Saturday night, so everyone knew about it. Even today, I know a lot of players that smoke. The French ones especially." Maybe this is why Geoff Twentyman decided not to recommend him to Liverpool in 1982 or Glasgow Rangers in 1986. "Some people say smoking affected my game and made me struggle with fitness," Garner adds, "but I always tell those people that I couldn't run more than 50 yards anyway…"

Had Liverpool moved for Garner it would have been for his goalscoring ability rather than his all-round attributes. He came alive in the penalty area and did little out of it. Few of his goals would gain points in aesthetics, but he was always there, sliding across a penalty box with the ball usually rippling the back of the net, typically via a deflection.

Twentyman watched Garner over several years – the last time coming in a game that Blackburn lost by a single goal to West Bromwich Albion, a club Garner later signed for. He had no idea that Twentyman was scouting him in 1986 when he was 27, or even five years earlier at 22, although he wouldn't be surprised if other First Division clubs were lurking around Ewood Park too.

"Maybe I had lots of offers that I didn't know about. I was scoring goals regularly, so naturally scouts would probably have a look at me. The club told me that they would be honest and if anyone came in for me they would let me know. Maybe they didn't.

"But hey, I have no regrets about anything at all. When I signed for Blackburn, it was my ambition to be the club's top scorer, to play at Wembley and to play in the First Division. Although I didn't achieve the last one, it was my choice not to."

Blackburn achieved promotion to the Premier League via the play-offs in 1992 after Kenny Dalglish was appointed at Ewood Park. Although Garner was offered a deal to stay, he was now nearing his 32nd birthday and decided to prolong his career elsewhere.

"Kenny was honest and told me that I could stay if I wanted to, but I wouldn't be playing regularly in the first team. I thought that because I was 31 and understood that football was a short career, I needed to be playing. When West Brom came in, I was ready to go because Ossie Ardiles was manager and I wanted to play for him. I'd played with Ossie at Blackburn and I liked him so I thought I might as well go for it."

Garner says he was privileged in his career to play under so many great managers. Before Dalglish arrived, he enjoyed spells with Jim Smith, Howard Kendall, Bobby Saxton and Don Mackay. "I learnt something under every manager I played for. Ninety-nine per cent of it was good stuff as well." Despite Dalglish being his favourite player of all time, he adds that Saxton was the best manager he worked for because of the number of goals he scored while under his stewardship. "Bobby had no money to spend and he did a great job at Rovers so I would say him. Kenny was great too, but he had it a little easier because he had money.

"I would have said Kenny was my favourite manager but he dropped me in his first proper game in charge. When he took over, he let Tony Parkes pick the team in a match against Plymouth and I scored two. The next week, I was left out! We did have a lot of good strikers on the books by then, though. You could tell early on at Wycombe that Martin O'Neill was destined to become a great manager too."

Born in Lincolnshire, Garner started playing for a Sunday league team owned by the secretary of Boston United, who were then managed by Howard Wilkinson. At 16 he joined Blackburn as a trainee after previous Pilgrim boss Jim Smith had asked the secretary to recommend any promising players to him. Rather than sign for Boston, or Scunthorpe who also made him an offer, Garner followed the call of Smith.

Soon after moving to Lancashire, however, his career was threatened by youth team boss John 'Pick' Pickering, who was unimpressed with his apprentice's already rabid smoking habits and proposed to Smith that he be sacked and packed off back across the Pennines. Rather than bring his Rovers career to a premature end, the Bald Eagle called the youngster into his manager's office and advised him not to get caught smoking in future, offering him a cigar on his way out – a present he duly accepted. Within two years he'd made his first team debut, scoring eight times in his first season. "I have a lot to thank Jim for," Garner chortles. "It would have been over for me there and then and I probably would have ended up playing non-league football or something. But Jim had seen me score and believed in me. He told me that he was taking a gamble on me, and that made me want to prove him right."

Garner played alongside many strikers during his time, from John Radford to Duncan McKenzie (who he points out also smoked more than a Moroccan bazaar), then Steve Archibold to Mike Newell. "Drinking and smoking relaxed me," he says. "In them days, teams went out a lot more together than they do now and were also a lot closer to the fans than what they are now. I lived in Blackburn, right in the centre of the town, so I knew a lot of fans and socialised with them. Probably now, not a single player lives there. I think they all commute from Cheshire."

As Garner points out, he lived with and for the people. He earned good money (£600 a week at its peak), but not silly money. He lived in the town, not in leafy Cheshire. He drove a smart car (not a Smart car), and certainly not something out of a Bond film. He never staged dramatics. No pretension off the pitch, and no dives in the box. And if Blackburn were a goal or two to the bad, and time was ticking on, there was always a chance that Garner would turn it around by popping in a couple of scrappy ones.

When his autobiography was released in 2005, the predictably named *There's Only One Simon Garner*, the Lancashire Evening Post noted: 'Above all, in the pre-Jack Walker days, the club's fans knew that if there was a Blackburn occasion, good or ill, then there would be Garner, chest puffed out, doing his level best... He was there when Jim Iley arrived ("very dour... he made Howard Wilkinson look like Ken Dodd"), he played and drank with Howard Kendall, and was with Bobby Saxton's side when, in a vital game against Wolves, their manager, Tommy Docherty, sat in on the Blackburn team-talk and then calmly stood up saying: "Don't worry about our lot; they're crap." He was there for the descent into the Third Division, the climb out of it, and those agonising seasons when, three years in a row, Blackburn reached the play-offs, only to lose. Even Garner's high times had a Blackburnish quality: a win at Wembley in 1987, but it was only the Full-Members' Cup final; and as Garner broke the club's scoring record in 1989 the celebrations had hardly started before news came through of an unfolding disaster across the Pennines at Hillsborough.'

"My suffering is minuscule compared to those at Hillsborough and their families. So there's absolutely no point talking about my feelings that day," Garner says firmly on the issue.

During his 14 years at Ewood Park, Garner scored 168 times in 455 league games. Had those goals been scored after 1992 in the Premier League, he would have been remembered on a nationwide level as one of the league's all-time folk heroes in much the same way Matt Le Tissier is today (although they were completely different in style). Instead, his infamy is only really recognised in Lancashire.

"I believed I was good enough to play for anyone," he adds. "If a winger put the ball in the box, I always thought I'd get on the end of it. It's an attitude you have to adopt if you're a striker." On the FA Cup tie against Liverpool in 1991, a game in which he opened the scoring, he concludes: "We were robbed that day. I reckon Liverpool fans know that too…"

JIM MAGILTON

Magilton was a midfielder who spent four seasons at Liverpool as an apprentice alongside the likes of Steve McManaman and Mike Marsh. He never played a senior game for the club, and was sold to Oxford United in 1990.

Signed: *As an apprentice for free in 1986*
Age when signed: *16/17*
Total LFC appearances/goals: *0/0*
Seasons spent at Liverpool: *4*
Birthplace: *Belfast*
Other clubs: *Oxford United, Southampton, Sheffield Wednesday, Ipswich*

THERE are surprsingly few Northern Irish players in Liverpool's history that can be labelled as legends. Only Belfast-born goalkeeper Elisha Scott can be afforded such a title having made 468 appearances in 21 years at the club. Dixie Dean described him as his toughest opponent. After Scott, there's only really the ironically named Sam English who scored an impressive 26 goals in 50 games shortly before the Second World War.

It could have been different, especially if ball-playing midfielder Jim Magilton had broken through into Kenny Dalglish's first team towards the end of the 1980s. Magilton, it seemed, had everything in his game to become an archetypal Liverpool player of his time. He had a far-ranging passing ability, he could move quickly from box to box and he boasted a healthy goal ratio. All of this, however, was only proven after leaving Anfield, as Magilton made more than 500 league appearances with Oxford, Southampton, Sheffield Wednesday and Ipswich as well as gaining half a century of international caps.

Now manager of Ipswich, Magilton says that he was simply not good enough to replace those players in front of him. "You just need to look at the list of midfielders we had. There was variation and versatility as well, so it was always going to be very difficult for me." When you consider that Steve McMahon, Ronnie Whelan, Ray Houghton, Jan Molby and even Steve Nicol, who mainly operated as a full-back, were all in the reckoning for midfield berths, it is easy to understand Magilton's previous concern.

Magilton was originally spotted playing for the youth team of Distillery by Jimmy McAlinden, who'd previously won an FA Cup winners' medal with Portsmouth in 1939. "He was a highly recognisable figure in Irish football," Magilton says. "From Geoff's time at Ballymena, he struck up a really good relationship with Jimmy – they were really good friends. Jimmy was always watching youth football and luckily, he liked me. Jimmy came to me one night after a game and said to me: 'Would you like to go to Liverpool?' I was a mad Liverpool fan with posters on my walls and I was 16, so I thought: 'Yeah, what game am I going to watch? Lovely.'

"But then Jimmy said to me: 'No son, you're going there to play. They're going to take you and have a good look at you.' I couldn't believe it, I was like: 'What – you're serious?' I was overjoyed. I was Liverpool-daft and Kenny had just become player-manager and he was my absolute idol, so I couldn't believe they were interested in looking at me. I know

Geoff spent a lot of time in Northern Ireland, but I'm not sure whether he actually came over to watch me there. I was so young, I never in a million years thought anyone would bother watching me, but obviously Geoff and Jimmy saw something they liked and they went for it."

When Magilton flew to Liverpool his first contact at the airport was Twentyman. Only now did he learn of his role within his trial. "I stayed in Geoff's house for the week. The plane was like a washing machine with wings. It was a propeller job...Buddy Holly Airways and it was the first time I travelled by plane so I was frightened. I remember there was lots of fog over Merseyside and I thought: 'F**k me, I'm never going to make it.' I trained well in the week, so they invited me back again and Geoff was there at the airport to pick me up, so I stayed in his house for a second week. At the end of that I was offered a six-month apprenticeship followed by a two-year pro contract. Without Jimmy or Geoff's influence, I doubt I'd have ever made it.

"Because I was such a young lad and I didn't know anyone in the city, Geoff would tell me all kinds of stories to pass the time away. He loved a story. I would sit there and listen with awe because he was talking about Bill Shankly and the time he spent at Ballymena. Jimmy was telling me similar stories too when I got home. I couldn't believe I was privy to all these great tales. F**k me, I mean, I was 16 years old!"

Magilton's enthusiasm when talking about his time at Liverpool is evident, even over a telephone conversation. Despite his Ipswich team being in the midst of a busy pre-season schedule when he talks (signing Dutch defender Pim Balkestein after putting the phone down), he takes time to explain what life was like at Anfield in a distinctive Belfast brogue.

"Geoff took me into the changing rooms as well as meeting the players. One week I was watching these players on 'Match of the Day', the next week I was cleaning up after them. Although there were some shitty jobs, it was an absolute pleasure to do it as an apprentice. Liverpool were flying, the club was bouncing and the education I got there has stood with me throughout my whole career. Working with pros day in day out who were the elite of their profession was the most amazing experience of my life."

It also quickly became apparent to Magilton that every single player at the club knew of Twentyman's presence – especially the younger ones who were keen to impress him. "From the senior pros right down to the 16-year-old trialist like me, everyone knew his name, but few people realised if he was watching a game because he kept such a low profile, even during the trial games. I suppose that explains why I don't know whether he came over to Northern Ireland in the first place. He was inconspicuous. Looking from the side of the game that I am involved in now, people still talk about him and know what he did for Liverpool. He's regarded as one of the great talent spotters in British football. His reputation is that he could spot a player a mile off. That's my claim to fame. Geoff Twentyman and Liverpool Football Club spotted me. Even though I didn't kick a ball for Liverpool, I always cling on to the fact that Geoff spotted me."

Magilton was one of Twentyman's last signings for Liverpool before the scout left the club. "Maybe I got him the sack!" Magilton jokes. "If he was still around today, maybe he wouldn't look as favourably at me as I do at him. Geoff had a tremendous amount of faith in me because I'm told he only recommended who were three-quarters of the way towards the first team. I was only 16, so that shows you how much faith he had in me. Only a year after I signed I went away with the first team on a pre-season tour, so he must have nearly been right. Probably it all happened a bit too quickly for me and that's why I never made a competitive appearance..."

Despite not making the grade at Liverpool, Magilton believes that his time at the club prepared him for a 15-year playing career before entering management. "The stuff I learnt off the likes of Roy Evans, Ronnie Moran and Kenny is ingrained in me. I was lucky to work with those people. Back then, their young players were taught how to play the game by senior pros. By that, I mean that the senior pros used to talk players through games. It's different now, because the system is different and you don't get as many senior players playing in the reserves, so maybe you don't learn as quickly. Our reserve team was really strong too. There was Stevie Mc, Steve Staunton, John McGregor, Ken de Mange, Mark Seagraves, Alex Watson, Mike Hooper and people of that ilk. The standards were high and Phil Thompson was manager of the reserves and he had a massive influence on me as well."

Since taking charge at Portman Road in 2006, Magilton has led the club to the fringes of the Championship play-offs. He says that he has been trying to implement the beliefs honed at Liverpool onto his team as the club attempts to return to the halcyon days of the late '70s when Bobby Robson was in charge. Although Ipswich have recently received financial investment which will safeguard the club's immediate future, he insists that he must act wisely in the transfer market if he wants the club to progress in the next few years. This means building a strong trust with his scouting system.

"The thing I tell all my scouts is that you must find an attribute that you really like about a player," he says. "If you hang around too long, you are likely to find negatives so you have to find something that really stands out. We don't have a set of rules that are rigid. We don't sit down and say: 'We want a right 6ft 2in right-back who can run 14km in a game.' First and foremost, we say: 'Can they pass and control?' Yes. 'Let's see what his options are – will he pick out the right one and is there something we can work on?' Ultimately, if we are going to sign a player, there has to be something we really like. I say we, because I take into consideration everything my scouts say to me. The only plan that we have is that the player must be able to pass and move – just like Liverpool. We want defenders who can defend, but pass as well. We like midfielders who are all comfortable in possession and we want strikers who are clever.

"For instance, I re-signed Pablo Counago, the Spaniard, because he has something that I like and he reminds me a little bit of Kenny [Dalglish].

He can see a pass, is good using his back and he has vision. We also need players with energy, and all the great Liverpool teams and players had that. The opposition hate it when you can run all day and that's what I look for in a player at Ipswich. Everyone at Liverpool had the same ideas and Geoff Twentyman understood what Liverpool managers wanted. I look for scouts who share the same vision as me."

Note: Jim Magilton has since left Ipswich Town.

TIM FLOWERS

Flowers' career began at Wolves in 1984 before he joined Southampton and then Blackburn, where he helped the club win the league title in 1995. His other honours comprised a League Cup winner's medal in 2000 while at Leicester, and 11 England caps.

Birthplace: *Kenilworth*
Position: *Goalkeeper*
Clubs: *Wolverhampton Wanderers, Southampton, Swindon Town (loan), Blackburn Rovers, Leicester City, Stockport County (loan), Coventry City (loan), Manchester City (loan)*

HAD Kenny Dalglish and Liverpool moved to sign Tim Flowers in 1986, then Bruce Grobbelaar's natural successor would have been found. Of course, a player of Flowers' talents might have become restless with waiting for a chance in the first team and left, considering it was a time when three substitutes were permitted in the matchday squad and few managers bothered using a goalkeeper on the bench.

Equally, it was a period when goalkeepers would play for the same club for decades in some cases. Grobbelaar didn't leave Liverpool until 1994, when he was 35, before departing for Southampton, where he incidentally replaced Flowers as the club's first choice after he moved to Kenny Dalglish's Blackburn Rovers. Flowers' transfer north earned

Southampton a reported £2.4m, a record fee for an English goalkeeper. The following season Flowers played a major role as Rovers became the first and only provincial club to win the Premier League since its inception in 1992.

Flowers later became a regular in England squads, and only David Seaman's consistent form throughout the '90s, as well as further competition from the equally reliable Nigel Martyn, prevented him from making more than 11 caps (a frustratingly low total considering Paul Robinson, a keeper with more flaws than a department store, played 41 times under Sven-Goran Eriksson and Steve McClaren).

It has often been suggested (albeit by fans of rival clubs) that Liverpool players are looked on more favourably by international bosses than other players who are perhaps more deserving of a chance. They point towards much-maligned players such as Emile Heskey and Peter Crouch, who before and after Liverpool weren't England regulars, but as soon as they pulled on the Red shirt, they also wore the white of England. With this in mind, does Flowers think his international career would have turned out differently had he signed for Liverpool?

"It's an amazing thought," Flowers says, who at the time of interview was assistant manager at QPR. "If I was Liverpool's number one and Liverpool were doing well, England couldn't have ignored me. What has happened has happened. I don't know what would have happened if I'd signed for Liverpool. All I do know is that anyone who has played for Liverpool is a very lucky person because they are a monster club. When I was a kid, they ruled the world. I grew up watching Liverpool smash the opposition to bits every single weekend. They were so good..."

After a long pause, he continues: "Jesus Christ, to think about going there would have been fantastic. Eventually I got to work with Kenny, so it wasn't so bad. I will always remember the supporters at Anfield and how they were with the visiting goalkeeper. You don't get that kind of reception that you do in front of the Kop at any other ground in the world. It's probably because the fans realised how stupid all these goalkeepers

Above: Pictured with colleague at Ballymena United, Norman Clarke. The hand-written description on the back of the photo reads 'The Kray Twins'

Silver service: With the European Cup at Anfield

Above: Football card from the 1950s of Twentyman as a Liverpool player

Son Geoff Twentyman junior gets in the famous orange club Cortina once owned by Shankly

The players 1967-1986

Kevin
Beattie

Alec
Lindsay

Davie
Cooper

John
Connolly

Steve
Heighway

Trevor
Francis

Steve
Ogrizovic

Larry
Lloyd

Phil
Neal

Alan
Birchenall

Joey
Jones

Gerry
Francis

Andy
Gray

Ray
Clemence

Francis
Lee

John
Toshack

The players 1967-1986

Bruce
Grobbelaar

Gary
Gillespie

Peter
Reid

Steve
Nicol

John
Gregory

Michael
Robinson

Jim
Magilton

Ian
Rush

Kevin
Sheedy

John
Gidman

Alan
Hansen

Graeme
Souness

Simon
Garner

Paul
Walsh

Tony
Cascarino

Paul
Rideout

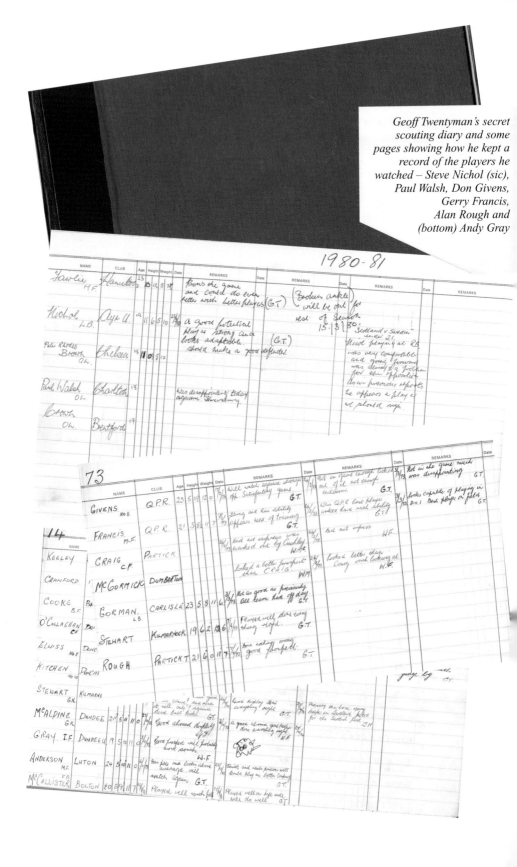

Geoff Twentyman's secret scouting diary and some pages showing how he kept a record of the players he watched – Steve Nichol (sic), Paul Walsh, Don Givens, Gerry Francis, Alan Rough and (bottom) Andy Gray

1980-81

NAME	CLUB	Age	Height	Weight	Date	REMARKS	Date	REMARKS	Date	REMARKS
CONNOLLY	St. Johnstone IF	21	5'9	11 0	3/1/70	Very impressive eg W.F. Very impressive eg. a bit open				
STEVENSON	Chesterfield GK	20	5'11	11 0	18/1/70	Good young G.K. well inside class grade. AB	24/1/70	Good practical help in area. AB	21/1/70	Be a everything right. Looks the part. GT
TILER	Chesterfield R.B.	19			18/1/70	Green green's back. AB. hard following	24/1/70	Looks following's AB in figure	21/1/70	Not enough to aa GT
ECCLESHARE	Bury. R.B.	20	5'11	6	18/1/70	Bury's best player. Too footed Good prospect.	GT 27/1/70	looks well and firm will 6/1/70 touch in	1/1/70 look again 1/1/70 Not enough 6 aa GT for judging	GT 8/1/70 Not Good enough GT
McDERMOTT	Bury. IL	18	5'9	10.12	24/1/70	A good footed I.L look earling	X		X	
TOSHACK	Cardiff I.L.	21	6'02	11.12	31/1/70	Box awkard to deal AB EH 3 goals. good enough. AB.1	1/1/70	Very good in the air GT does a job as usual	X	
HILL	IPSWICH C.F.	22	5'11	11 0	31/1/70	Not a Score dangerous VG End. J like the player				
BROWN	Albion No 10	22	5'9	11 0	31/1/70	Green no plus class GT End good Eso-I: Hards well				
EVANSON	Oxford No 6 midfield	23	5'8	11 0	7/1/70	Played well in attacking 28/1 well worth watching etc GT	28/1/70	Played well enough will follow up. AB	28/1/70	Not analysis and watching? AB
RODGERS	Bristol No 6	18	6'1	12 0	21/1/70	Raw but slender enforce worth small fee. AB				
ALLDER	Millwall OL	19			24/1/70	Looks a promising player AB				

Page including notes on future Liverpool stars John Toshack and Terry McDermott. Also on this page - John Connolly and Tony Brown

NAME	CLUB	Age	Height	Weight	Date	REMARKS	Date	REMARKS	Date	REMARKS	Date	REMARKS
HARDCASTLE	SKELMERSDALE	22	5 10	11		Does not look out of class	VG						
MILLINGTON	RHYL	18	5 10	10 0		Promising player VG to be followed up		Played well				
O'NEIL	DISTILLERY	18	5 10	11 7		Very good display TD must be watched		Not good as JD		Not enough drive		
DONNELLY	DISTILLERY	20	5 9	10 7		Plays a part well ID attack and defence		Not impressed				
DAVIES.F	RHYL	18	6 0	12 0		Seems good with pace good VG		Not a good game VE		Shown interest VG		Very poor not good enough GT
ASHCROFT	WREXHAM	18	5 11	12 0		Not impressed. A lot to learn GT		Needing to class NJ		Not a good game VG to judge		
FRANCIS	BIRMINGHAM	18				very promising player E.B						
BROWN L.R	HIBS	19	5 10	11 7		Can do better would GT have to see again		Against a good OL JM		Done all can to ADGT good action strong player		
BRACKPOOL	SPENNYMOOR	19	5 6	10 7		Shows promise would following up						
KEEGAN	SCUNTHORPE	21	5 8	10 6		a good player shows a lot of promise AB		This player is financed by A. Beattie. X				
TUNKS	ROTHERHAM	22	6 0	12 0		a very useful GK						

NAME	CLUB	Age	Height	Weight	Date	REMARKS	Date	REMARKS	Date	REMARKS	Date	REMARKS
PRENDERGAST	SHEFF.W.	23	6	9	11/7/74	None well scored two goals. KK.	16/8/74	Coming find on way a live prospect.	13/9/74	Books ag. through being crude. G.T.		
MORLEY, M.F.	PRESTON	18	5 8	10.12	9/1/74	Always however will talk An eye on. G.T.	13/9/74	Played well will follow thro' closely G.T				
CANT M.F.	HEARTS	21	5 9	11 6	20/1/74	Strong with good ball control. Looked useful G.T	27/1/74					
GLAVIN N.F.	PARTICK T.	20	5 8	11 0	2/1/74	Played well in attack. Most often injured G.T						
-75												
NEAL P. X	NORTHAMPTON	25	5 11	11 6	18/1/74	One will have a good game Satisfactory game G.T	2/6/74	One well alround for employed. G.T	5/7/74	Played as a central defender Came well.		
STARLING	NORTHAMPTON	25	5 11	11 0	18/1/74	Home well in good morch checking G.T	2/6/74	?				
GREGORY	NORTHAMPTON	21	6 0	11 2	18/1/74	Well worth watching at G.T	2/6/74	?				
FINNEY	ROTHERHAM	18	5 8	10 0	5/1/74	Small but looks useful can improve					Promising player.	

Phil Neal is included in this page from the 1974-75 season. Neal went on to become Liverpool's most decorated player

The Liverpool Football Club
& Athletic Grounds Plc
Deysbrook Lane, Liverpool L12 8SY
Tel: 0151 282 8888 Fax: 0151 252 2206
www.liverpoolfc.tv

Melwood Training Ground

18 February 2004

Mrs G Twentyman
299 Northway
Maghull
Merseyside
L31 0BN

Dear Pat

I was very sorry to hear the sad news that Geoff had passed away. Although I never met Geoff, I do know that he was a well liked and highly respected member of the staff and served this Club well as Chief Scout for many years.

On behalf of all the players and staff of Liverpool Football Club, may I offer you and your family our sincere condolences and deepest sympathy.

Our thoughts are with you at this sad time.

Kind regards.

Yours sincerely

Gérard Houllier

Right: Letter from Gerard Houllier after Twentyman's death in 2004. Below: Son William Twentyman in his barber's shop in Crosby, giving a shave to Jamie Carragher in 2008

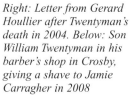

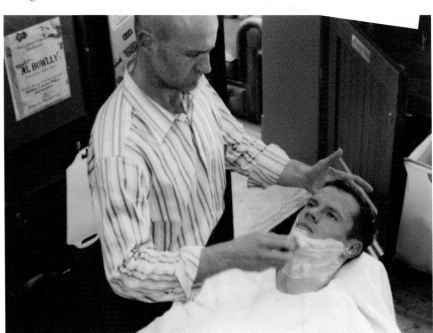

looked when they were constantly picking the ball out of the net. I was a Coventry fan as a kid and I used to travel everywhere to watch them. I went to Anfield a few times and I always thought the atmosphere there was better than anywhere else. I went to watch a game in the FA Cup and we actually got a 2-2 draw at Anfield. Larry Lloyd played for Cov and I thought we had a good chance back at Highfield Road. But Liverpool battered us. They were like a machine and there were no doubts about their confidence even after we held them at Anfield."

Flowers was only 16 when he played his first Football League game for Wolverhampton Wanderers. At that stage of his career, the prospect of winning Premier League titles and international caps with England were a long way from his thoughts. "The situation at Wolves was desperate. I started off as an apprentice cleaning the boots and then John Burridge who was the goalkeeper got the hump and decided he wanted to leave. Budgie wasn't getting enough money so off he went. Then Wolves went into administration and they had no money to bring another goalkeeper in, so they had nobody else to play but me. I was fresh out of school shorts and into league football getting my head kicked in every week. In those days there was always a massive centre-forward looking to knock you into next week."

In his first full season at Molineux, Wolves finished bottom under Tommy Docherty. But it wasn't all bad news for Flowers, who was now the youngest established goalkeeper in league football. "We were a very bad side and deserved to get relegated. We conceded more than 90 goals, too, but I was voted player of the year," he jokes. "That shows you how bad we were."

It would be fair to believe that Flowers' form led clubs further up the league pyramid to flock to the West Midlands. But he says that he wasn't aware of interest from anywhere else. "Tommy Doc was a great bloke, but he would never have told me if another club were having a sniff. The next season, Wolves came out of administration and managed to sign another goalkeeper, Scott Barrett [who later played for an array of London clubs in the lower leagues], and my form suffered. I was still only 17, so it didn't matter too much."

According to Norman Clarke, it was at this point he went to see Flowers play in a match against Charlton or Crystal Palace at Selhurst Park (they ground-shared at the time). Clarke says that he saw Flowers make a 'world class save' given the slippery conditions, and although he wasn't a specialist with scouting keepers, he felt Flowers would be good enough to challenge Grobbelaar for a first-team place at Anfield.

"I had absolutely no idea that Liverpool were looking at me," he says with genuine surprise. "All I know is that Southampton came in and realised my potential by spending 70 grand on me. As it happens, Peter Shilton was the first choice keeper down there, and looking back I didn't get the best deal because I was on £100 a week and £100 for each appearance at Wolves, then Southampton offered me the same weekly wage but with a £200 appearance fee. I was too thick to realise that I was never going to play because Peter Shilton was there. It was like that for two years until Shilts left for Derby. So I ended up earning less money there than I was on at Wolves."

Despite his early frustration, Southampton soon sold Shilton (who earned 125 caps for England) to Derby County and Flowers went on to make more than 200 appearances for the club over the next seven years. "Southampton was a fantastic club who coached me well and looked after me. Then I went to Blackburn where I played underneath Kenny – what a manager and what a person – and obviously a Liverpool legend. Liverpool's a magnificent football club and, like I say, whoever has had the chance to play for them has been very lucky. It's a hell of a long time since they were looking at me, so it's hard to judge how I feel because my career panned out alright. But it would have been nice to be able to say that I was a goalkeeper for Liverpool."

One of the reasons why Liverpool supporters have always been quick to welcome opposition goalkeepers is because they understand the importance of the position. Before 1990, the club was blessed with a series of greats to have donned the green number one shirt. Over a 30-year period, Liverpool had Tommy Lawrence, Ray Clemence and Bruce Grobbelaar. Between them they made 1,683 appearances. Before that, there was Elisha Scott, arguably the finest keeper of his generation and someone who alone played nearly 500 times for the club.

Yet in the 18 years since Liverpool last won the title, Mike Hooper, David James, Brad Friedel, Sander Westerveld, Chris Kirkland, Jerzy Dudek and Pepe Reina have all had a go at becoming an established first choice. Although Reina is now rightly regarded as one of the top five keepers in the world, the six that went before him never made the position their own and the team struggled partially as a result. Had Flowers succeeded Grobbelaar, then maybe things would have turned out slightly differently.

"What's definite is that I wouldn't have let that one bobble in at Ewood Park," Flowers jokes, in reference to Stan Collymore's shot in 1996 that hit a divot before bouncing agonisingly over his shoulder. "Liverpool is a dynasty and I love hearing about all their history with the bootroom. In my opinion, that is the way football clubs should be run – just like they were with Liverpool back in the '60s, '70s and '80s. My affinity is more with that side of the game, people running a football club who are just obsessed by the game and just want to talk football and aren't too arsed by which companies are on the advertising boards around the side of the pitch. I can't stand the commercial side of football."

TONY CASCARINO

After making his name at Gillingham, Cascarino was bought by Millwall in 1987 for £225,000. He was a prolific goalscorer at both clubs, and after brief, underwhelming stints at Villa, Celtic and Chelsea, he regained his form in France. Cascarino won 88 caps for the Republic of Ireland, scoring 19 goals.

Birthplace: *Orpington*
Position: *Striker*
Clubs: *Gillingham, Millwall, Aston Villa, Celtic, Chelsea, Marseille, Nancy, Red Star 93*

BACK in 'them' days, when footballers were real people and ate real food, steak and chips were regularly on the matchday menu at club canteens. Even at Anfield, players would enjoy a breakfast of fried egg and sausage on toast, before catching the bus to Melwood for training. Tony Cascarino, Millwall's telescopic-legged striker from the mid-'80s, took this level of gluttony to new levels of ill health as he waited to make his home debut for Gillingham.

"We were playing Wimbledon at home," he told the *Guardian* in 2007. "In them days you only had two subs, and they always named a 14th man in case someone came down with an illness or got hurt on the morning of the game. So I was the 14th man, and I arrived at Gillingham station about 10 to one, and I'm thinking, 'I don't really know what to do with myself now'. I didn't know the players that well, so I didn't want to get there early, so I went into Wimpy and ate a double cheeseburger and chips, and then a Knickerbocker Glory.

"Then I get to the stadium about 10 to two, and I get named as a substitute. So I'm thinking: 'Oh my God.' I'm thinking I might have to go be sick in the toilet; I'm feeling absolutely bloated. Then after 15 minutes a midfielder has a bad injury, and gets carried off, and I had to go on. We ended up winning 6-1 and I scored on my home debut. I was feeling absolutely wretched but all I could think was: "That's my pre-match meal" – double Wimpy and chips and a Knickerbocker Glory."

If Cascarino had signed for Kenny Dalglish's Liverpool in the mid-'80s, he needed only to visit the Wimpy in Williamson Square for his pre-match feast, one of only a few fast-food restaurants around in the city at the time. Instead, Cascarino enjoyed a nomadic career, playing in three different countries before settling in France for the best part of the

'90s, where he became a cult-figure at Marseille (after their demotion to the Second Division for their part in a match-fixing scandal), then Nancy. He's a likeable guy, who responds to my interview request by email before ringing later the very same day.

When asked about his initial feelings towards Liverpool's interest, his response is blunt and honest: "Gutted." Like a lot of kids around the country in the '70s, Cascarino enjoyed a teenage diet of watching Liverpool march to league title after league title. "Although I was born in south London and Millwall was my local team and I used to go to the Den quite a lot, my real love affair was with Liverpool Football Club.

"I grew up watching Toshack and Keegan. One of my earliest memories was sitting in my bedroom that was plastered with Liverpool memorabilia, listening to Liverpool beat Wolves on the radio when they won the title in '76. If I'd gone to Liverpool it would have been as good as it gets as a footballer. It would have been my dream move. I grew up watching Liverpool like a lot of young kids grew up following Man Utd today, dare I say it. I am not ashamed to tell you that. But life pans out funny for everyone, doesn't it? I am just pleased to know that they were impressed. The highlight of my career was playing for Millwall in front of the Kop and my favourite player of all time was Kenny Dalglish."

Given that Dalglish was on the verge of retirement when Cascarino was viewed as a potential signing, it is possible that the faux Irishman (he represented Ireland at international level without having any direct Celtic bloodline relatives), could have been the heir to the King's throne. Cascarino doubts this theory, however. "The only thing me and Kenny have in common is that we both have a big arse!" he says with hysterical laughter. "There's no way I could have come in for him because I was a big lad and he was small and skilful."

A move for Cascarino certainly would have seen a change in direction for Liverpool whose last striker with better ability in the air than on the ground only lasted 12 months at the club. Tony Hateley may have scored nearly 30 goals in 1967/68, but Bill Shankly bombed him out for not being adept enough with the ball at his feet. "My main attribute was my heading ability," Cascarino admits. "But I was a far better athlete than I was given credit for. My biggest strength was that I was a good partner for other strikers. I always did well with players who made intelligent runs because I could create a lot of chances if they worked off me. My partnership with John Aldridge was perfect because Aldo was the ultimate sniffer wasn't he?

"It's all hypothetical, but it would have been lovely to have a go at Liverpool. Kenny Dalglish was the first kind of second striker and it proves they were miles ahead of their time because everyone plays that way now. If you look before 1990, Liverpool always had really great forward partnerships that ultimately went a long way to making them successful. If I'd signed, maybe I could have worked well with Rushy, Aldo – we did well with the Ireland together – or even Robbie Fowler later on. I felt sorry for Robbie because him and Stan [Collymore] never really clicked. If he had someone else up-front, he would have scored even more than he did for Liverpool. I was enjoying an Indian summer in France by then, so maybe we'd have done ok together even though I was probably too old by then."

Despite the many doubters (and there will be many that disagree with this), Cascarino could have been a success at Anfield. Although he thrived on aerial bombardment and it was sacrilegious to adopt a kick-and-rush approach at the time as a Liverpool team or player, his successful partnership at Millwall with Teddy Sheringham proved that he could play with a player similar in style to Dalglish (although Sheringham was a lesser player than Kenny).

"When I got thrown in the deep end, I usually did alright. I probably would have fitted in from a team-building point of view, but maybe I would have struggled due to my style of play. I was better with the long ball, but Liverpool fans don't take to that too kindly – look at what happened when Houllier was there. So maybe Liverpool fans wouldn't have appreciated what I would have brought to the team, and quite rightly so because they wanted it on the ground.

"I was at Anfield when they beat Tottenham 7-0 and the quality of the passing that day was incredible. I watched the game from the Kop with a mate from London who was a Spurs fan. For the whole match, he was trying to talk in a Scouse accent, but it wasn't working. I thought that day that a young lad like me would find it hard if I wanted to play for Liverpool."

Admitting that it would have taken some transition fitting into the Liverpool way – "I would have been roughly 25 when they were looking at me, so it would have had to adapt pretty quickly," Cascarino says – he also reveals that Manchester United made an enquiry about him while he was at Aston Villa in the late '80s. "It was flattering and nice, but joining United would have been second fiddle for me compared to Liverpool, which sounds incredible after what has happened since."

The reason that nothing came of Liverpool's interest, is because Twentyman was not impressed. The original tip-off came from Tom Saunders but when Twentyman followed the lead up, he ruled out any possible bid.

Cascarino himself admits that he didn't always stand out when scouts came to watch him. He says: "I fell down sometimes because I had to be on the top of my game to look like I was any good." Indeed, he had to wait until he was in his mid-20s before any clubs higher up the leagues paid interest in him. "I was still very raw and naïve. Even at 22, I was all physical and I would just attack the ball. There was no guile in any kind shape or form about my game; then, by 25 at Millwall, I started to get a lot fitter and I was taking things a lot more seriously at that time. The trainer Jon Docherty knew that he had to work my backside off to get the best out of me, so he whipped me into shape. I was always very ungainly but when I was fully fit I could be very effective. But like all big centre-forwards, if I put a few pounds on, I struggled because I looked leggy and cumbersome."

After moving to Aston Villa from Millwall, Cascarino played for Celtic and Chelsea before deciding to try his hand in France. Only at this point, he says, did he begin to understand how important it was to take care of himself away from the training ground. "Liverpool were tea and biscuits before training and all the lads there loved a drink, so I am not sure whether they were that professional when you compare them to other teams. That was just the done thing.

"I just took football very seriously when I went to France. I gave everything to the game, got myself at a perfect weight. I was playing like a fighter on top of everything all the time and the French defenders couldn't deal with that approach. Because I dedicated my life to improving my game, I got an inner confidence. I remember scoring against Juventus in Europe and that was when I realised that I had wasted a lot of years not taking caring of myself. When I was fit I was a different animal. I could get the better of a lot of very good centre-halves in England. But when I was off my game and not at my peak, I was a mediocre player and unfortunately that happened all too often. Big Jack at Ireland got the best out of me out of all the managers I worked under because he liked my aggression and made the team play to my strengths."

Cascarino scored 19 goals in 88 games for Ireland, adding to the 248 he scored in 629 league games. Although his international record isn't as impressive, it is worth bearing in mind that he played when Niall Quinn was Ireland's premier striker and they were similar in style. Maybe if Quinn hadn't been around, he would have scored more for his country.

Jack Charlton, though, undoubtedly got the best out of his Ireland side. Playing Wimbledon-style long-ball, they specialised in abject chaos, trying to boot everything that moved (in some cases, even opponents) into the penalty area. It was dreck, but at least it was successful. Most importantly, John Aldridge, Ray Houghton, Steve Staunton and Ronnie Whelan all adapted from pass and move at Liverpool to the shovelling tactics with Ireland. If they could adapt, then maybe Cascarino could too.

Cascarino finishes by saying that he learnt a lot from the Liverpool players in the Irish squad and believes they were cut from a different cloth in terms of character. "The Liverpool lads were always the harshest critics," he says with a tremor in his voice. "I always found them quite funny because they gave each other stick for fun. I remember Steve Staunton as a 19-year-old telling Ronnie Whelan, Ray Houghton and Aldo to f**k off because they asked him to make them a cup of tea. I found that hilarious because Stevie was such a young lad and he had the confidence to take the older players on. Aldo was in bits when he said that. It took a certain type of character to play for Liverpool because as an outsider looking in, they seemed to mock each other at every opportunity. It was quite strange seeing players from a team that was so successful actually hammer each other so much.

"Little Ray was the biggest moaner I ever played with in football. Non-stop arguing, screaming and moaning all the time during games and in the changing rooms. He was the same in training. It seems to me that Liverpool players weren't afraid to say what they thought. Maybe that's what drove them on, because they would never accept someone making a half-hearted effort. Maybe I would have found it hard to adjust to that side of the mindset because I'm a big softy at heart."

9. Leaving Liverpool

Doubting Lineker, a changing game
and back to Scotland

GRAEME SOUNESS is in a self-imposed solitary confinement. He waits in a dimly lit corner. Legs crossed and arms folded, Liverpool's former captain and manager gathers his thoughts while the rest of the studio is submerged in football banter. There's a topless Richard Keys – the obvious fuzz-related jokes are fired in his direction. Jamie Redknapp wears a figure-hugging slate grey suit and burnished wingtips. Dion Dublin closes his eyes while make-up is applied to the shinier parts of his dome-shaped crown. All the while, Andy Gray is perforating everyone's eardrums by cackling "off, off, off" directly down Redknapp's ear-hole.

It's 11.10am on Saturday 13 September 2008 and Liverpool are three hours away from completing their first league victory over Manchester United since Rafa Benitez took charge. Souness is in Anfield's Sky Sports studio and he ready to talk about Geoff Twentyman. "You want to keep an eye on Keysey," he barks from his slumber. "He's a Liverpool supporter, you know. Not many people know that."

"Don't be controversial just for the sake of it," responds Keys, the Sky anchor, raising those distinctive eyebrows. "I am completely impartial – professionally and emotionally." Keys takes a moment to fix his tie. "I look as sharp as a tack today." Then he watches 'Soccer AM', which is on the small monitor in front of him. It's showboat time and Robinho is displaying numerous futile tricks while on international duty with Brazil the previous week. "That's entertainment, isn't it," he asks rhetorically.

But Souness responds: "That's not good play. That's not entertainment." Followed by a scowl. End of argument.

Keys: "People come to watch football to be entertained – what about when Jim Baxter was playing for Scotland against England – he juggled the ball and all the Scots thought it was great..."

Souness refuses to back down. "How can you call it entertainment when he's going to give the ball away? Where's the cross for the goal coming from Richard? I don't see it. Absolute rubbish."

Then Keys, in his best TV presenter's voice, looks directly into the camera with a hand pressed to his ear: "Teams are coming...Clemence, Neal, Hansen, Lawrenson, Avi Cohen – there's a surprise – no Souness too... Sammy Lee takes his place today..."

Souness issues Keys with an icy glare before turning away. "This is only the second time I have been back here other than when I have been working with a team," he says quietly. "It's different with the media because you can enjoy the game more. When I've been here as an opposing manager, I have been too busy preparing my team but when I am here with Sky, my blood pressure doesn't go through the roof as much – although I will get animated when the game starts because I am desperate for a Liverpool win today."

Critics say Souness has an ego and his belittling of Keys's opinion might suggest as much. As a player, he was probably Liverpool's most dynamic midfielder of all time (Steven Gerrard pushes him very, very close). Jamie Carragher recently said Souness had the tenacity and strength of Roy Keane and the hypnotic skills of Zinedine Zidane. He was a complete footballer. Yet as manager of the club, he failed, and his agreement to sign a deal with *The Sun* to serialise his heart bypass ordeal in 1992, which was eventually published three years to the day after the same paper printed disgusting bile and lies about Kopites at Hillsborough, made some fans boycott matches while he was in charge.

Peter Hooton, singer from The Farm and season ticket holder on the Kop, was one of them. "When Souness made Mo Johnston the first

Catholic to sign for Rangers, I never thought that was anything to do with equal opportunities. That was to do with him saying: 'I am Graeme Souness and I can do anything I want.' That spelt danger for me and after he came to Liverpool, I stopped going because the *Sun* thing was a disgrace and it ruined his reputation as one of Liverpool's all-time greats."

What is certain is that there is definitely an aura about Souness. A lone sliver of light shines underneath a tinted window. It slices across the room and across his stony face, which is otherwise covered deep in shadow, making him look like a prisoner in some Vietnam War movie. He wears a frosty pale blue shirt and starkly coloured black tie. There's a glint in his eye that sparkles almost demoniacally when he talks about serious matters. And when he does talk, it's mostly in a whisper, almost as though he fears being overheard. But for all this, his Edinburgh accent is soft, when one would imagine it would be caustic like a Glaswegian. His words on Twentyman, too, are humbling: "Nobody did a better job in the whole of Britain. His contribution was enormous. When I heard he'd left Liverpool, I couldn't move quick enough to get him up to Scotland with me at Rangers. It was a steal."

Twentyman left Liverpool in 1986. Within months, Souness was handed his first managerial appointment at Ibrox. Rangers hadn't won the league in eight years and Celtic and Aberdeen were dominating Scottish football. His squad was in need of a major overhaul. "I picked up the phone and called Geoff straight away. It was desperate times for Rangers and I wanted to change things quickly. We managed to win the league in my first season and although Celtic wrestled it away in the second year, after that we took a stranglehold of Scotland. Rangers ended up winning the league nine times in a row between 1989 and 1997. Even though I left for Liverpool in '91, Geoff deserves some of the credit for helping me build the foundations for that team."

*****

TWENTYMAN maintained his record of unearthing riches from beneath unlikely Scottish and English lower-league stones in the early 1980s. Steve Nicol and Ian Rush arrived from Ayr United and Chester City respectively, while Gary Gillespie, a player Twentyman had been watching for more than five years, signed from Coventry City. Phil Neal, Alan Kennedy and Alan Hansen, meanwhile, were all still integral parts of the squad throughout the period.

Liverpool continued to dominate domestically and in Europe. Even at the end of the '80s, long after Twentyman left the club, it seemed inconceivable that Liverpool would not win a league title for 18 years (and counting at the time of writing). The only difference in the '80s was where the challenge for titles and cups was coming from. Throughout the '70s, Derby County, Leeds United, Nottingham Forest, Aston Villa and, to a lesser extent, Manchester City all tussled with Liverpool both domestically and in Europe. English clubs dominated the European Cup, and for six years in succession the competition's eventual winner hailed from these shores.

By the early '80s, though, a new challenger had emerged. Howard Kendall was on the verge of being sacked as Everton manager in December 1983, but six months later his team won the FA Cup, and they reached the final for the next two years as well, only to lose on both occasions. Their victory over Watford, however (spurred by an Andy Gray goal that should have been ruled out for a foul on the goalkeeper), spurred them on in the league the next season, and they finished top ahead of Liverpool in second. Although Liverpool reclaimed their crown in 1986 (with Everton in second place), the Blues won the league again in 1987, with Liverpool finishing as runners-up.

Behind the scenes, Everton's success had a profound effect on Twentyman's position at Anfield. His judgement was questioned a few years earlier when Ian Rush (ironically, an Evertonian) didn't score a single first-team goal in his first full season after signing. Although Rush soon proved that Twentyman was correct in his decision to recommend him to Liverpool, a stigma, it appears, had taken hold. Norman Clarke, one of Twentyman's closest confidants in football, and someone who watched hundreds of players on his behalf, believes that several board members at Liverpool were unhappy with the chief scout for failing to realise the potential of Gary Lineker, a player who signed for Everton and promptly scored 40 goals in his one and only season at Goodison Park.

"Lineker finished Geoff off," Clarke says. "Everyone in scouting circles knew about Gary because he was what we called a 'one-touch finisher'. If you asked Gary to run with the ball or beat a man or even beat a defender over six yards then finish, he couldn't do it. But if you asked him to sprint onto a ball and finish in one touch, he found it easy. Everton signed Lineker in '85 and he started scoring straight away and kept them at the top of the league. Unfortunately, Geoff didn't fancy Lineker and told Liverpool so a few years earlier. Even though Liverpool ended up winning the double at the end of that season, Liverpool got rid of two people. One was Chris Lawler and the other was Geoff.

"Geoff told me that he'd arranged to see John Smith [the chairman] not long before the end of that season. Mr Smith made him wait outside his office for one hour like he was some kind of servant. When he was called in, Mr Smith's first question to Geoff was: 'Tell me, Mr Twentyman, how is it that Everton are signing all these good players?' To Geoff, that was like accusing him of beating his wife. It was like saying: 'Everton are signing these players, why aren't we?' That was very hurtful to him and he realised that he was expendable."

If the Liverpool board were unhappy about missing out on Lineker, it's a good job that they probably didn't know Twentyman scouted Peter Reid and Andy Gray (Lineker's predecessor) in the '70s, without insisting that Liverpool signed them as well. "That's football, though," insists Clarke. "There are always going to be one or two that slip through. You can't sign everyone, can you? At that time Liverpool probably had better players than Reid, Gray and Lineker, too."

In his early days as a player, Clarke was compared to George Best, making his Irish League debut as a 17-year-old. He later moved to Sunderland for £6,000 where, as we have already dicovered, he played in the same team as Brian Clough, someone who he later scouted for, despite never liking. "He still owes me money from when I did a bit of scouting for him," Clarke moans. "He was a master at getting the public on his side. But behind the scenes he was very manipulative."

A knee injury forced Clarke to retire early, and after returning to Ballymena in the late '60s as manager, he became a networker for Twentyman when he moved back to England in the '70s. Clarke's main area of concern for Liverpool was in the Midlands and London area where he lived. "It was 1983/84, 1984/85 when things really began to change for Geoff," he insists. "All of a sudden, people at the club were beginning to ask questions about why Everton were almost equalling Liverpool. When it's a team that's from somewhere else in the country, the daily pressure of being reminded who's at the top isn't as intense in each individual city, but when Liverpool and Everton were top, the scrutiny of certain aspects of each club is a lot tougher.

"Personally, I recognised a difference in Geoff. He phoned me once on a Sunday morning and asked me to go to watch a goalkeeper play at Wimbledon that very day because Everton were allegedly looking to sign him as a back-up for Neville Southall. Geoff wanted to check this keeper out too and make sure Liverpool didn't miss out. It was when Wimbledon were in the Fourth Division. The player I was watching was in goal for Wolves who were dire underneath Tommy Docherty. It was a really wet day, but this goalkeeper made a save that I thought would have been good if he tipped it round the post. Instead he held it. With the right guidance, I felt this keeper could be an all-time great in the future.

"For the first time ever, Geoff phoned me the next morning. He asked me about how this goalkeeper did. I told him that never bloody mind being a stand-in for Southall, if he wasn't in the top four goalkeepers in England in the next few years, I would eat my hat. The goalkeeper's name was Tim Flowers.

"Not long after Geoff had finished at Liverpool, he told me why he had called on the Sunday. John Smith, the chairman, would usually come in on a Monday morning and ask Geoff who he watched on the Saturday. Usually Geoff would tell him, but in the mid-'80s, Mr Smith started asking for reports on his desk on the Monday. Geoff quite honestly explained that because there was no post on a Sunday, it was impossible to do that and he would have to wait until Tuesday and listen to what the rest of the scouts had told him verbally. John Smith then started saying to Geoff: 'Well are we going to sign these players?' Geoff was getting a bit on edge about this kind of inquisitorial type of grilling. The next day, Geoff went in to see Mr Smith and said that he had Tim Flowers watched and he was going to be a very good goalkeeper. But nobody signed Flowers. Within three years he'd moved to Southampton before going to Blackburn for a record fee for a goalkeeper, also becoming an England player too. Liverpool could have signed him for £50-100,000."

One player that Liverpool did eventually sign, "somewhat against the wishes" of Twentyman, was Paul Walsh. Clarke had watched Walsh play for Charlton Athletic in a reserve match while scouting for Liverpool-born Len Ashurst who was managing Sunderland. "I would go and watch for Sunderland, but if I thought a player was good enough for Liverpool, I would mention it to Geoff who was fine with the arrangement. It was common for scouts who were almost freelance like me to do this kind of thing.

"I was watching Garth Crooks for Len when I saw Paul Walsh. So I told Geoff about Paul and said that he was small, but very quick and had a keen eye for goals. Geoff went to see him the following week when Charlton played in the cup against Shrewsbury. Unfortunately he didn't do very well and Geoff didn't fancy him. I told Len about him too after that, but he didn't seem interested either. Ironically, he went to Luton and although Geoff wasn't always that struck on him, Liverpool ended up signing him for a big fee – a lot more than they would have paid if they'd signed him earlier. I was later told that Liverpool signed Walsh because they needed a quick replacement for Ian Rush who was injured. It was against Geoff's recomendation and he was a bit annoyed by that."

Liverpool fought hard to sign Walsh who was also wanted by Manchester United. Despite scoring barely seconds into his Anfield debut against West Ham United, a mix of bad injuries at the worst times and a modest goalscoring record (37 in 112 games) meant that although he contributed to Liverpool's success in the mid-'80s, he never really established himself as a first pick. The £700,000 Liverpool spent was a huge investment for someone who'd act as a back-up to Ian Rush, a player that cost £300,000.

According to Clarke, Walsh wasn't the only player Twentyman didn't rate as good enough for Liverpool. "A member of the coaching staff at Liverpool was under the impression that Tony Cascarino could play, but Geoff wasn't so convinced," Clarke explains. "Tom Saunders rang me one day and asked me to go to Gillingham to watch him. In that match, he didn't actually look too bad. He was decent on the ground, he hovered in the air and won all the flick-ons, but he was a bit clumsy. His game was starting to improve so Geoff went for a second look but came away distinctly unimpressed, saying he'd never be good enough for Liverpool.

"Another player I went to see was Garry Parker. I mentioned him to Lenny [Ashurst] and to Geoff, but they weren't all that keen. He was playing for Luton and he couldn't half pass a ball over a distance. He was 18 at the time. Parker ended up going to Hull for 65 grand and did ok for two seasons before Brian Clough came from nowhere to sign him for a quarter of a million for Forest. Apparently when Graeme Souness became manager of Liverpool, he then tried to sign Garry for a quarter of a million. That's just football, though. I thought: 'F**k me, I told them about him 10 years ago when they could have got him for peanuts.' But this kind of thing happens all of the time."

It was around six months into Kenny Dalglish's reign as Liverpool manager when Twentyman was moved on from the club. Dalglish, who appointed Ron Yeats as his replacement, says that he asked Twentyman's advice when he made Steve McMahon his first signing in September 1985. "Everybody knew about Steve so he wasn't one that needed much scouting," Dalglish says. The Scot, who signed from Celtic in 1977, and is arguably Liverpool's most revered player, isn't sure whether Twentyman had a role in his move south. "I know big Jock [Stein] knew Bob [Paisley] and they arranged the move between them. Whether Geoff had a look at me before that and spoke to Bob, I honestly don't know."

Like all Liverpool greats, Dalglish has a simple analysis for why Twentyman achieved so much success at the club. "The biggest mistake you can make in football is to not make a decision," he explains. "The most difficult thing to do is to say yes or no on any issue in the game. That was Geoff's primary role. 'Sign him or don't sign him.' There's a lot of pressure that goes with that. The beauty of Liverpool Football Club was that everybody in that period who was appointed in whatever position they were in at the club, was appointed for a very good reason. They were all good, if not the best, at their job. Everyone's job at the club, though, was just as important as anyone else's. So the job Geoff did was equally as important as the coaches, the management, the reserve-team staff and so on. The difference was that Geoff and every-one else at Liverpool were doing their jobs better than people in the same positions at other clubs. And that's why we had success."

Unlike the managers before him, Dalglish asked Twentyman to spy on opposition teams during their year together as manager and scout. "He did a superb job with that and really helped me. I think he delegated a bit with the scouts working underneath him and asked some of his most respected colleagues to have a look at teams and their tactics for me. In many ways that was harder than scouting for players because as a scout he would have to watch closely what the oppo were doing on set-pieces. Noticing little deficiencies was the difference between winning and losing sometimes. He didn't have the benefit of TV cameras or coverage to check things back on a Saturday night because 'Match of the Day' only featured extended highlights of one game in the '80s. You were lucky if you even saw the goals from the other matches."

Although Dalglish insists that Twentyman left Liverpool "on very positive terms," adding that his arthritis was making it difficult for him to travel long distances, especially in cramped cars, Norman Clarke believes that Twentyman felt he was being encouraged to leave Liverpool against his wishes. "By the mid-'80s he was having physical problems, but they weren't affecting his ability to do his job properly. People at the club behind the scenes believed they could use back problems as an excuse to force him into early retirement. He was only 57 when he left Liverpool and that was extremely young, especially for a scout, where experience tells probably more than in any other field away from the pitch.

"Geoff realised that things had reached their natural end as it was the start of a new beginning under a player-manager – something that hadn't been tried before – but he was upset by the way it all finished. He always used to say to me that the fella who discovered Billy Liddell would never be out of a job because he had found the one player that would help him keep his reputation for life. Look at the players Geoff signed. He wasn't saying that he considered himself in the same light as the guy who scouted Billy Liddell or any other scout for the matter, because he was very humble, but he never expected it to end like that."

Clarke says that Twentyman told him that in his final weeks at Liverpool, even though he was spending more time conducting operations from Anfield, the tensions around Melwood were so great because of Everton's success and changes on the club's board that some members of the coaching staff and club directors ignored his presence when he went for his constitutional walk around the training ground.

"Geoff felt he'd been snubbed. On the whole, though, I think it was probably decided that things needed freshening up at the club," concludes

Clarke. "Football was changing in the '80s and it was becoming more of a business by then, so business decisions were made. Geoff was from the old school and he believed in honesty and trust, but some people at the club wanted paperwork and hard evidence of work. But that's football. Everything changes quickly and soon he was gone."

*****

BACK at Sky Central, Souness explains how he ended up signing for Liverpool. Unsurprisingly, Twentyman played a role in it.

"Bob Paisley was friendly with a guy who ran a garage called the Wheatsheaf," he explains. "This guy was mates with Phil Boersma who had been sold to Middlesbrough. I think Bob learnt about my progress off him and sent Tom Saunders up to see me play along with Reuben Bennett a couple of times before Geoff came as well, I think. It was done very quickly."

Souness says that his immediate perception of Twentyman was that of a serious man. "I could tell that straight away. But he was very popular. All the players could have a laugh with him, too – sometimes at his expense because of his accent. All the players would ask him who he was looking at: 'Who's going to take my position?' was every player's question to him. He'd never give anything away but he had a sense of humour too…"

Souness, laughing, then becomes the umpteenth footballer to slightly embarrass himself with another improvised impersonation of Twentyman's peculiar accent: "Caaaaarlisle," he screeches, with an emphasis on the first syllable.

Andy Gray finally exits the room after making so much noise. "See ya Andy. Have a good one," Souness says, almost like he's preparing to face United himself. Souness left Liverpool in 1984 days after captaining his side to a European Cup victory against Roma in the Eternal City. He enjoyed two years in Italy with Sampdoria before returning to Scotland where, at 33, he became player-manager of Glasgow Rangers. One of his first acts was to appoint Twentyman as his chief scout in England – ironic, given that most of his greatest finds for Liverpool were from Scotland.

"I couldn't believe Liverpool let him leave," says Souness with a reflective pause. "When I played for Liverpool, we were so successful because we had a group of players who were in their mid-to-late 20s that had grown up together since their early 20s when we were spotted, usually by Geoff or Tom Saunders, and quickly signed. Opponents have said to me that they feared playing Liverpool because we appeared to be men. All our most important players were between 26 and 29 years old, and we all had experience and hunger on our side and people feared that. The management knew which players they wanted and knew that we would grow up together and have the attributes to be successful with the right nurturing. The building of these teams started when we were scouted. Geoff and Tom must have taken a lot of satisfaction when their players came through to form a successful team.

"When I asked Geoff to come to Rangers with me, I wanted him to do exactly the same things he'd done at Liverpool. He was so well known, he had great contacts. I honestly believed I was getting the best scout in Britain. The experience he had was unparalleled in scouting terms. What other scouts can say they have played a part in 20 or so years of success at Liverpool in their greatest period? Geoff was the kind of guy that epitomised the bootroom spirit and he was definitely the kind of person I wanted at my club."

It's appropriate that Souness recognises the 'bootroom spirit'. It is a common misconception that he personally ordered the bootroom to be destroyed during his time as manager of Liverpool, when really it was a result of club directors trying to shape Anfield into a stadium fit enough to host matches at Euro '96. The old bootroom has since been a media room – a basic demand of UEFA for any European ties. Not that Souness wants to talk about that today. "Geoff was still relatively young when he came up with me and there was no reason for him to 'retire.'

When you think he wasn't even 60 and the fact that Ronnie Moran was there until the late '90s, it seems strange that they would allow someone with such experience to leave. I have absolutely no idea why they did. All I cared about was that he brought the best players available to Rangers."

Twentyman was given a free reign on Rangers' scouting system and Souness rarely even asked him where he was going every Saturday. Twentyman would travel to Glasgow once every three weeks, usually via train and according to his notebook, he looked at Kevin Pressman, a goalkeeper at Sheffield Wednesday, along with Nigel Worthington, David Kelly at Preston and Neil Pointon at Everton. Souness says that he signed Mark Walters on Twentyman's recommendation from Aston Villa – a player whom he later brought to Liverpool with limited success. But as Souness points out: "Our remit to Geoff was slightly different to what it would have been at Liverpool because the Scottish League wasn't as strong as it was down south." Just because Walters was good enough for Rangers, it didn't mean he was automatically good enough for Liverpool. Twentyman may have recommended someone else if he was still scouting for Kenny Dalglish. Walters, however, was a success at Ibrox, scoring an average of one in three from a wide-right position.

"You have to remember that Rangers were big, big spenders back then. We already had a brand spanking new stadium at a time when a lot of English clubs were rebuilding theirs or were yet to do so and we were playing European football every season so we could tempt a lot of players up north by offering them more money and spending more on transfer fees. That put a bit of extra pressure on Geoff and he came through with some excellent bits of advice on players."

Aside from Walters, Twentyman encouraged Souness to move for Trevor Steven, Terry Butcher and Mark Hateley, believing each player would fit in with the winning mentality Souness was devising at the club (although it's worth remembering that each player by then was already a fully fledged international and didn't need a lot of scouting).

"Before making a move, I'd always ask Geoff what he thought," Souness adds.

In his five years as manager at Rangers, Souness won four league titles. He laid the foundations for his successor, Walter Smith, later the manager of Everton, to win nine SPL titles in a row. "Geoff decided to retire in 1989," Souness says. "He was tired of all the travelling by then and decided to stay at home to be closer to his wife, Pat. His help was invaluable and I thought about asking him back with me when I returned to Liverpool as manager. But I felt Ron Yeats was doing a good job so I decided not to change it."

One of the few things he didn't change at Anfield, then.

10. Scouting Today

From Skem to Brazil, a matter of character
and the foreign invasion

ARBROATH, midwinter. Forfar Athletic are the visitors: the Angus derby. Rain, sleet, wind and anything else the North Sea can summon is gobbed towards the closest football ground in Britain to a coastline, Gayfield Park. Geoff Twentyman would take residency in one of the three uncovered terraces to avoid detection. As if it was ever needed at such a northerly outpost. No half-time complimentaries in the Main Stand. He'd make do with muddied Bovril or dishwater tea from a van. In a plastic cup.

When Twentyman was chief scout of Liverpool Football Club, trips to eastern Scotland were about as exotic as it got. When you consider he saw Steve Heighway playing at Skelmersdale Utd, it proves that he didn't even have to go that far to scout potential. He was not privy to the delights scouting dignitaries allegedly enjoy today where an overnight stay in a five-star hotel would be just the start of it. Twentyman made do with B&Bs. "He must have had a tart up in Scotland, he was up there so much," jokes son, William. "But he always made it home in time when he needed to. He never missed any family events."

Locations and overnight accommodation aren't the only differences between now and then. Before some computer nerd invented the internet and well before you could find anything about any person in the public eye on Google (or any footballer on Wikipedia), finding information on players was a laborious chore. "It was all about a profound knowledge of the game," Kevin Keegan told me prior to leaving Newcastle United for a second time as manager. "Now, if you want to know about a player, you just ask TV companies for DVDs of games. You can have as many as you want and it's never a problem. I get videos every single day of players from Brazil and Argentina. Everyone is dying to sell to you, so it's accessible to look at players no matter where they're from.

"There was no TV coverage of any of the games Geoff would be watching in Division Three and Division Four. Guys like Geoff had to go there and watch and write. They never had the benefit of replays or having it on film. Certainly none of my games at Scunthorpe were ever on TV. I think there's only a bit of footage that still exists that shows me in a Scunthorpe shirt. We played Arsenal in the League Cup and lost 6-0. I scored 70-odd goals for Liverpool, but only 40 of those were recorded. Now you can be a fan of a Conference team and if you can't get to the game on a Saturday, you can see the goals on TV on a Sunday morning."

Even at lower levels today there is a thought that different scouts are required by clubs to search for players in specific positions, when in the past, one scout was enough to watch all. Twentyman's son Geoff Jnr followed his father into scouting when he became assistant manager to Ian Holloway at Bristol Rovers in 1996. Rovers were struggling at the foot of the Division Two table. Without a goalscorer, Holloway and Twentyman agreed that they would continue to toil, so Twentyman used his contacts in non-league football to find a bargain.

"The first time I went I actually wondered what my dad would be looking for," he said. "I tried to trust my own judgement. The hard thing for me was that I was a centre-half and I felt that I only knew that position. My dad had the ability to spot any position. I ended up signing Barry Hayles from Stevenage. We knew Marcus Stewart was moving on because his reputation was rising, so I called Graham Roberts [former Spurs and Chelsea] who was the manager of Yeovil in the Conference. I asked him who was the best striker in non-league football. So when we went to watch Barry, he was outstanding. We signed him for £200,000 and Ollie (Ian Holloway) was panicking, saying: 'What will happen if he's rubbish?' I said we'd probably get the sack. Luckily the next season he scored 25 goals, got us in the play-offs, then we sold him for more than £2 million quid, so we made a profit on him. Inwardly it made us feel great because it put him on the path to success and a comfortable way of life. My dad did that with dozens of people, but we could have done with someone who knew their strikers."

Today, the role of a scout is incalculably different. Liverpool's current head scout Eduardo Macia says that he uses lots of traditional scouting methods to spot talent, although the areas where he searches are far-flung compared to when Twentyman was at the club. "I have been all over the world," he told *LFC* magazine last year. "Nowhere is too far."

Despite advancements in travel as well as logistics (Macia uses jets, while Twentyman used Shankly's 'hand-me-downs'), Macia believes that the fundamental approach to scouting hasn't changed a great deal. "Our idea has three parts," he explained. "First of all we've brought in a lot of young players in the last few years. Guys who are 16, 17, 18. Now we are hoping to add more players of that quality. In Spain it would be described as a 'B' team. The plan is to provide first-team players for the future so that when they are 20, 21, 22 they are ready for the Premier League."

The second part of Macia's programme involves players that are slightly older. "Guys like Lucas who was one of the best youngsters in Brazil, and Ryan Babel," Macia continued. "Both of them are in their early 20s and are players for the years to come, although they're already capable of playing in the first team. Then on the next level it's Javier Mascherano, Fernando Torres, Martin Skrtel and Daniel Agger.

"They are also still young – 22, 23, 24 – when they came here, but have lots of experience and can go straight into the first team without too many problems. We hope that in the future we'll be bringing through enough players that the manager might only need to buy one or two every summer. Hopefully he won't need to go out and sign four or five then."

Macia said that Benitez is trying to mimic and improve upon the system he installed at Valencia – a system that provides stability and continuity for the club. "We won the league [twice] with a fantastic team. A lot of young players such as Carlos Marchena, Ruben Baraja, Vicente and David Albelda combined with the veterans like Amedeo Carboni and Jocelyn Angloma to bring success. We knew we had a good foundation with the older guys and added to it in the right way to bring trophies."

Valencia's success in La Liga is made all the more impressive when you consider the opposition they finished ahead of. "It was done despite the fact that Barcelona, Real Madrid, Deportivo and Atletico all had more money than us. But we were working with a clear idea and got it right. Now we want to do the same here at Liverpool. To be perfectly honest it's not possible for us to spend £200m to win the Premier League. We can't do that so we have to find another way. Steven Gerrard, Jamie Carragher and Sami Hyypia are all fantastic veterans. We've added to that group in the right way by bringing in some of those I mentioned earlier. Now Rafa is happy with the young players we have and wants to continue improving the senior squad. I think the squad we have now, along with some of the young players coming through, is the best I've seen during my time in the game. I think it's got the potential to be better than the Valencia team of '04. That was nearly five years ago and the level of football has gone up since then. The game has progressed a lot in such a short space of time. That's what we've got to keep doing: improve. If you're not, then you're going backwards. Even when you win something you've still got to try and become better by bringing in more quality."

With this in mind, how does Macia identify those he thinks will make it to the very top? "The mentality is the most important thing. There are probably a million players with good quality in the world. That's not enough. I don't want someone who is fantastic in September and

October. I want someone who is fantastic all year round. If you want to be a successful team you need players who can still be at their best when it comes to the end of the season and the big games arrive almost every few days. It's not just a matter of quality. You can improve a player's fitness, technique and make them tactically better. What you can't do is give them the mentality. You can be a fantastic player at a lower-level team but if you want to come here then you've got to be a winner. When you play for a big club – particularly in the Premier League – everyone else will be doing their utmost to beat you every weekend. You've got to be able to deal with that and produce your best."

'Mentality' is a word that has been frequently used by Benitez since he arrived on Merseyside nearly five years ago. A positive 'mentality' is essential if a player is ever to play for Liverpool's first team under the Spaniard. Macia illustrates his point: "For example, Lucas says: 'Give me the ball; even if I make a mistake, I'm not afraid to take responsibility in big games.' That's what we require. They are strong-minded individuals who can think for themselves and don't need to be told what to do; clever guys who can make their own decisions on the pitch and help you win. When you combine that with good quality then you've got the best players."

It is obvious that football has changed infinitely in the time between the eras of Twentyman and Macia. Given that Twentyman searched first and foremost at players that could 'strike the ball properly', like Phil Neal, and Macia looks at 'mentality', like Lucas – who is yet to win over the Liverpool fans – it is clear to me which mandate should be followed. Then again, cultures are different, football is more popular and the demands are heavier these days. Maybe Phil Neal wouldn't have had the 'mentality' to see through his darkest moments as a Northampton player if he was a professional now. Unlikely as it may seem.

Gordon McQueen, who now works as the European scout for Middlesbrough, said that Twentyman's success as a scout was undeniable, but if he worked today, he would find different problems to the ones he experienced back then. "It's unbelievably difficult because all the clubs which have similar resources in the Premier League are all looking at the same players," he argued. "The market has gone absolutely cuckoo when you look at what's going on at Man City compared to other clubs which have had the same amount of money in recent seasons. The financial side is the hardest thing now, but knowing whether a player will adapt to the Premier League quickly is the most difficult thing because it's such a strong league – a lot stronger than it ever has been."

Macia agrees and says that there are numerous hidden demands that the average football fan wouldn't even begin to think about. "They [the scouts] have to live in the country that they cover, that's the way we like it to be," he explained. If you are based in England and just travel over to watch the player, you don't get the full picture. It's easy to see if someone is performing well or not, but that's not enough. We want to know everything about the player, not just how his form is. I never stop. Even at the weekends I am still going to watch a game on a Saturday and Sunday. It could be an U17 or U19 UEFA tournament. Or during the season I might be attending a Champions League game on Tuesday and Wednesday and then a UEFA Cup game on a Thursday. It's a special job that you have to love a lot. If you don't, then it would become impossible.

"It's definitely not a typical office routine. It varies greatly from day to day. Scouting is not a nine to five job. When you are looking for players everything can change quickly. For example, you might plan to watch an U18 game but if the player you are checking on doesn't feature, then you can't work. It means you always need a plan b and sometimes even a plan c. You have to be able to adapt in an instant."

There are also other criteria Macia seeks in those he employs with a scouting task – none of whom are his friends. Twentyman often used Norman Clarke, a person he could trust through their long-standing solidarity, but Macia believes that friendships in the football business when it comes to scouting rarely work.

"Our scouts have got to be totally professional. We use guys who have worked for big clubs like Real Madrid or been a sporting director in Italy or been at the biggest club in Brazil. They are all very experienced, strong people. They don't say 'maybe', they give definite answers on players. They are usually the best scouts in each country. I think the best scouts should find you the best players."

Despite the differences, there is one main similarity that Twentyman and his second successor share in their approach to spotting talent. "Discretion," Macia said. "Nobody can know who you are. I try to stay out of the spotlight because it's more beneficial if people don't recognise my face. I don't like to be in the newspaper. That's not beneficial for me. If they know you then they will probably be able to figure out what player you are looking at. You have to be almost like a secret agent. You are working for your club – nobody else – so it's important not to show other teams what you're doing. Most of the time you will have Manchester United, Chelsea, Arsenal, Real Madrid, Barcelona, Inter, Milan, Juventus, Bayern Munich and Lyon all chasing the same talents. They are all powerful clubs with a lot of money so you have to make sure everything you do is top secret. The scouts can't be telling anyone they work for LFC. So if you can stay discreet it helps."

This Cold War approach to scouting means unseen battles between the world's super clubs take place all over the planet on a daily basis. Decisions must be made instantly if Macia is to be successful – something that seems different to Twentyman's era when there was maybe less competition to sign players, at least in terms of spending power and the sheer number of European clubs interested in targets.

"Sometimes we might watch them five times, sometimes 10," Macia continues. "On other occasions you'll only need to see them twice and you are sure because you already know everything about him. On average I'd say we watch them five or six times. But it's not just about that. Lucas, our scout watched him and asked lots of different people about him. Then I spent two weeks in Brazil watching him training as well as playing. From all that we hope to be certain about a player. Of course you can still make a mistake but this method reduces the chances. Sometimes, even when you know everything, you can still get it wrong. There are lots of factors to consider, such as language, wife or girlfriend not settling in a new country, and a different style of football. You can still get it wrong, but with our method we hope to make the least number of mistakes. Football is not a science, therefore scouting can't be either. It's all about decisions and relationships. So a scout can never be 100 per cent certain that a player will go on to be a success in the first team. But you've got to find those who have all the requirements to do so."

After all Macia's work, a final report is given to the manager. But even then his job is still not complete. "When you hand the info to Rafa you have to be certain. I have to convince him that this player is right for Liverpool. And he is always the most difficult one to convince. You have to believe in the player's capabilities. If Rafa isn't sure, and you're not convinced either, then the player will never be signed. Making a decision with the scout, talking with Rafa and then finalising the move with Rick Parry. It's a very long process." Only after all that is complete can Macia actually take a breather.

"When you are watching an unveiling press conference here at Melwood everyone is very happy. You are relaxed. That is a fantastic feeling. People are very happy when the player signs and is standing there posing in a Liverpool shirt. They say: 'Yes, we've got a new player.' But if they knew exactly what goes on behind the scenes and how much work goes into it all they'd be absolutely ecstatic."

Macia indicates that the fundamental approach to scouting is no different to what it was in the 1960s. Only the desires of those in charge at the top have altered. Bill Shankly, Bob Paisley, Joe Fagan and Kenny Dalglish all shared similar beliefs on how football clubs should be run, how the team should play, and which type of players are included in the make-up of that team. Twentyman listened to their wishes and searched for the appropriate players – just as Macia does today. The main difference is that Twentyman was searching for players that had grown up on Arbroath beach. Macia looks for fledglings of the Copacabana.

Indeed, there was a time when every English club could boast a backbone of Scottish granite. Jordan, Bremner and McQueen at Leeds; Burns, Gemmill and Robertson at Forest; Burley, Brazil and Wark at Ipswich Town. For Liverpool, see Kenny Dalglish, Graeme Souness and Alan Hansen.

A celtic invasion had seen the English leagues rife with Scots in the '60s, '70s and '80s. At any given ground on any given Saturday, fans would reliably see a sprinkling of Scottish talent slugging it out on First Division pitches. A quick look at any Panini sticker album from that decade indicates so. In 1979, there were more than 50 players of Scottish blood in English squads. When you consider there were only 13 players in each squad (according to the number of stickers on each Panini spread), that number is even more prevalent.

Compare that with the number of Scottish starters in the Premier League today and it looks like Hadrian's Wall has been re-fortified and the infantry have been sent in across the borders. On the opening day of the 2008/09 season, only six Scottish players were included in matchday squads, one of them being Calum Davenport from West Ham United, who had only recently been called up by Craig Burley to represent 'his country,' despite being born in Bedford and having represented England Under-21s on eight occasions. The other players were Darren Fletcher (Manchester United), Craig Gordon (Sunderland), Iain Turner (Everton's substitute goalkeeper), Graeme Dorrans and Craig Beattie (both subs for West Bromwich Albion).

When it comes to championing Scottish talent, Liverpool aren't exactly pioneers in this era either. A Scot hasn't represented the club consistently since Gary McAllister left six years ago. In 2008/09, only one Scot was issued with a squad number by Rafa Benitez – Falkirk-born midfielder Ryan Flynn got the less-than-prestigious number 35 shirt.

Now this is not to say that English clubs should be including Scottish players purely out of misty-eyed tradition. It is highlighting how football has changed in the time since Geoff Twentyman was scouting for Liverpool. His knowledge of the Scottish scene was unparalleled and his success rate in uncovering pearls such as Steve Nicol was prolific. He wasn't alone in looking north of the border, though, with Everton's Harry Cooke plucking several players from relative obscurity before presenting them with a stage in the First Division. "Geoff obviously did a lot of his scouting up in Scotland and his record stands head and shoulders above any other scout in the game," says Nicol. "In life, everyone has a talent, but to get to the top, you always need someone there to recognise you have a talent and open doors for you. Most people probably think it's easy to spot players, but it's a lot more difficult than that. Geoff's record is second to nobody else and his track record is phenomenal."

Given the lack of Scottish players in the Premier League now, does that mean that the scouts aren't looking in the right places? Does it mean that it has become less fashionable to shop in Scotland? Does it mean that clubs are becoming less patient with nurturing British talent? Or does it simply indicate a decline in Scottish football? When you consider that in September 2008 Scotland were only one place below England in the FIFA World Rankings (15th and 16th), the latter certainly can't be applied, at least at international level.

Gary Gillespie says that scouts traditionally had success in Scotland, particularly Liverpool and Geoff Twentyman, because Scots and Scousers share similar characteristics. He added that it is now vogue to go abroad when looking to sign new players. He's probably right, too. Fans and the media get more excited about the signing of a boy from Brazil than a bairn from Brechin, regardless of their talent.

"Just look at Arsenal," barks John Connolly, who was scouted by Geoff Twentyman before moving to Everton. "Traditionally there were a few Scottish players in the squad. But now, even in the reserves, there are a lot of West African boys in there – as well as French/Moroccans."

Connolly knows more than most about this issue. Now scouting for a number of clubs, he also works as a delegate for the Scottish Premier League. "It seems to be a thing where Scottish players aren't big enough physically to make it to the top. If you look at the Arsenal team, they're all giants and the modern-day footballer is 6ft 2in or 6ft 3in. They're all well built and can run for fun. All the Scots are small and it's become so much more difficult. It's the same case with the English lads. The talent is still up here, it's just there are more Championship and lower-league clubs looking at us rather than Premier League. In the last few years, only Alan Hutton has gone down to Spurs for big money. Shaun Maloney was a good player and it didn't work for him, as was Ross Wallace, who played for Sunderland [now at Preston North End], but they're both very small and maybe physically it didn't work out for them. I think Scottish players these days have a better chance in theory if they go to the Championship, get noticed and progress from there.

"My worry technically when I look at all the UK sides, especially when we play international football, is that we are behind. The opposition always seems to be better technically. When you see the calibre of player England have, whenever they are put together in a team, the other side consistently shows better technique, regardless of the result. Scotland might end up winning games because of their up-'n'-at-'em attitude, but even against the Norways and Icelands, we're still behind them technically."

Connolly believes the problem with the lack of Scottish talent, particularly with younger players, is endemic across Britain – and it's not entirely down to football. "I seriously think it comes down to changes in society. When I was young – without trying to sound like an old fogey – I came home and went out with a ball straight away. I would play with the bigger boys and learn a lot that way. These days, that just doesn't happen. If things aren't organised these days, kids won't do it. It's laziness, and whether they want it enough is debatable. Keegan in the '70s was maybe not technically the best player in the world, but he fought harder than any other player I have seen to reach the top. He worked his socks off to become a better player. During the week in training, he worked harder than any other player – but you don't get many kids with that attitude these days. It's true that it's easier to sign kids from abroad – just as it is for any person to move to Britain because of the lack of restrictions – but I think it's also true that foreign kids want it more, too."

11. What Price Now?

The modern-day value of
Twentyman's signings

"IT is easier to compare players and where they have come from, rather than the fee they were signed for. Therefore the only team Shankly's can be compared to today is Arsene Wenger's Arsenal, because of their similar attitudes in the transfer market," says Dr Rory Miller, a specialist in football business and finance from Liverpool University.

There is a case for arguing that Wenger's approach to the transfer system is like that of Bill Shankly in the 1960s and '70s. Unlike Manchester United and Chelsea, for the most part, Arsenal, like Liverpool, have signed unfashionable and equally obscure players from the game's lesser clubs. The main difference being that Wenger casts his eye across a wider net of players, whereas Shankly only searched in the north of England and Scotland. Steve Rowley, Arsenal's current chief scout, like Twentyman, has scouts posted in different regions. Whereas Twentyman had different positions for Cumbria, the north-east, the Midlands and Yorkshire, Rowley has one in each of South America, North America, central Europe and southern Europe.

It could be argued that most big clubs in the modern era have similar networks, but few have enjoyed the success of both Shankly and Paisley's Liverpool and Wenger's Arsenal. That, in itself, is another similarity, as Liverpool were able to sign the best youngsters because they had a calling card stamped 'Bill Shankly'; they knew they would eventually get the chance to play. Arsenal now have their own trump in Arsene Wenger.

"One can only maintain and develop players by communicating a culture, a culture which passes from generation to generation," Wenger said at the start of the 2008/09 season. Prospects such as Cesc Fabregas, Theo Walcott, Denilson and more recently Carlos Vela go straight into the senior squad after arrival, but then spend time learning the 'Arsenal way' in the reserves or by going out on loan. Vela has only this season arrived in England after three years in Spain. Shankly and Paisley after him adopted a similar approach, with Terry McDermott, Steve Nicol, Gary Gillespie and John Toshack all being bought and then learning the 'Liverpool way' before establishing themselves as first-team regulars. This system was repeated year after year with one or two players coming in each summer before reaching the first team later, thus creating continuity and safeguarding the long-term future of the club. Perhaps this is more of a description of philosophy at each respective outfit, but the players that are targeted in the transfer market dictate the way in which the football side is run at any club.

Vela's arrival at Arsenal again has its comparisons with numerous Liverpool signings who were spotted before Twentyman moved stealthily to sign them. In September 2008, the *Times* reported how Arsenal's chief scout, Rowley, received a phone call in the early hours of the morning from his South American expert, Sandro Orlandelli. He was at the World Youth Championships in Peru and told him: "Turn on your television." Vela starred in a preliminary game. Rowley immediately booked a flight that took him to Lima via Miami. He watched the final as Vela's Mexico defeated Brazil with the striker also the competition's highest scorer. With other Spanish clubs hovering, yet dithering, Rowley contact Vela's club, Chivas, and a day later a deal was agreed.

Scouting has saved Arsenal hundreds of millions. In 2007, Premier League clubs spent £120m on players aged 21 or younger. Vela cost only an initial £125,000. Fabregas was earlier signed for £700,000. While Chelsea have spent vast sums on players recommended by more than 60 scouts (a network that was streamlined to less than a dozen in late

2008), not a single one has broken through to claim a regular first-team place. According to newspaper reports in 2006, they spent around £5m alone on taking 16-year-old Leeds United pair Tom Taiwo and Michael Woods to Stamford Bridge. Although Woods has played twice against lower-league opposition in the FA Cup, Taiwo has since been sent to Port Vale for an ultimately unsuccessful loan spell and is now a free agent. Liverpool, too, have spent a reported £20m to bring 30 foreign youngsters into their youth ranks and first-team fringes, with few making any kind of lasting impression. Critics might argue that these fees are small change in football today, but Arsenal have proven that you can snare the best youngsters for relatively little money providing that a club has an adept scouting network.

There are, of course, differences between the Liverpool way and the Arsenal way. Wenger signs players mainly when they are still in their teenage years, whereas Liverpool signed them when they had a bit more experience. (There have been some, though. In the summer of 2008, Wenger signed 21-year-old Samir Nasri, for instance, a player who he'd been scouting for more than six years.) Equally, Wenger is doing it at a time when the financial climate in football has encouraged managers to spend, spend and spend some more. Liverpool's success, however, came when there were fewer reasons to have so many youngsters and indeed so many players in the squad. Then again, Wenger's approach is a result of (financial) necessity being the mother of (youthful) invention. Arsenal have built a new stadium in recent years, but how many other managers could have produced a team on such meagre resources that sells out a 60,000-seater arena on a habitual basis?

Liverpool signed players such as Hansen, Neal, Clemence and Nicol, and played them for more than a decade, winning everything before them. As it stands, Wenger has won nothing with his kids and has increasingly struggled to keep hold of some. Ashley Cole and Alexander Hleb moved on in recent years, and with the Gunners winning nothing again in 2008/09, it is reported that Fabregas will go too (aged 22, he is currently their longest-serving player). Conversely, we don't live in a time where players spend a considerable amount of time at one club, unless you are playing for the club you supported in a city you grew up in, like Steven Gerrard. Arsenal, though, are in danger of becoming a selling club, whereas the only player Liverpool sold at his peak in their heyday was Kevin Keegan.

What is certain is that if both models are to be truly compared, Arsenal must start winning things. Only if their success in the transfer market is replicated by welcoming trophies into their cabinet will it be fair to compare the two approaches to the transfer market. After all, Liverpool's success in the market was backed up by glory on the field. The two factors are not mutually exclusive.

Wenger has said: "I feel we have the quality to be successful with this group. What has changed is patience levels have become shorter and we are in a situation where people say: 'You haven't won anything for three years, you need to win the championship.' Yes, that's true, but what I believe is right and leave people to judge…and I feel I can be successful this way." At Liverpool, or any other top club in Europe, Wenger would not have been allowed four trophyless seasons without clear signs that silverware is waiting for them in a short period of time. Shankly and Wenger may be two completely different characters but they both won trophies early on in their careers at each club. This ultimately relieved early pressure and enabled both managers to foster a legacy.

*****

"YOU couldn't put a price on the players Geoff signed in today's climate," Phil Thompson says, which is quite literally right. Trying to establish an accurate value of how much Twentyman's Liverpool signings would be worth in the modern game is no easy task – mainly because the price of footballers doesn't rise simply with inflation.

"It's quite noticeable that a lot of economists have tried to work out a method for predicting transfer fees, especially up until 1998," says Dr Miller. "But the Bosman ruling made everything so much more difficult because players were moving for nothing, sometimes at an age when they were coming into their peak."

Even in the years immediately before Bosman, it was difficult to ascertain a precise figure of modern worth, mainly because there was a ruling deeming that players such as Ian Rush and Dean Saunders, who were both Welsh internationals and had played in England for their whole careers, were still considered as foreigners, therefore distorting their value. And deals are now even more intricate, so it is unsurprising that Rick Parry, Liverpool's soon to be former chief executive, consistently refers to the "complexities of transfers".

Dr Miller adds: "The market today depends on so many different factors. More so after the Webster case [where Hearts defender Andy Webster bought himself out of a contract and moved to Wigan]. Players can now legally renege on their contract with up to three years to run and move elsewhere." If someone is under 28, the ruling says that you can buy that player out for what their remaining salary is. For example, recently the case of Jonas Gutierrez at Newcastle has led to a dispute over his transfer fee. This is partly because he is half-owned by Real Mallorca and Velez Sarsfield in Argentina, but also because he has tried to buy out his own contract under the Webster ruling rather than pay the full amount that the clubs would want. Frank Lampard is another player who could have moved under the Webster ruling before he signed his new contract.

"In some cases it is becoming more difficult to put a price on players. We've seen Emmanuel Adebayor valued at £35m and Cristiano Ronaldo at £70m. Let's say Adebayor goes for £20m and Ronaldo goes for whatever, then where do you value a Dimitar Berbatov among that? The Webster ruling can make clubs a little bit more cautious on both the buying and the selling side."

UEFA have insisted that clubs must submit a squad maximum of 25 for European matches, eight of whom must have been reared through the youth system of any club within that team's domestic league, and four of those eight must be from the actual side that is competing in European competition. Yet if a player has been brought in from elsewhere in Europe, but has been at an English club between the ages of 18 and 21, they fall into the home-grown category too. That means that Cesc Fabregas and Philippe Senderos of Arsenal are considered 'home-grown' because they were both at the club by the time they were 18 and have since remained for a period of three years or more.

In summary, the first distortion of the transfer market came with Bosman. Then the Webster ruling arrived and changed things again. And now, UEFA's new edict makes it even more difficult to establish the true value of a player. Dr Miller says: "Leeds United threw the whole market and theories in the air because at their height a respected economist called Bill Gerrard valued them at £180m. The whole team went for less than £60m."

Promotions, relegations, European qualification and board takeovers, not to mention fluctuating financial climates, also have an impact. With all that in mind, it seems unlikely that there is really a correct way to figure out how much players such as Phil Neal, Kevin Keegan and Alan Hansen would be worth today.

But Dr Miller has another idea: "The best bet is to try and find the value of the nearest equivalent player in the modern game and look at their transfer record. You look at age because a player is going to reach his maximum transfer value at 27 or 28. You obviously look at his position, then you have a look at his number of international caps. When considering strikers as well, you need to have a look at the number of goals scored. Strikers will command the biggest fees and attacking midfielders will go for more than defensive midfielders.

"Central defenders will go for a reasonably high value, Rio Ferdinand for example. Full-backs are not going to be as valuable because it's easier to replace a full-back than a central defender. Goalkeepers also won't be as valuable, which is surprising given how important they are to the team."

Again, however, this is difficult to assess, as no two players are the same in style, ability, nationality or age when they are bought or sold. It is worth considering that Liverpool traditionally signed players and used them until they could run no more. Only Kevin Keegan left when he was at his peak. Most, such as Phil Neal and Alan Hansen, remained at the club until they retired, in turn making it difficult to guess how much they were worth even at their peak. That means you can only compare the fee for which they were signed. However, unlike today where there is an obsession with buying established players from other top clubs, it is unlikely that Rafa Benitez will do any of his shopping in the lower leagues of Scotland and risk playing them in the Premier League. The trend of where you spend your money has polarised the market.

"It would be easier to do it on the basis of what salaries the players were earning because you can be more sure about certain figures," Dr Miller concludes. "If you take Alan Hansen, for example, you can look at any one of the top four and be able to compare what he is earning. William Gallas at Arsenal, for example, has played for his country without winning anything, but has had an integral level of importance for his club side."

Maybe Ray Clemence can be contrasted with Pepe Reina in that the pair have been first choice for Liverpool, yet haven't won as many caps internationally as they probably should, owing to the standard of goalkeeping in their respective nations. While Clemence was fighting for the number one jersey with Peter Shilton, Reina has a similar predicament with Iker Casillas. Reina, though, was signed from Spanish Primera Liga side Villarreal, who reached the Champions League semi-final the season after he left. Now that's hardly Scunthorpe, is it?

*****

"FOOTBALL is a simple game. It doesn't change a great deal," Ronnie Moran tells me. "It's only made complicated by people who don't really know it." Ronnie is not wrong. Although he's not totally right either. Time has changed. Football is played at a greater pace now than it was even 10 years ago. And whereas 20 years ago coaches were trying to mould footballers into athletes, now they're trying to mould athletes into footballers. Momo Sissoko, for example, would never have been a Premier League or Serie A footballer two decades ago, while Xabi Alonso would surely have been considered as an undisputed world-class midfielder rather than someone who would be if he wasn't a yard short of pace. Professionalism in the game has also improved, and booze cultures are all but extinct from football clubs, from the Premier League to the Conference.

Like the game on the field, the discipline of scouting shares the same fundamentals it always has, albeit with a few changes that have already been mentioned in this book. What has remained the same is that having a competent scout is imperative if a club is to build success and sustain it over a long period of time. "The sort of lad I'm looking for here is a kid who'll try to nutmeg Kevin Keegan in a training match... but then step aside for him in the corridor," Bob Paisley once said. It was the Liverpool way and the same values should still be applied today. If a manager has blended a squad of players that share the same talent, desire and ambition, he is going to enjoy success a lot more than he suffers defeat.

It would probably be unfair to compare Twentyman and Eduardo Macia's success rate with players in the transfer market, owing to the fact that Twentyman was at the club for 19 years as chief scout, while Macia has been at Liverpool for less than half a decade so far. Twentyman outlined his potential for success early on, however, by discovering Ray Clemence and Larry Lloyd from the lower leagues. While Macia has enjoyed seeing players such as Fernando Torres and Martin Skrtel cement their positions as potential future Liverpool greats (it is too early to be certain just yet – even with Torres), his record with lesser-known players has been moderate at best. David Ngog, Sebastian Leto and the mysterious Vitor Flora are just a few foreign youngsters who have been signed for considerable transfer fees or signing-on fees before expressing through their languid body style that they have little interest in making a name for themselves. It seems as though by merely signing for Liverpool, they feel they have already found fame, success and fortune.

The issue of nationality is irrelevant by comparison. Although it is important for scouts to find a sprinkling of Scousers good enough to play for the club (which is another issue for the Academy altogether), Liverpool has always been a club with more of a commonwealth feel to it. In the team that won the 1986 FA Cup final against Everton, the only Scouser, or Englishman for that matter, was on the bench – Steve McMahon. Even in the most successful decade in the club's history, the '70s, the only local footballers to play regularly were listed as Phil Thompson, Ian Callaghan (who'd been there for years beforehand), Jimmy Case, Sammy Lee and David Johnson. Macia is, remember, only acting upon his manager's wishes. If the manager told him to try and find the best British talent he would simply be narrowing the pool of talent, but Macia would nevertheless have to fulfill those demands.

Macia, though, has been responsible for more experienced misfits such as Charles Itandje and Andriy Voronin. At the moment, Philip Degen has done little to suggest he will ever make any sort of positive impact at Anfield, while the £7m to bring Andrea Dossena from Italy looks like money lost, especially when you consider John Arne Riise (who admittedly wasn't up to the mark), was more accustomed to English football and was sold for half the price. In reserve-team football meanwhile, Emmanuel Mendy, looks like someone who has only recently been introduced to a football.

Even though it could be argued that Liverpool, and football clubs in general, were spending less money in Twentyman's time, there were fewer risks financially and fewer observers analysing it. Plus there is simply more transfer activity now because clubs need bigger squads for European competitions that are saturated with fixtures and therefore there are more opportunities for deals not to work out. Still, Twentyman didn't make as many expensive mistakes, and when he did make one, Liverpool rarely made a loss when they sold the player on. When you consider the technology scouts have at their disposal today, it makes Twentyman's record with signings all the more remarkable. Modern scouts have a databank of potential targets at the touch of a computer button while Twentyman had to rely on word of mouth, a diary and a battered old motor.

"When Geoff Twentyman put his name to a player, that player was good enough to play for Liverpool," says Kevin Keegan. "Whether that is the case [with scouts] now, I am not so sure. I know Geoff did make mistakes with a few, and sure they signed players that didn't quite fulfill their promise, but there is bound to be a failure somewhere along the line. He may have missed out on one or two – players that became greats elsewhere – but hey, you can't collect all the pebbles on the beach, can you?"

12. Scout's Honour

A proud record and life after football

VISIT Melwood on any given weekday and it is staggering how many random extras there are buzzing around. Most of them are dressed in official club attire and wear personalised flip-flops with their initials. Sometimes the letters are golden.

There are hundreds of people that work behind the scenes of a football club and each one contributes to the club's success and failure in any small way. Ultimately, it's the manager and players that receive the adulation or flak when it comes, but without the work of others, success, at least, wouldn't be possible.

In 1982, Twentyman said: "I am proud to say Liverpool have never fallen from grace. The club has qualified for European competitions either by winning trophies or through high league positions every year. No other top club has enjoyed such continued success. All the greats – Manchester United, Spurs, Arsenal and Leeds – have slipped when one great team has aged. Liverpool have shown the way in staying at the top."

Four years after Twentyman left Liverpool for Rangers, Liverpool won the league title for the 18th time. They haven't won it since.

Before Sky's TV and its money, football had a tendency to run in cycles, and Liverpool's slip from the zenith of English football is a result of several different factors. One of them was their lack of success in the transfer market – something directly linked to Twentyman's departure. For four years between 1986 and 1990, only four players signed for Liverpool that could undeniably be described as a success. Those players were John Barnes, Peter Beardsley, Ray Houghton and John Aldridge. Glenn Hysen had his merits, but he lacked pace and was certainly not an adequate replacement for Alan Hansen.

In the months before Twentyman left the club, Alan Kennedy and Phil Neal also departed, two players who between them had racked up more than 1,000 appearances and collected countless trophies along the way. They simply weren't replaced. Steve Nicol was a fine player (another Twentyman signing), but his versatility meant he was more useful further up the pitch than at full-back. Barry Venison was a good professional but wasn't on the same level of ability as either Neal or Kennedy.

During this time, Nicky Tanner, Nigel Spackman, David Burrows, Jimmy Carter, David Speedie and Ronny Rosenthal were also signed, some for exorbitant fees. Carter in particular cost nearly a million pounds from Millwall. All, again, were simply not up to the standard of the players they were replacing.

After that, it got even worse, with Souness bringing in overpriced misfits such as Dean Saunders, Mark Walters, Istvan Kozma, Paul Stewart, Torben Piechnik, Neil Ruddock, Julian Dicks and Michael Stensgaard (a £400,000 signing who never played a single game). Experienced legends such as Jan Molby, Steve McMahon, Steve Nicol, Ian Rush, Ronnie Whelan and Bruce Grobbelaar were allowed to leave (admittedly at the right time as they were coming towards the end of their peak) but once again were replaced inadequately.

By now the game had changed and more money was involved in transfers generally, so the fees are relative. But the mismanagement in the transfer market continued with Roy Evans: Phil Babb, John Scales and Mark Kennedy were brought in, none of whom were good enough for Liverpool. Later Stan Collymore signed for a club record £8,500,000 and didn't have the mental strength to deal with a weekly shopping trip to the supermarket, never mind play in front of 45,000 fervent fans.

Between 1990 and 2000, Liverpool won two major trophies. For a club used to feeding off success and achieving more, the results were lean gruel. You can blame the managers in charge or the scouts that spotted some of the hidden 'diamonds' (Ron Yeats and his team must have mined in the wrong quarry when they dug out Jimmy Carter) but one of the main reasons why Liverpool were overtaken in the '90s by Manchester United and Arsenal was their impotence in spotting the right talent, replacing former greats appropriately, and making the correct big-money moves for the good of the team. Somewhere along the line, the wrong advice was being given to the management and the wrong decisions were being made at the top.

It is difficult to comprehend it now, but the squad that delivered the league championship and the European Cup in 1977 was assembled on a pittance. A Liverpool player today and even in the mid-'90s would earn in a few months what Shankly and Paisley spent to give the Reds immortality.

Some of the players in that squad were maybe not individually the very, very best, but the balance was right. Anyone can pick out the best players from a match, but Twentyman had the Midas touch of picking future stars from mediocre performances. He was an expert at spotting talent that would complement others already at the club. When he left, his foresight disappeared.

*****

GEOFF TWENTYMAN'S encyclopaedic memory of locations meant he never used a map whenever he travelled to watch a player. On 11 May 1985 he was due to look at a target from Lincoln City who was in action at Bradford. Fortunately, he never made it to the match. Fifty-six people lost their lives when a flash fire engulfed the Main Stand at Valley Parade. Had Twentyman been there, he might have been elsewhere in the stadium anyway, given his penchant for mixing it with the fans rather than the dignitaries. But according to his friends, Twentyman wasn't as sharp in locating grounds as he used to be. He missed the turning for Bradford on the motorway and went elsewhere to watch another match.

Maybe Liverpool saw he was ageing and decided it was time for a change in the scouting system, because less than a year later he'd left Anfield and moved to Glasgow Rangers, remaining there until the end of the 1991/92 season when Walter Smith had taken over from Graeme Souness, who was then in charge at Liverpool. A UEFA ruling that meant only four foreigners were permitted in the matchday squads across European domestic leagues eventually forced Rangers to dispense with Twentyman's services. Rangers had dominated Scottish football since the mid-'80s with a squad filled with 'foreign' English players, who'd left their clubs south of the border in search of European football after Heysel and the ban that followed it. From 1991, Rangers needed to dispense with English players, not sign them. So Twentyman, a scout that operated in northern England and the Midlands, left Ibrox.

"Dad didn't seem to mind, and everything was amicable," says son William. "He was more disappointed he had to leave and stare at the car he'd not long been issued by Rangers in the front drive every day rather than use it for work. It was a brown Austin Montego 1600."

For the first time in almost half a century, Twentyman was out of football. Just like he was before Shankly offered him an Anfield lifeline all those years ago. This time it was the end. Although he never made the conscious decision to leave the game, there were no more offers of a return and he slipped into retirement.

The last 10 years of his life were slow and painful. "Football was his world," William adds. "He had no other interests to occupy his mind."

Ivor Broadis said that when he played for Carlisle at the end of the 1940s he had trouble reaching the near post from a corner when it was wet. "The ball was so heavy back then, it was like kicking a basketball around," he chuckles.

Broadis calculated that an average centre-half would head the ball at least seven times or more each game. That means a player would use his forehead to clear something of considerable weight with all his might – remember a defender's job back then was firstly to clear it rather than lay it on to someone else – an average of 30 times a month. Geoff Twentyman, a centre-half with an agricultural approach to the game, had more blows to his head than a heavyweight boxer on a losing streak. In a professional career lasting 16 years he must have headed the ball more than 4,000 times.

This surely had an effect on his brain. Whether or not it resulted in Alzheimer's later on in life is uncertain. What is certain is that by the end of the '90s, Geoff Twentyman's memory became so bad that he had to move into a nursing home. His nadir came when he was found wandering near the Leeds-Liverpool canal, many hours after leaving his house in Maghull. He'd always enjoyed afternoon strolls around the billiard-like fields of Melwood before his retirement, but this was different. William, his son, said that when the police found him, his feet were bleeding. He'd spent hours walking on gravel paths in old boots. His father was completely oblivious to what was happening.

Like Bob Paisley before him, who also suffered from Alzheimer's, Geoff Twentyman's deterioration was agonising. When he died in 2004 William said that his mind was so vegetated by the end that he didn't recognise his own family, let alone remember being part of the Liverpool backroom staff that lifted 29 major trophies in 19 years.

Twentyman was a man who had given honesty and loyalty to Bill Shankly, the most revered football manager in Liverpool's history, then Bob Paisley, the most successful manager in English football. But by the end of his life, he had lost every recollection of Liverpool's greatest nights, nights fuelled by the players that he spotted.

He was never given a testimonial for his work.

A Close Shave

Final word: By William Twentyman

MY dad didn't have a bad word to say about anyone. Apart from Ron Atkinson. He really disliked Ron – as a player at least. I don't know whether he went to watch him at Oxford United in the late '60s, but if he did, he must have come away unimpressed by the man they nicknamed the 'Tank'.

"Atkinson's got big fat thighs like a woman," my dad would say. "He'd wear tight shorts and roll them up to show off his legs, then lather them up in oil to make himself look bigger and better than his opponents… but he had the touch of a blacksmith and would never have been good enough to play for Liverpool."

Dad could have said plain and simple that Atkinson was shi*e. But he would always have a way of saying something you'd remember – even if it were negative. I never heard him swear once, though. He was always well presented and never wore jeans. Maybe that's one of the reasons why Liverpool Football Club were so happy with him for so long. The way in which he conducted himself represented the club's values. Understated and humble.

You would expect that being the son of a Liverpool employee would have its perks. But we never regularly received tickets for the match or anything like that – mainly because dad would be working away at weekends, watching future targets. On the rare occasions we did go to Anfield we usually managed to get into the players' lounge. I remember

Jimmy Case using the old 2p payphone and speaking at the top of his voice while wearing a distinctive brown suit. He was always very kind to me when I was a kid.

Most of the times I went to Anfield, however, was to accompany dad while he completed some menial tasks. I remember him once showing me a hole in the Anfield Road End roof where a groundsman had taken a shot at a pigeon and missed. Sometimes, he'd be trusted with banking and would take cash from gate receipts to a vault somewhere in Bootle. Everyone at Liverpool mucked in together. Joe Fagan and Bob Paisley would often sweep changing rooms after the game rather than hire a cleaner. If a job needed doing, nobody was special enough to let it pass.

My dad was always very proud and appreciated basic qualities in people. Honesty was more important to him than anything else in life. He always felt that if you told someone the truth, things would never be as bad as they could be. That was a great principle he drilled into me.

Even long after he was diagnosed with having Alzheimer's, he still lived by his morals, despite the disease taking hold of his frail body. When we found him that day on Warbreck Moor many hours after leaving home, he had to move into an EMI unit. I went there early one morning and he was in need of a shave. All of the elasticity in his face had gone and his chin was like a raw chicken carcass. His hair had grown grey and tatty and it was in need of a cut.

He only had a blunt throwaway Bic razor with him and even though I knew what I was doing because of my job, it was going be painful. Like many of the players he nearly recommended for Liverpool, it was the closest of shaves.

I could tell he knew it was going hurt as his vacant eyes staring into the distance squinted when I approached him with the razor. "You've got to be cruel to be kind," I told him, just like he warned me when I was a child. We'd come full circle.

His mind was completely gone. He'd lost all grasp of reality by the end. For a father who'd done so much for me and a man that had contributed so much to Liverpool Football Club, a callous, more, pitiful destiny is impossible to envisage.

At his funeral, which was attended by many of the players he scouted, I spoke about what he was like as a person and my brother used his football know-how to talk about his professional life. We both reached the same conclusion. Everyone we'd chatted to about dad well before and after his death said how he was universally liked. He was the type of guy that people had nothing but kind words for.

I get strangers coming up to me all the time in the street asking if I am related to Geoff Twentyman. It's one of those surnames that people remember, in football especially. Only the other week a guy stopped me outside my barber's shop and told me about how dad used to attend all sorts of kids' football team presentations to hand out awards. Years ago, when I visited Australia, an officer stopped me at passport control and asked me the same question. I couldn't believe it.

Few people, however, know of his significance to the history of Liverpool Football Club. Dad was at Anfield for the best part of 35 years. To my knowledge, only Ronnie Moran and Roy Evans have spent as much time at the club.

People remember who he was but not what he did. Dad had a technique of making young footballers very successful yet he was never one for self-appreciation so few knew the full extent of his work.

I am tired of punters coming into the shop and telling me half-baked stories about how players like Phil Neal or Alan Hansen were spotted by Liverpool without them knowing the whole truth.

That's why I wanted this book to be written because I think it's about time people learnt about his achievements. Dad's story is one of the last untold tales of Liverpool's era of glory because he is rarely mentioned in the history books.

I think it's a unique and fascinating story, too, although if he was here now he'd go mad if he knew about this book.

That was just him.

Barbershop banter

August 2008

A KNIFE which is more like a jailor's torture device is pressed against
the throat of Jamie Carragher. It scrapes back and forth the way a mace
would on the sandstone that Liverpool is built upon. A slip of the wrists
and Red Scouse blood spills. The kind of red that Bill Shankly said used
to strike fear into Anfield opponents. The tension is palpable. But
Liverpool's vice-captain is relaxed. Today he is enjoying a cut-throat
shave at WE Twentyman's in Waterloo.

Carragher has been visiting here for the last six months since his wife,
Nicola, bought him a gift voucher for Christmas. It seems like a present
of convenience when you consider she runs her own beauty spa just over
the road. Although he continues to stay loyal to the barber in Bootle that
has always cut his hair, Carragher visits Twentyman's every couple of
weeks for an hour of pampering. Fellow Crosby resident Peter Hooton
from The Farm does the same, although he just gets his ears lowered.

"I'd never tried anything like this before," Carragher says, gargling
nervously while the blade caresses his stubble-covered neck. "I don't
like a fuss and I didn't think I'd be into it. I thought it was a load of
nonsense, but I tried it and it was relaxing so I have kept coming back.
I live just round the corner, so it's handy."

In a world where Premier League footballers sport highlights,
Mohicans and ponytails (although Andriy Voronin has since returned to
Germany), all fashioned at high-end grooming boutiques, Carragher's

approach to his appearance is refreshingly modest. Twentyman's offers everything from short back and sides to full-body massages, but this place is not Toni & Guy. Carragher wouldn't have it any other way, though. A Scouser to the core, he keeps it local. Twentyman's is a humble setting and a traditional barbers.

"Even when I go shopping, I'd always go to Liverpool rather than Manchester," he explains with a wry smile. "I'd rather spend my money in my home town, and if someone's going to get it, I'd rather they be local. I always think about that and I'd say I am quite passionate about Liverpool as a city. Not just from a football point of view, but from a business side as well. If I ever spend a few bob, like booking a holiday, I will try and book it through someone I know so they will benefit financially. I think everyone should do that if they can. We should all look after each other."

And that is exactly what he is doing today. Carragher understands the value of community spirit. As a former employee of the local newspaper, the *Crosby Herald*, I was always aware that Carragher would do almost anything to help those less privileged around him. Every other week he would appear in its pages, pictured at charity events and sporting fundraisers. Not that he demanded the publicity. His constant representation in the paper was craved by its editors who probably believed it would sell more copies with his mugshot on the front or back page handing over some kind of gong to a local hero or kids' football team. Carragher always obliged. His presence would not only give the people he was pictured with a day to remember, but also mean that more papers would be sold around Crosby, in turn keeping people like me in a job at a time when sales figures in all local paper media were on its knees and begging for collective redemption. I was grateful for that.

To me Carragher has always oozed Shanklyesque values, and as a local hero – the kind of yesteryear – today he is once again looking after one of his own: a former employee of Liverpool Football Club, chief scout Geoff Twentyman. The father of William E Twentyman.

Prostrate and body taut, Carragher transforms into head and trabs – gleaming white Stan Smith's like a proper Scouser. Covered shoulders-to-ankles in towels, turquoise, black and blue, he relaxes while William lightly applies the shaving cream first to his chin and then to the neck. Ducking and darting around the body like a cross between a Renaissance sculptor weighing up his masterpiece and the Demon Barber of Fleet Street (or Oxford Road in this case), he uses an implement as sharp as a rapier sword to remove the lotion. Carvery completed, Carragher's head is turbaned with a hot wet towel. Then, a five-minute break.

Signed shirts hang on the wall. One is from Carragher himself – he wore it against Inter Milan in the 2-0 Champions League victory at Anfield – and another from Ian Callaghan, retro, marked by signatures from a thick-tipped felt pen. Opposite, there is a copy of the *Liverpool Echo* from 1954 with the headline of 'Twentyman fits the bill'. An array of boxing memorabilia decorates the ceiling. Another punter, delighted to be in the company of a Liverpool great, chatters nervously – the type of inane barbershop banter you would expect at most gentlemen's hairdressers. "See ya later lad," says Carragher when the customer departs.

Downtime elapsed, Carragher is indulged in steam treatment and a face mask of rosemary (it's for rehydration, apparently) before leaning forward into the white basin in front of him. It looks like he's going to throw up. Maybe it's a delayed reaction to Liverpool's abject performance against Standard Liege the previous night. Then after a wash of hair Carragher finally emerges with a smile that stretches from ear to ear. Even Scouse granite can embrace male grooming products from time to time.

Later, sitting in the back of the shop, a clean-shaven Carragher explains how he came to realise that his local barber's is an unrecognised relic of Liverpool Football Club history. "The name Twentyman rang a bell when the missus gave me her present on Christmas Day. Then one of my mates confirmed it. I have known about Geoff Twentyman for a long time because he's one of those famous names linked to Liverpool's past. There are the famous names like the managers and players that get all the plaudits and the fame and fortune in their day, although it's not the same as it is today, but Geoff was one of those people working in the background that played a major part in the success story of Liverpool Football Club. There are a lot of people in football that work behind the scenes that don't get the credit they deserve purely because they aren't in the papers or in front of the camera. Sometimes the people in the background are just as important as the people that front the success."

Although Carragher has since received national recognition for his performances in a Red shirt, he too was once one of those people that toiled desperately for the cause without receiving much adulation. I always felt he was a player who would only be truly appreciated if he ever left the club. For so long, he performed consistently and honestly without the plaudits. It was only when Rafa Benitez took charge of the club in 2004 and promptly made him a permanent fixture in the centre of Liverpool's defence (he'd played there before under Roy Evans and Gerard Houllier before being moved elsewhere across the backline), that fans (many Kopites included), the written press and mass media started to realise his ability as a world-class defender.

Carragher is a player that all the celebrated managers in Liverpool's history would have selected in their team. He is now regarded as a Red great, having won every major competition bar the Premier League since making his debut in 1997 (at the time of writing). For Geoff Twentyman, who was a man that prided himself, as well as the men he scouted and signed, on honesty and endeavour, Carragher is a player and a person that would have represented the eminent Liverpool sides of Shankly, Paisley, Fagan and Dalglish. So it's appropriate that Carragher recognises the work of Geoff Twentyman.

"What Geoff did for Liverpool will never be repeated again," Carragher continues. "To spot the players that he did at lower league clubs and see these players end up winning European Cups just doesn't happen now. It's a special ability in itself to spot potential and being able to judge whether a player will fit into a club and a team. It's not about just looking at a player and seeing if he plays well, its how they fit in and the characters they are as well. If I ever take up management after I retire, I would make sure my scouts research a player's character before I think about signing him – just like Geoff Twentyman did. I've seen a lot of players come and go at Liverpool who didn't have enough mental strength or character to fit in with the demands or suit the culture of the club. That rarely happened in Geoff's time because he was a good judge of people and knew what would suit the Liverpool way."

Twentyman's assignment was to scout players between the ages of 20 and 23. Carragher was scouted a lot younger, as a schoolboy for Bootle boys. He signed for Liverpool before he'd even joined secondary school and went straight into the system that Tom Saunders, the club's former youth development officer, created.

When Twentyman looked at a player, he made himself as inconspicuous as possible by watching matches from the terraces with the fans. Today, and even when Carragher was reaching adulthood 12 years ago, every kid knew the face of their local scout. Carragher says: "There was a scout for each area and the one for Bootle was a fella called Harry Hodges. He scouted Stephen Wright as well. We were aware of him and his reputation. I was picked up at the start of the '90s when football was beginning to change. I tried to play my own game when I knew Harry was watching, but it is always in the back of your mind that you need to impress. When Geoff went he did it without anyone knowing who he was. He probably wore a fake nose and glasses back then."

Twentyman's clandestine approach to scouting made him different from any other talent spotter. Most would mill around together in the main stand of whatever ground they were at, supping on complementary Oxo at the half-time interval (today it might be "champagne and caviar", one scout later told me). But Twentyman would stand and chat to the local fans and get the inside story about the player he was looking at. His strengths. His weaknesses. His mental ability. His family life. His choice of tipple. Liverpool, like Twentyman, did everything differently to other clubs and that was what set them apart.

"In the '70s and '80s Liverpool's approach to everything was unique," Carragher insists. "Liverpool signed players who'd been regulars at their clubs and bedded them into the Liverpool system or the Liverpool way for up to 12 months before giving them a game in the first team. No other clubs did that. Maybe it would be difficult to do that now with the egos and different pressures in the game. It's also different now with a lot of young foreign players that pack the reserves up. The Liverpool team at the time was so successful, so players understood that they had to fit into Liverpool and not the other way around. That's what's unique about the club."

When Twentyman became Liverpool chief scout in 1967, his brief was simple: to found a scouting network that would bring Britain's best young talent to the club. A quick glance at the list of players that he spotted before persuading Shanks to sign them suggests he easily fulfilled that remit – and continued to do so after the great man retired and passed away. Indirectly, his keen eye landed many of the 29 trophies that were placed in the Anfield trophy cabinet during his 19 years at the club (he was there for another five as a player). Yet like most scouts, he is rarely mentioned in the honours lists.

Shankly, though, would have said that Geoff Twentyman was one of his most important appointments and undoubtedly a person that contributed to the Liverpool success story that was masterminded by Shankly and the bootroom. Although Twentyman rarely entered the bootroom on a matchday – the nature of his job meant he'd be watching other teams and targets – he would spend many a morning and afternoon at Melwood. His relationship with Shankly in particular was one of unbreakable respect, but he was also frequently found spending time with Bob Paisley, Joe Fagan, Reuben Bennett, Roy Evans and Ronnie Moran, where football would be the only topic of conversation.

This was the spiritual creation of the bootroom, something Carragher concludes is a part of Liverpool Football Club that might never return. "Over the last few years, only one or two assistant managers have taken over from the manager at different clubs and it hasn't really worked out. At Liverpool, they always promoted from within, but that trend is dying across football now. The bootroom was a massive part of that and it brought a lot of success to the club.

"A lot of people have asked me whether I will go into management one day. They ask me whether I'd manage Liverpool. If I did, I'd take a lot of things learnt from people who were involved in the bootroom when I signed professional forms – people like Roy Evans, Doug Livermore, Steve Heighway and Ronnie Moran. A lot of the values from the bootroom were instilled in me. It's not just about football, it's about how you conduct yourself by not getting too carried away with things and having humility. I think that's been bred into me, and if I stayed on at the club, I would try and instil that into other people.

"I know times have changed and the bootroom has gone, but there are certain things about life that footballers need to learn and I would be keen to show them that. There aren't enough people like Bill Shankly, Bob Paisley, Joe Fagan or even Geoff Twentyman involved in the game anymore.

"I would love to try and change that."

THE following is a comprehensive list of the players noted in Geoff Twentyman's Scouting Diary who are not included in the player interview section earlier in this book. The period of the diary covers 1970/71 to 1986/87, although some seasons are not included and certain periods are more expansive than others. The details for each player listed are not always consistent, although Twentyman meticulously notes their age, height and weight as a matter of course. Diary notes are dated and other Liverpool scouts may have watched the player – indicated by the initials in brackets after the comments. Apart from chief scout Geoff Twentyman (GT), other scouts referred to are Andy Beattie (AB), Verdy Godwin (VG), Norman Clarke (NC), Jimmy McAlindon (JM), Tom Whitfield (TW), Walter Flaherty (WF), Tom Saunders (TS), Reuben Bennett (RB) and A McCrae (AM). The identity of Twentyman's scouts was a closely guarded secret and many worked on an ad hoc basis, so we cannot be sure who the following initials refer to: (FO'D), (KK), (JD), (WJ), (RB), (WMc), (BJ), (JB), (FMc) and (DW). Not all players' future careers could be reliably tracked.

1970/71 SEASON

G DAVIES (CF)
Wigan
Age: 21 Height: 5ft 11in Weight: 12st

12.09.70: 'Played well good prospect worth looking at' (VG)
12.09.70: 'A good performance worth following up' (FO'D)
16.09.70: 'Not impressed didn't look in our class' (GT)

TERRY CONROY (No 7)
Stoke
Age: 24 Height: 5ft 10in Weight: 11st 6lbs

19.09.70: 'A ready made player easy to recommend' (GT)
30.09.70: 'Had a fair game' (GT)
03.10.70: 'Not as good as in past games (VG)
10.10.70: 'Satisfactory game made a lot of chances' (GT)

After appearing for Glentoran, the Republic of Ireland international spent most of his career at Stoke City, where Twentyman watched him, and he scored 66 goals in 333 appearances for the club, winning a League Cup winners' medal in 1972. After Stoke, he played briefly for Bulova in Hong Kong, Crewe Alexandra, Waterford United and Limerick. He has since worked for the Irish FA.

MALCOLM MACDONALD (CF)
Luton
Age: 20 Height: 5ft 9.5in Weight: 11st 6lbs

12.09.70: 'Useful around the box. Could hold his own in 1st D.' (AB)
10.10.70: 'Scored 3 goals, useful in box, improved' (AB)

When scouted by Liverpool, Macdonald was in a rich vein of form for Luton – he scored 49 league goals in 88 appearances before moving to Newcastle in 1971 and then Arsenal in 1976. At both clubs he averaged around a goal in every two league games. Macdonald is also remembered for scoring all five goals when England beat Cyprus 5-0 in 1975. His career was cut short in 1979 owing to a knee injury.

NORMAN PIPER
Portsmouth
Height: 5ft 7in Weight: 10st

Born in Devon, Piper was a midfielder who joined Plymouth Argyle in 1965 and scored 35 goals in his five years at the club. He then moved to Portsmouth, where he played for eight years, aiding the team in their fight to maintain Division Two status by scoring 51 league goals. He left after the team were relegated, and moved to America to play for Fort Lauderdale Strikers.

QUINTIN YOUNG (OR)
Ayr U
Age: 20 Height: 5ft 8in Weight: 11st

26.09.70: 'Shows a lot of ability must see against B. oppos.' (GT)
26.09.70: 'Looks a good prospect, worth watching' (VG)

Young, who played outside-right, spent two years at Ayr United before moving to Coventry City in 1971 and then Rangers in 1973. His peak came with a goal away from home against Ajax in the European Super Cup. Young saw out his playing days at East Fife between 1976 and 1980.

LEE BROGDEN (OR)
Rotherham
Age: 20 Height: 5ft 8.5in Weight: 10st 10lbs

'Shows improved form, a live prospect' (KK)

Brogden was a traditional right-winger who joined Rotherham as a teenager in 1967. In his second season at the club he made 36 league appearances and scored seven goals. After four-and-a-half years there, he joined Rochdale where he played for three seasons and maintained a strong goals-to-games ratio for a winger.

STEVE DEERE (No 4)
Scunthorpe
Age: 22 Height: 5ft 11in Weight: 11st

15.09.70: 'Looks a player capable of playing in 1st Div' (AB)

Originally employed as a striker at Scunthorpe with mixed success, the lanky East Anglian was shifted into central defence by manager Ron Ashman, and he was ever-present in the team for three out of the next five seasons. Deere joined Hull in 1973 after Scunthorpe's relegation, but returned to the club in 1978 after also spending time at Scarborough (where he won FA Trophy medals). He only missed four more games before retiring in 1980.

ROY McDONALD (GK)
Distillery
Age: 18 Height: 6ft 2in Weight: 13st

'A very good young GK. Looks certain for top D' (JD)
02.10.70: 'Not as good as reported from Ireland'
23.01.71: Shaped well, very keen and brave' (GT)

McDonald played in every game of the 1970/71 season for Distillery, helping the team to Irish Cup victory. After 84 games, he was involved in a half-time argument that led to him leaving the club – he was sold to Crusaders for £300. McDonald played for Crusaders against Liverpool in the first round of the 1977 European Cup. He is currently goalkeeping coach at the club.

RIKKI FLEMING (No 4)
Ayr U
Age: 20? Height: 5ft 11in Weight: 11st 7lbs

26.09.70: 'A very good defensive player could become great' (GT)
26.09.70: 'Played well, good material' (VG)
11.08.73: 'Strong in all departments, a good back player' (GT)
14.08.73: 'Done well, kept Gordon of Hibs quiet, looks a dedicated defender' (GT)

Fleming played at centre-back for Ayr United for 10 years after signing from Rangers (for whom he didn't play a first-team game). He made 287 league appearances before moving to Hibernian in 1978 and Berwick Rangers a year later. He retired through injury.

JIMMY KERR (No 11)
Blackburn
Age: 21 Height: 5ft 8in Weight: 10st 12lbs

03.10.70: Played well in 2nd half right side in midfield (GT)

Twentyman did well to get to see Jimmy Kerr at all. Blackburn paid a club record fee of £60,000 for him in 1970, and he only played 11 games for the club before injury ended his career. Blackburn suffered relegation to the Third Division that season.

ALAN STEVENSON (GK)
Chesterfield
Age: 20 Height: 5ft 11in Weight: 11st

17.10.70: 'Good young GK will make the grade' (AB)
24.10.70: 'Good potential keep in mind' (AB)
21.11.71: 'Did everything right, looks the part' (GT)

Stevenson graduated from Chesterfield's junior team in October 1969 and swiftly became the club's finest goalkeeper, helping them to the Division Four championship in 1969/70. Scouts from Leeds and Brian Clough's Derby were circling around the same time as Twentyman had his eye on Stevenson, but he eventually moved to Burnley, with whom he had previously had an unsuccessful trial. With Stevenson the foundation, Burnley won the Third Division and Second Division titles, but he was released when just two games short of the club's record for appearances by a 'keeper. He played for Rotherham and Hartlepool, and has since moved into the commercial side of the game.

PLAYERS' GLOSSARY

KENNY TILER (RB)
Chesterfield
Age: 19

17.10.70: *'Good young back. Worth following' (AB)*
24.10.70: *'Worth following in the future' (AB)*

Tiler spent four years at Chesterfield between 1970 and 1974, making 139 appearances and scoring one goal. He was apparently "moved on" with several other players after they went public with complaints over poor pay in the 1974/75 season. Tiler played for Brighton and Hove Albion until 1979, when he switched to Rotherham United.

KEITH ECCLESHARE (RB)
Bury
Age: 20? Height: 5ft 9in Weight: 11st 6lbs

17.10.70: *'Bury's best player. Two footed, good prospect.' (GT)*
27.02.71: *'Kicks well and good tackler, watch again' (WJ)*
06.03.71: *'Not enough to do for judging' (GT)*
08.03.71: *'Not good enough' (GT)*

Eccleshare's loyalties were divided between football and cricket – he was both a solid defender and a superb bowler. In his time as a footballer he played for Bury from the age of 15 to 21, representing England's youth team several times, before playing on semi-professional terms for Fleetwood, Macclesfield Town, Northwich Victoria (where he enjoyed a glorious FA Cup run in 1976/77, reaching the fifth round) and Chorley. He retired from football at the age of 30. As a cricketer, he enjoyed great success, winning seven league championships and taking 2,500 wickets.

MICK HILL (CF)
Ipswich
Age: 22 Height: 5ft 11in Weight: 11st

31.10.70: *'Not a good display but I like the player' (VG)*

Mick 'The Flick' Hill was a traditional target-man who joined Ipswich Town from Sheffield United in 1969 after just 37 appearances in four years. At Ipswich, he scored 20 league goals in 77 games before leaving for Crystal Palace in 1973, where he scored six times in 45 appearances. Capped twice by Wales.

TONY BROWN (No 10)
West Bromwich Albion
Age: 22 Height: 5ft 9in Weight: 11st

31.10.70: *'Good midfield player big heart ready made' (GT)*

Tony 'Bomber' Brown was actually 25 when Twentyman made a note of him in his scouting book, and he had been playing for West Brom for seven years, since 1963. He'd been part of the side that won the League Cup in 1966 and the FA Cup in 1968, and he was the First Division's top scorer in the 1970/71 season. West Brom suffered relegation in 1973, but Brown helped them gain promotion in 1976. In all, he made 720 appearances for the Baggies and scored 279 goals – both club records. Brown saw out his career with the New England Tea Men, Torquay United and Stafford Rangers.

JOHN EVANSON (No 6 midfield)
Oxford
Age: 23 Height: 5ft 8in Weight: 11st

07.11.70: *'Played well in attacking role, worth looking at' (GT)*
26.12.70: *'Played well enough, will follow up' (AB)*
02.01.71: *'Not satisfied with tackling' (AB)*
11.09.71: *'Injured 1st min' (GT)*

Newcastle-born Evanson was promoted from the juniors to the Oxford United first team, and he scored 11 goals in 179 appearances for the club. He moved to Blackpool in February 1974 before spells at Miami Toros, Fulham and Bournemouth.

DAVID RODGERS (No 6)
Bristol C
Age: 18? Height: 6ft 1in Weight: 12st

21.11.70: *'Raw but should improve, worth small fee' (AB)*

The Bristol-born central defender signed professional terms with his local club in 1969 and scored on his first-team debut in the League Cup win over Leicester City in November 1970. Rodgers scored 15 goals in 192 league games before the 'Ashton Gate Eight' crisis in 1982 – Bristol City were declared bankrupt and eight first-team players, including Rodgers, accepted redundancy to save the club. He then played for Torquay United, Lincoln City and Forest Green Rovers.

303

DOUG ALLDER (OL)
Millwall
Age: 19

21.11.70: 'Looks a promising player' (AB)

Allder, a left-winger, made 332 appearances in his career – 201 of these were at his first club, Millwall, which he signed for in 1969. He scored 10 goals for the club. Allder moved to Leyton Orient in 1975, playing 41 times, and after month-long trials at Torquay and Watford, he joined Brentford in October 1977, helping them to promotion that season. He left in 1980 and played for several lower-league teams before retiring.

PETER HARDCASTLE (MF)
Skelmersdale
Age: 22 Height: 5ft 10in Weight: 11st 7lbs

16.01.71: 'Does not look our class' (VG)

After leaving Skelmersdale, Hardcastle played for Blackpool, Plymouth Argyle and Bradford City.

GRENVILLE MILLINGTON (GK)
Rhyl
Age: 18 Height: 5ft 10in Weight: 11st

21.11.70: 'Promising player, to be followed up' (VG)
28.11.70: 'Played well, worth bringing for Central Lge.' (VG)
05.12.70: 'Played well. Good enough to contact.' (VG)

Millington was on Chester's books before moving to Rhyl in 1969, and he returned to City in 1973, where he became a mainstay between the sticks. He was ever-present in the 1974/75 season when Chester reached the League Cup semi-finals and won promotion from Division Four, and in total he made 290 appearances for the club. In 2005 he was voted the club's BBC cult hero. Brief stints at Oswestry Town and Wrexham rounded off his career.

MARTIN O'NEILL (IF)
Distillery
Age: 18 Height: 5ft 10in Weight: 11st 7lbs

05.12.70: 'Very good display, must be watched' (JD)
19.12.70: 'Not as good as previous, scored good [goal]' (JD)

23.01.71: 'Not enough pace. Does not strike the ball' (GT)

The current Aston Villa manager started out playing Gaelic football before switching to soccer and starred for Distillery, where he won the Irish Cup in 1971 and then scored against Barcelona in a 3-1 Cup Winners' Cup defeat. He was signed by Nottingham Forest that same year and played a key part in the the club's subsequent success, winning promotion to the top flight, two League Cups, the league title, two European Cups (though he only played in one final) and the European Super Cup. O'Neill also captained Northern Ireland and played briefly for Norwich City (twice), Manchester City and Notts County before moving into management.

MARTIN DONNELLY (LH)
Distillery
Age: 20 Height: 5ft 9in Weight: 10st 7lbs

09.12.70: 'Played very well, attack and defence' (JD)
23.01.71: 'Not impressed. Looks a Cheshire Lge player.' (GT)

Donnelly made his debut for Distillery in September 1969, and soon was their established left-half. He helped the team to win the Irish Cup in 1970/71, and was an uncompromising tackler – in 1972 he was suspended for two months owing to bookings and sending offs. Donnelly scored nine goals in 140 appearances for Distillery before moving on to Kidderminster and Waterford.

E DAVIES (IR)
Rhyl
Age: 18 Height: 6ft Weight: 12st

14.12.70: 'Scored good goal, work rate good' (VG)
19.12.70: 'Not a good game, player compressed' (VG)
26.12.70: 'Moved around no support' (VG)
27.01.70: 'Very poor not good enough' (GT)

BILLY ASHCROFT (CF)
Wrexham
Age: 18 Height: 5ft 11in Weight: 12st

17.10.70: 'Not impressed lot to learn' (GT)
02.01.71: 'Nothing to show' (WJ)
02.01.71: 'Not a good game to judge' (VG)

Ashcroft served Wrexham for seven years before joining Middlesbrough, where he made his debut in September 1977. He moved to FC Twente in 1982 before returning to the UK in 1985, signing for Tranmere Rovers.

JOHN BROWNLIE (FB)
Hibs
Age: 19 Height: 5ft 10in Weight: 11st 7lbs

16.01.71: 'Can do better would have to see again' (GT)
16.01.71: 'Against a good OL would watch again' (JM)
23.01.71: 'Done all had to do good kicker strong player' (GT)
04.09.71: 'One of the best FB seen' (JM)
30.10.71: 'Not happy on left side' (GT)

Brownlie played at Hibs for nine years as a full-back, winning the Scottish League Cup in 1972. Crossing the border in 1978, he plied his trade at four clubs in the north-east – Newcastle United, Middlesbrough, Hartlepool United and Berwick Rangers respectively. Brownlie won seven Scotland caps.

BRACKPOOL
Spennymoor
Age: 19 Height: 5ft 10in Weight: 10st 7in

16.01.71: 'Shows promise worth following up'

ROY TUNKS (GK)
Rotherham
Age: 22 Height: 6ft Weight: 12st

16.01.71: 'A very useful GK' (KK)

Born in Worthing, Tunks served an apprenticeship at Rotherham before working his way into the first team – his debut was in 1968 but he had to wait until 1970 to become first choice. After a couple of strong seasons he had to fight with Jim McDonagh for his position. Tunks joined Preston North End in 1974, where he made 277 league appearances, and then Wigan Athletic in 1981, where he made 245.

DAVID CROSS
Rochdale
Age: 20? Height: 5ft 11in Weight: 11st 7lbs

27.02.71: 'Worth following up' (VG)
31.09.71: 'Disappointed will watch again' (GT)
03.10.71: 'Not strong enough in any asset' (GT)

Cross played as a forward for a host of different clubs: Rochdale, Norwich City, Coventry City, West Bromwich Albion, West Ham United, Manchester City, Oldham Athletic, Vancouver Whitecaps, Bolton Wanderers, Bury and finally AEL Limassol in Cyprus. His high points were winning the Second Division championship with Norwich in 1972, then again in 1981 with West Ham, and he played as the lone striker in the Hammers' victory over Arsenal in the 1980 FA Cup final.

GEORGE LYALL
Preston
Height: 5ft 7in Weight: 11st

08.03.71: 'Looks an improved player worth checking' (GT)

Lyall made his Preston debut in 1966 against Charlton and went on to make 115 appearances, scoring 16 goals. He then moved to Nottingham Forest in 1972, where he scored 24 goals in 116 appearances before transferring to Hull City and finally Scarborough.

KIRK
Glentoran
Age: 18 Height: 6ft Weight: 12st

06.03.71: 'Very good prospect' (VG)

GRAHAM WATSON
Doncaster
Age: 21 Height: 5ft 11in Weight: 11st 7lbs

20.03.71: 'Looks useful worth looking at' (GT)

Watson was in his second spell at Doncaster Rovers when Twentyman made a note of him – he had also spent time at Rotherham United where he had been employed in several positions but never settled. The midfielder left Doncaster in 1972 for Cambridge United, where he made 210 appearances.

ALEXANDER CROPLEY
Hibs
Age: 19 Height: 5ft 9.5in Weight: 10st 12lbs

10.04.71: 'A good-looking player, brains craft ability'
07.09.71: 'Playing well' (JM)
30.10.71: 'Would be good in a better side' (GT)

Cropley, born in Aldershot, made 195 appearances for Hibs and scored 50 goals between

1968 and 1974. The midfielder then moved south of the border to Arsenal, but struggled to make a name for himself after two leg-breaks. He signed for Aston Villa in 1976 and scored seven goals in 67 appearances before spells at Newcastle (on loan), Toronto Blizzard and Portsmouth.

WILLIAM GREEN (CH)
Hartlepool
Age: 20 Height: 6ft 1in Weight: 12st

14.08.71: 'A lot to learn yet' (GT)
08.08.71: 'Very raw' (TW)

Green joined Hartlepool United after school and spent four years at the club, racking up 131 league appearances. The centre-half also had spells with Carlisle United, West Ham United, Peterborough United, Chesterfield and Doncaster Rovers. Green briefly managed Scunthorpe United, Buxton and – for one game – Sheffield Wednesday, and is now a European scout at Derby County alongside Nigel Clough.

ROBERT HATTON (IF S)
Carlisle
Age: 24 Height: 5ft 10.5in Weight: 12st 6lbs

07.09.71: 'Strong forward scores goals. Not clever when crowded' (GT)
'Scores goals looks as though he can play in better class' (GT)

Before Hatton arrived at Carlisle United he'd been at Wolverhampton Wanderers, Bolton Wanderers and Northampton Town, but it was at the Cumbrian side that he finally proved his worth, scoring 37 goals in 93 league matches. Not long after Twentyman had watched him, Birmingham City triggered a release clause in his contract, paying a club record fee of £80,000 to take him to the Midlands at the end of 1971. In five years at Birmingham he scored 58 goals in 175 league games, and Hatton continued his goalscoring form to the end of his career at Blackpool, Luton Town, Sheffield United and Cardiff City.

DENNIS MARTIN (IF S)
Carlisle
Age: 23 Height: 5ft 10.5in Weight: 11st 4lbs

07.09.71: 'Useful player moves around. Shows pace' (GT)

Edinburgh-born Martin played for Kettering Town and West Bromwich Albion before Bob Stokoe took him to Carlisle United in the summer of 1970. Martin could play as both a striker and a winger, and he settled on the right-flank at Carlisle. He made 311 appearances at the club in seven years, scoring 57 goals as Carlisle enjoyed promotion to Division One and then suffered a double relegation to Division Three. Martin moved to Newcastle United in 1978, where he played for six months before being sold to Mansfield Town. He also played in Denmark before returning to Kettering where he finished his career.

TOMMY WALKER
Arbroath
Age: 19 Height: 5ft 10in Weight: 11st 10lbs

11.08.71: 'Promising player' (JM)
15.08.71: 'Looks good material' (WF)

Walker was a midfielder who scored 17 times for Arbroath in 74 appearances before being sold to Airdrie for a Second Division record fee of £16,000 in the 1971/72 season. He stayed at Airdrie until 1982 (although he was loaned back to Arbroath for the 1973/74 season), scoring 34 goals in 376 appearances for The Diamonds. Walker finished his career at Stirling Albion.

ALAN WEST
Burnley
Age: 20 Height: 5ft 9in Weight: 11st 6lbs

18.09.71: 'Good midfield player' (GT)

West was a product of the Burnley youth system, and he played for the first team between 1969 and 1973. He was close to a move to Sunderland when doctors told him he had to stop playing or risk being crippled. West carried on regardless, moving to Luton Town in 1973 where he dominated the midfield and became club captain. He finished his career at Millwall in 1983.

DON GIVENS
Luton
Age: 22? Height: 5ft 11in Weight: 11st 10lbs

25.09.71: 'Would like to see in a striker roll [sic] not mid' (GT)
20.11.71: 'Still in midfield not suited to this position' (GT)
17.02.73: 'Will watch against stronger opp. Satisfactory game' (GT)

24.02.73: '*Not in game enough looked
out of it not enough endeavour*' *(GT)*
03.03.73: '*Not in the game much was
disappointing*' *(GT)*

After a brief stint at Manchester United, Givens
moved to Luton Town in 1970 and spent two
years there, playing 83 league games and scoring 19 goals. Perhaps QPR spotted what
Twentyman had already senn– that Givens was
made for a striking role. The London club
signed him in 1972 and he scored 77 goals in
242 appearances, helping QPR to push
Liverpool all the way for the First Division
championship in 1975/76. He was sold to
Birmingham City two years later, and he also
spent time with Bournemouth (on loan),
Sheffield United and Neuchatel Xamax in
Switzerland. Givens was picked 56 times for
the Republic of Ireland, and is best remembered for his hat-trick against the USSR in
1974, the first hat-trick by an Irish player in 40
years. The following year he scored four goals
against Turkey. He is currently the manager of
the Republic's U-21s.

GARRY JONES
Bolton
Age: 19 Height: 5ft 9in Weight: 10st 7lbs

08.09.71: '*Played well looked
a good prospect*' *(GT)*
27.12.71: '*Not so effective*' *(GT)*

Jones was a striker who starred for Bolton
Wanderers between 1968 and 1979, scoring 41
goals in 203 appearances. He also played for
Sheffield United, Blackpool and Hereford
United.

ROY GREAVES
Bolton
Age: 24 Height: 5ft 11in Weight: 11st 7lbs

08.09.71: '*Played well showed more
pace, is a possible*' *(GT)*
27.12.71: '*Worked hard would like
to see him in midfield*' *(GT)*
08.01.72: '*Playing no 9 was Bolton's
best forward*' *(GT)*
08.02.74: '*Does a good job alround [sic]
a player who can cover most positions*' *(GT)*

Greaves began his career at local club Bolton
Wanderers, where he was employed up front
but after relegation to Division Three and the
appointment of Jimmy Armfield in 1971, he

was moved into midfield. He helped the club to
win the Third Division championship in
1972/73 and promotion to the top division in
1977/78. After relegation two seasons later,
Greaves moved to the Seattle Sounders and
then Rochdale before retiring. He scored 66
goals in 495 league games during his time at
Burnden Park.

IAN BUCKLEY
Oldham
Age: 17/18 Height: 5ft 10in Weight: 11st 7lbs

18.12.71: '*Very raw with no support*' *(GT)*

Buckley was a full-back who played for
Oldham Athletic, Rochdale, Stockport County
and Cambridge United.

KEN BEAMISH
Tranmere
Age: 24 Height: 5ft 10.5in Weight: 11st 10lbs
17.12.71: '*Much improved looks useful*' *(GT)*

Birkenhead-born Beamish was a striker who
scored 159 goals in 555 league games. He
played for Tranmere Rovers (twice), Brighton
and Hove Albion, Blackburn Rovers, Port
Vale, Bury and Swindon Town, and he is currently the commercial manager at Blackburn
Rovers.

IAN WOOD
Oldham
Age: 23 Height: 5ft 9in Weight: 11st

18.12.71: '*Not our class not enough fire*' *(GT)*
08.01.74: '*Good display. Two good
feet & enthusiasm*' *(GT)*

Wood was a full-back who joined Oldham
Athletic from Park Lane Olympic and scored
22 goals in 524 appearances between 1965 and
1980. Wood then spent a season at Burnley
before becoming player/coach at Radcliffe
Borough.

PAUL JONES
Bolton
Age: 21? Height: 5ft 11in Weight: 11st 7lbs

08.01.72: '*Steady player, worth keeping
in mind*' *(GT)*

Jones spent the vast majority of his career,
which began in 1970, at Bolton Wanderers –
the defender made 445 league appearances and

scored 38 goals for the club. Between 1983 and 1990 he played for Huddersfield Town, Oldham Athletic, Blackpool, Rochdale and Stockport County.

DAVID MILLS
Middlesbrough
Age: 21? Height: 5ft 10in Weight: 11st

15.01.72: 'Looked useful, worth following up' (GT)
17.04.72: 'Showed pace and fitness, will watch again' (GT)
26.11.72: 'No support but still a lively prospect' (GT)
10.02.73: 'Would be better in a good team' (GT)

Mills, a striker, had just become a regular at Boro when Twentyman watched him. He was part of the team that won the Second Division title in 1973/74, scoring the goal that secured promotion against Luton Town. In 1979 Ron Atkinson paid £500,000 to take Mills to West Bromwich Albion, which broke the British transfer record and made him Britain's first half-million-pound player. Injuries, lack of form and a deployment in midfield limited his opportunities, and he was loaned out to Newcastle United in 1981. Subsequently, he moved to Sheffield Wednesday before returning to the north-east to see out his career at Newcastle, Middlesbrough and Darlington.

WILLIE MADDREN
Middlesbrough
Age: 21 Height: 5ft 10in Weight: 11st 5lbs

15.01.72: 'Looked a good defender, hard worker' (GT)
26.11.72: 'Hard player could do a job in better team' (GT)
10.02.73: 'Not as good as previously' (GT)

Maddren spent his whole career at Middlesbrough. Initially he was used as a striker before switching to central defence. When Boro won the Second Division championship in 1973/74, with Jack Charlton at the helm, they conceded just 30 goals, keeping 25 clean sheets in 42 games. Boro more than held their own in the top division the following season, finishing five points behind champions Derby County in seventh and missing out on Europe by one place. An unsuccessful knee operation in 1977 led to his retirement at the age of 26.

STAN BOWLES
Carlisle
Age: 22 Height: 5ft 9in Weight: 10st 7lbs

29.01.72: 'Showed skill will watch again' (GT)

Bowles had already played for Manchester City, Bury and Crewe Alexandra before signing for Carlisle United, and it was at the last two that he began to show his abilities as a creative attacker. Bowles signed for QPR in 1972, replacing Rodney Marsh, and he played a vital role as the club finished league runners-up in 1975/76. He joined Nottingham Forest in 1979 but didn't fit into Brian Clough's plans and was sold to Leyton Orient in 1981. Bowles finished his career at Brentford. One of football's larger than life characters, his autobiography in 1996 revealed that he enjoyed excessive drinking, womanising and gambling throughout his career.

JOHN GORMAN
Carlisle
Age: 22 Height: 5ft 8in Weight: 11st

29.01.72: 'Looks best FB this season' (GT)
03.03.73: 'Not as good as previously. All team had off day' (GT)

After failing to make the Celtic first team, Gorman was signed by Carlisle United where he made 261 league appearances in six years and was almost ever-present in their season in the First Division. He went on to play for Tottenham Hotspur but injury limited his chances there, and he chose to move to Tampa Bay Rowdies in 1979. He has since moved into management and coaching.

DON SHANKS (LB)
Luton
Age: 18 Height: 5ft 7in Weight: 10st 12lbs

25.09.71: 'Disappointing' (GT)

Shanks left Luton Town for QPR in November 1970 and went on to make 180 league appearances in the club's defensive line. He later played for Brighton and Hove Albion.

ERIC McMORDIE (MF)
Middlesbrough
Age: 25 Height: 5ft 8in Weight: 10st 10lbs

25.09.71: 'Best player on view' (GT)

15.01.72: *'Played well used the ball with cutting passes' (GT)*

An attacking midfielder, McMordie travelled over from Belfast with George Best to have a trial at Manchester United in 1961, but both players became homesick and returned home. Only Best could be persuaded to return. McMordie played for his local part-time side Dundela, where he was spotted by Middlesbrough, and McMordie became a regular on Teesside for eight seasons before he was muscled out of the team by Graeme Souness. After a loan period at Sheffield Wednesday in 1974, he finished his career at York City and Hartlepool United.

DAVID WATSON (CF)
Sunderland
Age: 25 Height: 5ft 10.5in Weight: 12st

16.10.71: *'Took my eye, looked above average' (WJ)*

Watson played as a striker for Notts County and Rotherham United before moving to Sunderland, where he was switched to the role of central defender. Watson won the FA Cup in 1973 when Sunderland beat Leeds United despite being in the Second Division at the time, and after that he became a regular for England. He moved to Manchester City in 1976, winning the League Cup in his first eason, and becoming club captain two seasons later. After City, Watson played for Werder Bremen (for six months), Southampton, Stoke City, Derby County and the Vancouver Whitecaps.

JOHN HAMILTON (IF)
Hibs
Age: 19 Height: 5ft 8.5in Weight: 11st 6lbs

10.10.71: *'Looks a very good prospect' (GT)*
'Reports being a flatterer'

A hard-working midfielder, Hamilton scored 18 goals in 95 appearances for Hibernian before moving to Glasgow Rangers in 1973, Millwall in 1978 and St Johnstone in the same year.

BILL GARNER (CF)
Southend
Age: 21 Height: 6ft 2in Weight: 12st

06.11.71: *'Not good enough on floor' (GT)*

Garner played a couple of games for Notts County before joining Southend United in 1969, where he scored 41 goals in 102 league appearances. The centre-forward then signed for Chelsea after an impressive display against them in the League Cup. Chelsea were relegated to the Second Division in 1975 and Garner suffered injury problems, but he still scored 31 goals in 105 league games for the club. He subsequently signed for Cambridge United on a free transfer in 1978 and finished his career with Chelmsford City and Brentford.

DAVE CLEMENTS (LF)
Sheff W
Age: 26 Height: 5ft 9.5in Weight: 11st 12lbs

13.11.71: *'Quiet but efficient' (GT)*

Clements played for Wolverhampton Wanderers and Coventry City before joining Sheffield Wednesday in 1971 – he'd scored 30 goals in 255 appearances for Coventry. His solid play at Sheffield Wednesday earned him the nickname 'Tank', and it was during his time there that he received attention from bigger clubs. Clements signed for Everton in 1973 and was made club captain in 1974/75, a season when Everton were odds-on to win the league championship but lost out to Derby County in the run-in. While at Everton he briefly became player-manager of Northern Ireland before moving to America in 1976 to see out the remainder of his career.

TOMMY CRAIG (MF)
Sheff W
Age: 21 Height: 5ft 8.5in Weight: 11st 2lbs

13.11.71: *'Disappointing' (GT)*
12.01.74: *'Stronger and matured, was Sheff W best player'*
16.03.74: *'This player is having his best spell in poor team'*
13.04.74: *'Best player on field, craft and brains' (GT)*

Craig moved to Sheffield Wednesday from Aberdeen in 1968 and scored 38 goals in 214 league games for The Owls. The club were relegated to the Second Division, and battled with further relegation while Craig was there, but he jumped ship before they succumbed to the drop, moving to Newcastle United in 1974. He struck 22 goals in 124 league games for Newcastle before moving on to Aston Villa (where he lasted two years), Swansea City, Carlisle United and finally Hibernian.

ARTHUR MANN (LB)
Man C / Blackpool
Age: 22 Height: 5ft 9in Weight: 11st 2lbs

20.11.71: 'Not good enough' (GT)

Mann was born in Falkirk and began his career at Heart of Midlothian before signing for Manchester City in 1968 for a club record fee. In four years he only made 35 appearances for the club – he reportedly had a fear of flying, which limited his opportunities to take part in City's European travels (they won the Cup Winners' Cup in 1970) and therefore restricted his first-team chances. Mann went on loan to Blackpool in 1971, when Twentyman presumably watched him, and then signed for Notts County in 1972, where he made 253 league appearances and scored 21 goals. He also played for Shrewsbury Town and Mansfield Town before moving into coaching.

DAVIE CAIRNS (LB)
Cowdenbeath

20.11.71: 'Promising player' (WF)
27.11.71: 'Not up to our standard' (GT)

Cairns was an overlapping left-back who joined Cowdenbeath from Forfar Athletic in 1970. He made 170 appearances, scored seven goals and became the club captain. He joined Raith Rovers in 1974 (which Cairns has since described as "the worst decision I ever made"), then Berwick Rangers in 1976 and Brechin City a year later.

McCULLOUGH (LB)
Alloa
Age: 23 Height: 5ft 11in Weight: 12st

27.11.71: 'Looked useful' (GT)

ALAN HARDING (F)
Darlington
Height: 5ft 8.5in Weight: 11st 5lbs

04.11.71: 'Moved well up front, worth looking at' (GT)

Harding was a winger who scored 38 goals in 129 league appearances for Darlington before joining Linoln City in 1972. He stayed there

until 1979 (209 apps, 38 goals) when he joined Hartlepool United, where he finished his league career.

SAMMY MORGAN
Port Vale
Height: 6ft 1in

'25 years age'

Twentyman's note on Morgan was brief. The forward made 114 appearances for Port Vale, scoring 25 goals and being named player of the year in 1972, before moving to Aston Villa in 1973, where he scored nine in 40 league matches. Morgan then played at Brighton and Hove Albion, Cambridge United and Sparta Rotterdam in Holland.

IAIN PHILLIP (CH)
Dundee
Height: 5ft 11in Weight: 11st 6lbs

03.01.72: 'No 5. Played at back, never showed' (GT)
10.01.72: 'Played in same roll [sic] as previously' (GT)

Phillip had two spells at Dundee between 1970 and 1978 – in between he spent a season at Crystal Palace. He also played for Dundee United, Raith Rovers and Arbroath, racking up a total of 432 league appearances and winning three Scottish League Cups.

DAVE BOOTH (LB)
Barnsley
Age: 21 Height: 5ft 9in Weight: 11st 6lbs

27.12.71: 'Not improved since last season' (GT)

Booth was a left-back who played for two clubs: Barnsley (1968-1972) and Grimsby Town (1972-1978), playing 364 games.

JIM HENRY (MF)
Dundee U
Height: 5ft 10.5in Weight: 11st 7lbs

03.01.72: 'Showed up quite well, worth another look' (GT)

Signed from Carnoustie Juniors in 1967, Henry played in 94 games for Dundee United (seven goals). A move to Fulham fell through in 1972, and Henry moved to Aberdeen instead two years later. He had two spells in America and finished his career at Forfar Athletic.

GRAHAM HONEYMAN (OL)
East Fife
Age: 19

'Injured early on'

Honeyman spent seven seasons at East Fife before moving to Australia in 1976. He briefly returned to Scotland to play for Dundee United in 1978/79 before heading back down under.

GEORGE ANDERSON (CH)
Morton
Age: 19 Height: 5ft 11in Weight: 12st

'Good prospect' (RB)

The central defender had two spells at Greenock Morton (1969-1980 and 1985-1987), and appeared for Airdrie in between. Made 384 league appearances (22 goals).

BERNIE WRIGHT (No 10)
Walsall
Age: 19 Height: 5ft 11in Weight: 11st 7in

05.02.72: 'Strong big heart, useful will watch again' (GT)

'Bernie the Bolt' scored two goals for Walsall in 15 appearances before being sold to Everton in 1971. He only lasted 11 league games with the Blues before having his contract terminated for 'serious misconduct'. The story goes that he took exception to being dropped and chased the manager around Bellefield, Everton's training ground. He subsequently returned to Walsall – it is in this spell that Twentyman made a note of him – where he scored 38 goals in 152 appearances. He also played for Bradford City, Port Vale, Kidderminster Harriers and Cheltenham Town and now still lives in the Midlands.

MARK WALLINGTON (GK)
Walsall
Age: 19 Height: 6ft Weight: 11st 7lbs

05.02.72: 'Done well for first game' (GT)

Wallington won England Schoolboys caps before he was picked up by Walsall. He managed just 11 games there before being snapped up by Leicester City – the club at which he spent the vast majority of his career. Wallington trained as Peter Shilton's understudy, and when the latter left for Stoke City in 1974, Wallington became Leicester's undisputed number one. He was ever-present between 1975 and 1981. After making 460 appearances for The Foxes, Wallington played for Derby County (helping them to win promotion to the Second Division in 1986 and the Second Division title in 1987 before being dropped for his former teammate Peter Shilton), Lincoln City and Grantham Town.

DAVID SHAW (IF)
Oldham
Height: 5ft 9in Weight: 11st 7lbs

26.02.72: 'Very good game gave alround [sic] performance' (GT)
04.03.72: 'Showed up well with pace and strength satisfactory' (GT)
31.03.72: 'Always dangerous, might have scored 3' (GT)

Shaw played for Huddersfield Town before joining Oldham Athletic in 1969. In his first spell with Oldham he scored 70 goals in 155 league games before moving to West Bromwich Albion in 1973. Shaw returned to Oldham two years later and bagged 21 more goals in 59 matches for The Latics before deciding to hang up his boots.

KEN MACKIE (IF)
Dunfermline
Age: 16 Height: 5ft 11in Weight: 12st

11.03.72: 'Very good display for his age' (GT)
07.10.72: 'Raw but could improve, will watch again'
03.02.73: 'Looks to have improved, useful in the air may be transferred shortly' (WF)

Mackie scored 46 goals in 119 appearances for Dunfermline between 1971 and 1976. He moved to Falkirk but only struck three times in 38 matches there before he joined East Fife, where his ratio improved to roughly a goal every three league games.

ALEX McGREGOR (IF)
Ayr
Age: 19 Height: 5ft 10in Weight: 11st 7lbs

'Not forceful enough'

A winger born in Glasgow, McGregor joined Ayr United from Troon in 1969 and scored one goal in 29 league appearances for the club. After a brief period at Hibernian, he moved on to Shrewsbury Town and Aldershot – he spent six years at the latter, scoring 17 goals in 177 league games.

BOYSOCK (CF)
Forfar
Age: 19 Height: 5ft 10in Weight: 11st

19.08.72: 'Promising player, worth looking at' (FMc)

STUART KENNEDY (RB)
Falkirk
Age: 20 Height: 5ft 9in Weight: 11st

19.08.72: 'Worth following, shows a lot of promise' (WMc)

Kennedy spent five years at Falkirk, making 110 league appearances before moving to Aberdeen in 1976. He won the Scottish League Cup in 1976/77, the league title in 1979/80 and the Scottish Cup in 1981/82 at Aberdeen, and was integral to the side that won the Cup Winners' Cup in 1983 – an injury picked up in the semi-final prevented him from playing in the final against Real Madrid, but his manager at the time, Alex Ferguson, named him on the subs' bench to ensure he received a medal. Kennedy never played again.

KENNY THOMPSON (RH)
Dunfermline
Age: 20 Height: 5ft 10in Weight: 10st 12lbs

19.08.72: 'Showed up well, worth keeping an eye on' (JM)
07.10.72: 'Played as sweeper looks useful, an easy runner' (GT)

Thompson spent the vast majority of his career at Dunfermline Athletic – between 1970 and 1982 he made 253 appearances. He also had a six-year spell at Alloa Athletic, three at St Johnstone and finished his career at Cowdenbeath.

JIM WALLACE (LB)
Dunfermline
Age: 18 Height: 5ft 8.5in Weight: 11st

07.10.72: 'Good left foot lacks defensive qualities will watch again for improvement'

Wallace stayed with Dunfermline until 1975,

when he moved to Aldershot. He also played for Alloa Athletic.

ALAN SUTHERLAND (LB)
Forfar
Age: 19 Height: 5ft 7in Weight: 10st 12lbs

02.09.72: 'Shows promise worth following up' (JM)

Sutherland played for Forfar Athletic between 1971 and 1974, making 39 league appearances.

JOHN GRAY (OR)
Motherwell
Age: 18 Height: 5ft 8in Weight: 10st

09.09.72: 'Not enough in the game to pass judgement' (GT)

Gray left Motherwell in 1974 having scored two goals in 25 league games. He joined Ayr United and only made two appearances before moving into non-league football.

ARTHUR THOMSON (IF)
Airdrie
Age: 18 Height: 5ft 9in Weight: 10st

09.09.72: 'Young player of promise, worth keeping in mind' (GT)

Between 1972 and 1974, Thomson made 19 league appearances without scoring for Airdrie. It is unknown where he moved to after that.

STEWART KENNEDY (GK)
Stenhousemuir
Age: 21 Height: 5ft 11in Weight: 11st 6lbs

26.08.72: 'Good GK playing well' (JM)

Kennedy was signed by Glasgow Rangers in 1973 after a successful two-year spell at Stenhousemuir. He was employed mainly as back-up to Peter McCloy, but in his five years at the club he still managed to make 131 appearances and keep 45 clean sheets. Kennedy was ever-present for Rangers in the championship-winning season of 1974/75, their first for 11 years. Regularly rotating with McCloy from then on, he won another league title in 1978 and also picked up two Scottish League Cups, in 1976 and 1978. Kennedy moved to Forfar on a free in 1980, and he played there until he was 40, racking up a massive 281 league appearances over a period of 11 years.

MICK PRENDERGAST (IF)
Sheff W
Height: 5ft 9in Weight: 10st 13lbs

'Best forward for Sheff W. Works hard,
good in air must be watched' (GT)
09.03.74: *'Done well scored two goals' (KK)*
16.03.74: *'Coming back after injury,*
a live prospect' (GT)
13.04.74: *'Broke leg through being*
brave' (GT)

It was a case of what might have been for Mick Prendergast, who played for Sheffield Wednesday for 12 years, scoring 53 goals in 183 league appearances. He was hit by several injuries during his time at the club, including internal bleeding in his knee and a broken leg in 1974 (presumably the incident Twentyman witnessed), and Wednesday suffered relegation twice. Prendergast moved to Barnsley in 1978 but only made 12 full appearances before going on loan to Halifax and then moving to non-league teams Mexborough Town Athletic and Denaby United. He was forced to retire on medical grounds, had to have a hip replacement at 36 and is now registered as disabled.

DAVE SUNLEY (No 11)
Sheff W
Age: 20 Height: 5ft 9in Weight: 10st 12lbs

'Scored from close in but did little,
lacks a bit of devil' (GT)

Sunley was an apprentice at Sheffield Wednesday before making the first team in 1970, and in 145 appearances for The Owls he scored 26 goals. After a brief loan spell to Nottingham Forest, Sunley moved to Hull City in 1975, Lincoln City in 1978 and Stockport County in 1979.

STUART PEARSON (CF)
Hull
Age: 21 Height: 5ft 8.5in Weight: 11st 7lbs

'A bouncy bustler, a little disappointing
after good reports' (GT)
08.04.74: *'Straight forward a question*
in 1st Div at the price' (GT)

Born in Hull, Pearson played for his hometown team until 1974, bagging 44 goals in 129 league games. He was signed by Manchester United, who had just been relegated to the Second Division, and he proved instrumental in helping the club to regain their top-flight status, scoring 17 goals in his first season. Pearson played a vital part in Man Utd's 1977 FA Cup final win over Liverpool, scoring the first of their goals in the 2-1 win. In all, he scored 55 goals in 139 league games for Utd before signing for West Ham in 1980, where he again won the FA Cup – his cross-cum-shot enabled Trevor Brooking to head the winner against Arsenal. Pearson retired in 1982.

DOM SULLIVAN (OR)
Clyde
Age: 21 Height: 5ft 8in Weight: 10st 12lbs

'A lot of skill, ? against indurence [sic]' (GT)

Sullivan spent six years at Clyde, scoring 16 goals in 174 appearances before moving to Aberdeen in 1976. He struck 10 goals for the Dons in 98 league games before earning a move to Celtic in 1980, where he netted 15 times in 119 games and became an unsung hero in Celtic's back-to-back league championship wins in 1981 and 1982. Released in 1983, having been nudged out of the first team by Paul McStay, Sullivan went on to play for Greenock Morton and Alloa Athletic.

PHIL ROBERTS (RB)
Bristol R
Age: 21 Height: 5ft 9in Weight: 11st 7lbs

21.10.72: *'Good player could play*
in better class' (GT)

After 175 appearances in the Bristol Rovers defence between 1968 and 1973, Roberts moved to Portsmouth. He spent four seasons there and won four Wales caps, but he could not prevent Portsmouth from falling from Division Two into Division Four between 1976 and 1978. Roberts ended his career with a brief period at Hereford and a longer spell at Exeter, where he made over 100 appearances.

PETER SPIRING (No 10 S)
Bristol C
Age: 22 Height: 5ft 10in Weight: 11st

21.10.72: *'Played well up front*
worth looking at' (GT)
10.02.73: *'Just back and still looks useful' (GT)*

Spiring arrived in the Bristol City first team from the juniors, and he struck 16 goals in 63 appearances before Twentyman's scouting brought him to Liverpool in 1973. However, the winger only made the bench twice and never made an appearance for the Reds' first team before he was offloaded to Luton Town in 1974. After 15 games there he was sold to Hereford United, where he played 227 league games and scored 20 goals.

GEOFF MERRICK (6 BF)
Bristol C
Age: 21 Height 5ft 8in Weight: 11st

21.10.72: 'Good back four player' (GT)
10.02.73: 'Was troubled by wind on high ball but still quick and good back four player' (GT)

A strong centre-back, Merrick spent his entire professional career at Bristol City from 1968 to 1982, and was adored by the fans. He was part of the team that took Bristol City back into the top flight in 1976 under Alan Dicks's steward-ship. Merrick made 367 appearances and scored 10 goals, and he was one of the leg-endary 'Ashford Eight' who tore up their con-tracts in 1982 to enable the club to survive.

DAVE ROBERTS (4 BF)
Oxford
Age: 21? Height: 5ft 9in Weight: 11st 5lbs

21.10.72: 'Good back four player' (GT)

Central defender Roberts joined Oxford United from Fulham in 1971 after 22 appearances with the Londoners. A rock in the Oxford defence, he made 176 appearances and scored eight goals. After leaving the club in 1975, Roberts played for Hull City (86 apps) and Cardiff City (41 apps) before moving to Hong Kong.

KEITH FEAR (No 10)
Bristol City
Age: 19 Height: 5ft 7in Weight: 10st 12lbs

19.11.72: 'Lot of ability but would be better in midfield' (GT)

Bristol-born Fear was a striker with Bristol City between 1969 and 1978, scoring 32 goals in 151 league games. He had loan spells at St Louis Stars, Hereford United and Blackburn Rovers in 1977 before signing with Plymouth Argyle the following year. He scored nine goals in 46 games for The Pilgrims, went on loan to Brentford in 1979, and then moved on to Chester City in 1981. Fear saw out his career at Wimbledon and Bangor City.

TREVOR TAINTON (No 7)
Bristol
Age: 24 Height: 5ft 8in Weight: 11st 7lbs

16.11.72: 'Played well' (KK)
19.11.72: 'Shows ability and strength as previous' (GT)
10.02.73: 'Looked the best player afield [sic]' (GT)

Tainton played out almost his entire career at Bristol City, making 581 appearances between 1967 and 1982 – he is second to John Atyeo in City's all-time appearance-makers list. He fin-ished his professional career with a season at Torquay United, making 19 appearances.

PETER SUDDABY (No 6)
Blackpool
Age: 22 Height: 5ft 11in Weight: 11st

09.12.72: 'A sweeper not impressed as a CH' (GT)

Suddaby had a decade at Blackpool (1970-80), during which he made 331 appearances in the league before moving to another seaside club, Brighton. After 23 league games on the south coast, Suddaby subsequently moved on to Wimbledon and Wycombe Wanderers, retiring in 1983.

ALAN AINSCOW (No 11)
Blackpool
Age: 19 Height: 5ft 9in Weight: 11st

09.12.72: 'Good in patches took his goals well' (GT)

Beginning his career at Blackpool, Ainscow played in 192 league games for the club, scoring 28 goals. He was a versatile player who was employed on either flank until he was dropped deeper into the midfield. In the 1972/73 season – when Twentyman noted him – he was the club's joint top scorer with Alan Suddick. In 1978 he was sold to Birmingham City for £40,000, where he helped the club to promotion from the Second Division in 1979/80. Everton took him to Goodison Park in 1981 for £250,000, but despite a return of three goals in 28 games he failed to make a name for himself, and he was loaned to Barnsley a season later. After a brief stint playing in Hong Kong, Ainscow returned to the UK to play for Wolverhampton Wanderers, Blackburn Rovers and Rochdale.

JOHN MITCHELL
Fulham
Age: 20 Height: 5ft 11in Weight: 12st

*30.12.72: 'Honest but did nothing
to recommend' (GT)*

Mitchell, a forward, was at Fulham between 1972 and 1978, and he averaged just under a goal in every three league games – 57 in 169 appearances. He moved across London to join Millwall, where he scored 18 in 81 games before retiring in 1981.

DAVID IRVING (IF)
Workington
Age: 21 Height: 5ft 10in Weight: 12st 5lbs

*06.01.73: 'Heavy in build but has
good qualities will watch again' (GT)*

Irving spent three years with Workington, who were in Division Four at the time, scoring 16 goals in 65 league games. Several scouts were clearly circling when Twentyman went to watch him – he ended up signing for Everton in 1973 for £30,000. However, he only made six league appearances for The Toffees before being farmed out to Sheffield United on loan. He secured a permanent move to Oldham in 1976, where he struck seven times in 21 league matches. In 1978 he moved to America and spent the final years of his career at various clubs there and also at Shamrock Rovers in Dublin.

MIKE LESTER (MF)
Oldham
Age: 19 Height: 5ft 9.5in Weight: 11st

*03.02.73: 'Promising player' (GT)
17.02.73: 'Looks a bit one paced for
midfield not really impressed'*

We must presume that Twentyman meant "Lester" even though he wrote "Lister" – there has only been one Lister who played for Oldham Athletic, and that was Bert Lister, a forward who left the club in 1965. Twentyman must have been watching Mike Lester, a midfielder at Oldham between 1972 and 1974 who scored two goals in 27 league appearances before moving to Manchester City. Lester was on City's books until 1977, when he moved to Grimsby Town, although he also spent time at Stockport County and Washington Diplomats on loan. Lester only made two league appear-

ances for City. He also played for Barnsley, Exeter City, Bradford City, Scunthorpe United, Hartlepool United and Blackpool.

KEITH HICKS (CH)
Oldham
Age: 19 Height: 5ft 11.5in Weight: 12st 4lbs

*03.02.73: 'Keep an eye open for
improvement' (GT)
17.02.73: 'Not commanding enough in the air'*

Hicks was a centre-half who played in more than 450 league matches during the 1970s and '80s. He had nine years at Oldham Athletic (242 appearances, 11 goals), five years at Hereford United (201 apps, two goals) and two years at Rochdale (32 apps, one goal). Hicks is currently football in the community officer at Rochdale.

MAURICE WHITTLE
Oldham
Age: 23? Height: 5ft 9.5in Weight: 11st 4lbs

*03.02.73: 'Good left foot quick and
honest played well'
17.02.73: 'Had plenty of room to attack,
does well going forward useful'*

Oldham Athletic signed Whittle from Blackburn Rovers in 1969, where he'd been an apprentice and made seven first-team league appearances. The full-back spent the majority of his career with The Latics, notching up 312 league appearances and 39 goals between 1969 and 1977. He then moved to America to play for Fort Lauderdale Strikers before returning to the UK to finish his career at Barrow and Wigan Athletic.

JOE CRAIG (CF)
Partick

*24.02.73: 'Did not impress was marked
out by Cushley' (WMc)
24.02.73: 'Did not impress' (WF)*

Craig signed for Partick Thistle in 1972 from Sauchie and enjoyed a successful time with the club, scoring 44 goals in 112 league games and helping them to the First Division title in 1975/76. This prompted a move to Scottish giants Celtic for £60,000, and he spent two seasons there, scoring 22 times in 55 league matches and winning the Scottish Cup and league championship in his first year. While at

Celtic, he won his only Scotland cap, coming on as a substitute in the 75th minute against Sweden and scoring with his first touch of the game – a header. Craig moved on to Blackburn Rovers in 1978, where he scored eight goals in 48 games before finishing his career at Hamilton Academical.

ROY McCORMACK
Dumbarton

'Looked a better prospect than Craig' (WM)
24.02.73: 'Looked better than Craig
worth looking at' (WF)

Noted as "McCormick", we must assume the scouts meant Roy McCormack, a striker who played for Dumbarton between 1966 and 1975, scoring 108 goals in 246 games. He then moved to Australia to play for APIA Leichhardt.

JIM STEWART
Kilmarnock
Age: 19 Height: 6ft 2in Weight: 12st 6lbs

07.04.73: 'Played well done everything
right' (GT)
06.10.73: 'Done everything well,
good hands, brave, and reads it well.
Only ? against dead ball kicks' (GT)
20.10.74: 'Good display done
everything right' (GT)
27.10.74: 'Probably the best young keeper in
Scotland picked for the Scottish pool' (JM)

A beanpole goalkeeper, Stewart made 175 appearances for Kilmarnock in six years before trundling across the border to Middlesbrough in 1978. After a couple of seasons he returned to Scotland to join Rangers – between 1980 and 1984 he played 56 league games. Stewart also spent time on loan at Dumbarton before finishing up at St Mirren and Partick Thistle. He won two caps for Scotland.

ALAN ROUGH
Partick T
Age: 21 Height: 6ft Weight: 11st 7lbs

07.04.73: 'Done nothing wrong,
good prospect' (GT)

Rough was another goalkeeper that Twentyman looked at. He spent the majority of his career at Partick Thistle – 409 league appearances between 1969 and 1982 – but also

played 175 times for Hibernian between 1982 and 1988. He then had brief stints with Celtic (five games), Hamilton Academical and Ayr United before becoming player-coach of Glenafton Athletic in 1990.

JOHNNY DOYLE (OR)
Ayr
Height: 5ft 9in Weight: 10st 7lbs

11.08.73: 'Plenty of skill, has pace and
guts a good prospect' (GT)
14.08.73: 'Not as good tryed [sic] to
do to [sic] much' (GT)

Doyle was a winger who began his career with Ayr United, playing in 155 league games and scoring 24 goals for the club before moving to Celtic in 1976, where he won two league titles and one Scottish Cup in five years. Doyle's life was cut short in 1981, at the age of 30, when he was electrocuted while working on his new home.

BOBBY TYNAN (IF)
Tranmere
Height: 5ft 10in Weight: 10st 12lbs

01.09.73: 'Got everything just needs
strength and indurance [sic]' (GT)
15.09.73: 'Looked jaded, heavy ground' (GT)

Tynan made 195 league appearances for Tranmere Rovers, scoring 26 goals, before being sold to Blackpool for £100,000 in 1978. However, before the next season started, Tynan got a severe knee injury that ended his professional career.

STUART LEE (IF)
Bolton
Height: 5ft 9in Weight: 10st 12lbs

03.09.73: 'Neat control and looking
for chances worth following' (GT)
10.09.73: 'Takes good positions
will score goals' (GT)
18.01.75: 'Played well quick
good control' (GT)

Lee played for Bolton Wanderers between 1971 and 1975, scoring 20 goals in 85 league games. He then moved to Wrexham for a couple of seasons (12 goals in 54 appearances) before going to Stockport County (21 goals in 49 apps) and Manchester City (two goals in seven apps). Lee then headed to America.

PLAYERS' GLOSSARY

ALLY McROBERTS (No 6)
Airdrie
Height: 5ft 9in Weight: 11st

01.09.73: 'Promising player,
wants covering' (JM)

A forward who averaged a goal every three
league games for Airdrie (31 in 91). He moved
to Falkirk in 1977, and stayed there until 1982,
bagging 35 goals in 129 games before heading
to Dumbarton for a brief spell. McRoberts also
played for Stirling Albion and Stenhousemuir.

BRIAN AHERN (LH)
Clyde
Age: 20 Height: 5ft 9in Weight: 11st 2lbs

01.09.73: 'Player worth looking at' (JM)
12.09.73: 'Not enough physically only a
neat player' (GT)

Ahern had two spells at Clyde, 1971-81 and
1983-87. Operating mostly from midfield, he
scored 63 goals for the club in 420 league
games. Between those periods, Ahern played for
Ayr United (nine goals in 70 league games), and
ended his professional career at Albion Rovers.

IAN McDONALD (IF)
Workington
Age: 20 Height: 5ft 9in Weight: 11st 7lbs

15.09.73: 'Promising player, will watch
again' (GT)
23.09.73: 'Shows good promise but must
win the ball better' (GT)
12.01.74: 'Promising display, above
average in this division' (KK)
20.01.74: 'Done well worth buying
if right price' (GT)

Liverpool followed up Twentyman's interest in
McDonald, signing the forward in 1974 after
two years at Barrow and two more at
Workington. He never made an appearance for
Liverpool's first team and was sent to
Colchester United on loan before being sold to
Mansfield Town in 1975. He made 56 appear-
ances for Mansfield but enjoyed much longer,
more fruitful spells at his final two clubs – York
City (175 league apps, 29 goals) and Aldershot
(340 games, 50 goals).

BILLY JENNINGS (IF)
Watford
Age: 21 Height: 5ft 9in Weight: 11st

08.09.73: 'Useful worth looking at' (TS)
15.09.73: 'Quiet game never
showed much' (BJ)
08.12.73: 'Scored only goal,
useful in box' (GT)

The London-born striker spent four years at
Watford, grabbing 33 goals in 92 league
games. He signed for West Ham United in
1974 for £110,000, and was part of the FA Cup-
winning team of 1974/75 and the side that
reached the final of the Cup Winners' Cup the
following season. Jennings suffered an Achilles
injury in 1977 and subsequently lost his place
in the team, so after scoring 34 goals in 99
league games he was sold to Leyton Orient in
1979. He continued to score(21 league goals in
67 games) before he moved on to the final
league club of his career – Luton Town.

CHRIS GUTHRIE (CF)
Southend
Age: 20? Height: 6ft 1in Weight: 12st 7lbs

11.09.73: 'Looks useful will
watch for progress' (GT)
22.09.73: 'Did not show anything,
fought a lone battle' (WJ)

Guthrie had spent an unremarkable season at
Newcastle before arriving at Southend. In three
seasons with The Shrimpers, he made 108
appearances and struck 35 goals. Guthrie then
spent two seasons at Sheffield United (60
league games, 15 goals) and Swindon Town
(45 league games, 12 goals) before brief stop-
offs at Fulham and Millwall.

O'NEIL
Oldham
Age: 23 Height: 5ft 11in Weight: 11st 12lbs

11.09.73: 'No pace nothing to
recommend this player' (GT)

NOLAN KEELEY
Scunthorpe
Age: 20 Height: 5ft 10in Weight: 11st

14.09.73: 'Worth looking at,
will follow up' (KK)

Midfielder who spent eight years at Scunthorpe
United, making 259 league appearances and
scoring 37 goals. He moved to Lincoln City in
1979 for two seasons, playing in 52 league
games and scoring three goals.

ALAN CRAWFORD
Rotherham
Age: 19 Height: 5ft 8in Weight: 10st

*23.09.73: 'To be watched looks
a good prospect' (KK)*

Crawford was a schoolboy fan of Rotherham United and became an apprentice with the club at 16. The left-winger was loaned out to Mansfield Town in the 1972/73 season, but swiftly returned to his parent club, where he firmly established himself in the side over the next few years, scoring 49 goals in 237 league games between 1973 and 1979. His 31 league and cup goals in a single season (1976/77) is a record for a winger at Rotherham. Ever-present for three seasons, a disagreement with the manager led to him being sold to Chesterfield, where he played just shy of 100 league games and scored more than 20 goals – a feat he repeated at Bristol City between 1982 and 1985. He spent his final season at Exeter City.

JOE COOKE (BF)
Bradford City
Age: 20 Height: 5ft 11in Weight: 11st 7lbs

*03.10.73: 'Good in the air but looked out
of position up front more suited to defence'*

Cooke was a Dominican who spent his entire career in the UK. Although he started out as a striker, Twentyman was right to spot that he'd be better in defence – that was where he ended up. In his first spell at Bradford City (as a striker) he managed to score 62 goals in 204 league games. He then jumped around clubs, playing for Peterborough United, Oxford United, Exeter City, Bradford City (again), Rochdale and Wrexham.

BRENDAN O'CALLAGHAN (CF)
Doncaster
Age: 18 Height: 6ft 2in Weight: 12st 7lbs

*22.09.73: 'Promising player good in air,
to be followed' (GT)*

In five seasons at Doncaster Rovers, O'Callaghan scored 65 goals in 187 league games. He was sold to Stoke City in 1978, where he scored one of the fastest debut goals of all time – coming on as a substitute in the 75th minute when Stoke were waiting to take a corner against Hull, he ran into the penalty area and headed in the cross. He stayed at Stoke until 1985, scoring 44 times in 265 league matches before moving on to Oldham Athletic. After 10 league appearances there, he suffered a serious knee injury and was forced to retire. O'Callaghan also played six times for the Republic of Ireland.

MIKE ELWISS (No 8)
Doncaster
Height: 5ft 8in Weight: 11st

22.09.73: 'Useful may improve' (GT)
08.12.73: 'Worked hard without success' (WJ)
*13.10.73: 'Had a frustrating game,
one shot nothing else' (WJ)*
*03.02.74: 'Quiet game not much to
judge by' (GT)*
*At Preston: 'Has improved tremendously since
Doncaster R. Has the heart and determination
to win but most of all can play with movement
into space and always prepared to have a go at
goal a handful for any defender to handle'*

Elwiss played for Doncaster Rovers for three seasons as a forward, scoring 30 goals in 97 league appearances. He moved to Preston North End in February 1974 where he became a hit with the fans, winning player of the year twice and scoring 60 goals in 192 league games. Elwiss then moved to Crystal Palace in 1978, where he struck seven times in 20 league games before getting injured. He went back to Preston on loan, but the injury got the better of him and he was forced to retire.

PETER KITCHEN (No 10)
Doncaster
Height: 5ft 11in Weight: 11st

*22.09.73: 'Quite lively scored two goals,
will watch again' (GT)*

Kitchen spent seven years at Doncaster Rovers, scoring 89 goals in 228 league appearances before spending two seasons apiece at Leyton Orient, Fulham and Cardiff City, scoring fairly regularly at each. Kitchen went back to Leyton Orient in 1982 before ending his league career at Chester City on a non-contract basis.

HAMISH McALPINE (GK)
Dundee
Age: 21? Height: 5ft11in Weight: 11st

27.10.73: 'Good alround [sic] display' (GT)
*03.11.73: 'A good alround [sic]
goalkeeper done everything right' (WF)*

McAlpine kept net at Dundee United for 20 years between 1966 and 1986, racking up 477 league appearances. He even managed to score three goals when he enjoyed a run as Dundee United's penalty taker. While at the club, they won two Scottish Cups and the league championship in 1982/83. Early in his time at Dundee United he spent a season on loan at Montrose, and at the end of his time there he played a single game on loan at Dunfermline. He moved to Raith Rovers in 1986, where he made 72 league appearances and scored another goal, this one directly from a goal kick. McAlpine finished his career with Arbroath, retiring in 1989.

PETER ANDERSON (MF)
Luton
Age: 24 Height: 5ft 10in Weight: 11st

06.11.73: 'Has pace and looks above average will watch again' (GT)
22.12.73: 'Quick and reads positions well could play in better company' (GT)

Born in Hendon, Anderson was a winger who spent most of his career at Luton Town. Between 1970 and 1976 he notched 34 goals in 181 league appearances for the club. He was integral to Luton's successful promotion bid in 1973/74, when they fought their way into the top flight for only the second time. Anderson was then sold to Royal Antwerp in Belgium in 1976 – the year that Luton were again relegated from the First Division. In 1978, he began jumping across the Atlantic, playing for San Diego Sockers and Tampa Bay Rowdies before returning to the UK to play for Sheffield United. In one season there, he scored 12 goals in 30 league matches. Anderson then went back to the Tampa Bay Rowdies before returning to play for Millwall, where he finished his career.

DON McALLISTER (FB)
Bolton
Age: 20 Height: 5ft 9.5in Weight: 11st 7lbs

29.09.73: 'Played well worth foll[owing]'
17.11.73: 'Played well on left side, will do well' (GT)

Spurs scouts were obviously watching McAllister too – they snapped up the full-back in 1975 after he'd been at Bolton Wanderers for five years (156 apps, two goals). He enjoyed mixed success at Tottenham. McAllister was part of the 1977 team that got relegated from

the top flight, and the 1978 team that narrowly scraped to promotion. He made 202 appearances in all competitions and scored 10 goals before moving to Charlton Athletic in 1981, where he played for two seasons. McAllister latterly spent brief periods with Tampa Bay Rowdies (USA), Vitoria Setubal (Portugal) and Rochdale.

STEVE FOLEY (CF)
Colchester
Age: 19 Height: 5ft 10in Weight: 11st

14.11.73: 'Looks useful to be followed up' (GT)
15.12.73: 'Scored two goals, still shows promise' (GT)

Foley spent his entire playing career at Colchester United. Between 1971 and 1982 he made 283 appearances in the league, scoring 54 goals. He has since moved into management and coaching – Foley is currently specialist skills coach at Ipswich Town.

DAMIEN RICHARDSON (CF)
Gillingham
Age: 19 Height: 5ft 10in Weight: 11st 7lbs

17.11.73: 'Sent off after 20 mins will watch again' (KK)
22.12.73: 'Seen in patches not a display above average' (GT)

After nine years at Shamrock Rovers, Dublin-born Richardson moved to Gillingham in 1972. Another nine-year spell brought 94 goals in 323 league games before he was released. He won three caps for the Republic of Ireland between 1971 and 1979, and has since spent time in management and punditry.

DICK TYDEMAN (MF)
Gillingham
Age: 19 Height: 6ft Weight: 12st

17.11.73: 'Strikes ball & takes good positions. ? against pace. Will watch again' (KK)
22.12.73: 'Played in space good kicker and passer worth following up' (GT)

Tydeman enjoyed two spells at Gillingham during his career (1969-77 and 1981-84), notching up 371 league appearances and 15 goals, although he apparently considered dropping football in 1971 to become a teacher. In between those two periods, Tydeman followed former Gillingham manager Andy Nelson to Charlton Athletic, where he made 158 league appearances in five years. He also played for Peterborough United before moving to several non-league sides in Kent.

ALAN WALDRON (MF)
Bolton
Age: 20 Height: 5ft 9in Weight: 11st

05.12.73: 'Played well showed pace
and strength will follow' (GT)
08.12.73: 'Bolton's best player 2nd half
good prospect will recommend' (GT)

Waldron made 141 appearances in the league for Bolton Wanderers, scoring six goals, between 1970 and 1978. He then moved to Blackpool, Bury and York City (on a non-contract basis) before heading overseas to Australia.

ALAN CURTIS
Swansea
Age: 19 Height: 5ft 9in Weight: 11st 7lbs

19.01.74: 'Not impressed
on this showing' (WJ)
'Has a lot of ability and strength
has a tendency to relax, if his enthusiasm
was 100% could be a good player'

Curtis played not once, not twice, but three times for Swansea during his career, featuring in the 1980s First Division sides. The Welsh international (35 caps, six goals) and forward-thinking midfielder also played for Leeds United, Southampton, Stoke City (on loan) and Cardiff City, notching up over 570 appearances and 116 goals between 1972 and 1990.

ROBBIE JAMES
Swansea
Age: 20 Height: 6ft Weight: 12st 7lbs

19.01.74: 'Showed up in patches,
not really impressed' (WJ)
'A player who is improving and could be
ready for the higher grade this season'

Another Swansea player who helped lift the club to heady heights in the 1980s, James played twice for City – in his first spell (1972-83) he made 394 league appearances and scored 99 goals, and in his second (1987-1990) he scored 16 goals in 90 games. Apparently he

had a trial at Arsenal in the 1974/75 season but failed to impress. James also played for Stoke City, Queens Park Rangers, Leicester City, Bradford City and Cardiff City, and he won 47 caps for Wales, scoring seven goals.

JEFF KING (MF)
Albion R
Age: 19 Height: 5ft 10in Weight: 11st

12.01.74: 'Shows promise,
best player on view' (JB)
20.01.74: 'Not a good display taken
off at HT' (WMc)

King was a journeyman. His career spanned 12 years, from 1972 to 1984, and in that time he played for Albion Rovers, Derby County, Notts County (on loan), Portsmouth (on loan), Walsall, Sheffield Wednesday, Sheffield United and Chesterfield (on a non-contract basis). In total, he made 209 league appearances and bagged 21 goals.

STEVE HETZKE (WH No 6)
Reading
Age: 18 Height: 5ft 11in Weight: 11st 7lbs

03.02.74: 'Promising player will follow' (KK)
17.08.74: 'Home to Cambridge,
reports as on form' (GT)
24.08.74: 'Away to Rotherham,
report given on form' (GT)

Wiltshire-born Hetzke was a defender who twice won promotion from Division Four with Reading, and after 11 years at the club (1971-82) he received a testimonial before joining Blackpool. In all, he scored 23 goals in 261 league games for Reading; at Blackpool he managed 18 in 140. The final years of Hetzke's career were spent at Sunderland, Chester City and Colchester United – he retired in 1989.

ERIC MARTIN (GK)
Brechin
Age: 19 Height: 6ft Weight: 12st

03.02.74: 'Not as good as
recommendation' (FMc)

Not to be confused with his namesake who kept goal for Southampton in the early 1970s, this Eric Martin dipped in and out of Scottish league football between 1972 and 1995. He played for Brechin City twice and Arbroath three times (once on loan), also spending time at non-league clubs Elgin City and Arbroath Victoria. He made just 96 league appearances.

TONY MORLEY (MF)
Preston
Age: 18 Height: 5ft 8in Weight: 10st 12lbs

09.03.74: 'Shows promise,
will keep an eye on' (GT)
13.04.74: 'Played well,
will follow next season' (GT)

Morley was a skilful left-winger who enjoyed a fruitful career. After four years at Preston North End (84 apps, 15 goals) and three at Burnley (91 apps, five goals), he transferred to Aston Villa in 1979 and was moulded by Ron Saunders into a fearsome attacker. Between 1979 and 1983 he played 180 matches in all competitions for Villa, scoring 34 goals – his strike against Everton at Goodison Park during 1980/81 was named goal of the season. He was part of the teams that won the league championship in 1980/81, the European Cup the following year and the European Super Cup. Despite winning six England caps he failed to make a name for himself and didn't play at the 1982 World Cup. In 1983 he signed for West Bromwich Albion, where he scored four goals in 33 games, before moving on to Birmingham City (on loan) and Den Haag in Holland, then back to West Brom and Burnley (on loan).

JIMMY CANT (MF)
Hearts
Age: 21 Height: 5ft 8in Weight: 11st 6lbs

27.04.74: 'Strong with good
ball control looked useful' (GT)
18.09.74: 'Report v Oldham (GT)

Edinburgh-born midfielder Cant played 74 games for Hearts in all competitions and scored three goals. He moved to Australia in 1977.

RONNIE GLAVIN (MF)
Partick T
Age: 20 Height: 5ft 8in Weight: 11st

27.04.74: 'Played well in flashes,
must show more' (GT)

An attacking midfielder, Glavin spent six years at Partick Thistle and scored 35 goals in 136 league games. He was signed by Celtic in 1974 and went on to win the league championship with the club in 1977, when he was scoring reg-

ularly from midfield. In five years at Parkhead he scored 35 goals in 101 league matches before moving to Barnsley in 1979. Racking up 176 appearances and 73 goals there, he had a brief spell at Belenenses in Portugal before returning to Barnsley as player-coach. He moved into a similar role at Stockport County before finishing his playing days at Cowdenbeath. He now manages non-league Wakefield FC.

SEASON 1974/75

ALAN STARLING
Northampton
Age: 23 Height: 5ft 11in Weight: 11st 10lbs

18.09.74: 'Done well in goal,
worth checking' (GT)

Starling was a goalkeeper who played for Luton Town, Torquay United (on loan), Northampton Town and Huddersfield Town. His longest spell was at Northampton, where he played in 258 league games. In April 1976 – his final year at the club – he scored a penalty against Hartlepool United which meant that every regular player for Northampton that season had scored at least one goal. He spent three years at Huddersfield and played in 112 league matches.

RICHARD FINNEY (OR)
Rotherham
Age: 18 Height: 5ft 8in Weight: 10st 10lbs

05.10.74: 'Small but looks useful can improve'
24.08.74: 'Home to Reading,
report as on form' (GT)
'Promising player worth keeping an eye on'
'Promising little player time will decide'

Finney was a winger who spent his entire career at Rotherham, from 1973 to 1981. He scored 68 goals in 236 league appearances.

BOBBY ROBINSON (MF)
Dundee
Age: 23 Height: 5ft 8in Weight: 10st 12lbs

31.08.74: 'Away to Airdrie,
report as on form' (GT)

Robinson played in midfield for Falkirk for two seasons before joining Dundee. He played 149 league games for Dundee and scored 16 goals before moving to rivals Dundee United in

1977/78. Robinson went on to play for Hearts and Raith Rovers.

DAVE McWILLIAMS (GK)
Airdrie
Age: 21 Height: 6ft Weight: 11st 6lbs

*31.08.74: 'Home to Dundee
report on form' (GT)*

McWilliams joined Airdrie from Alloa Athletic in 1973. He played 106 times for Airdrie between 1973 and 1978, going on loan at the end of this period to Hamilton Academical before being sold to Forfar Athletic. McWilliams also played for Clyde.

JOCKY SCOTT (MF)
Dundee
Age: 26? Height: 5ft 8in Weight: 11st

*31.08.74: 'Away to Airdrie
report as on form' (GT)*

Scott had been an appretice at Chelsea before joining Dundee in 1964. Although noted by Twentyman as a midfielder, he was mainly used as a forward, scoring 113 goals in 275 league games for Dundee between 1964 and 1975. He moved to Aberdeen for a couple of seasons before returning to Dundee to see out his career, and he is currently manager there. Scott won two Scotland caps.

BOBBY HOUSTON (LH)
Partick
Age: 22?

*17.08.74: 'Home to Dumbarton.
Very good performance by this player' (JM)*

Houston spent seven seasons at Partick Thistle, scoring 18 times in 186 league games before moving to Kilmarnock for two seasons and Greenock Morton for four.

BURKE (CF)
Dumbarton
Age: 19 Height: 6ft Weight: 11st 7lbs

*17.08.74: 'Raw in a lot of his work
but worth following' (JM)*

CAMERON (GK)
Queen of the South

'Showed up well worth following' (JM)

LAURIE WILLIAMS (GK)
Dumbarton

'Very good game worth following' (JM)

Williams was on Dumbarton's books from 1969 to 1980, making 296 league appearances, and was loaned out at the end of this period to Motherwell and Dundee.

DAVIE JOHNSTON (LB)
Dundee
Age:21 Height: 6ft Weight: 12st

*31.08.74: 'Confident display
although he prefers right foot' (GT)
31.08.74: 'Looked very useful
on this showing' (JM)*

Johnston played for Dundee for 10 years between 1968 and 1978, making 219 appearances and scoring nine goals. He subsequently moved to Montrose for two season before heading overseas to Hong Kong.

BOBBY HUTCHINSON (CF)
Dundee
Age: 20 Height: 5ft 9in Weight: 10st 12lbs

*31.08.74: 'Report as given on
report form Away to Airdrie' (GT)*

Hutchinson was more often used in midfield than up front. Between 1971 and 1988 he played for Montrose, Dundee, Hibernian, Wigan Athletic, Tranmere Rovers (twice), Mansfield Town, Bristol City, Walsall, Blackpool (on loan) and Carlisle United (on loan). He played 449 league games and scored 74 goals.

GRAHAM BELL (MF)
Oldham
Age: 19 Height: 5ft 10in Weight: 10st 12lbs

*31.08.74: 'Home to Bristol City,
report as on form' (DW)*

Bell made 107 league appearances for Oldham Athletic before moving to Preston North End in 1979, where he played in 143 games. He scored nine league goals for each club. Bell also played for Huddersfield Town (on loan), Carlisle, Bolton Wanderers and Tranmere Rovers.

RONNIE MOORE (CH)
Tranmere
Age: 21 Height: 5ft 11.5in Weight: 11st 10lbs

PLAYERS' GLOSSARY

31.08.74: *'Home to Aldershot, report as on form'*

Tranmere Rovers legend Ronnie Moore started and finished his career at the club, and during his playing days he was used as both a central defender and a forward. In 249 appearances he scored 72 goals in his first spell at Tranmere before moving to Cardiff City for two seasons. He moved to Rotherham United in 1980 – in 125 games there he hammered in 52 goals. Moore also played for Charlton Athletic and Rochdale before returning to Prenton Park to finish his career. He currently manages the club.

KENNY WATSON (LH)
Montrose
Age: 18 Height: 6ft Weight: 11st 7lbs

31.08.74: *'Home to East Stirling, report as on form' (FMc)*

Watson spent two years at Montrose before signing for Glasgow Rangers in 1975. He made 62 league appearances for Rangers in five years, scoring five goals and winning the league championship and the Scottish Cup before moving to Partick Thistle, where he spent the majority of his career. Watson was there between 1980 and 1989 – 254 league games, 47 goals – before he retired through injury.

HENNIGAN (LB)
South Liverpool
Age: 18 Height: 5ft 10in Weight: 11st 7in

03.09.74: *'Useful worth having a look at' (GT)*

STEVE EMERY (RB)
Hereford
Age: 18

31.08.74: *'Report as on form, home to Peterboro' (RB)*

Emery was more regularly used in midfield during his career, and he had two spells at Hereford United (1973-80 and 1983-85) – in all, he made 279 league appearances for the club and scored 12 goals. He also played for Derby County (four goals in 75 games), Newport County and Wrexham.

BILLY GILLIES (LB)
East Fife
Age: 18 Height: 5ft 10in Weight: 11st 7lbs

25.09.74: *'Report v Cowdenbeath' (WF)*

Gillies had seven years at East Fife, playing in 165 league games and scoring 16 goals before moving to Forfar Athletic in 1980, where he played for a season. He subsequently moved to non-league team Kelty Hearts.

JOHN LOVE (MF)
East Fife
Age: 20 Height: 5ft 9in Weight: 10st 12lbs

09.11.74: *'Report v Hamilton' (JB)*

East Fife was Love's only league side, and he served them between 1971 and 1977, playing in 116 league games and scoring nine goals.

JOHN WARD (No 8 S)
Lincoln
Age: 19 Height: 5ft 10in Weight: 11st

09.11.74: *'Report v Darlington' (TW)*
16.11.74: *'Report v Barnsley' (GT)*

Ward was a useful forward player who was on Lincoln City's books between 1970 and 1979. He appeared 240 times and scored 91 league goals. He spent time at Workington on loan during the 1972/73 season. Ward moved to Watford in 1979, and in a season there he bagged six goals in 27 games. The forward saw out his career at Grimsby Town and then Lincoln City for a second spell, and has since been involved in coaching and management.

BOBBY DOYLE (MF 4)
Barnsley
Age: 20? Height: 5ft 10in Weight: 11st

'A good right foot but not as mobile as expect, plays in one area on the right not able to dictate enough'

Doyle came through the ranks at Barnsley and played in the first team for four years, notching up 149 league appearances and 16 goals before joining Peterborough United in 1976. In three years there he played a further 130 league games, scoring 10 times, but was sold to Blackpool in 1979. Doyle signed for Portsmouth in 1981 (177 apps, 16 goals), then Hull City in 1986. He retired a year later.

MICK BUTLER (No 10 S)
Barnsley
Age: 22 Height: 5ft 8.5in Weight: 11st

SECRET DIARY OF A LIVERPOOL SCOUT

Butler played for Barnsley, Huddersfield Town, Bournemouth and Bury, scoring a total of 113 league goals in 350 games. His longest spell was at Barnsley, where he stayed for four years between 1972 and 1976.

JIM CLARK (No 4)
Stirling A
Age: 20

Clarke had six years at Stirling Albion (176 appearances, 22 goals) and another six at Kilmarnock (173 appearances, eight goals) before short spells at Motherwell and Meadowbank Thistle. He briefly returned to Kilmarnock in 1986 before moving to Australia.

CRAWFORD BOYD (CH)
Queen of S
Age: 19 Height: 5ft 11in Weight: 11st 12lbs

30.11.74: Done nothing wrong against poor opposition' (JB)

Boyd had two spells at Queen of the South, the first being the longest. Between 1972 and 1979 he played in 215 league games and scored six goals for the club before moving to Hearts for two seasons. He then returned to Queen of the South for a 38-game stretch.

DICK TAYLOR (GK)
Huddersfield
Age: 19 Height: 5ft 10in Weight: 11st 6lbs

30.11.74: 'Useful. Needs experience good on reflex work' (GT)

Taylor only had a short career, and he spent nearly all of it at Huddersfield between 1973 and 1982. He had a brief loan spell at York City in 1979/80. Taylor was forced to retire through injury after 105 league games for Huddersfield.

GRAHAM McGIFFORD (RB)
Huddersfield
Age: 20 Height: 5ft 9in Weight: 11st

30.11.74: 'Looks useful kicks well, tackles well and shows pace' (GT)

McGifford played for Huddersfield, Hull City and Port Vale, enjoying only limited success at each. In all, he only made 63 league appearances between 1972 and 1978.

BOBBY HOY (OR)
Huddersfield
Height: 5ft 6in Weight: 10st 7lbs

30.11.74: 'Lot of skill uses ball well' (GT)

Hoy was a winger who rose up the ranks at Huddersfield after signing as an apprentice. Between 1966 and 1974 he played 144 first-team league games and scored 18 goals before moving to Blackburn Rovers for two seasons. He then moved to Halifax Town and York City before ending up in Rochdale in 1978, where he finished (66 league games, 12 goals).

DAVE SMALLMAN
Wrexham
Age: 21 Height: 5ft 9in Weight: 10st 12lbs

18.11.74: 'Not seen a lot but knows where goal is, always looking for an opening' (GT)

After 101 appearances and 38 goals for Wrexham, Smallman was indeed snapped up by a Merseyside club – Everton. Signing in 1974, Smallman struggled to make a name for himself at Goodison, constantly battling with injury. He made 21 league appearances for the Blues and scored six goals but was moved on in 1977 to Bangor City.

BRIAN HORTON (MF)
P Vale
Age: 24 Height: 5ft 10in Weight: 11st 7lbs

21.12.74: 'Hard worker with a fair amount of ability watch again' (GT)

Horton had a successful career, with long stints at Port Vale, Brighton and Hove Albion and Luton Town (where he helped David Pleat's team avoid relegation in 1983) before becoming player-manager at Hull City. He made a total of 610 league appearances and scored 74 goals, and has since been in charge of teams in more than 1,000 games.

DAVIE COOPER (OL)
Clydebank
Age: 18 Height: 5ft 7.5in Weight: 10st 12lbs

04.01.75: 'A lot of skill will watch again' (GT)
11.08.75: 'Very good player gifted with skill, a real crowd pleaser'
12.08.75: 'A promising player who can take on defenders and is comfortable with both feet' (GT)

324

'Plays on the flanks can pick up a ball any part of the field and beat defenders. A very useful player' (GT)
'A good player in possession can beat defenders easily and crosses a good ball' (GT)

Twentyman watched Rangers legend Cooper while he was a skilful left-winger starting his career at Clydebank, where he won the second division championship in 1975/76. He signed for Rangers in 1977 for £100,000, and played for the Scottish giants for 12 years, winning three league championships and three Scottish Cups, and scoring 49 league goals in 376 games. After losing his first-team place he moved to Motherwell in 1989, where he scored 17 goals in 157 games and again won the Scottish Cup in 1991. Cooper finished his career by returning to Clydebank in 1994. He also won 22 Scotland caps and scored six goals. Cooper suffered a brain haemorrhage in 1995 while making a kids' coaching film with Charlie Nicholas at Broadwood Stadium, and he later died in hospital. He was 39.

FOSTER (MF)
Mansfield

Twentyman's note is brief, and there were two Fosters playing at Mansfield Town at this time – Colin and Barry. The latter was a full-back who spent his entire career at Mansfield. Colin Foster was a centre-back who had periods at both Mansfield Town and Peterborough United.

BILLY BELL (FB MF)
Rochdale
Age: 21 Height: 5ft 8in Weight: 11st

Bell was only at Rochdale for a season on a non-contract basis – he made six appearances for the club between 1974 and 1975. Bell played for several non-league clubs.

PAUL SMITH (MF)
Cambridge
Age: 22 Weight: 5ft 6in Weight: 9st 12lbs

Smith was an apprentice at Huddersfield Town and played for their first team twice between 1972 and 1974 before moving to Cambridge United. At Cambridge he appeared 38 times and scored three goals before leaving the club in 1976. It is unclear what happened to him after that.

DAVID GREGORY (S)
Peterborough

Gregory started and finished his 14-year professional career at Peterborough United, making a total of 173 league appearances for the club and scoring 40 goals. In between those spells, he also played for Stoke City, Blackburn Rovers (on loan), Bury, Portsmouth and Wrexham. In four years at the latter, he made 153 appearances and scored 31 goals.

CHRIS TURNER (CH)
Peterborough

The central defender played 314 league games for Peterborough United between 1969 and 1978, scoring an impressive 37 goals. He then moved to Luton Town for a season, where he scored five times in 30 league games. Turner had two spells with the New England Teamen in America, and two with Cambridge United. He also played for Swindon Town (on a non-contract basis) and Southend United before becoming manager at Cambridge.

LYONS (S)
Port Vale

IAN MacDONALD (CH)
St Johnstone

MacDonald spent four years at St Johnstone, then five at Carlisle United. He also spent shorter periods at Dundee and Arbroath – in total, he played 391 league games and scored 13 goals.

REID
St Mirren

It's difficult to know which Reid Twentyman was noting here, as between 1974 and 1976 both Bobby Reid and Ian Reid were on St Mirren's books, and both of them played in defence. Bobby was a centre-back who played for St Mirren between 1973 and 1980 before retiring, and Ian was a full-back who came to the club from Partick Thistle and then left in 1976 to play for non-league side Carluke Rovers.

TREVOR (MF)
Worcester
Age: 18

SEASON 1975/76

DAVID NAREY (D)
Dundee U
Age: 20

*'Looks a useful alround [sic] defender
prepared to defend and attack nicely built'*
*'Good build with right movement knows
his job reads situations well and can pass
the ball correctly looks very good player'*

Narey spent 21 years at Dundee United during
their most successful era, making 603 league
appearances and scoring 22 goals. He won the
league championship in 1982/83 and two con-
secutive Scottish League Cups in 1979/80 and
1980/81 (Dundee United's first-ever major trophies). Narey's performances in defence and
midfield won lots of attention – Derby
County's assistant manager Frank Blunstone
was fined for making an illegal approach to
sign him in 1978 – and they were integral to
Dundee United's run to the UEFA Cup final in
1987. He was released in 1994 and joined Raith
Rovers, helping the club to the First Division
title (and promotion) that season, and winning
yet another League Cup medal as Raith were
surprise winners over Celtic on penalties.
Narey won 35 caps for Scotland and was
awarded an MBE in 1992.

WILLIE PETTIGREW (F)
Motherwell

*'Difficult to assess, a sneak around goal
but does little else' (GT)*

Pettigrew won five Scotland caps while at
Motherwell between 1972 and 1979 and
scored two goals. He struck 80 goals in 146
league appearances for his club before joining
Dundee United for £100,000. While at
Dundee, Pettigrew won two Scottish League
Cups but was sold to Hearts in 1981, where he
scored 25 goals in 68 games. He saw out his
career at Greenock Morton and Hamilton
Academical.

PETER BURKE (CH)
Barnsley
Age: 19

*'Could become a strong stopper, good in the
air and not easily drawn out, worth watching
for progress'*

Burke played for three lower-league clubs during his career. He started out at Barnsley and
then played for Halifax Town and Rochdale.

MICK PICKERING (CB)
Barnsley
Age: 19

*'Typical Barnsley player strong and positive
could become a good player with time'*

Pickering reached his century of league appearances at Barnsley before moving to
Southampton and then Sheffield Wednesday –
he played 110 league games for the Sheffield
club. Pickering also played for Norwich City
(on loan), Bradford City (on loan), Barnsley
(on loan), Rotherham United (102 apps, one
goal), York City and finally Stockport County.

MARK RHODES (MF)
Rotherham
Age: 18

'Promising player will need time to tell'

Rhodes came through the Rotherham United
apprenticeship scheme, and he was on the
club's books between 1975 and 1982, helping
the club to the Division Three championship in
1980/81. He wasn't a prolific scorer – 13 goals
in 258 league appearances for Rotherham – but
he was an important part of the midfield. He
went to both Darlington and Mansfield Town
on loan before finishing his career at Burnley,
where he made 13 league starts.

KEVIN JOHNSON (MF)
Hartlepool
Age: 23

'Not in my opinion first Div material'

A Sheffield Wednesday apprentice, Johnson
played for them, Southend United, Gillingham
(on loan) and Workington before arriving at
Hartlepool United, where he made 61 first-
team appearances and scored eight goals before
switching to Huddersfield Town. He was more
prolific in front of goal at Huddersfield, scoring
23 times in 81 games. Johnson moved to
Halifax Town in 1978 before returning to
Hartlepool two years later.

DUNCAN SHIELDS (CH)
Albion
Age: 24

'Not the player he was made out to be,
disappointing in his games when watched'

Shields had two spells at Albion Rovers, the first from 1973 to 1979 and the second from 1981 to 1982. In between he played for Queen of the South and Stranraer.

BRIAN WILLIAMS (MF)
Bury
Age: 20
Height: 5ft 8in
Weight: 11st 7lbs

'An improved player with good work rate
and endurance links well in midfield one
of the more matured young player good
material' (GT)

Williams switched between left-back and mid-field. He spent six years at Bury, making 159 league appearances and scoring 19 goals before a brief stint at Queens Park Rangers during the 1977/78 season. From there he enjoyed solid spells at both Swindon Town (99 apps, eight goals) and Bristol Rovers (172 apps, 21 goals), as well as slightly shorter periods at Bristol City and Shrewsbury Town.

ANDY ROWLAND (S)
Bury
Age: 21 Height: 5ft 10in Weight: 11st 12lbs

'Can do very well abroad, has games
where he doesn't show but this stems
mainly from lack of support'

Initially on Derby County's books, Rowland didn't make a first-team appearance for the Rams before moving to Bury, where he played in 174 league games and banged in 58 goals. He moved to Swindon Town in 1979, and he remained there until 1986 (345 apps in all competitions, 98 goals) when he retired and became club coach.

MERVYN CAWSTON
Newport
Height: 6ft Weight: 11st 7lbs

'A young looking keeper who took the eye
with his alround [sic] display'

Cawston was on loan at Newport County when Twentyman watched him – he was on Norwich City's books and had already spent a season on loan at Southend United. In 1976, he moved on

to Gillingham, but when the team's form dipped, Cawston's contract was cancelled and he went to America to play for Chicago Sting. It was Southend that brought him back and gave him a decent run, and he repaid them – he broke several records at the club during the 1980/81 campaign when The Shrimpers won the Division Four title, including most clean sheets in a single season (25). After becoming injury-prone, he left for Stoke City but returned briefly a season later to help keep Southend in the Fourth Division.

RALPH CALLACHAN
Hearts
Age: 20 Height: 5ft 10in Weight: 11st

'A promising player, to be followed'

After a successful period at Hearts, during which Callachan and his teammates reached the 1976 Scottish Cup final but lost to Rangers, Callachan moved to Newcastle United in 1977. However, he only played nine league matches for the Magpies before moving back to Edinburgh to play for Hibernian. Callachan made 218 league appearances for Hibs, scoring 26 goals, and he reached another Scottish Cup final in 1979 only to be vanquished by Rangers again. He saw out his career at Greenock Morton, Meadowbank Thistle and Berwick Rangers – in his final two years at the latter, he became player-manager.

JASON SEACOLE
Oxford
Age: 16½

Twentyman only noted Seacole's name, age and club, so we don't know what he made of him. The forward played for Oxford United between 1976 and 1982, coming up the ranks as an apprentice and scoring 22 goals in 120 first-team league games before moving to non-league side Witney Town. Seacole also spent two seasons at Wycombe Wanderers (1986-88), scoring 14 goals in 56 appearances in all competitions.

JEREMY CHARLES
Swansea
Age: 17 Height: 6ft 1in

'A young player who has a big heart.
Good in the air and tackles well. Which will
be his best position is the question. Looks
sure to get a good living out of football'

02.11.76: 'Having a second look against good opposition. Has the strength and endurance of a 21-year-old. A good bet to make the grade in some position'

Charles was an apprentice at Swansea who went on to make a name for himself in the first team, making 247 league appearances between 1976 and 1983 and scoring 53 goals. The forward moved to Queens Park Rangers (12 apps, five goals) for a season before joining Oxford United, where he hit 13 goals in 46 league games. He scored for Oxford in the 1986 League Cup final when they defeated Charles' former club, QPR. He won a total of 19 caps for Wales and scored one solitary international goal.

COLIN METHVEN (CH)
East Fife
Height: 6ft 1in Weight: 12st 6lbs

'Rawboned strong player looks a late developer but can tackle and promises to be good in the air, recovers well for his build, tackles stronger from left' (GT)

Indian-born defender Methven played for East Fife between 1974 and 1979, making 154 appearances and scoring 15 goals before joining Wigan Athletic. He made just shy of 300 league appearances for The Latics, scoring 21 goals and becoming club captain. Blackpool swooped for his services in 1986, and he had another impressive period there (175 apps, 11 goals) – he was voted player of the year twice. Against the will of the fans, Methven was shunted out on loan to Carlisle United during the 1990/91 season and then sold to Walsall, but that decision came back to haunt Blackpool as he helped Walsall to a 2-0 win over his former club on the final day of the 1990/91 season, thus denying Blackpool automatic promotion. He finished his 20-year career at Barrow in 1994.

GREGOR ABEL (LB)
Clydebank
Height: 5ft 10in Weight: 11st 7lbs

'Quick – two footed attacks on the flanks and recovers well, has makings of a good back'

Abel had played for Falkirk for a couple of seasons before joining Clydebank in 1972. He stayed there for eight years, playing in 235 league games before signing for Alloa Athletic.

MIKE LARNACH (CF)
Clydebank
Height: 5ft 10in Weight: 11st 4lbs

'Big hearted player with plenty of enthusiasm can take chances, worth keeping a close watch'

Larnach was a trialist at East Stirling before joining Clydebank in 1972. He made 167 appearances for Clydebank, scoring 63 goals, and other scouts must have been watching him alongside Twentyman – he was signed by Newcastle United in 1977. His time there was brief, however, and he made just 13 appearances before moving back across the border to Motherwell. Larnach also played for Ayr United and Stenhousemuir but finished his career back at Clydebank, where he made another 86 appearances and scored 20 goals before joining the coaching staff.

PAUL HART (CH)
Blackpool
Age: 24 Height: 6ft 2in Weight: 13st

'After playing midfield and a sweeper, is most suited to the centre of defence. About the best outside Div 1' (GT)

Appointed as caretaker manager of Portsmouth at the end of the 2008/2009 season, Hart is still very much involved in the game. As a player, he had three years at Stockport County before moving to Blackpool in 1973, where he played in 143 league games and scored 15 goals. As Blackpool headed for relegation, Hart escaped to Leeds United as a replacement for Gordon McQueen. In five years there he made 191 appearances in the league and scored 16 times. Moving to Nottingham Forest in 1983, Hart played in the controversial 1983/84 UEFA Cup semi-final against Anderlecht when his goal was unjustly ruled out for no clear reason – Anderlecht later admitted to bribing the official. Hart moved on to Sheffield Wednesday a year later, and finished his career with stints at Birmingham City and Notts County.

IAN ATKINS
Shrewsbury
Age: 20
Height: 5ft 10in Weight: 11st 5lbs

'Plays as a sweeper but takes part in build up and does a very good job. Gives everything

he's got and looks about the best I've seen in this roll [sic] in the 3rd Division' (GT)

Atkins played 279 times for Shrewsbury Town in the league and scored 55 goals. The club won the Third Division championship in 1979 and Atkins helped them avoid relegation for the next three seasons. He moved to Sunderland in 1982, playing in 77 games over two years, and then to Everton for £70,000. Everton won the league and Cup Winners' Cup that year, but Atkins only played a very small part, making just seven league appearances before moving on to Ipswich Town. In his later years, he played for Birmingham City twice, Colchester United, Cambridge United and Doncaster Rovers. At all of these clubs he held the position of player-manager.

GRAEME PAYNE
Dundee U
Age: 21 Height: 5ft 7in Weight: 10st 7lbs

26.10.77: *'Has improved and no doubt is one of the best midfield players in Scotland. Very good control and vision, passes are inch perfect and this player has the instinct to take on players when necessary. Other than his size, his only fault is not being prepared to shoot at goal when getting into good positions outside the box' (Ayr v Dundee Utd, Partick v Dundee Utd)*

The first winner of the Scottish PFA's Young Player of the Year award (in 1977/78), Payne was a winger who spent 11 years at Dundee United where he made 200 league appearances, scored 12 goals and won two Scottish League Cups. He spent a season on loan at Greenock Morton before leaving Dundee United for Arbroath. He also played for Brechin City and St Johnstone.

BILLY RONSON
Blackpool

'Another small stocky midfield player who has reached nearly his peak. In my opinion could play in a good 1st Div side has the brains to give the above average pass and also capable of breaking through and scoring. Not as near as Payne but comes to mind quickly when thinking of midfield players'

In the season Twentyman watched him (1977/78), Ronson and his Blackpool team-mates would find themselves in a relegation battle – a battle they lost as they departed Division Two. He stayed with the club for one more season, taking his match tally to 128 and goal tally to 12, before joining Cardiff City. After two seasons there and one more at Wrexham, where he again suffered relegation, Ronson joined Barnsley. In the final years of his career, he played for Birmingham City (on loan), Blackpool again (on a non-contract basis) and featured for several teams in America.

RICKY THOMSON
Preston
Age: 21 Height: 5ft 9in Weight: 11st

'Good alround [sic] player moving into midfield and attacking positions has the strength to work and score goals also his build up work is good'

Thomson was a forward who only played for Preston North End. He came through as an apprentice and played for the first team between 1974 and 1980, scoring 20 goals in 71 league games before retiring through injury.

DOWNIE (FB)
Meadowbank

'Not matured enough to judge'

JIM MELROSE (IR)
Partick

Melrose played for a host of different clubs – his peak was probably a season with Celtic in 1983/84 when he made 30 league appearances and scored seven goals, and was on the losing side in the Scottish League Cup final. After five years at Partick Thistle he moved around swiftly. He played for Leicester City, Coventry City, Celtic, Wolverhampton Wanderers (on loan), Manchester City, Charlton Athletic, Leeds United and Shrewsbury Town. In total, he played in 390 league matches and scored 99 goals.

DAVIE DODDS (CF)
Dundee U

Dodds signed for Dundee United on schoolboy terms and then gradually worked his way into the first team at a time when the club enjoyed its most successful period. While he missed out on the Scottish League Cup final in 1979, the

SECRET DIARY OF A LIVERPOOL SCOUT

striker scored in the final the following year when they retained the trophy, and he played an important part in the league championship triumph in 1982/83. He scored 102 league goals for the club in 243 games. Dodds spent a short period on loan at Arbroath in 1977/78, and in 1986 he moved abroad, to Swiss club Neuchatel Xamax, although that only lasted for a couple of months before he returned, joining up with Alex Ferguson at Aberdeen. He played 73 games for Aberdeen, then moved to Rangers, where he finished his career.

JOHN McNEIL (MF)
Morton

McNeil was a right-winger who spent almost his entire career at Greenock Morton, playing in 328 games and scoring 67 goals between 1975 and 1991. In the 1982/83 season he played one game on loan for Dundee United in their championship year.

JAMIE FAIRLIE (MF)
Hamilton
Age: 23 Height: 5ft 7.5in Weight: 10st 12lbs

'Knows the game and could do
even better with better players' (GT)
15.03.80: *'(Broken ankle) will be out*
for rest of season'

Fairlie spent his entire career in Scotland and played for Hamilton Academical twice – 1974-84 and 1987-89. He also played for Airdrie, Clydebank, Motherwell and Clyde.

PETER RHODES-BROWN (OL)
Chelsea
Age: 18 Height: 5ft 10in Weight: 11st

Rhodes-Brown spent five years at Chelsea as a winger, scoring four times in 96 league games before joining Oxford United. He made 112 appearances for Oxford, scoring 13 times, before retiring through injury.

PAUL WALSH (OL)
Charlton
Age: 18

'Was disappointing today against Shrewsbury'

Walsh had successful spells at Charlton Athletic (87 apps, 24 goals) and Luton Town (80 apps, 24 goals) before Joe Fagan signed him for Liverpool in 1984. He settled in well,

scoring crucial goals as Liverpool defended their European crown in the 1984/85 season, but they lost the infamous final in Heysel. Injuries disrupted Walsh's time at Liverpool, meaning he only played a bit part until Dalglish bought Aldridge and Beardsley and he knew his time was up after scoring 25 goals in 77 league games. Walsh moved to Tottenham Hotspur but again found himself superseded by another striker – in this case Gary Lineker. After a loan spell at QPR, he played for Portsmouth (twice) and Manchester City before retiring through injury. Walsh won five England caps, scoring once.

DAVE CROWN (OL)
Brentford
Age: 19

During Crown's 13-year career he played for seven teams – Brentford, Portsmouth, Exeter City (on loan), Reading, Cambridge United, Southend United and Gillingham. At the last three, he averaged just shy of a goal in every other league game: 44 goals in 106 games for Cambridge, 61 in 113 at Southend and 38 in 86 for Gillingham.

RAY BLAIR (OL)
Dumbarton

'Shows promise' (AM)

Blair ran the right wing for seven years at Dumbarton, making 188 appearances and scoring 46 goals before moving to St Johnstone. He played over 50 times in the league for them, Motherwell and East Fife before going to Australia.

JOE COYLE (IL)
Dumbarton

'Shows promise' (AM)

In two spells at Dumbarton, Coyle scored 37 league goals for the club and played in 205 games. He also played for Airdrie, Greenock Morton, Arbroath and Stranraer.

GEORGE McCLUSKEY
Celtic

'A good player with a lot of ability
and skills. Moves into positions and
would be worth an enquiry if ever
buyable' (A McCrae)

McCluskey had eight years at Celtic and was fruitful in front of goal – he scored 54 times in 145 league matches. Leeds United bought him in 1983, and he scored 16 goals in 73 games for the club before returning north to Hibernian. He also played for Hamilton Academical (where he average around a goal every three league games), Kilmarnock and Clyde.

PAUL RIDEOUT
Swindon

'A young forward playing in a moderate team has a chance but at the moment doesn't do enough to prove anything' (GT)

Rideout's career covered the globe, taking in Merseyside on its way. He was at Swindon Town for three years before brief spells of mixed success at Aston Villa, Bari in Italy and Southampton, from where he returned on loan to Swindon. Rideout had spells at Notts County and Rangers before landing at Everton. In five years with The Toffees he played 112 league games and scored 29 goals, though he is best remembered for his winning goal in the 1995 FA Cup final against Manchester United. His time at Everton came to an end as he struggled to make the first team, and he travelled to China and America before returning to play for Tranmere Rovers.

DAVE CALDWELL
Mansfield
Age: 22 Height: 5ft 10in Weight: 11st 7lbs

'Has a good turn of foot but doesn't use it right lacks the necessary craft to make a good 1st Division player' (GT)

After a solid five-year stretch with Mansfield Town (157 appearances, 57 goals), Caldwell jumped around between clubs, spending time at Carlisle United and Swindon Town on loan, longer periods at Chesterfield and Torquay United, a season overseas at KW Overpelt in Belgium, and then second spells at Torquay (on loan) and Chesterfield.

SEASON 1986/87

IAN McPARLAND (F)
Notts C
Height: 5ft 8in Weight: 11st

18.10.86: 'Showed good pace & takes on defenders worth watching again' (GT)

McParland had his most successful period at Notts County, scoring 69 times in 221 league games. After a reasonable spell at Hull City (47 games, seven goals), McParland's career took him to seven clubs in as many years – Walsall (on loan), Dunfermline Athletic, Lincoln City (on a non-contract basis), Northampton Town, Instant Dict in Hong Kong, Hamilton Academical and Berwick Rangers. Twentyman scouted McParland and all other players in this period for Glasgow Rangers.

DAVID THOMPSON (RM)
Notts C
Height: 5ft 9in Weight: 11st 5lbs

18.10.86: 'Worth following up, strong on the ball with good runs into the opponents' half' (GT)

Thompson top-and-tailed his professional career at Rochdale, making 266 appearances for the club and scoring 24 league goals. In between, the right-winger played for Notts County, Wigan Athletic, Preston North End and Chester City, making a total of 555 league appearances. He later played non league football with Southport and Marine.

KEVIN PRESSMAN (GK)
Sheff W
Height: 6ft Weight: 11st 7lbs

21.10.86: 'Did well quick reaction, kicks and punches well, good alround [sic] performance' (GT)

Pressman made 513 league appearances in his career, the vast bulk of which were at Sheffield Wednesday, whom he signed with in 1985 and made his debut for two years later. Wednesday reached three cup finals in three years – the League Cup in 1991 (which they won), then the FA Cup and League Cup in 1993 (both of which they lost to Arsenal) – but Pressman was only a substitute in those games and did not play. He spent 19 seasons at the club, playing in a total of 404 league games – more than 200 of which were in the Premiership – and fending off competition from Chris Turner, Chris Woods and Pavel Srnicek. While at Sheffield Wednesday he had loan spells at Stoke City and West Bromwich Albion, and when he left in 2004 he went on to play for Leicester City, Leeds United, Coventry City, Mansfield Town and Portadown. He is currently player/goalkeeping coach at Scunthorpe United.

MIKE GALLOWAY (BF)
Halifax
Height: 5ft 10in Weight: 11st

*25.10.86: 'Best back four player on the field
reads it well and good competitor' (GT)*
04.11.86: 'Had a good steady game'

A left-footed central defender, Galloway began
his career at Berwick Rangers before moving
to Mansfield Town in 1983 and then Halifax
Town in 1986. After a year there he joined
Hearts and helped them push Celtic all the way
in the 1987/88 championship race. His performances sealed a switch to Celtic in 1989,
and in seven years at the club he made 136
league appearances, scoring eight goals and
winning a Scotland cap. He was in and out of
the team, though, owing to inconsistent performances, and after he fell out with manager
Lou Macari he was loaned to Leicester City.
Galloway was involved in a car crash that
ended his footballing career.

CHRIS CUTLER (LM CF)
Crewe
Height: 5ft 10in Weight: 11st

*25.10.86: 'Looked useful going forward
on the left, pending on age' (GT)*

Cutler arrived at Crewe Alexandra from Bury
in 1985, where he had scored three times in 23
games. He spent five years at Crewe, netting 24
goals in 140 league matches before joining
Northwich Victoria.

DAVID LONGHURST
Halifax
Height: 5ft 8in Weight: 10st 12lbs

*25.10.86: 'Good control holds the ball
well and is worth another look'*
*04.11.86: 'Doesn't do a lot but
always threatens'*

Longhurst was on Nottingham Forest's books
for three years before joining Halifax Town
but didn't make a first-team appearance. The
forward was fruitful at Halifax, scoring 24
goals in 85 league games, but left for
Northampton Town in 1987. He also played
for Peterborough United and York City, and it
was when playing for the latter that he died
suddenly, on the pitch, of a heart attack. He
was only 25. One of the stands at York City has
been named after him.

PAUL STEWART (CF)
Blackpool
Height: 5ft 10in Weight: 11st 7lbs

*18.10.86: 'Plenty of movement with
good pace I feel he would do well in a
good team'*

Stewart was in great form for Blackpool, on
his way to scoring 56 goals in 201 league
games and he proved just as effective at
Manchester City between 1987 and 1988,
scoring 26 times in 51 league matches. He was
then sold to Tottenham Hotspur, where he
began brightly as a striker but was converted to
an impressive-looking midfielder when he
stopped scoring, and he won three England
caps in this position. Liverpool spent £2.5m on
Stewart in 1992 but he failed to impress, scoring just three times in 42 appearances in all
competitions, and he also struggled with
injuries. In his last two years at the club he was
mostly out on loan – at Crystal Palace,
Wolverhampton Wanderers, Burnley and
Sunderland. He made his move to the north-
east permanent in 1996 and saw out his career
at Stoke City and Workington.

DAVID KELLY (CF)
Walsall
Height: 5ft 10in Weight: 11st

*01.11.86: 'Shows control & skill,
lacked support to really do anything'*

After recovering from Perthes disease as a
child, Kelly forged a successful, if unsettled,
career. He began with a tally of 63 goals in 147
league games for Walsall before moving to
West Ham United, Leicester City and then
Newcastle United. He helped the latter to gain
promotion to the Premiership in 1993, finishing
the season as their top scorer with 25 goals. He
moved to Wolves after the return of Peter
Beardsley and struck 26 times in 83 league
matches for the Midlands club before heading
to Sunderland. His form there slumped drasti-
cally – in 1996/97 he failed to score a single
league goal despite playing in nearly all of the
team's fixtures – and he was subsequently sold
to Tranmere Rovers where he regained his eye
for goal. Kelly latterly played for Sheffield
United, Motherwell, Mansfield Town and
Derry City, and won 26 caps for the Republic
of Ireland during his career, scoring nine goals
(including a memorable winner against
England).

NEIL POINTON (FB)
Everton
Height: 5ft 10in Weight: 11st 10lbs

29.10.86: 'Ready made for the league stuff'

Presumably Twentyman was watching Pointon with a view to taking him to Scotland from his former Merseyside rivals, Everton. The left-back was struggling for a place in Howard Kendall's team, as he competed with Pat van den Hauwe and Paul Power. However, he still played enough games to win a championship medal in the 1986/87 season, and he was consistent whenever chosen over the next couple of years, eventually becoming first choice when Van den Hauwe was sold to Spurs. Pointon left Everton in 1990 to rejoin Kendall at Manchester City, where he was a regular, before moving to Joe Royle's Oldham Athletic. During his time there, Oldham suffered relegation from the top flight and a desperate defeat to Manchester United in a 1994 FA Cup semi-final – Pointon's goal looked to have sealed Oldham's place in the final, but Mark Hughes equalised with the last kick of the game in injury time. United easily won the replay. Pointon also played for Hearts, Walsall, Chesterfield and Hednesford Town, and he had begun his career at Scunthorpe United.

NIGEL WORTHINGTON (LB)
Sheff W
Height: 5ft 11in Weight: 11st 7lbs

08.11.86: 'Has improved a lot. A gutsy player who can go forward and do a good job'

Now a respected manager with Northern Ireland, Worthington was regularly capped internationally throughout his career. The left-back played for Ballymena United and Notts County before joining Sheffield Wednesday, where he spent most of his career. Between 1983 and 1994 he made 338 appearances for the club, scoring 12 times and winning the League Cup and promotion to the top flight in 1990/91. He also played in the League Cup and FA Cup final defeats in 1993. Worthington went on to feature for Leeds United and Stoke City, and was player-manager at Blackpool before spells in charge at Norwich and Leicester City.

Other notes from the scouting diary:

YOUNG PLAYERS DATES OF BIRTH

BILLY RUSSELL
Doncaster, 14.09.59
Played for: Everton, Celtic, Doncaster Rovers, Scunthorpe United, Rotherham United.

DARAL PUGH
Doncaster, 05.06.61
Played for: Doncaster Rovers, Huddersfield Town, Rotherham United, Cambridge United (loan), Torquay United.

STEVE LISTER
Doncaster, 18.11.61
Played for: Doncaster Rovers, Scunthorpe United, York City (loan).

K MABBUTT
SCHOOLBOYS 1972/73
GARY OWEN
Warrington Schools

A ROBERTSON, D WILLIAMS, A CLARKE
Flintshire Boys

BOLO GLENNIE, COLIN WILLIAMSON
GRAHAM MOSSOP, BILLY McKAY
GARY MARSHALL, PETER REID

ROLL OF HONOUR

The players that Geoff Twentyman and his band of scouts spotted and recommended to Liverpool catapulted the club into a period of unparalleled success. Between 1967 and 1987 Liverpool lifted 29 senior titles and 14 reserve league championships.

First Division Champions
1972-73, 1975-76, 1976-77, 1978-79, 1979-80, 1981-82,
1982-83, 1983-84, 1985-86

European Cup winners
1976-77, 1977-78, 1980-81, 1983-84

FA Cup winners
1973-74, 1985-86

UEFA Cup winners
1972-73, 1975-76

League Cup winners
1980-81, 1981-82, 1982-83, 1983-84

Charity Shield winners
1974, 1976, 1977*, 1979, 1980, 1982, 1986*
* Charity Shield shared

European Super Cup winners
1977

Reserve League winners
1968-69, 1969-70, 1970-71, 1972-73, 1973-74, 1974-75, 1975-76,
1976-77, 1978-79, 1979-80, 1980-81, 1981-82, 1983-84, 1984-85

Geoff: Father to Susan, Margaret, Geoffrey and William and Grandpa to eight grandchildren and four great grandchildren

GEOFF TWENTYMAN FINALLY LEFT
LIVERPOOL IN THE SUMMER OF 1986.
THIS WAS THE LEAGUE TABLE
IN THE FIRST DIVISION

	P	W	D	L	F	A	PTS
1 LIVERPOOL	**42**	**26**	**10**	**6**	**89**	**37**	**88**
2 Everton	42	26	8	8	87	41	86
3 West Ham United	42	26	6	10	74	40	84
4 Manchester United	42	22	10	10	70	36	76
5 Sheffield Wednesday	42	21	10	11	63	54	73
6 Chelsea	42	20	11	11	57	56	71
7 Arsenal	42	20	9	13	49	47	69
8 Nottingham Forest	42	19	11	12	69	53	68
9 Luton Town	42	18	12	12	61	44	66
10 Tottenham Hotspur	42	19	8	15	74	52	65
11 Newcastle United	42	17	12	13	67	72	63
12 Watford	42	16	11	15	69	62	59
13 Queens Park Rangers	42	15	7	20	53	64	52
14 Southampton	42	12	10	20	51	62	46
15 Manchester City	42	11	12	19	43	57	45
16 Aston Villa	42	10	14	18	51	62	44
17 Coventry City	42	11	10	21	48	71	43
18 Oxford United	42	10	12	20	62	80	42
19 Leicester City	42	11	8	23	54	76	42
20 Ipswich Town	42	11	8	23	32	73	41
21 Birmingham City	42	8	5	29	30	73	29
22 West Bromwich Albion	42	4	12	26	35	89	24

Other publications produced by Sport Media:

Story of Bill Shankly
as told by his family

The players' stories
behind the pictures

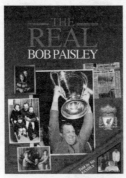

Story of Bob Paisley
as told by his family

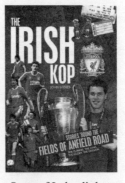

Story of Ireland's love
affair with LFC

CD book – featuring
rare Shankly interview